THE GLOBAL ENVIRONMENT

THE GLOBAL ENVIRONMENT

INSTITUTIONS, LAW, AND POLICY

Third Edition

Edited by

Regina S. Axelrod
Adelphi University

Stacy D. VanDeveer
University of New Hampshire

David Leonard Downie
Fairfield University

CQ PRESS

A Division of SAGE
Washington, D.C.

CQ Press
2300 N Street, NW, Suite 800
Washington, DC 20037

Phone: 202-729-1900; toll-free, 1-866-4CQ-PRESS (1-866-427-7737)

Web: www.cqpress.com

Cover design: Anne Kerns, Anne Likes Red, Inc.
Composition: C&M Digitals (P) Ltd.

⊚ The paper used in this publication exceeds the requirements of the American National Standard for Information Sciences—Permanence of Paper for Printed Library Materials, ANSI Z39.48–1992.

Printed and bound in the United States of America

14   13   12   11   10   1   2   3   4   5

Library of Congress Cataloging-in-Publication Data

The global environment : institutions, law, and policy / edited by Regina S. Axelrod, Stacy D. VanDeveer, David Leonard Downie.—3rd ed.
     p. cm.
 Includes bibliographical references and index.
 ISBN 978-0-87289-966-7 (alk. paper)

 1. Environmental law, International. 2. Environmental policy. I. Axelrod, Regina S. II. VanDeveer, Stacy D. III. Downie, David Leonard. IV. Title.

 K3585.G58 2011
 344.04'6—dc22

2009043265

For Lenny, Gregg,
Renee and Sam,
and
little Sienna,
Laryssa, and Sarah

Contents

Part I. International Environmental Institutions and Regimes

Part II. Global Environmental Policy: Cases and Questions

Part III. Implementing Global Policy: Cases and Controversies in Sustainable Development

Preface

This volume is designed to meet the need for an authoritative collection of readings on international environmental institutions, laws, and policies at the beginning of the twenty-first century. Although there are numerous texts in individual disciplinary fields, we brought together essays by a distinguished group of international scholars spanning the traditional boundaries of political science, international relations, international law, policy studies, and comparative politics. Only by integrating perspectives from diverse fields can we begin to address the enormous complexities of global environmental problems and their governance.

The introductory chapter explains some of the most important concepts derived from these fields for the study of international environmental law and policy. These include basic perspectives on international cooperation drawn from international relations theory, the nature of international institutions and policy regimes, and the concept of sustainable development. The first two sections of the book focus on the development of global environmental institutions, laws, regimes, and policies. The third section presents case studies of national and regional implementation of international environmental and sustainable development policies. Linkages among national and international actors as well as among public institutions, firms, and nongovernmental organizations are discussed throughout the book.

In one sense, all serious environmental threats are now international in scope, given that nearly all forms of pollution, use of resources, and destabilization of natural ecosystems have implications for the sustainability of life as we know it. Global biogeochemical cycles circulate materials and energy throughout the planetary biosphere, and losses of Earth's inherited biodiversity and mineral resources are irreversible. The consumption of resources by one country or group of people ultimately affects the life chances of other—and much larger—segments of the human population, including those in future generations.

The nations of the world began to deal with many of the most obvious environmental threats during the past century, particularly since the twin imperatives of ecological sustainability and development of the world's poorest economies were put on the global agenda at the United Nations Conference on the Human Environment, held in Stockholm in 1972. The concept of sustainable development, articulated in the 1987 report of the World Commission on Environment and Development and in the United Nations Conference on Environment and Development, held in Rio de Janeiro in 1992, established a broad intellectual framework and agenda for action by the international community. Commitments to the implementation of this agenda were discussed by representatives of 191 nations at the World Summit on Sustainable Development, held in Johannesburg in 2002.

Despite this progress, the prospects for attaining the levels of international cooperation necessary to manage the impact of humans on the natural life-support systems of the planet remain grim. Chapter authors were asked to evaluate initial steps toward strengthening international policies and institutions to achieve the goals of sustainable development set out in 1992. Although some advances are documented, the record to date is not encouraging. The political will to make substantial economic and political changes appears to be lacking in most parts of the world. The declining leadership of the United States in international environmental policy making has been even more striking than it was when the first edition of this book was published in 1999. Only time will reveal whether changes in U.S. political leadership can reverse this trend.

Disagreements over the meaning of sustainable development as well as problems in implementing environmental policies are evident throughout this book. Several contributors note the persistence of deep cleavages among developed, developing, and transitional states in various regions of the world. Political differences among the United States, Europe, and the developing world have often widened rather than narrowed in recent years (Chapters 7, 10–12). Projects such as the expansion of nuclear power in the Czech Republic and around the world (Chapter 14), rapid economic development and increasing energy demand in China (Chapter 13), and the ever-growing demands of consumer societies on the Earth's finite resources and fragile ecosystems (Chapter 15) raise profound questions about the trade-offs that may be required to achieve sustainable development—and about the role of international financial interests in promoting incompatible forms of development. An expected human population of between seven and nine billion people will not be able to consume the Earth's resources like the average North American; neither should billions be expected to settle for a life in poverty.

We hope this third edition will be even more useful as a text in college and university courses than the previous editions were, and that this edition will also be of interest to a broad range of scholars, professionals, and citizens concerned about the state of the global environment. Attentive readers will notice that our publisher follows style guidelines set forth in the fifteenth edition of *The Chicago Manual of Style* in capitalizing the names of legislative, administrative, and judicial entities only upon mention of the full name of such entities.

We wish to acknowledge the support of our colleagues and staff at Adelphi University and the University of New Hampshire, without whom we would not have been able to complete the project. Regina S. Axelrod owes thanks to the National Science Foundation for a grant (SBR-9708180) that allowed her to study nuclear power development in the Czech Republic; to colleagues at Charles University, the University of Economics, and the Czech Institute of International Relations, Prague; and to the many public officials there and in the Environment Directorate of the European Commission, who facilitated her research. Stacy D. VanDeveer is grateful for support from the European Union's Jean Monnet program, Brown University's Watson Institute for International Affairs, and the University of New Hampshire's College of Liberal Arts's London Program for supporting aspects of his research. He also wishes to thank his undergraduate and graduate students at UNH, Brown, Harvard, and Regent's College (London) for inspiring his continuing interests in environmental, energy, and resource politics. Finally, the editors express their appreciation to Elise Frasier, Brenda Carter, and Charisse Kiino of CQ Press for their encouragement and assistance throughout this project. They also extend their gratitude to manuscript editor Mary Marik and senior production editor Lorna Notsch, also of CQ Press. Any remaining errors are, of course, the authors' responsibility.

Regina S. Axelrod
Stacy D. VanDeveer

Selected Acronyms in Global Environmental Policy

AMAP	Arctic Monitoring and Assessment Programme
AOSIS	Alliance of Small Island States
AU	African Union
CAFE	U.S. corporate average fuel economy
CATARC	China Automotive Technology and Research Center
CBD	Convention on Biodiversity
CDM	Clean Development Mechanism
CEC	Commission for Environmental Cooperation
CEE	central and eastern Europe
CERs	certified emissions reductions
CEZ	Ceske energeticke zavody
CFCs	chloroflourocarbons
CITES	Convention on International Trade in Endangered Species of Wild Fauna and Flora
CLRTAP	Convention on Long-Range Transboundary Air Pollution
CMA	China Meteorological Administration
COCF	Center for Our Common Future
COP	Conference of the Parties
CSD	Commission on Sustainable Development
DDT	dichlorodiphenyl trichloroethane
DOE	U.S. Department of Energy
ECJ	European Court of Justice
EEA	European Environment Agency
EIA	Environmental Impact Assessment
EIONET	European Environment Information and Observation Network
EU	European Union
Euratom	European Atomic Energy Authority
FAO	Food and Agriculture Organization
FTAA	Free Trade Area of the Americas
G-77	Group of 77 (developing countries)
GATT	General Agreement on Tariffs and Trade
GEF	Global Environment Facility
GHG	greenhouse gases
GM	General Motors
GMOs	genetically modified organisms
GRID	Global Resource Information Database
IAEA	International Atomic Energy Agency
ICLEI	International Council for Local Environmental Initiatives
IDA	International Development Agency

IGO	intergovernmental organization
ILO	International Labour Organization
IMO	International Maritime Organization
INC	Intergovernmental Negotiating Committee (for a Framework Convention on Climate Change)
INGOs	international nongovernmental organizations
IPCC	Intergovernment Panel on Climate Change
ISO	International Organization for Standardization
ITLOS	International Tribunal for the Law of the Sea
IUCN	International Union for the Conservation of Nature
JI	joint implementation
JV	joint venture
MAI	multilateral agreement on investment
MDG	Millennium Development Goals
MEAs	multilateral environmental agreements
MOP	Meeting of the Parties
NAFTA	North American Free Trade Agreement
NAM	Non-Aligned Movement
NATO	North Atlantic Treaty Organization
NDRC	National Development and Reform Commission
NGO	nongovernmental organization
NICs	newly industrialized countries
NIEO	new international economic order
NRC	Nuclear Regulatory Commission
ODS	ozone-depleting substances
OECD	Organization for Economic Cooperation and Development
OEWG	open-ended working group
OPEC	Organization of Petroleum Exporting Countries
PCBs	polychlorinated biphenyls
PHARE	Poland-Hungary: Assistance for Restructuring their Economies
PIC	prior informed consent
POPs	persistent organic pollutants
REACH	Regulation on the Registration, Evaluation, Authorization and Restriction of Chemicals
RGGI	Regional Greenhouse Gas Initiative
RoHS	Restriction of the Use of Certain Hazardous Substances in Electrical and Electronic Equipment
SAICM	Strategic Approach to International Chemicals Management
UN	United Nations
UNCED	United Nations Conference on Environment and Development
UNCHE	United Nations Conference on the Human Environment
UNCLOS	United Nations Convention on the Law of the Sea
UNDP	United Nations Development Programme
UNECE	United Nations Economic Commission for Europe
UNEP	United Nations Environment Programme

UNESCO   United Nations Educational, Scientific and Cultural
                Organization
UN FCCC United Nations Framework Convention on Climate Change
UNIDO   United Nations Industrial Development Organization
UNITAR   United Nations Institute for Training and Research
WEEE   Waste Electrical and Electronic Equipment
WMO   World Meteorological Organization
WSSD   World Summit on Sustainable Development
WTO   World Trade Organization
WWF   World Wildlife Fund

Global Environmental Policy: A Brief Chronology

1900   First multinational treaty to protect endangered species signed

1909   Treaty between the United States and Great Britain Respecting
        Boundary Waters; International Joint Commission formed

1911   Treaty for the Preservation and Protection of Fur Seals

1933   London Convention on the Preservation of Fauna and Flora
        in Their Natural State

1940   Convention on Nature Protection and Wildlife Preservation in
        the Western Hemisphere

1941   Final decision of Trail Smelter arbitration

1944   United States and Mexico adopt Treaty on Colorado and
        Tijuana Rivers

1945   United Nations created

1946   International Bank for Reconstruction and Development (World
        Bank) created;
        International Convention on the Regulation of Whaling

1948   International Maritime Organization (IMO) created;
        International Union for Conservation of Nature (IUCN) founded

1949   International Convention for the North-West Atlantic Fisheries;
        United Nations Conference on Conservation and Utilization
        of Resources

1950   World Meteorological Organization (WMO) created;
        International Convention for the Protection of Birds

1952   Four thousand people die in the worst of the London "killer fogs"

1954   International Convention for the Prevention of Pollution of Sea
        by Oil

1957   International Atomic Energy Agency (IAEA) created;
        Treaty of Rome establishing European Economic Community

1961   World Wildlife Fund established

1963   Agreement for the Protection of the Rhine against Pollution;
        Nuclear Test Ban Treaty

1965   United Nations Development Programme (UNDP) created

1971   UNESCO's Man and the Biosphere program launched;
       Ramsar Convention on Wetlands of International Importance;
       Greenpeace established

1972   United Nations Conference on the Human Environment (often
           referred to as the Stockholm Conference), the first global
           environmental conference;
       United Nations Environment Programme (UNEP) created;
       UNESCO Convention Concerning the Protection of the World
           Cultural and Natural Heritage (World Heritage Convention)

1973   Convention on International Trade in Endangered Species of
           Wild Fauna and Flora (CITES);
       International Convention for the Prevention of Pollution from
           Ships (MARPOL)

1974   World Population Conference, Bucharest;
       M. J. Molina and F. S. Rowland publish their theory that CFCs
           threaten the ozone layer

1976   Convention for the Protection of the Mediterranean Sea against
           Pollution;
       United Nations Conference on Human Settlements, Vancouver

1977   UNEP International Register of Potentially Toxic Chemicals
           (IRPTC);
       UN Conference on Desertification

1978   CFCs in spray cans banned in the United States

1979   Convention on the Conservation of Migratory Species (CMS);
       Convention on Long-Range Transboundary Air Pollution
           (CLRTAP)

1980   Convention on the Conservation of Antarctic Marine Living
           Resources

1982   United Nations Convention on the Law of the Sea (UNCLOS)

1983   International Tropical Timber Agreement

1985   Vienna Convention for Protection of the Ozone Layer;
       Discovery of the Antarctic ozone hole

1987   Montreal Protocol on Substances That Deplete the Ozone Layer;
       World Commission on Environment and Development publishes
           Our Common Future (Brundtland Commission Report)

1989   Basel Convention on the Control of Transboundary
           Movements of Hazardous Wastes and Their Disposal;
       Oil spilled in the Gulf of Alaska by the *Exxon Valdez*

1991   Global Environment Facility (GEF) created;
        Convention on the Ban of the Import into Africa and the
            Control of Transboundary Movement and Management of
            Hazardous Wastes within Africa

1992   United Nations Conference on Environment and Development
            (UNCED), also known as the Earth Summit, Rio de Janeiro;
        United Nations Framework Convention on Climate Change
            (UNFCCC);
        Convention on Biological Diversity (CBD);
        Rio Declaration on Environment and Development Agenda 21;
        Maastricht Treaty establishing the European Union;
        Commission on Sustainable Development created

1993   North American Free Trade Agreement (NAFTA) signed

1994   United Nations Convention to Combat Desertification
            (UNCCD);
        United Nations Conference on Population and Development,
            Cairo;
        World Trade Organization (WTO) established

1997   Kyoto Protocol to the FCCC

1998   Rotterdam Convention on the Prior Informed Consent (PIC)
            Procedure for Certain Hazardous Chemicals and Pesticides
            in International Trade;
        CLRTAP Persistent Organic Pollutants (POPs) Protocol;
        CLRTAP Heavy Metals Protocol

2000   Millennium Development Goals adopted in UN Millennium
            Declaration

2001   Stockholm Convention on Persistent Organic Pollutants

2002   UN World Summit on Sustainable Development
            (Johannesburg Summit)

2005   Millennium Ecosystem Assessment published;
        European Union Emissions Trading Scheme (EU ETS) launched

2006   UNEP-coordinated Strategic Approach to International
            Chemicals Management (SAICM) launched

2009   United Nations Climate Change Conference (Copenhagen
            Summit)

Contributors

Regina S. Axelrod is professor of political science and chair of the political science department at Adelphi University. She has published numerous articles and books on environmental and energy policy in the United States, the European Union, and Central Europe, including *Conflict between Energy and Urban Environment: Consolidated Edison versus the City of New York* (1982) and *Environment, Energy, Public Policy: Toward a Rational Future* (1981). She has lectured at Charles University, Prague; University of Economics, Prague; and University of Budapest on nuclear power and the transition to democracy. She is an academic associate of the Atlantic Council and past president of the New York Political Science Association. In 2007, she lectured at the University of Economics, Prague, on theories of public policy and on international environmental policy on a Fulbright Senior Specialist grant.

Michele M. Betsill is associate professor of political science at Colorado State University, where she teaches courses in international relations, global environmental politics, and research methods. Her research focuses on the governance of global environmental problems, especially related to climate change. She is author and coauthor of numerous book chapters and articles on climate change politics from the global to the local level. She is coauthor (with Harriet Bulkeley) of *Cities and Climate Change: Urban Sustainability and Global Environmental Governance* (2003) and coeditor of two books: *Palgrave Advances in International Environmental Politics* (2006; with Kathryn Hochstetler and Dimitris Stevis) and *NGO Diplomacy: The Influence of Nongovernmental Organizations in International Environmental Negotiations* (2008; with Elisabeth Corell).

Elizabeth R. DeSombre is Frost Professor of Environmental Studies and professor of political science at Wellesley College, where she directs the Environmental Studies Program. Her research is on global environmental politics, particularly relating to issues of the global commons, especially protection of the ocean and atmosphere. Her recent books include *Flagging Standards: Globalization and Environmental, Safety, and Labor Regulations at Sea* (2006) and *Global Environmental Institutions* (2006). Her first book, *Domestic Sources of International Environmental Policy: Industry, Environmentalists, and U.S. Power* (2000) has won several prizes.

David Leonard Downie is director of environmental studies and associate professor of politics at Fairfield University. His research focuses on the creation, content, and implementation of national and international environmental policy.

The author of numerous publications on a variety of topics, his most recent works include *Climate Change: A Reference Handbook*, with Kate Brash and Catherine Vaughan; *Global Environmental Politics*, 5th ed., with Pam Chasek; and *Northern Lights against POPs: Combating Toxic Threats in the Arctic*, coedited with Terry Fenge. He has attended more than one hundred global environmental negotiations on climate change, stratospheric ozone protection, toxic chemicals, and sustainable development. During many negotiations on ozone protection and toxic chemicals, he has worked with the treaty secretariats to draft in-session and summary documents.

Daniel C. Esty is Hillhouse Professor of Environmental Law and Policy at Yale University with appointments in the School of Forestry and Environmental Studies and the Law School. He serves as director of Yale's Center for Business and the Environment as well as the Yale Center for Environmental Law and Policy. He is the author or editor of nine books and a number of articles on the environment and coauthor of a recent prize-winning book, *Green to Gold: How Smart Companies Use Environmental Strategy to Innovate, Create Value, and Build Competitive Advantage.* Prior to taking up his position at Yale, he was a senior fellow at the Institute for International Economics and served in a variety of senior positions in the U.S. Environmental Protection Agency.

Michael G. Faure became academic director of the Maastricht European Institute for Transnational Legal Research and professor of comparative and international environmental law at the law faculty of Maastricht University in September 1991. He still holds both positions today. In addition, he is academic director of the Ius Commune Research School and member of the board of directors of Ectil. Since February 2008, he has been half-time professor of comparative private law and economics at the Rotterdam Institute of Law and Economics of the Erasmus University and academic director of the European Doctorate in Law and Economics program. Since 1982 he has also been an attorney and member of the Antwerp bar. He publishes in the areas of environmental (criminal) law, tort and insurance, and economic analysis of (accident) law.

Kelly Sims Gallagher is associate professor of energy and environmental policy at the Fletcher School of Law and Diplomacy. She directs the Energy, Climate, and Innovation research program in Fletcher's Center for International Environment and Resource Policy. She is also senior research associate and a member of the board of directors of Belfer Center for Science and International Affairs at Harvard University, where she previously directed the Energy Technology Innovation Policy research group. She focuses on energy and climate policy in both the United States and China and is particularly interested in the role of policy in spurring the development and deployment of cleaner and more efficient energy technologies, domestically and internationally. She is the author of *China Shifts Gears: Automakers, Oil, Pollution, and Development* (2006), editor of *Acting* *in Time on Energy Policy* (2009), and author of numerous academic articles and policy reports.

Jürgen Lefevere is policy coordinator of international climate change negotiations at the European Commission in Brussels. He is responsible for coordinating the European Commission's input in international climate change negotiations and represents the European Commission in bilateral and multilateral negotiations. He has played a key role in the design and implementation of the European Union emissions trading system and, since 2004, in every major European Commission proposal on the international climate change negotiations. Prior to joining the Commission in October 2003, he was director of the Climate Change and Energy Programme at the London-based Foundation for International Environmental Law and Development. From 1993 to 1998 he was a research associate on European Union environmental law at Maastricht University.

Joanna I. Lewis is an assistant professor in the Science, Technology, and International Affairs program at Georgetown University's School of Foreign Service. Her research focuses on the renewable energy industry and policy development and mechanisms for low-carbon technology transfer in China as well as international climate change policy. She serves as an international adviser to the Energy Foundation's China Sustainable Energy Program in Beijing and as a research adviser to the Asia Society's Initiative for U.S.-China Cooperation on Energy and Climate. She is a member of the National Academies Committee on U.S.-China Cooperation on Electricity from Renewables and is also a member of the strategic advisory board of the U.S.-China program of the American Council on Renewable Energy. She previously was a senior international fellow at the Pew Center on Global Climate Change, a researcher in the China Energy Group at Lawrence Berkeley National Laboratory, and a visiting scholar at Tsinghua University.

John McCormick is professor of political science at the Indianapolis campus of Indiana University. His research and teaching interests focus on the European Union, transatlantic relations, and environmental policy. He is the author of ten books, including *Environmental Policy in the European Union* (2001), *Comparative Politics in Transition,* 6th ed. (2009), and *Europeanism* (forthcoming).

Adil Najam is Frederick S. Pardee Professor of Global Public Policy and director of Boston University's Pardee Center for the Study of the Longer-Range Future. His research focuses on developing countries in global governance and on sustainable development. He has also taught at the Fletcher School of Law and Diplomacy, Tufts University; Massachusetts Institute of Technology; and University of Massachusetts. He was a lead author for the third and fourth assessments of the Intergovernmental Panel on Climate

Change, and he serves on the UN Secretary-General's Committee for Development Policy. He is a recipient of MIT's Goodwin Medal for Effective Teaching and the Fletcher School Paddock Teaching Award. In 2009 the president of Pakistan conferred on him the medal Sitara-i-Imtiaz for services to education and environment.

Jacqueline Peel is an associate professor with the Melbourne Law School. She holds a doctorate from the University of Melbourne and will soon publish her thesis on risk assessment in international law. She earned a master's of laws from New York University, where she studied as a Fulbright Scholar and where she was also a Hauser Research Scholar. Her research focuses on the areas of domestic and international environmental law, including climate change, the intersection of law and science, and the precautionary principle. She has written widely on these topics, including an environmental law text and a book on the implementation of the precautionary principle.

Miranda A. Schreurs is director of the Environmental Policy Research Center of the Free University of Berlin and a member of the Advisory Council on the Environment, a consultative committee of the German federal government. She was selected to be the 2008–2009 faculty leader of the Fulbright New Century Scholars Program and to cochair (with Ilan Chabay) the Scientific Planning Committee on Knowledge, Learning and Societal Change under the auspices of the International Human Development Programme in Global Environmental Change. Her recent books include *Transatlantic Environment and Energy Politics* (2009, coedited with Stacy D. VanDeveer and Henrik Selin), *The Environmental Dimensions of Asian Security* (2007, coedited with In-taek Hyun), and *Comparative Environmental Politics* (2007, in Japanese).

Henrik Selin is an assistant professor in the department of international relations at Boston University, where he teaches classes and conducts research on global and regional politics of the environment and sustainable development. He is the author and coauthor of more than two dozen journal articles and book chapters; the author of *Global Governance of Hazardous Chemicals: Challenges of Multilevel Management* (2010); and coeditor of *Changing Climates in North American Politics: Institutions, Policymaking, and Multilevel Governance* (2009) and *Transatlantic Environment and Energy Politics: Comparative and International Perspectives* (2009).

Marvin S. Soroos is professor emeritus of political science and former department head at North Carolina State University in Raleigh, where he taught courses on global problems and policies, with an emphasis on environmental issues. He is the author of two books, *Beyond Sovereignty: The Challenge of Global Policy* (1986) and *The Endangered Atmosphere: Preserving a Global Commons* (1997), in addition to numerous articles in the field of international environmental law and policy. He has been a visiting professor at Williams College and the American University in Bulgaria.

Stacy D. VanDeveer is associate professor of political science at the University of New Hampshire. His research interests include international environmental policy making and its domestic impacts, the connections between environmental and security issues, and the role of expertise in policy making. In addition to authoring and coauthoring more than fifty articles, book chapters, working papers, and reports, he has coedited several books, including *Comparative Environmental Politics* (forthcoming), *Changing Climates in North American Politics* (2009), *Transatlantic Environment and Energy Politics* (2009), *EU Enlargement and the Environment* (2005), and *Saving the Seas* (1997).

Norman J. Vig is Winifred and Atherton Bean Professor Emeritus of Science, Technology and Society at Carleton College. He has written extensively on comparative politics, science and technology policy, and environmental politics and is coeditor with Michael E. Kraft of *Environmental Policy: New Directions for the Twenty-First Century*, 7th ed. (2009).

1

Introduction: Governing the International Environment

Regina S. Axelrod, Stacy D. VanDeveer, and Norman J. Vig

Humans change their environments. Environmental change is driven by the things we eat, build, make, and buy and by the decisions we make as citizens and voters. During the past few decades we have acquired the power to change the planet's climate. The early twenty-first century finds the Earth's physical and biological systems under unprecedented strain. The human population was over 6.7 billion in 2009 and is projected to increase to about 9 billion in the next half century. The United Nations estimates that one-third of the world's people live in countries with moderate to high shortages of fresh water and that this percentage could double by 2025. Many of the world's largest cities are choked by pollution. As carbon dioxide and other greenhouse gases build in the atmosphere, the average surface temperature of the Earth has reached the highest level ever, measured on an annual basis, as glaciers and polar ice recede. The biological diversity of the planet is also under heavy stress. Scientists believe that a mass extinction of plants and animals is under way and predict that a quarter of all species could be pushed to extinction by 2050 as a consequence of global warming alone. Without question, the human impact on the biosphere will be one of the most critical issues of the century.[1]

Threats to the Earth's flora and fauna, water systems, and atmosphere have been recognized by scientists and conservationists for more than a century, but it is only in the past four decades that nations have begun to address these issues on a global scale. The 1972 United Nations Conference on the Human Environment in Stockholm, Sweden, attended by 113 states, marked the beginning of organized international efforts to devise a comprehensive agenda to safeguard the environment while also promoting economic development.[2] Although no binding treaties were adopted at Stockholm, the United Nations Environment Programme (UNEP) was established, creating a permanent forum for monitoring global environmental trends, convening international meetings and conferences, and negotiating international agreements. Among its most important achievements are the 1985 Vienna Convention for the Protection of the Ozone Layer and the binding 1987 Montreal Protocol on Substances That Deplete the Ozone Layer.[3] In 1987 the World Commission on Environment and Development (known as the Brundtland Commission, after its chair, the former Norwegian prime minister Gro Harlem Brundtland) issued its historic report, *Our Common Future,* calling for a new era of "sustainable development."[4] To begin implementing this strategy,

1

the UN Conference on Environment and Development (UNCED), known as the Earth Summit, was convened in Rio de Janeiro, Brazil, in June 1992. The conference produced major international treaties on climate change and biodiversity, as well as two declarations of principle and a lengthy action program (Agenda 21) for implementing sustainable development throughout the world. Ten years later, in August 2002, 191 nations attended the World Summit on Sustainable Development (WSSD) in Johannesburg, South Africa, to reassess and renew commitments to sustainable development.[5]

As a result of these and other diplomatic achievements, a system for global environmental governance now exists. This system consists of three main elements:[6]

- intergovernmental organizations such as UNEP, the UN Development Programme, the Commission on Sustainable Development, the World Meteorological Organization, and dozens of specific treaty organizations (see Chapter 2)
- a framework of international environmental law based on several hundred multilateral treaties and agreements (see Chapter 3)
- financing institutions and mechanisms to carry out treaty commitments and build capacity in developing countries, including the World Bank and specialized lending agencies such as the Multilateral Fund and the Global Environment Facility

In addition, hundreds of bilateral and regional treaties and organizations such as those involving the United Nations Regional Seas Programme and the European Union (see Chapter 11) deal with dozens of transboundary and shared resource issues. By one count, there are more than 900 international agreements with some environmental provisions.[7]

Particularly since the 1990s, a host of nongovernmental organizations, including international environmental interest groups, scientific bodies, business and trade associations, women's groups, and indigenous peoples' organizations, have also come to play an important role in international environmental governance (see Chapter 5). These organizations participate in international negotiations, help to monitor treaty compliance, and often play a leading role in implementing policies. At the Johannesburg summit, more than 20,000 individuals registered as participants and countless others attended a parallel Global People's Forum and summit of indigenous peoples.[8] The increased access to and transparency of international environmental governance is one of the most remarkable achievements of the emerging global environmental governance system.

Despite these strides, there is a growing perception that the current international governance system remains weak and ineffective.[9] Many of the international environmental institutions lack adequate funding and effective enforcement mechanisms. Because no world government or sovereign political authority exists, international agencies often work at cross purposes and must rely on individual states to carry out their policies. States are reluctant to relinquish their sovereignty and right to pursue their own national interests. Consequently, many trends and patterns of global environmental degradation have not been reversed and may result in devastating ecological crises unless global institutions are strengthened and many other actors (including private organizations and citizens) take on far more responsibility for environmental governance.[10]

The role of the United States in international environmental diplomacy has been especially disappointing in recent years. Although the Clinton administration signed the 1997 Kyoto Protocol, which set targets and timetables for reducing greenhouse gas emissions that cause global warming, neither this treaty, nor others such as the Convention on Biological Diversity, the Basel Convention on the trade in hazardous wastes, and agreements covering biosafety and a host of transboundary air pollutants were ratified by the U.S. Senate. President George W. Bush repudiated the Kyoto Protocol in 2001 and showed little interest in other multilateral environmental agreements and institutions. U.S. support for many international environmental programs has declined over time. This indifference has resulted in deep divisions between the United States and both the European Union and the developing nations of the "South" (see Chapters 10–12).[11] Yet even here the picture is more complex than it might seem at first glance. Although environmental policy development was largely abandoned by the U.S. federal government in the early years of this century, many U.S. states and cities continued to make policy in response to international environmental challenges. Many states, for example, enacted policies to combat climate change and expand renewable energy generation even when the federal government was opposed to doing so.[12] In 2009, the Obama administration arrived in Washington, D.C., pledging to return to domestic environmental policy making and to steer the United States toward a re-engagement in global environmental cooperation (and in other areas of multilateral politics). Such changes take time and require the support of Congress and the American people. Time will tell if a new era in U.S. domestic and international environmental politics has arrived.

This book presents an overview of the development of international environmental institutions, law, and policies and attempts to assess their adequacy. The authors analyze developments since World War II, with special emphasis on trends since the 1992 Earth Summit. They share some of the current concern and pessimism about trends in both global environmental degradation and governance in the past two decades, but they also take a longer view in evaluating the new environmental regimes that are emerging. Most authors in this volume argue that there are important lessons to learn and reasons for hope. However, more serious attention to global environmental governance is required of citizens and governments alike if disturbing and dangerous trends are to be reversed.

The last twenty-plus years have seen dramatic and often surprising political and economic changes, and this volume tries to assess some of these and learn from them. In addition to two large global summits on the environment and sustainable human development, the past twenty-five years witnessed developments such as the end of apartheid in South Africa, the collapse of Soviet-style communism in Eastern Europe and across the Soviet Union, and a host of other transitions to democratic rule in Latin America and elsewhere. These changes brought unprecedented growth in the number of democracies in the world. The same era witnessed the deepening of European integration and expansion of the European Union from twelve countries to twenty-seven Member States (with more applicants in the wings). China, India, and a few other developing countries have roared into the global economy, reshaping aspects of their domestic politics, international relations, and global resource and environmental trends. These developments can both affect and inspire global environmental governance. So, for example, many of these political and economic changes have helped drive ever-increasing use of the Earth's resources (along with the seemingly never-ending growth in North American consumption). However, if Europeans can overcome generations of war to build a unified Europe and citizens can demand their democratic and basic human rights and replace dictators with elected officials, then it may be possible to reverse global environmental degradation and build effective global environmental governance institutions to engender sustainable development around the globe.

The next two sections of this chapter provide a brief overview of the theoretical context for studying international environmental governance. The first of these summarizes the most important perspectives from international relations theory relevant to the emergence of international environmental institutions and law. The second section discusses the concept of "sustainable development," which became the dominant ideological framework for global environmental policies in the 1990s. The third section of the chapter outlines the organization and contents of the book, briefly discussing each of the three parts: (I) international environmental law, institutions, and regimes, (II) global environmental policies and policy implementation, and (III) national and regional case studies and controversies in sustainable development. A short conclusion summarizes some of the themes of the book.

International Relations, Regimes, and Governance

A large body of international relations theory is applicable to the development of international environmental institutions and agreements (see Chapter 4).[13] The study of international relations has traditionally been dominated by two broad theoretical schools: realism and liberalism. "Realists" view the world as an anarchic collection of sovereign nation-states, each of which is a unitary actor in pursuing its unique national interests. These interests are largely defined in terms of relative power and security compared with other states. In this perspective, nation-states do not cooperate with one another unless it is clearly in their self-interest to do so, and cooperative behavior will continue only so long as the parties perceive this condition to be met. International laws and institutions are thus essentially instruments for promoting or defending national interests and have little or no independent effect on the behavior of nations. Indeed, they can usually function only if strong or hegemonic states maintain them and enforce their decisions against weaker members or other states. The potential for international cooperation is therefore quite limited, and international laws and institutions are likely to be fragile and impermanent.[14]

This anarchic, state-centered perspective has been increasingly challenged in recent decades by a variety of "liberals," "neoliberals," and "liberal institutionalists." While most of these theorists concede that states are the primary actors on the international level, they hold that the traditional view of state sovereignty and unitary interest cannot explain the steady growth of international cooperation or the persistence of many specialized international institutions in the contemporary world. Although there are many strands of thinking, most liberal theorists hold that states are interdependent and, in fact, have many common interests that lead them to cooperate; moreover, they believe that international institutions not only serve these common interests but create further incentives for cooperation.[15] In other words, institutions matter, and they influence the preferences and behavior of states by allowing them to improve collective welfare outcomes by cooperating. Whereas realists focus on *relative* status gains (especially regarding military security), liberals tend to emphasize *absolute* benefits (especially mutual economic gains) made possible by international agreements and institutions that solve collective action problems.

Over the last generation, a third, broad theoretical perspective has joined realism and liberalism in the pantheon of common theoretical approaches to understanding global environmental politics: constructivism.[16] Constructivism focuses attention on the influence of ideas, collective values, and identities and norms in international politics. Constructivism refers to the argument that social reality is "constructed" through social interaction: that humans, collectively, construct the world in which they live through their identities and debates about values and norms (about what is justified or appropriate). Because of constructivism's attention to the influence of ideas and values, some international relations theorists view it as the contemporary variant of idealism.[17] For constructivists, international cooperation is more than mere ad hoc coalitions or a reflection of shared interests. It reflects who the participants are (or believe they are), and it can shape how they see themselves over time and what they view as appropriate. In other words, cooperation has the potential to be transformative in constructivism. For example, political scientist Peter Haas argues that a constructivist understanding of the effectiveness or impacts of conferences like the global environmental and sustainable development summits in 1972, 1992, and 2002 focuses more on how such meetings shaped actor understandings, raised awareness, and brought political actors to agreement on norms, values, and ideas (on which they may act later).[18]

In other words, global environmental politics both reveals and shapes emerging, collectively held consensus positions and norms—about policies, problems, and how we understand the global environment and our place in it (and the place of international politics). For example, constructivists might examine scientific and policy debates around climate change to better understand how some actors reach consensus or agreement while others continue to question widely held views or understandings. They might also explore the role and use of language and discourse in such debates.

During the past two decades many environmental policy scholars have turned to the concept of "regimes." International environmental regimes are composed of the international treaties and agreements, intergovernmental organizations, binding and nonbinding norms and principles, relevant national and local government institutions, and associated nongovernmental and private institutions that define and implement policies in different issue areas such as climate change, maritime oil pollution, or endangered species protection. In Chapter 4, David Downie explains regime theory in more detail and discusses many prominent examples of international environmental regimes. Drawing on other strands of international relations theory and systems theory, he also analyzes the obstacles to effective international cooperation. His chapter thus reveals the real difficulties of achieving effective international environmental policies.

Some theorists are more optimistic about the potential for a global governance system comprising an increasingly dense and interactive network of international regimes.[19] "Governance" in this sense does not presuppose a central government; rather, that coordination of action can occur through many different institutions, including private social and economic systems and nongovernmental organizations, as well as a variety of governmental institutions at different levels. This concept often presupposes some kind of global "civil society" or decentralized network of autonomous social institutions that represent citizens and organized interests and engage in cooperative actions to achieve broad goals such as sustainable development. Increased communication and exchange of information among individuals and groups around the world through the Internet and other means can magnify the impact of such civic action to the point where common ideas and values begin to influence the actions of governments from the bottom up.[20]

This brief discussion highlights the fact that whatever one's basic theoretical perspective, the development of international environmental cooperation has become one of the most fruitful and dynamic fields of international relations. Although there is no consensus among scholars on the nature of the world system or the autonomy and durability of current international environmental institutions, laws, and policies, it is undeniable that the global environment has become a principal concern of political actors as well as scholars around the world. From this broader vantage point, the halting and confused human response to gathering evidence of potential ecological catastrophe may be less discouraging than short-term observations suggest.

Sustainable Development

Cutting across theoretical disputes are the realities of world economic and social development. Environmental threats are the product not only of population growth and ignorant or careless individual actions; they are deeply embedded in our religious, cultural, economic, and social systems. Perhaps the most obvious realities are that these systems are highly fragmented and differentiated and that global economic development is grossly uneven. The gap between the world's richer and poorer nations is enormous and growing. So, for example, while GDP per capita in the United States is more than $46,000, about a billion people, concentrated mostly in the world's fifty poorest countries, live on less than one dollar per day. These differences among nations at various stages and levels of development have profound implications for the global environment. Recognized at least since the Stockholm conference is the fact that the needs and agendas of developed nations (the "North") and developing countries (the "South") are fundamentally different, making it difficult to reach consensus on international policies that benefit all parties (see Chapter 12). Essentially, while the North gives substantial attention to environmental issues that threaten ecological stability, the South has placed greater emphasis on immediate needs for economic growth to raise standards of living. Indeed, developing countries at the Stockholm conference feared that environmental protection was a plot by the North to limit their development—a concern that still echoes through all international negotiations.[21]

The North-South division raises fundamental issues of international equity.[22] Developing countries rightly argue that the developed countries have benefited from environmental exploitation in the past and are responsible for most of the world's pollution and resource depletion, including that leading to ozone depletion and climate change; therefore it is primarily their responsibility to deal with these problems. Furthermore, developing countries are not willing to foreclose opportunities for economic growth that would permanently lock them into poverty and dependency while the peoples of the North engage in profligate consumption. Representatives of developing countries (organized as the Group of 77 in the United Nations since 1964 but now actually including more than 130 states) thus usually condition their willingness to participate in international environmental treaties and agreements on concessions from the North, such as guarantees of special funding and transfer of technologies to enable them to reduce their impact on the environment while increasing economic growth.

Another fundamental dimension of global environmental protection concerns intertemporal, or intergenerational, equity. That is, policies must consider not only the needs of the present generation but those of the future. Edith Brown Weiss, a leading scholar of international environmental law, defines three essential principles: (1) each generation should be required to conserve the diversity of the resource base so that it does not unduly restrict the options available to future generations; (2) each generation should maintain the planet's overall quality so that it is bequeathed in no worse condition than it was received; and (3) members of every generation should have comparable rights of access to the legacy of past generations and should conserve this access for future generations.[23] The third principle implies a degree of intragenerational equity as a condition for intergenerational equity; that is, no group should either be denied a right to present environmental resources or be asked to bear a disproportionate share of environmental burdens (a principle often referred to as *environmental justice*).

The concept of sustainable development was born of these concerns. First set out in *World Conservation Strategy*, published by the International Union for the Conservation of Nature (IUCN) in cooperation with the World Wildlife Fund and UNEP in 1980, the concept was popularized in the Brundtland Commission report of 1987. The famous definition of sustainable development is from this report: "Sustainable development is development that meets the needs of the present without compromising the ability of future generations to meet their own needs." This was immediately followed by the explication of two key concepts embedded within it: "the concept of 'needs,' in particular the essential needs of the world's poor, to which over-riding priority should be given"; and "the idea of limitations imposed by the state of technology and social organization on the environment's ability to meet present and future needs."[24]

Several elements in this definition are critical for an understanding of sustainable development. First, the concept clearly represents an attempt to bridge the concerns and interests of developed and developing nations, but it applies to both (that is, industrial as well as less developed countries must change their production and consumption patterns). Second, it attempts to reconcile economic growth and environmental protection, not view them as trade-offs; indeed, the Brundtland report argues that neither is possible without the other. Third, the concept is strongly anthropocentric. It starts from the premise that human needs must be met in order to address environmental problems. Thus improvement in the living conditions in poor countries, and especially of women and marginal social and economic groups, is an essential precondition for ecological preservation. Fourth, the limits to growth are not ultimately physical or biological but social and technological; it is assumed that environmental problems can be solved. Finally, the concept is extremely general, lacking specific content on how sustainable development is to be attained or who is responsible for achieving it. This vagueness was deliberate: it allows the idea to be adopted by virtually everyone as a way of bringing people together to seek common ground. In this formulation it is clearly a political and social construct, not a scientific concept or blueprint.[25]

Sustainable development can be defined in numerous other ways; by one count at least seventy definitions are in circulation.[26] These formulations reflect the different values and priorities of the holders. For example, in 1991 the IUCN published a sequel to *World Conservation Strategy* entitled *Caring for the Earth*, which put emphasis back on ecological limits: sustainable development was defined as "improving the quality of human life while living within the carrying capacity of supporting ecosystems." The more general idea of "sustainability" has also been the subject of considerable controversy; *Caring for the Earth* defines it simply as "a characteristic of a process or state that can be maintained indefinitely."[27] This implies such basic principles as "rates of utilization of renewable resources must not be greater than rates of regeneration"; "waste emissions must not be greater than the assimilation capacities of the environment"; and "rates of use of non-renewables must not be greater than the rate of creation of renewable substitutes."[28]

Whatever the conceptual and ideological differences below the surface, there have been numerous attempts to translate sustainable development into policy initiatives. The most important political effort to do so occurred at the UN Conference on Environment and Development in 1992 in Rio de Janeiro. UNCED produced both a general declaration of principles (Rio Declaration on Environment and Development) and Agenda 21, a massive effort to define strategies and policies for implementing sustainable development. Governments around the world pledged to formulate sustainable development plans and programs, and a new Commission on Sustainable Development was established by the UN General Assembly to monitor these commitments. Many other regional, national, and local organizations, including the European Union, have adopted the principles and goals of sustainable development since 1992. Organizations such as UNEP, the IUCN–World Conservation Union, the World Bank, the Organization for Economic Cooperation and Development, and the U.S. National Academy of Sciences have also been actively working to identify specific empirical "indicators" for measuring progress toward sustainable development.[29]

Despite these efforts, there is a general sense of disappointment, if not despair, regarding implementation of Agenda 21 since the Rio summit. International aid flows for sustainable development projects have failed to come anywhere close to the levels considered necessary in 1992; indeed, official development assistance has *declined* in absolute terms.[30] A sense of pessimism thus pervaded the World Summit on Sustainable Development held in Johannesburg on the tenth anniversary of UNCED. The WSSD understandably focused on implementing existing obligations rather than launching new programs, although some new policy goals, financial commitments, and public-private partnerships were agreed upon. The summit also produced a Johannesburg Declaration on Sustainable Development and a Plan of Implementation to guide future investments.[31]

Most of the chapters in this book discuss efforts to incorporate the idea of sustainable development into international environmental institutions, treaties, and policies. The case studies in Part III evaluate particular national and regional policies and projects from this perspective, further illustrating the obstacles to realizing sustainable development in both North and South.

Overview of the Book

This section outlines the main themes and concepts of the three parts of the book and briefly summarizes each of the individual contributions.

International Environmental Institutions and Regimes

International environmental organizations take many forms. Some of the oldest, like European river basin commissions or the International Joint

Commission formed by the United States and Canada in 1909 to preserve the Great Lakes, are bilateral or multilateral bodies created to encourage cooperation in managing a shared resource. Some, like the International Whaling Commission and International Tropical Timber Organization, concern the worldwide harvesting and trade of specific categories of living resources, while others protect "common pool" resources such as Antarctica and the high seas that are beyond national jurisdictions. The International Maritime Organization regulates shipping to reduce pollution as a result of both normal operations and accidents. Still others, like the World Meteorological Organization, conduct scientific research and monitor environmental change on a global scale. Finally, many are essentially ad hoc organizations, such as the secretariats and conferences of the parties (COPs) that are created to monitor and develop detailed protocols to treaties and conventions.

Most of these international bodies are *intergovernmental* organizations (IGOs), meaning that they are created by member states and are accountable to them. In most cases member states are formally equal in governing (though not financing) these institutions, but in some (notably the World Bank and the International Monetary Fund) weighted voting procedures are used that reflect donor contributions. This has become a contentious issue in negotiations over multilateral funding mechanisms to channel special economic assistance to the South. The Global Environment Facility, which provides funding primarily for implementation of the climate change and biodiversity conventions in developing countries, was restructured after 1992 to give recipient countries more influence in financial decisions.

In Chapter 2, Marvin S. Soroos looks at the evolution of global institutions since the Stockholm era and focuses on the record and current state of five principal IGOs: the United Nations General Assembly, the United Nations Environment Programme, the Intergovernmental Panel on Climate Change (IPCC), the Global Environment Facility (GEF), and the World Bank. Overall, he finds substantial accomplishments in regard to focusing worldwide attention on environmental problems; framing new principles, policies, and laws; facilitating international treaties and agreements; coordinating environmental monitoring and promoting scientific research; and providing modest technical and financial support for sustainable development projects. But the picture is quite mixed. Newer institutions like GEF have gotten off to a slow start in promoting sustainable development. And, while the World Bank has made considerable efforts to develop environmentally sensitive loan policies, it continues to support many destructive projects, so that it is doubtful whether, on balance, it can be viewed as furthering sustainable development. Overall, despite great progress since the 1960s, it appears that the state of critical environmental IGOs has deteriorated rather than improved in the post-Rio period. Soroos suggests that a new central UN agency such as an Environmental Security Council may be needed to deal effectively with coming problems, but he doubts that agreement can be reached on creating such an institution. The alternative is to strengthen existing institutions and improve coordination among them.

There are at least 200 multilateral environmental agreements (MEAs) or treaties of global significance.[32] These international agreements have established a fairly comprehensive body of international environmental law covering the atmosphere, oceans and seas, international watercourses, hazardous wastes and materials, wildlife conservation, biodiversity and habitat protection, desertification, the polar regions, and outer space.[33] International law differs from domestic law, however, in that it is normally binding only on participating states and it applies to national governments, not individuals or corporations. (There are some exceptions, for example, in human rights law.) Moreover, international courts cannot force states to comply with their obligations. The International Court of Justice, or World Court, hears cases and renders opinions that carry great weight, but sovereign states must ultimately agree to accept them. Nevertheless, even nonbinding declarations and principles (often called "soft law") can influence the behavior of governments.

Jacqueline Peel provides a history of the development of international environmental law and its most important principles in Chapter 3. She points out that before the establishment of the United Nations in 1945, there was no international forum in which to raise international environmental issues. Although the UN Charter does not explicitly mention the environment or conservation of resources, the UN convened its first environmental conference in 1949 and hosted many negotiations prior to the Stockholm conference in 1972. Most existing environmental treaties were signed between 1972 and 1992, and recent decisions of the International Court of Justice confirm that the environment is now considered within the mainstream of international law. Peel explains the sources of international law, the role of different actors in formulating and implementing it, and the most important emerging principles of environmental law. She outlines the development of international legal standards in six broad fields: protection of flora and fauna, the marine environment, freshwater resources, air quality, waste management, and hazardous substances. Finally, Peel concludes that implementation and enforcement of this body of international law will be the most critical issue in the next phase of its development, suggesting that both international courts and nonjudicial bodies such as tribunals of the World Trade Organization are playing stronger roles than heretofore.

Chapter 4 by David Leonard Downie analyzes the nature of international environmental policy regimes. Building on previous scholarship, Downie defines such regimes as "a set of integrated principles, norms, rules, procedures, and institutions that actors create or accept to regulate and coordinate action in a particular issue area of international relations." He explains in detail the meaning of each of these terms, using as an example the global regime to protect the ozone layer. He also outlines the structure of ten other environmental regimes before he discusses a wide range of political, economic, procedural, scientific, and cultural factors that can undermine the effectiveness of regimes and make international cooperation difficult. While not denying the success of some existing regimes, his chapter casts a cold eye of realism on the strategic difficulties in achieving effective international policy.

In Chapter 5, John McCormick argues that the failure of the nation-state system since World War II—including its dependent environmental organizations—has led to the rapid rise of local, national, and international nongovernmental organizations (NGOs) to fill the vacuum. These groups, ranging from thousands of local grassroots organizations to large federations of national organizations such as the International Union for Conservation of Nature and the World Wide Fund for Nature, play an increasingly important role in setting the environmental agenda, participating in negotiations that create environmental regimes, and monitoring the implementation of treaties and agreements and environmental conditions generally. NGOs are now essential actors in international environmental regimes, whether or not they have official status. Collectively, McCormick and others argue, they provide the backbone of an emerging global civil society in which the loyalties of individuals transcend national boundaries. The enlarged roles of environmental NGOs in the international arena have been controversial because of their challenge to the nation-state. The lack of accountability and ambivalence about whom they actually represent raises questions about their legitimacy. Nevertheless, they remain important and credible actors with increasing influence.

This does not mean that international NGOs are homogeneous in their beliefs, goals, or methods. McCormick distinguishes several different philosophies of environmentalism, as well as basic differences between groups in developing and developed countries and among different socioeconomic groups. Focusing on some of the larger international NGOs, he provides numerous examples of how they carry out different functions and specialize in different issue areas. They also collaborate with one another and with IGOs in various campaigns, often forming broad international alliances (for example, to save tropical rain forests and endangered species). They are also handicapped, however, by the lack of any central environmental authority on the international level, by the consequent need to influence a large number of national governments, by the power of countervailing interest groups, and by the weakness of international legal enforcement.[34]

Global Environmental Policy: Cases and Questions

The range of international environmental policies currently in force is vast, covering, among other things, protection of endangered plants and animals; protection against transboundary pollution of air, water, and soil; protection of the atmosphere against acidification, ozone depletion, and climate change; protection of the oceans against oil spills and the dumping of radioactive and other hazardous materials; conservation of fisheries; regulation of trade in dangerous chemicals, pesticides, and hazardous wastes; measures to combat desertification; and protection of Antarctica. In addition, new policies are emerging for consideration of environmental protection under the rules of international trade and for promoting sustainable development initiatives pursuant to Agenda 21.

Policies may take the form of binding treaties or secondary legislation, or they may take the form of policy declarations or voluntary programs to achieve certain results. They usually require implementation by actors at many levels, including businesses, local governments, and grassroots organizations as well as national governments. Evaluation of the *effectiveness* of policies is complex and can be measured in many ways: for example, by whether states are in legal compliance with treaties, whether monetary and other resources are being spent on programs, or by the actual results of the policy measured in terms of environmental improvements. Policies are also *learning processes* in that the actors involved continually gain new knowledge about problems and engage other parties in parallel efforts to achieve goals.

Climate change resulting from a gradual buildup of greenhouse gases (GHGs) in the Earth's atmosphere is perhaps the most serious, complex, and contentious of all international environmental policy issues. In Chapter 6, Michele M. Betsill traces the origins of concern over this problem and analyzes policy responses since the First World Climate Conference in 1979. She discusses the development of scientific research as a basis for negotiations leading to the Framework Convention on Climate Change (FCCC) in 1992. The chapter explains the principles underlying this historic agreement before analyzing the first binding agreement restricting GHG emissions made pursuant to the FCCC, the Kyoto Protocol of 1997. Although the United States neither ratified nor implemented the Kyoto treaty, the protocol came into legal force because of other states' ratifications. Betsill argues that the Kyoto agreement and subsequent negotiations have had many important indirect effects on policy actors at many levels of government and in the private sector—in the United States and in ratifying states. For example, many states and cities and private corporations (in the United States and around the globe) have adopted GHG reduction strategies despite the lack of international consensus. As negotiations for a climate agreement to follow the Kyoto Protocol progressed, the role and actions of the United States, and of the largest developing country emitters, loomed large in global negotiations. Yet, Betsill's chapter makes it clear that global climate change governance is a complex, multilevel process that is not confined only to multilateral treaty making. Such multilevel governance, she argues, presents new opportunities to develop effective policy responses around the world.

A consequence of modern societies' reliance on chemicals and heavy metals is the release of hazardous substances that produce long-term environmental damage and pose significant health risks. Many international and regional treaties address these issues, and the UN has a prominent role. Chapter 7 by Henrik Selin focuses on the 1989 Basel Convention on the Control of Transboundary Movements of Hazardous Wastes and Their Disposal; the 1998 Rotterdam Convention on the Prior Informed Consent Procedure for Certain Hazardous Chemicals and Pesticides in International Trade; the 1998 Protocol on Persistent Organic Pollutants to the Convention on Long-Range Transboundary Air Pollution (CLRTAP); and the 2001 Stockholm Convention on Persistent Organic Pollutants. The Basel Convention seeks to regulate trade in hazardous waste through a notification scheme. The Rotterdam Convention focuses on transparency in the trade of chemicals by requiring notification to importers by exporters of such materials. The aim of the CLRTAP Protocol is to reduce the release and long-term transport of persistent organic pollutants. The Stockholm Convention regulates the production of persistent organic chemicals. Selin discusses problems incurred by these regulatory regimes and suggests means to strengthen them. Hazardous materials are still being produced in large quantities, and many states are suspicious of relinquishing national authority to international treaty regimes or organizations. His treatment of these issues also demonstrates the tremendous growth in international cooperation over time, from isolated and rather modest agreements to a large and complex set of governance regimes. The European Union has taken a leadership role in adopting regulations targeting hazardous chemicals and electronic waste, but countries all over the world are struggling to manage hazardous substances and wastes. Selin argues for more proactive and precautionary actions, including giving industry greater responsibilities for reducing hazardous waste and the development of green chemistry.

International trade in dangerous substances is only one example of how economic globalization has led to a host of new concerns over environmental impacts. Many environmentalists fear that international trade agreements such as the North American Free Trade Agreement (NAFTA) and establishment of the World Trade Organization (WTO) accelerate global environmental degradation in several ways: by the sheer increase in consumption of resources and production of wastes that will result from accelerated economic growth; by shifting capital and production to "pollution havens" with weak environmental laws; and by establishing rules of international trade that may conflict with and override existing multilateral environmental agreements and environmental legislation in individual countries. For example, laws restricting trade in endangered species or banning products harvested by environmentally damaging methods might be found to violate international free trade principles.[35]

In Chapter 8, Daniel C. Esty takes a somewhat more optimistic view of the potential for balancing international trade and environmental protection. He analyzes the concerns of environmentalists that liberalized trade and increasing competitive pressures will undermine existing environmental protections, and he summarizes the counterarguments of free trade advocates. NAFTA was the first such agreement to integrate aspects of environmental and trade policy. Esty evaluates the Environmental Side Agreement to NAFTA in some detail, generally finding it a more successful effort to balance economic and environmental goals than many critics have suggested.[36] Moreover, in the trade agreement negotiating authority granted to President George W. Bush in 2002 and in resolutions at the World Summit on Sustainable Development in Johannesburg, the linkage between trade and environmental protection was explicitly recognized. Recent U.S. trade agreements also include some environmental commitments. Still, Esty concludes that the WTO needs reform—especially to increase transparency and access by

NGOs—and that the underlying General Agreement on Tariffs and Trade may have to be revised to ensure the trade regime's compatibility with environmental treaties.[37]

The final chapter in Part II, by Michael Faure and Jürgen Lefevere, focuses on the broader problem of improving compliance with international environmental agreements.[38] The authors distinguish among treaty compliance, implementation, enforcement, and effectiveness. *Compliance* refers to the extent to which the behavior of states conforms to the rules set out in a treaty, whereas *implementation* involves specific actions taken by states within their own legal systems to make a treaty operative; *enforcement* denotes measures to force state compliance and implementation; and *effectiveness* focuses on whether the objectives of the treaty are actually achieved. Compliance does not guarantee effectiveness but is usually a necessary condition unless the treaty itself is so weak that compliance requires no changes in behavior.

Traditionally, international agreements have included some dispute settlement procedures or other provisions for invoking legal, economic, or political sanctions against noncompliant parties, but in practice such sanctions have rarely been enforced and are seldom effective in achieving treaty objectives. Faure and Lefevere discuss the many factors that can affect rates of compliance, including the number of parties involved, the capacities of national governments, the strength of NGOs, and the nature of the substantive provisions (primary rules) written into the treaties themselves. They show how there has been a shift from the traditional enforcement approach to a "managerial" or "facilitative" approach in some recent environmental agreements such as the Montreal Protocol on ozone-depleting substances and the Kyoto Protocol on climate change. These new "comprehensive noncompliance response" systems attempt to induce compliance through information and advice, technical assistance, and other incentives rather than by invoking negative sanctions. The nonadversarial approaches seem to be gaining in popularity, and they have been successful in some cases, yet it remains to be seen how effective these nonadversarial methods will be generally as international environmental law and governance shift toward a greater focus on implementation.

Implementing Global Policy: Cases and Controversies in Sustainable Development

Because the concept of sustainable development is broad and has quite different meanings when translated into different cultures and languages, it is difficult to evaluate national policies in terms of specific criteria or indicators of sustainability.[39] Some nations such as New Zealand and the Netherlands have adopted far-reaching sustainable development plans and programs, whereas others have dealt with sustainability issues in a piecemeal and ad hoc fashion, if at all.[40] But apart from rhetorical justification of selected measures under the sustainable development label, many policies and projects at the national and local levels do, in fact, have major implications for sustainability.

Decisions about energy supply or land use within a given country can impact other nations or the entire global system; this is especially true of very large nations such as China, Brazil, and the United States. Major projects within countries (even small states) also attract capital and technical support from international banks and corporations, thus involving the international community in what may appear to be local developments. It is important to study these linkages between national politics and international action as part of global environmental policy.[41]

Among developed nations, the United States has been among the most resistant to the idea of sustainable development and to ratification of multilateral environmental agreements in the past decade.[42] Although the leader in establishing many of the environmental treaties through the 1980s (including the Montreal Protocol), the United States has been an international laggard since the first Bush administration and became openly hostile to multilateral institutions and policies during the second Bush administration. American policy also reflected a shift to conservative majorities in the U.S. Congress between 1995 and 2007, making it virtually impossible to ratify any environmental treaties. Although Democratic majorities in Congress ushered in greater attention to environmental issues and regulation, by late 2009 they were not yet able to change in the record of U.S. environmental treaty ratification. Thus, the United States has not ratified (and is not a party to) the Convention on Biological Diversity and its Biosafety Protocol, the Kyoto Protocol, or the Basel Convention. American avoidance of certain kinds of international environmental agreements predates (and may outlast) the era of conservative ascendancy, requiring a deeper analysis of U.S. behavior.

Chapter 10 by Elizabeth R. DeSombre explores a wide range of hypotheses as to why the United States has initiated or supported some multilateral environmental agreements and opposed others over the past several decades. In particular, why has the United States taken a unilateral course on such major issues as climate change, biodiversity, trade in hazardous wastes, and the law of the sea? In search of a consistent causal explanation, DeSombre examines these cases as well as others in which the United States has preferred a cooperative approach, such as on combating ozone layer depletion and endangered species protections. After determining that most conventional explanations concerning American culture and ideology, scientific uncertainty, relative vulnerability to harm, and the projected costs of regulation fail to explain all cases, she suggests a more nuanced explanation that focuses on certain aspects of U.S. domestic politics. In general, the United States supports international agreements when it already has enacted domestic regulations in the same area and opposes international controls that go beyond domestic regulation or would be difficult to implement in the U.S. system. This pattern can in turn be explained by institutional peculiarities of the American system, especially the unique role that Congress plays in shaping foreign policy. DeSombre and others have noted that the Senate, especially, tends to be responsive to domestic business and industry pressures seeking to block international regulation. This pattern may be changing, however, as some sectors of industry now favor action on climate change and other issues and because international institutions may, over time, shape the preferences of U.S. domestic actors.

In contrast with the United States, the European Union (EU) has increasingly taken the lead on international aspects as well as many aspects of domestic environmental policy. Chapter 11 by Regina S. Axelrod, Miranda A. Schreurs and Norman J. Vig explains how the European integration process and its evolving institutional structure have contributed to this leadership role. Although the Treaty of Rome, which established the European Economic Community in 1957, made no mention of environmental policy, beginning in 1972 the Community adopted a series of environmental action programs and enacted numerous specific environmental laws as a way of harmonizing economic policies. Since 1986 several major treaty revisions have strengthened the legal capacity of the Community to legislate in the field of environmental protection. The Maastricht Treaty of 1992 transformed the European Community into a broader European Union, which has since grown from twelve to twenty-seven states. The Union has also explicitly incorporated the goal of sustainable development into the treaty and has taken an increasingly active role in international environmental diplomacy on matters such as climate change. In a number of environmental policy areas, EU and U.S. federal policymaking often diverged on global environmental issues during the past fifteen-plus years.[43] The EU has enacted a large set of innovative and ambitious environmental polices over the past ten or fifteen years on a wide range of issues, several opposed by the U.S. government and U.S. corporate actors. This growth, however, has also increased the implementation challenges in both the newer EU Member States and in longtime Member States.[44]

Chapter 11 describes the structure and evolution of the EU in detail and analyzes policy developments since 1992. Although the Union is still an intergovernmental organization in the sense that decisions must ultimately be approved by the Council of Ministers representing the Member States, in practice it functions as a supranational governance system in which most policies are adopted by majority voting in the council and the parliament. Moreover, the council's composition changes according to the subject at issue; thus it consists of environment ministers when it considers environmental legislation. As a result, EU environmental policies have been less subject to opposition group pressure than is the case in the United States. At the same time, the EU treaty requires integration of environmental policy into other policy sectors in order to promote sustainable development. Several new, innovative policies that go beyond measures in the United States are discussed in the chapter. Yet, as the authors make clear, the EU faces major hurdles in implementing sustainable development policies and in adapting governance structures and policy standards to both old and new Member States.[45]

Chapter 12 shifts the focus to the developing world, or the South, as opposed to the wealthy, industrialized North. Adil Najam argues that the South has a well-developed collective identity and sense of purpose dating back to the Stockholm Conference on the Human Environment and the quest for a "new international economic order" in the 1970s. This unity is manifest primarily in the Group of 77 bloc in the United Nations, now consisting of some 134 developing countries. Najam explains how preparations for the 1992 UNCED in Rio offered the South an opportunity to revive the North-South dialogue around the theme of sustainable development. From the South's perspective, the Rio conference provided a high point in its ability to shape the international agenda. Although most of its demands were not met, UNCED did link the economic development goals of the South to the environmental agenda of the North, and it established several important new principles of international environmental law such as the principle of common but differentiated responsibility. Nevertheless, in looking back at the decade between Rio and the World Summit on Sustainable Development in 2002, Najam concludes that these principles and the "Rio bargain" on sustainable development have largely been abandoned at the global level and have led to widespread disillusionment among developing countries.

Chapter 13 by Joanna I. Lewis and Kelly Sims Gallagher addresses energy, environmental, and sustainability issues in a rapidly developing county: China. The chapter presents a wealth of data about China's energy resources and use and its transportation and electricity generation infrastructure. It analyzes political institutions that shape energy issues in the country. As the authors make clear, providing energy for 1.3 billion people and a growing and modernizing economy in a sustainable manner is an enormous challenge. On one hand, the environmental and social costs of China's energy and transportation infrastructure are huge; on the other hand, the Chinese central government demonstrates growing environmental concern and growing interest in serious environmental policy and investment in renewable energy generation. The costs of moving China away from coal are also enormous, as is the challenge of implementing new environmental standards at the local level. Yet China's automobile efficiency standards are higher than those in the United States, and its investments in wind power have put it on track to be second in the world in terms of installed capacity. Lewis and Sims Gallagher make clear that China faces enormous obstacles in transitioning to a more sustainable society, but they also demonstrate that China's environmental politics and regulation are changing rapidly.

The formerly socialist countries of central and eastern Europe have also experienced rapid political and economic transformations during the past generation, moving from Soviet-style communism to capitalist democracies and EU Member States.[46] In Chapter 14, Regina S. Axelrod discusses one fascinating example: the political controversy surrounding the Temelin nuclear power plant in the Czech Republic. Her chapter also frames this case in the context of what many are calling the global renaissance of nuclear power, comparing aspects of Czech nuclear power controversies with ongoing debates in the United States. Western governments, banks, and corporations and various IGOs were involved in upgrading Soviet-designed nuclear power reactors such as Temelin in the central and eastern European countries to ensure their safety and continued operation and to provide alternatives to dirty coal-fired plants. As Axelrod explains, however, serious technical and environmental problems raise questions about the wisdom of this strategy and have led to protests both inside and outside the Czech Republic. She looks at the project in the broader context of sustainable development and the evolution of Czech democracy and society since 1989. She finds a troubling rejection of sustainable development policies by Czech governments since 1992, accompanied by an exclusion of environmental NGOs and the reassertion of state bureaucratic and technocratic methods of decision making. It does not appear that Czech citizens had either access to information or opportunities to participate in what are regarded as technical areas of regulation. Axelrod argues that nuclear power debates demonstrate that the concept of sustainability remains new and rather marginalized in both the Czech Republic and the United States.

Last, in Chapter 15, Stacy D. VanDeveer's contribution addresses the related issues of consumption, transnational commodity chains, and sustainability. Human consumption of the Earth's resources continues to grow as we use up ever-increasing amounts of material throughput. The chapter's analysis rests on some basic facts and arguments: that everything comes from somewhere, that all consumption uses things up, and that every transaction along the webs of social relations for any basic commodity or manufactured good consumes (or uses) resources. This ever-increasing material throughput of consumer societies—societies that are being rapidly replicated around the world—means that the ecological and humanitarian damage done by consumption is globalizing and increasing. The things we eat, drink, buy, use, or throw away in our everyday lives leave long trails of destruction, even if they also accrue benefits for their consumers and producers. The chapter offers a list of policies to combat or reduce such harm as well as some examples of ongoing efforts to meet the challenges posed by global consumerism and its costs.

The Uncertain Future

The contributions to this book convey rather mixed and sobering messages. Although great progress was made between the Stockholm and Rio conferences in establishing international environmental institutions, laws, and policies to address problems such as marine pollution and depletion of the ozone layer, global environmental governance has often faltered since 1992. The concept of sustainable development turned out to be enormously complex and difficult to implement in the two decades since the Rio summit, although efforts to do so continue at the global, national, and local levels around the world. Its most basic requirements for raising the living standards of the world's poor have not been met, nor can it be said that environmental concerns are being effectively integrated into most sectors of economic and social development. Even as the truly catastrophic outcomes of climate change loom in the not too distant future, states and societies around the world struggle to muster the political will to act to reduce the emissions causing climate change or adapt to the impacts of global climate change, or both.

Most international agencies, including the United Nations Environment Programme, Global Environment Facility, and Commission on Sustainable Development, are inadequately financed and torn by economic and political divisions and other ideological conflicts. With the exception of the European Union and certain specific policy regimes, international environmental governance remains weak. National governments also vary greatly in their interpretation of, and commitment to, the idea of sustainable development, but few have given high priority to environmental sustainability in the post-Rio period. While the EU often attempts to lead, the United States continues to struggle to define its role as a leader or a laggard in global environmental governance.

Despite this, local governments, private organizations, and a host of NGOs have become more important actors in defining the environmental norms of civil society. Also, without engagement and commitments from large and economically dynamic developing states such as China, global environmental governance is unlikely to succeed. The 2009 Copenhagen Climate Change Summit demonstrated the continuing inability of states to come to agreement on binding commitments.

The election of a new U.S. administration, with greater emphasis on building renewable energy infrastructure and industries and a greater willingness to support more stringent environmental policies on domestic and international issues, has given sustainability issues a new life in the United States. And many European, North American, and Asian leaders and citizens are again talking about the need for greater multilateral environmental cooperation and the benefits of competition to become leaders in renewable energy and cleaner technology development. In recent years, for example, large developing countries such as China, India, and Brazil have shown greater willingness than before to engage global environmental negotiations and governance. Growing awareness of environmental degradation and its public health, economic, and security implications may yet bring countries (North and South) into greater agreement about sustainability.

Whether globalization and rising global consumption can be made compatible with the integrity of the Earth's ecological systems remains to be seen. Overall, the early years of the twenty-first century have been a period of uncertainty and rather incremental development for international environmental governance. The European Union and some U.S. states and world leaders demonstrate that environmental policy leadership remains possible and beneficial. Successful cooperation around issues such as the protection of the ozone layer also demonstrates that global environmental governance can be efficient and effective. If worrisome environmental trends are to be reversed, such successes must become the rule rather than the exception.

Notes

1. World Resources Institute et al., *World Resources 1998–99* (New York: Oxford University Press, 1998), 141, 188–189; World Resources Institute et al., *World Resources 1996–97: The Urban Environment* (New York: Oxford University Press, 1996); James Gorman, "Scientists Predict Widespread Extinction by Global Warming," *New York*

Times, January 8, 2004; "Global Warming Called Growing Threat to Species," *Seattle Times,* January 8, 2004.

2. Lynton K. Caldwell, *International Environmental Policy,* 3rd ed. (Durham, N.C.: Duke University Press, 1996).

3. See esp. Richard Elliot Benedick, *Ozone Diplomacy* (Cambridge: Harvard University Press, 1998).

4. World Commission on Environment and Development (WCED), *Our Common Future* (New York: Oxford University Press, 1987).

5. On UNCED and WSSD, see Philip Shabecoff, *A New Name for Peace: International Environmentalism, Sustainable Development, and Democracy* (Hanover, N.H.: University Press of New England, 1996); and James Gustave Speth, "Perspectives on the Johannesburg Summit," *Environment* 45, no. 1 (Jan.–Feb. 2003): 24–29.

6. *World Resources 2002–2004: Decisions for the Earth: Balance, Voice, and Power* (Washington, D.C.: World Resources Institute, 2003), 138.

7. Edith Brown Weiss, "The Emerging Structure of International Environmental Law," in *The Global Environment: Institutions, Law, and Policy,* ed. Norman J. Vig and Regina S. Axelrod (Washington, D.C.: CQ Press, 1999), 111.

8. *World Resources 2002–2004,* 140–141.

9. Ibid., 138–139; James Gustave Speth, *Red Sky at Morning: America and the Crisis of the Global Environment* (New Haven: Yale University Press, 2004), esp. chap. 5, "Anatomy of Failure"; Hilary French, *Vanishing Borders: Protecting the Planet in the Age of Globalization* (New York: Norton, 2000); Ronnie D. Lipschutz, *Global Environmental Politics: Power, Perspectives, and Practice* (Washington, D.C.: CQ Press, 2004).

10. See Lipschutz, *Global Environmental Politics,* and Speth, *Red Sky at Morning.*

11. See also Miranda A. Schreurs, Henrik Selin, and Stacy D. VanDeveer, eds., *Transatlantic Environment and Energy Politics* (Farnham, Surrey, U.K.: Ashgate, 2009); and Norman J. Vig and Michael G. Faure, eds., *Green Giants? Environmental Policies of the United States and the European Union* (Cambridge: MIT Press, 2004).

12. See Henrik Selin and Stacy D. VanDeveer, eds., *Changing Climates in North American Politics: Institutions, Policymaking, and Multilevel Governance* (Cambridge: MIT Press, 2009).

13. Kate O'Neill, *The Environment and International Relations* (New York: Cambridge University Press, 2009); Paul F. Steinberg and Stacy D. VanDeveer, *Comparative Environmental Politics* (Cambridge: MIT Press, forthcoming).

14. See John J. Mearsheimer, "The False Promise of International Institutions," *International Security* 19 (1995): 5–49. Classic realist texts include Hans J. Morgenthau, *Politics among Nations: The Struggle for Power and Peace,* 5th ed. (New York: Knopf, 1978); and Kenneth N. Waltz, *Theory of International Politics* (New York: Random House, 1979).

15. For a standard text, see Robert O. Keohane and Joseph S. Nye Jr., *Power and Interdependence: World Politics in Transition* (Boston: Little, Brown, 1977).

16. O'Neill, *The Environment and International Relations;* Kate O'Neill, Joerg Balsiger, and Stacy VanDeveer, "Actors, Norms and Impact," *Annual Review of Political Science* 7 (2004): 149–175.

17. Jack Snyder, "One World, Rival Theories," *Foreign Policy* (November/December 2004): 52–62.

18. Peter Haas, "UN Conferences and the Constructivist Governance of the Environment," *Global Governance* 8 (2002): 73–91.

19. Oran R. Young, ed., *Global Governance: Drawing Insights from the Environmental Experience* (Cambridge: MIT Press, 1997); Oran R. Young, George J. Demko, and Kilaparti Ramakrishna, *Global Environmental Change and International Governance* (Hanover, N.H.: University Press of New England, 1996); and Paul F. Diehl, ed., *The Politics of Global Governance* (Boulder, Colo.: Rienner, 1997).

20. See, for example, Ronnie D. Lipschutz, with Judith Mayer, *Global Civil Society and Global Environmental Governance* (Albany: State University of New York Press,

22   Regina S. Axelrod, Stacy D. VanDeveer, and Norman J. Vig

1996); Margaret E. Keck and Kathryn Sikkink, *Activists beyond Borders: Advocacy Networks in International Politics* (Ithaca, N.Y.: Cornell University Press, 1998); and Lipschutz, *Global Environmental Politics*.

21. On the conflict preceding the Stockholm conference, see Caldwell, *International Environmental Policy*, 57–62.
22. See, for example, John Lemons and Donald A. Brown, eds., *Sustainable Development: Science, Ethics, and Public Policy* (Dordrecht, Netherlands: Kluwer Academic Publishers, 1995); Ian H. Rowlands, "International Fairness and Justice in Addressing Global Climate Change," *Environmental Politics* 6 (Autumn 1997): 1–30; and Keekok Lee, Alan Holland, and Desmond McNeill, eds., *Global Sustainable Development in the 21st Century* (Edinburgh: Edinburgh University Press, 2000).
23. Weiss, "Emerging Structure of International Environmental Law," 106–107. For a full discussion, see Edith Brown Weiss, *In Fairness to Future Generations: International Law, Common Patrimony, and Intergenerational Equity* (Dobbs Ferry, N.Y.: Transnational Publishers, 1989).
24. WCED, *Our Common Future*, 43.
25. For an excellent collection of essays, see Susan Baker, Maria Kousis, Dick Richardson, and Stephen Young, eds., *The Politics of Sustainable Development* (London: Routledge, 1997). See also Thomas M. Parris, "Toward a Sustainability Transition: the International Consensus," *Environment* 45, no. 1 (Jan.–Feb. 2003): 12–22; and John C. Dernbach, ed., *Stumbling toward Sustainability* (Washington, D.C.: Environmental Law Institute, 2002).
26. Thaddeus C. Trzyna, ed., *A Sustainable World: Defining and Measuring Sustainable Development* (Sacramento: California Institute of Public Affairs, 1995), 23 n. 1. See also David Pearce and Edward B. Barbier, *Blueprint for a Sustainable Economy* (London: Earthscan, 2000); Neil E. Harrison, *Constructing Sustainable Development* (Albany: State University of New York Press, 2000); and Simon Bell and Stephen Morse, *Measuring Sustainability: Learning from Doing* (London: Earthscan, 2003).
27. Trzyna, *Sustainable World*, 15.
28. Bell and Morse, *Measuring Sustainability*, 6.
29. Some of these are discussed in Trzyna, *Sustainable World*, and Bell and Morse, *Measuring Sustainability*. See also Joy E. Hecht, "Sustainability Indicators on the Web," *Environment* 45, no. 1 (Jan.–Feb. 2003): 3–4.
30. Paul G. Harris, *International Equity and Global Environmental Politics: Power and Principles of U.S. Foreign Policy* (Aldershot, U.K.: Ashgate, 2001); Harris, "International Development Assistance and Burden Sharing," in *Green Giants?* ed. Vig and Faure, 252–275; and Adil Najam et al., "From Rio to Johannesburg: Progress and Prospects," *Environment* 44, no. 7 (September 2002): 26–38.
31. World Resources Institute, *World Resources 2002–2004*, 140–141; Speth, "Perspectives on the Johannesburg Summit"; Speth, "Environment and Globalization after Johannesburg," in *Worlds Apart: Globalization and the Environment*, ed. James Gustave Speth (Washington, D.C.: Island Press, 2003), 155–165.
32. For a recent United Nations review of current treaties, see United Nations Environment Programme (UNEP), "Multilateral Environmental Agreements: A Summary," UNEP/IGM/1/INF/1 30 March (paper prepared for the Open-Ended Intergovernmental Group of Ministers or Their Representatives on International Environmental Governance, First Meeting, New York, April 18, 2001), www.unep.org/ieg/Meetings_docs/index.asp.
33. For an excellent legal text, see David Hunter, James Salzman, and Durwood Zaelke, eds., *International Environmental Law and Policy*, 2nd ed. (New York: Foundation Press, 2002).
34. See Thomas Princen and Matthias Finger, *Environmental NGOs in World Politics* (London: Routledge, 1994); Paul Wapner, *Environmental Activism and World Politics* (Albany: State University of New York Press, 1996); and Keck and Sikkink, *Activists beyond Borders*.

35. See Speth, *Worlds Apart,* for a collection of essays on the environmental consequences of free trade.
36. See John J. Audley, *Green Politics and Global Trade: NAFTA and the Future of Environmental Politics* (Washington, D.C.: Georgetown University Press, 1997); and Jerry Mander and Edward Goldsmith, eds., *The Case against the Global Economy* (San Francisco: Sierra Club, 1996). For a recent assessment of NAFTA, see John J. Audley et al., *NAFTA's Promise and Reality: Lessons from Mexico for the Hemisphere* (Washington, D.C.: Carnegie Endowment for International Peace, 2004).
37. See also Daniel Esty, "Toward a Global Environmental Mechanism," in *Worlds Apart,* ed. Speth, 67–82.
38. See David G. Victor, Kal Raustiala, and Eugene B. Skolnikoff, eds., *The Implementation and Effectiveness of International Environmental Commitments: Theory and Practice* (Cambridge: MIT Press, 1998); and Edith Brown Weiss and Harold K. Jacobson, *Engaging Countries: Strengthening Compliance with International Environmental Accords* (Cambridge: MIT Press, 2000).
39. For a comparison of European language translations, see Nigel Haigh, "'Sustainable Development' in the European Union Treaties," *International Environmental Affairs* 8 (Winter 1996): 87–91.
40. Huey D. Johnson, *Green Plans: Greenprint for Sustainability* (Lincoln: University of Nebraska Press, 1995). See also Tim O'Riordan and Heather Voisey, eds., *Sustainable Development in Western Europe: Coming to Terms with Agenda 21,* special issue, *Environmental Politics* 6 (Spring 1997); and William M. Lafferty and James Meadowcroft, eds., *Implementing Sustainable Development: Strategies and Initiatives in High Consumption Societies* (Oxford: Oxford University Press, 2000).
41. For some good examples, see Miranda A. Schreurs and Elizabeth A. Economy, eds., *The Internationalization of Environmental Protection* (Cambridge: Cambridge University Press, 1997).
42. See Gary C. Bryner, "The United States: 'Sorry—Not Our Problem,'" in Lafferty and Meadowcroft, *Implementing Sustainable Development.* There have been many sustainable development projects at the state and local level, however; see Daniel A. Mazmanian and Michael E. Kraft, eds., *Toward Sustainable Communities: Transitions and Transformations in Environmental Policy* (Cambridge: MIT Press, 1999); Kent E. Portney, *Taking Sustainable Cities Seriously: Economic Development, the Environment, and the Quality of Life in American Cities* (Cambridge: MIT Press, 2002); and Barry G. Rabe, *Statehouse and Greenhouse: The Emerging Politics of American Climate Change Policy* (Washington, D.C.: Brookings Institution, 2004).
43. See Vig and Faure, eds., *Green Giants?* and Schreurs, Selin, and VanDeveer, *Transatlantic Environment and Energy Politics.*
44. JoAnn Carmin and Stacy D. VanDeveer, eds., *EU Enlargement and the Environment: Institutional Change and Environmental Policy in Central and Eastern Europe* (London: Routledge, 2005).
45. See also Susan Baker and John McCormick, "Sustainable Development: Comparative Understandings and Responses," in *Green Giants?* ed. Vig and Faure, 277–302.
46. For a survey of recent developments in this region, see Liliana B. Andonova, *Transnational Politics of the Environment: The European Union and Environmental Policy in Central and Eastern Europe* (Cambridge: MIT Press, 2003); and Carmin and VanDeveer, *EU Enlargement and the Environment.*

2

Global Institutions and the Environment:
An Evolutionary Perspective

Marvin S. Soroos

The past one hundred years saw the human assault on the planet's natural environment accelerate as the world's population quadrupled from 1.7 billion to 6.8 billion. The global push to industrialize and enhance material living standards has devoured immense amounts of natural resources and released huge quantities of pollutants into the environment. With the growing magnitude of human activities, environmental degradation, once largely localized within the borders of states, has increasingly taken regional, and even global, proportions.[1] Scientists warn that human beings have become the agents of fundamental changes in the Earth's natural systems, including depletion of the stratospheric ozone layer, global climate change, and loss of biological diversity.[2]

As these foreboding environmental developments were taking place, political authority around the world became more fragmented following the dissolution of the far-flung colonial empires of Britain, France, the Netherlands, Belgium, and Portugal and, more recently, the splitting up of the Soviet Union, Czechoslovakia, and Yugoslavia into multiple states. The proliferation of new states has been reflected in the growth of the United Nations from 51 member states in 1945 to 192 in 2009. That each of these states, regardless of the size of its population or economy, claims the exclusive right to dictate how its natural resources will be used, has significantly complicated the task of achieving international cooperation in addressing regional and global environmental problems. States also have a tendency to overuse or misuse realms beyond their territorial jurisdictions, such as the oceans and atmosphere, leading to what Garrett Hardin famously referred to as a "tragedy of the commons" on a global scale.[3]

The centrifugal tendencies of the nation-state system have been restrained to some extent by the emergence and maturation of international regimes, which provide a measure of international governance for addressing numerous environmental problems.[4] The concept "international regime" has been widely used to refer to the combination of international institutions, customary norms and principles, and resolutions and formal treaties that guide the actions of states in regard to a specific subject, problem, or region (see also Chapter 4).[5] For example, there are international regimes for preserving biological diversity, reducing transboundary air pollution in Europe, restricting the dumping of toxic substances in the oceans, regulating uses of outer space, conserving endangered species, and protecting the environment of Antarctica.

International institutions play a fundamental role in the creation, development, and operation of international environmental regimes. They include not only the global international governmental organizations (IGOs) of the United Nations system, but also regional ones, such as the European Union and the African Union (formerly the Organization of African Unity). Most of the IGOs that have played a role in the evolution of international environmental regimes were not established expressly to address environmental problems, but over time their missions evolved to include ecological concerns. A relatively small, but growing, number of IGOs were created primarily to address environmental problems, examples being the United Nations Environment Programme and the Global Environment Facility (which are described later in this chapter).

The work of these international institutions has been complemented by a rise in the number and influence of nongovernmental organizations (NGOs). Among these are scientific associations, such as the International Council for Science (formerly the International Council of Scientific Unions) and numerous environmental advocacy organizations, such as Greenpeace and the WWF (formerly the World Wildlife Fund). Collectively, NGOs are said to make up an international civil society in view of their roles in drawing together people and groups from multiple countries to further common interests or causes.[6]

This chapter reviews the roles of global institutions in addressing environmental threats posed by human activities. It begins with a historical overview of the subject, with emphasis on how other issues—in particular the quest by a growing bloc of developing countries for economic development and equity—have shaped the response of global institutions to environmental problems. The chapter then presents case studies of five global institutions that are key players in addressing environmental concerns. The concluding section asks whether these and other international institutions are adequate to cope with the challenges of responding to the increasingly serious and complex array of environmental threats and briefly considers alternative forms of global environmental governance that may be more effective in addressing these threats.

Historical Perspective

The rise of environmental issues on the agendas of international institutions can be understood by dividing the postwar period into three eras defined by two major landmark meetings—the United Nations Conference on the Human Environment, which was convened in Stockholm in June 1972, and the United Nations Conference on Environment and Development, otherwise known as the Earth Summit, which was held in Rio de Janeiro in June 1992. The first, or *pre–Stockholm era*, extends to 1968, the year in which the UN General Assembly adopted a resolution to convene the Stockholm conference four years later. The second, or *Stockholm era,* from 1968 to 1986, encompasses the 1972 Stockholm conference, including the numerous preparatory meetings in the years preceding it as well as the implementation of its recommendations over the following decade. The third, or *Rio de Janeiro era,* commenced in 1987 with the release of the influential report of the Brundtland Commission, entitled *Our Common Future,* which set the stage for the Earth Summit in 1992.[7] The Rio de Janeiro period continues through the Earth Summit and follow-up efforts to implement the summit's elaborate plan of action, including the World Summit on Sustainable Development in Johannesburg, South Africa, in 2002 and the annual sessions of the United Nations Commission on Sustainable Development. A new era seems to be emerging in response to growing worldwide concerns about the gravity of the threats to humanity and the planet's ecosystems posed by global climate change.

The Pre-Stockholm Era (Prior to 1968)

International institutions have addressed environmental problems for more than a century; among the earliest were the international commissions for the Rhine and Danube rivers, formed during the nineteenth century to foster cooperation among the riparian states on matters such as navigation, hydrology, flood control, and pollution.[8] Nevertheless, when the UN was established after World War II, there was little awareness of environmental problems. Even though the new organization was given a significantly broader mission than that of the League of Nations, especially on economic, social, and humanitarian matters, no mention was made of the natural environment in the UN charter.

In the decades that followed, a growing number of IGOs, in particular the largely autonomous specialized agencies loosely coordinated by the UN, added environmental problems to their missions. The Food and Agriculture Organization, whose broad portfolio includes the relationship between food production and the environment, has facilitated the development of a score of international fishery commissions to manage and conserve marine fish stocks. The World Health Organization has investigated the impacts of air and water pollution on human health, while the International Labour Organization has sought to protect workers from environmental perils, such as dust and pesticides. The International Maritime Organization has sponsored a series of international agreements designed to regulate pollution of the oceans from vessels, especially oil tankers. The United Nations Educational, Scientific and Cultural Organization (better known by its acronym UNESCO) has supported research on environmentally related topics, including the Man and the Biosphere Program. Outside the United Nations, the International Whaling Commission was established in 1946 to conserve threatened species of whales, since 1986 it has done so by a comprehensive ban on the commercial harvesting of whales.[9]

The international attention given to environmental issues through the 1960s was directed toward rather narrowly defined ecological problems, such as the prevention of certain types of pollution and the conservation of specific species of wildlife. No major international organizations existed whose primary mission was broadly environmental. In the economic realm, three powerful Bretton Woods institutions—the World Bank, the International Monetary Fund, and the General Agreement on Tariffs and Trade (which became the World Trade Organization in 1995)—have shaped the development of an increasingly globalized world economy. By contrast, the existing forms of international environmental governance were rudimentary and fragmented across many largely autonomous IGOs, for whom environmental issues were secondary to their central missions in sectors such as transport, labor, weather, health, resources, energy, and science.

The Stockholm Era (1968–1986)

A wave of public concern about the environment, led by NGOs in Europe and North America, rose during the late 1960s and peaked during the early 1970s. Among the specific problems receiving attention were the dispersion of DDT and other toxic substances through ecosystems, radioactive contamination from the above-ground testing of nuclear weapons, and damage to forests and aquatic life from acid deposition. The immense oil spill from the grounding of the supertanker *Torrey Canyon* in the English Channel in 1967 was described by political scientist Richard Falk as the "Hiroshima of the environmental age."[10] The devastating effect of warfare on the environment in Vietnam became a contentious issue at the Stockholm conference, during which Sweden introduced the term "ecocide" to refer to American use of environmental destruction as a tactic of war, such as by defoliating and bulldozing forests to deny guerrillas the cover of the jungle canopy.[11]

More significantly, this era saw a growing tendency to view the environment more holistically. This perspective had its origins in the International Geophysical Year of 1957–1958, an eighteen-month global scientific project sponsored by International Council of Scientific Unions, which added significantly to scientific knowledge about the more remote realms of the planet, including Antarctica, the oceans, the atmosphere, and outer space.[12] This holistic perspective was also inspired by pictures from the moon and orbiting satellites showing the planet Earth as a fragile sphere drifting through the dark vastness of space, an image that prompted Barbara Ward to coin the phrase "spaceship Earth."[13] By the latter 1960s there was a growing uneasiness about the prospect that exponential population growth and booming industrial development would rapidly deplete the planet's natural resources and severely degrade its environment.[14]

Swedish scientist Svante Odén's revelation that the increasing acidification of the environment in southern Scandinavia was being caused by air pollutants drifting from as far away as the British Isles and continental Europe prompted Sweden in 1968 to propose the United Nations Conference on the Human Environment, held in Stockholm in 1972. Following the recommendations of the conference, the UN General Assembly established the United Nations Environment Programme (UNEP) to be a focal point for UN programs on the environment. The Stockholm conference became the prototype for a spate of major world conferences, sometimes referred to as "global town meetings," which focused worldwide attention on major international issues. Among those on environmentally related subjects were the World Population Conference in Bucharest in 1974, the World Food Conference in Rome in 1974, the United Nations Conference on Human Settlements in Vancouver in 1976, the United Nations Water Conference in Mar del Plata (Argentina) in 1977, and the United Nations Conference on Desertification in Nairobi in 1977. In each case, including the original Stockholm conference, a series of preparatory meetings was held to draft official documents, typically a declaration of principles and a plan of action, which were revised and adopted toward the end of the conference. Most UN member states sent representatives to these conferences, as did UN agencies and other IGOs with an interest in the subjects being discussed. Numerous NGOs, some of which were given limited opportunities to participate in the official governmental meetings, organized simultaneous public forums that often had more interesting exchanges of ideas on the problems and solutions being considered.[15]

The surge in environmental concern in the early years of the Stockholm era came primarily from industrialized countries, which by the early 1970s had begun establishing environmental ministries, departments, or agencies (such as the U.S. Environmental Protection Agency) to address domestic problems such as air and water pollution. Developing countries were skeptical of the new environmental agenda because their more pressing priorities were their own economic development and the alleviation of poverty. They were also concerned that a presumption that the Earth's resources are finite and are rapidly being depleted or degraded, as suggested by the Club of Rome's influential book, *The Limits to Growth*, would become a rationale for denying them higher levels of development and consumption.[16] Moreover, by the time of the Stockholm conference, the developing countries were actively pressing demands for a "new international economic order" that would entail major reforms in the management of the global economic system. Thus, developing countries refused to enter into a serious dialogue on the ecological issues of concern to the industrialized countries without strong assurances that new international environmental initiatives would not be undertaken at the expense of their legitimate aspirations for economic growth nor freeze inequalities in the distribution of the world's wealth.[17]

The wave of international environmental concern that peaked about the time of the Stockholm conference dissipated by the late 1970s, a change reflected in a declining frequency of relevant world conferences. Despite limited and uncertain funding, however, UNEP made remarkable progress in implementing key parts of the action plan adopted at the Stockholm conference. Several of the UN specialized agencies took on additional environmental projects, often working in partnership with one another, UNEP, and NGOs such as the World Conservation Union (formerly the International Union for the Conservation of Nature and Natural Resources). A decade of negotiations led to the adoption of a comprehensive law of the sea treaty in 1982. Nevertheless, the response of the UN system to environmental problems during this period continued to be fragmented and largely uncoordinated. Furthermore, international efforts in the realms of environment and economic development proceeded for the most part on separate institutional tracks despite the persistent efforts of developing countries to link these two overarching priorities.

The Rio Era (1987 to the early 2000s)

A second major wave of international environmental concern began building during the latter half of the 1980s, reaching a climax as the Earth Summit was convened in Rio de Janeiro in 1992. The problems receiving most attention during this period included the depletion of the ozone layer, global climate change, destruction of tropical rain forests, loss of biological diversity, spread of deserts, and decline of marine fisheries. The scientific community embraced the term "global change" to draw attention to the ways that human activities were impacting the basic functioning of the Earth system, such as by altering the composition of the atmosphere in ways that moderate the flow of solar energy reaching the planet and the amount of heat radiated back into space. This perspective has guided the International Geosphere-Biosphere Program, a continuing global scientific research effort headquartered in Stockholm that was launched by the International Council of Scientific Unions in 1986.[18]

The Rio era also saw significant shifts in the responses by international institutions to environmental problems. The first was a move to adapt international environmental initiatives to the aspirations of the global "South" for economic development and equity, the overarching challenge being the pursuit of "sustainable development." This reorientation of UN environmental programs was proposed by the World Commission on Environment and Development, chaired by Norwegian prime minister Gro Harlem Brundtland and widely known as the Brundtland Commission. The group addressed the misgivings of developing countries about the UN's environmental agenda against the backdrop of their frustrations with the slow pace of economic development during the 1980s and the failure of the rich developed countries to respond to their demands for a reformed international economic order. The Brundtland Commission's report, *Our Common Future*, was notable for recognizing that poverty and underdevelopment in developing countries were important causes of environmental degradation. The report argued persuasively that environmental priorities could not be achieved without reducing poverty through sustainable economic growth in the developing countries and addressing inequities between rich and poor countries in the consumption of the planet's limited resources.[19]

The Brundtland Commission report became the intellectual framework for the Earth Summit, held in June 1992 on the twentieth anniversary of the landmark Stockholm conference. The conference was attended by 116 heads of state, the largest assemblage of world leaders at any event to that date, which testified to the rise of the environment in the constellation of global issues before the UN. The gathering adopted a revised set of principles and a detailed and ambitious plan of action entitled Agenda 21, as well as major international treaties on climate change and biological diversity and a statement of forest principles.[20] The UN General Assembly followed up by creating the Commission on Sustainable Development (CSD) to facilitate implementation of the broad range of proposals and recommendations set forth in Agenda 21.

In addition to the Earth Summit, several other global conferences convened during 1990s took up environmental issues within the context of a people-centered emphasis of the United Nations. These included the 1993 World Conference on Human Rights in Vienna, the 1994 United Nations Conference on Population and Development in Cairo, the 1995 World Summit on Social Development in Copenhagen, and the Fourth World Conference on Women in Beijing, also in 1995.[21] These conferences are also notable for the heightened involvement of NGOs at all stages, from the preparatory meetings through the implementation of the action programs that were adopted. The subsequent decade also witnessed follow-up meetings, usually held five and ten years after the original world conferences, to assess the progress toward implementing their recommendations, which was generally disappointing. Thus, the goal of the World Summit on Sustainable Development (WSSD), convened in Johannesburg in 2002, was not to propose ambitious new initiatives, but to revitalize efforts to advance the recommendations contained in Agenda 21 that was adopted at the Earth Summit ten years earlier. Environmental issues took a back seat to the development problems of the poorer countries, whose representatives argued that they were not sharing in the growth stimulated by economic globalization and that inequalities between the world's rich and poor nations were continuing to widen.[22]

The Rio era had run its course by the first years of the twenty-first century. A new era seems to be emerging in conjunction with a third wave of environmental awareness around the world, or what Thomas Friedman refers to as the energy/climate era.[23] Of particular concern have been the alarming indications that the pace of global climate change is accelerating more rapidly than had been anticipated, along with disturbing signs that the diverse and disruptive impacts of climate change are already taking place in many parts of the world. The gravity of situation was highlighted in the influential 2007 report of the Intergovernmental Panel on Climate Change (discussed later in this chapter). In recent years many of the industrialized countries intensified their efforts to reduce their greenhouse gas emissions in anticipation of the 2008 to 2012 period for achieving the limitations they agreed to in the 1997 Kyoto Protocol. Talks on the next phase of international efforts to address climate change began in December 2007 at a UN-sponsored conference in

Bali, Indonesia, where a road map was adopted for further negotiations toward a new major climate change treaty that was to have been adopted in Copenhagen in December 2009. Confronting the challenges posed by global climate change will require a fundamental transition away from fossil fuels toward renewable sources of energy and green technologies that will make much more efficient use of the energy they provide.

Major Global Institutions

This section profiles five global institutions from among many whose activities can have significant environmental implications. The UN General Assembly is not only the arena in which numerous environmental issues are first raised, but also the body that instigates and reviews the response to them within the UN. The United Nations Environment Programme coordinates and facilitates a broad range of environmental activities among the UN family of organizations, including the specialized agencies. The Intergovernmental Panel on Climate Change, a joint project of UNEP and the World Meteorological Organization, issues periodic reports for policymakers on the state of research on global climate change. The World Bank is a major global economic institution seeking to "green" its image in response to strong criticism for its earlier failures to take environmental consequences into account in funding large-scale development projects. The Global Environment Facility has become a key instrument for dispersing funding for environmental projects in developing countries.

United Nations General Assembly

The General Assembly is the only one of the six principal organs of the United Nations in which all member states are represented. Since 1945 it has been the central meeting place of the international community and the only permanent venue in which a full range of issues are raised, discussed, and debated. The institution is known as the world's preeminent debating society because it has provided the most visible forum for the clashing views of East and West during the Cold War and the often contentious North-South dialogue between the industrial and developing countries. The General Assembly is, however, much more than an arena for airing conflicting perspectives. Although the organ lacks the authority to make decisions that bind its members, it has played a key role in framing and implementing international strategies for addressing a wide array of problems.

The General Assembly sponsored most of the major world conferences that addressed environmental problems during the Stockholm and Rio eras. To the casual observer, these conferences may appear to be extravagant media events that have temporarily heightened interest in the problems at hand. The importance of these meetings cannot be fully appreciated, however, without viewing each of them as the most visible event in a much longer process that includes preparatory meetings that draft the documents to be taken up and adopted at the conferences, which normally last less than two weeks. Also, governments and international organizations take steps to implement the recommendations of the conferences. Thus, the significance of any global conference should be judged by the sum of the new institutions created, programs launched or expanded, international treaties and policies adopted— and, ultimately, the results of these initiatives.[24]

The General Assembly facilitates the creation of international treaty law by sponsoring negotiating sessions. Notable examples are the three United Nations Law of the Sea conferences of 1958, 1960, and 1973–1982, the latter culminating in the signing of the comprehensive Convention on the Law of the Sea (in international law a convention is a major treaty). The General Assembly also sponsored the negotiations that drafted the 1992 Framework Convention on Climate Change and a 1995 treaty on the conservation of straddling and highly migratory fish stocks. In addition, the General Assembly has adopted numerous resolutions setting forth nonbinding regulations and standards, which are commonly referred to as "soft law." For example, a 1992 resolution calls for a moratorium on large-scale drift-net fishing on the high seas, a practice that had taken a heavy toll on marine life.[25]

The General Assembly also plays a role in addressing environmental problems by delegating tasks and responsibilities to other institutions. It has created new IGOs, including those with key environmental responsibilities, most notably the United Nations Environment Programme and the Commission on Sustainable Development. The General Assembly also convenes independent panels of prominent international public officials and experts to investigate and make recommendations on how to tackle major international problems, examples being the Brandt Commission on international development issues and the Brundtland Commission on sustainable development.[26] The General Assembly frequently calls upon existing international organizations to assume additional environmental responsibilities. For example, a 1961 General Assembly resolution called upon the World Meteorological Organization to develop the World Weather Watch, an improved global weather monitoring and reporting system that would take advantage of technological advancements in the fields of satellites, computers, and telecommunications.[27]

The General Assembly has been the arena of choice for developing countries, not only because of the universality of its membership, but also because each country has one vote regardless of its economic or population size, level of development, or contributions to the United Nations budget. Thus, it has been possible for the more numerous developing countries through their coalition, the Group of 77 (which numbered 130 countries in 2008), to dictate the General Assembly's agenda and to routinely pass resolutions promoting their interests by large majorities. In the 1970s the General Assembly was the arena in which the developing countries pushed their proposals for a "new international economic order" (known as the NIEO), expressed in the Charter on the Economic Rights and Duties of States that was adopted by a vote of 120 to 6 (with 10 abstentions) in 1974.[28] During the

1980s the General Assembly oversaw the merging of the UN's environmental and development agendas under the rubric of sustainable development. The developing countries have been repeatedly frustrated, however, that their dominance in agenda setting and voting in the General Assembly has had limited results, especially in implementing the proposals contained in the NIEO, because the body's resolutions are not binding on the developed countries whose cooperation is needed to implement them.

The turn of the century was the occasion for the General Assembly to take the lead in refocusing the mission of the UN as a whole. Toward this end, it convened the 2000 Millennium Summit in New York City in 2000, where leaders from 189 countries adopted eight overarching Millennium Development Goals aimed at substantially improving the living conditions of much of the world's poor by 2015. Among these is the goal of "ensuring environmental sustainability," with the more specific objectives of incorporating sustainable development into the policies of governments, reducing the loss of environmental resources and biodiversity, and halving the number of people without access to safe drinking water and sanitation.[29] These and several other millennium goals, such as ending poverty and advancement of public health, were on the agenda of the 2002 World Summit on Sustainable Development and included in the plan of action that was adopted.

The United Nations Environment Programme

Following the Stockholm conference of 1972, the General Assembly established the UNEP to become the institutional hub for environmental activities within the UN system. To keep the new organization from competing directly with initiatives already under way elsewhere in the UN system, UNEP's role was to be limited to catalyzing, facilitating, and coordinating environmental programs by countries and other international organizations. In keeping with this limited mission, UNEP was given a small staff and budget and was headquartered in Nairobi, far from the principal centers of UN activity, such as New York, Geneva, and Vienna. The UNEP secretariat, which in 2007 had 890 staff members and an annual budget of $239 million, is dwarfed by the U.S. Environmental Protection Agency with its 17,000 employees and an annual budget of over $7 billion.[30]

Nevertheless, UNEP has undertaken a broad range of initiatives to promote and facilitate national and international efforts to address environmental problems. It has coordinated efforts by UN agencies to assess the state of the planet's environment and to provide timely warnings of developments that require urgent action. Toward this end, during the past two decades UNEP has coordinated the preparation of four comprehensive reports in its Global Environmental Outlook (GEO) series; the reports examine trends in the state of the planet's atmosphere, water, land, and biodiversity. The most recent of these reports, known as GEO-4, was released in 2007 after having been prepared by 390 experts and reviewed by another 1,000 specialists.[31] UNEP's Global Resource Information Database, based in Arendal, Norway, integrates and disperses environmental data for geographical units ranging from local to global levels in forms that are useful to planners and policymakers.[32]

One of UNEP's most significant roles has been to sponsor negotiations on major environmental treaties and, after they are adopted, to provide the secretariat that coordinates implementation of them. Among these treaties is the Convention on Protecting the Ozone Layer (1985), which was soon followed by the landmark Montreal Protocol on Substances That Deplete the Ozone Layer (1987). The latter document, as amended several times since its original adoption, provides a comprehensive response to the threat of ozone depletion and is arguably the most significant accomplishment to date in the field of international environmental law. Other significant treaties sponsored by UNEP include the Convention on International Trade in Endangered Species of Wild Flora and Fauna (1973), the Basel Convention on Transboundary Movements of Hazardous Wastes and Their Disposal (1989), the Convention on Biological Diversity (1992), the Stockholm Convention on Persistent Organic Pollutants (2001), and the Cartagena Protocol on Biosafety (2002). Collectively, these treaties have made the environment one of the most dynamic fields of international law in recent decades.[33]

Another major contribution of UNEP toward the development of international law and policy is its Regional Seas Programme. In the mid-1970s, UNEP brought together the diverse and conflict-prone states bordering the Mediterranean Sea to adopt a series of intergovernmental agreements that would reduce the flow of both vessel- and land-based sources of pollution contaminating the largely self-contained sea.[34] What is known as the Mediterranean Blue Plan became the prototype for similar projects that address the environmental problems of twelve other regional seas, including the Black Sea, Red Sea, Caribbean, Persian Gulf, West and Central African seas, South Pacific, and East Asian seas, which collectively involve more than 140 coastal states.[35]

UNEP has sought to be sensitive to development issues and continues to be the only global UN agency headquartered in a developing country. In 1982 UNEP's Governing Council proposed what became the Brundtland Commission to delve into the relationship between environment and development. Nevertheless, UNEP's role in the United Nations system was challenged when the environmental agenda of the United Nations was redirected toward the pursuit of sustainable development during preparations for the Rio de Janeiro Earth Summit. Developing countries looked upon UNEP as being too attentive to the concerns of the industrialized countries with global environmental problems, such as stratospheric ozone depletion and human-induced climate change, and not sufficiently responsive to the environmental problems of more concern to developing countries, such as diseases, desertification, and the urban quality of life, or to their aspirations for economic development. Thus, the General Assembly established a special negotiating committee for the climate-change negotiations beginning in 1991, rather than assigning the task to UNEP, which had a decade-long involvement with the issue. Moreover, rather than putting UNEP in charge of furthering the recommendations contained in Agenda 21, the General Assembly (led by developing countries) created a new body, the Commission on Sustainable Development (CSD), to assume this responsibility.[36]

The creation of the CSD made it possible for UNEP to concentrate on its original mission to be the environmental conscience within the United Nations system. Agenda 21 called on UNEP to continue its roles as both a coordinator and a catalyst of environmental activities within the UN system, to further develop the various components of the Earthwatch program, and to facilitate the drafting and negotiation of environmental treaties.[37] Nevertheless, UNEP's mission became a subject of considerable controversy between industrial and developing countries in ways that threatened the organization's future. The dispute came to a head in 1997, when the United States and several other developed countries threatened to withhold funds for the organization until reforms were made to strengthen the role of national environmental ministers in determining UNEP's direction and policies and concurrently weaken the power of Nairobi-based diplomats who tended to reflect the perspectives of developing countries.[38] Since then, UNEP has regained some of its footing under the leadership of two Germans, Klaus Töpfer (1998–2006) and Achim Steiner (2006 to present). The organization has been lauded for several less publicized projects, such as conservation and conflict management in the Carpathian Mountain region and restoration of the Iraqi marshlands, drained by Saddam Hussein.[39] The location of UNEP's headquarters in Nairobi continues to hinder its coordination with other UN agencies and projects, as does the fluctuating and uncertain levels of its voluntary financing. Larger questions remain about redefining UNEP's mission and, given its limited resources, whether the institution can be an effective focal point for efforts by the broader United Nations system to address the increasingly severe environmental problems of the twenty-first century.[40]

Intergovernmental Panel on Climate Change

In 1988 UNEP and the World Meteorological Organization partnered to establish the Intergovernmental Panel on Climate Change (IPCC) amid growing concerns of the scientific community that a pronounced trend toward warmer global average temperatures during the decade was attributable at least in part to human activities. The IPCC's mission was not to conduct or facilitate additional monitoring or research on these topics, but to review and assess the ongoing research in fields related to climate and to issue reports that would inform the decisions of policymakers.

Much of the work of the IPCC centers on the preparation of periodic comprehensive assessment reports, which are designed to be informative rather than prescriptive. The first of these IPCC reports was released in 1990 in advance of the Second World Climate Conference. It informed negotiations that began the next year to draft the United Nations Framework Convention on Climate Change, adopted at the 1992 Earth Summit. The second report, issued in 1995, lent urgency to negotiations on the Kyoto Protocol of 1997; while the third report, released in 2001, spurred efforts to finalize the protocol's rules at Marrakesh later that year. The fourth was circulated in 2007 in the face of alarming research findings about the pace of climate changes and their impacts and as negotiations were being launched in Bali, Indonesia, on a new climate change treaty to replace the Kyoto Protocol when it expires in 2012. In 2007 the IPCC was awarded the Nobel Peace Prize, along with the former U.S. vice president and climate-change activist Al Gore.

Preparation of the IPCC assessment reports takes place in three working groups. Working Group I (WGI) surveys historical data on climatic and environmental variables, such as global average air temperatures, ocean surface temperatures, precipitation patterns, and sea levels. To view recent trends in a much longer perspective, the working group reviews findings from paleoclimate research on the Earth's climate and atmosphere over hundreds of thousands of years as revealed by glacial ice cores and sea sediments. WGI also addresses the question of whether the recent global warming trend can be attributed to human activities that have added significantly to concentrations of greenhouse gases in the atmosphere. Finally, WGI reviews the projections of several major climate modeling groups on how much global average temperatures can be expected to rise over the next century on the basis of varying assumptions about future trends in human emissions of greenhouse gases.

Working Group II (WGII) is tasked to survey studies on a wide range of impacts of climate changes on natural and human systems. It reports not only on impacts that are already being observed, but it also forecasts on how impacts will evolve decades into the future. WGII also highlights how the impacts of climate change are playing out in each of world's geographical regions and the vulnerabilities of their populations to these impacts.

Working Group III (WGIII) is charged with identifying and evaluating the policy options that could be adopted to mitigate climate change by stabilizing greenhouse gases at certain levels, while taking into account how these strategies might advance or detract from the achievement of other priorities such as economic development.[41]

Turning to some of the highlights of the 2007 Fourth Assessment Report, WGI concluded that evidence of a warming of the climate system was "unequivocal," noting that global average temperatures had increased by 0.74°C during the past century. It further stated that most of the warming of the past half century was "very likely" (at least 90 percent certainty) to have been caused by increased concentrations of greenhouse gases in the atmosphere resulting from human activities. The report projected an increase in global temperatures in the range of 2° to 4.5°C by the end of the twenty-first century, with 3°C being the mostly likely increase.

WGII noted impacts of warming temperatures are already occurring, such as the shrinking of glaciers and appearance of new glacial lakes, thawing of permafrost, shifts in the range of species toward the poles and higher elevations, earlier occurrences of spring events, and increasing acidity of oceans. The report included numerous alarming projections of future impacts, such as increasingly severe water shortages in many parts of the world owing to the spread of deserts and declines in river flows and the vulnerability of millions to coastal flooding caused by anticipated rises in sea levels.

WGIII argued that major reductions in greenhouse gas emissions are economically feasible through an array of policies it listed in the sectors of energy supply, transport, buildings, industry, and agriculture. If temperature increases are to be limited to the range of 2.0° to 2.4°C above preindustrial levels, WGIII calculates that global emissions of greenhouse gases will have to peak no later than 2015 and be cut back by 50 to 80 percent from 2000 levels by 2050.[42]

The IPCC assessment reports are the products of a rigorous process designed to achieve a broad consensus among scientists on the state of climate change research. Governments nominate prominent scientists to serve as lead authors of the working groups, which are instructed to involve as many experts as possible from all regions of the world in preparing initial technical drafts for their assigned sections of the reports. When writing their drafts, the lead authors are expected to take into account the diversity of peer reviews, internationally available scientific research on the topics assigned to them, as well as reliable non-peer-reviewed literature. The initial drafts are then subjected to a review by experts from a broad variety of organizations, including industry, who are invited to submit comments on the completeness of the scientific content of the drafts as well as on their overall balance. Critical comments are taken into account by the lead authors as they prepare revised technical drafts, which, along with summaries for policymakers, are subjected to another round of reviews, this time by governments as well as by the authors and previous expert reviewers. Final drafts and summaries for policymakers are then prepared and submitted to a session of the sponsoring IPCC working group for approval. The process comes to a conclusion at plenary meetings of the IPCC at which the technical reports and summaries for policy makers of the three working groups are accepted by representatives of member governments. More than 3,000 experts from 130 countries served as authors or reviewers in the preparation of the 2007 assessment report.[43] The IPCC assessment reports are widely regarded around the world as the most definitive compilations of what is known about climate change.

Despite being the product of a review process designed to be objective, open, and transparent, the reports have drawn criticism not only from skeptics of climate change, who consider the reports excessively alarmist, but also from scientists who contend that the reports do not adequately convey the gravity of threats facing humanity. Skeptics have argued that the selection of lead authors is tilted in favor of scientists having a pessimistic persuasion about human impacts on the global climate and that opposing views were not adequately taken into account in drafting up the reports of the working groups. Alternatively, the 2007 assessment report has been criticized for not only being too cautious a document but also for being outdated by the time it was released.

Because it is a consensus-oriented report subject to approval by governments, critics argue the report fails to adequately alert policymakers of potentially catastrophic future developments for which the science is less definitive, such as the dramatic impact that the collapse of the ice sheets on Greenland and Antarctica would have on sea levels. Moreover, being based on peer-reviewed articles published up through mid-2006, the report does not reflect important new scientific findings, such as the accelerated loss of sea ice in the Arctic and disturbing indications that the warming oceans will not absorb as much carbon dioxide as had been previously anticipated. Finally, the assumptions on which the report's high-end business-as-usual projections of future temperature increases are based have been eclipsed by unanticipated growth in global greenhouse gas emissions.[44] These and other developments will be taken up in the fifth assessment report scheduled for release in 2013–2014.

The World Bank

The World Bank, the informal name for International Bank for Reconstruction and Development, actually functions more as a fund than a bank (in contrast with the International Monetary Fund, which is more of a bank than a fund). A specialized agency of the United Nations, the Bank was established in 1946 to jump-start the recovery of the war-devastated countries of Europe by providing funds to rebuild their damaged infrastructure, such as roads, bridges, dams, water systems, and power plants. After the Bank's original mission was largely accomplished, the World Bank redirected its mission to providing loans to assist in the development of the African and Asian countries emerging from colonialism during the late 1950s and 1960s. Since then, the largest share of the Bank's loans has gone to the relatively more economically viable of the developing countries at interest rates on a par with those of private banks. In 1960 the Bank created an affiliate known as the International Development Agency (IDA) to provide loans to the least-developed countries at zero interest and with extended repayment schedules.

Throughout its history, the World Bank has funded large projects designed to build up the infrastructure of developing countries in ways that would stimulate their economic development and make them more attractive to private investment. While infrastructure projects continue to be a major part of its portfolio, in recent decades the Bank has put increasing emphasis on reducing poverty and facilitating sustainable development in the world's poorest countries, in particular those that have emerged from destructive conflicts, have been impacted by natural disasters, or are in danger of an economic or political breakdown. Toward this end, substantial funds have been allocated to social projects, such as enhancing educational opportunities and containing the spread of HIV/AIDS, malaria, and other communicable diseases. In recent years, the Bank has reframed its overall mission to promote the achievement of the UN's Millennium Development Goals, among which are eradicating extreme poverty and hunger and ensuring environmental sustainability.[45]

As the world's largest source of development assistance, the Bank has done much to facilitate economic growth and development in the many countries receiving its loans. Nevertheless, it has also been one of the most criticized international institutions for funding numerous poorly conceived projects. Critics attributed the Bank's missteps in part to pressure to lend the large amounts of capital it has had available to projects that were inadequately reviewed at the proposal and implementation stages and thus ultimately proved to be of little benefit to the recipient countries. Such projects also often failed to generate the revenues needed to pay back the loans, thus adding to the debt burdens that have plagued numerous developing countries. Another frequently raised criticism was that the Bank's projects have tended to benefit the people who are already well-off in developing countries while they do little for the poorest, if not further impoverishing or displacing them.[46]

The World Bank has been strongly criticized in environmental circles for a failure to anticipate the ecological and social impacts of the projects it supported. During the 1980s the Bank teamed up with the Asian Development Bank to assist Indonesia's transmigration program, which eventually relocated upward of 3.6 million people from the densely populated island of Java to the nation's relatively underpopulated islands, including Sumatra, Kalimantan, Sulawesi, and West Papua. Unfortunately, the soils of these islands were not suitable for food crop rotations, leaving the settlers few options but to engage in slash-and-burn agriculture that, along with commercial logging, has devastated the forests of these islands. Moreover, incidents of violent conflict have broken out between the transplanted people and the indigenous inhabitants of the regions opened to settlement.[47]

At about the same time, the Bank funded two controversial projects in Brazil. The first, known as Polonoroeste, entailed the construction of a 1,500-kilometer highway deep into the northwestern Amazon state of Rodonia. Tens of thousands of settlers used the road to migrate to a region the size of the United Kingdom, where they engaged in slash-and-burn agriculture on lands with tropical soils that were unsuitable for sustained cultivation. The project accelerated deforestation of the region and the displacement of indigenous forest dwellers. Large tracts of Amazon forest were also destroyed by Brazil's Greater Carajas project, which included a large iron-ore mine, a 900-kilometer railway, and a deep-water port. The Bank provided more than $300 million to develop the infrastructure for the project.[48]

By the late 1980s, as concern grew over global climate change, critics began pointing to World Bank projects that would add significantly to anthropogenic greenhouse gas emissions. The Bank had been funding numerous energy-related projects such as the development of oil and gas fields and coal mines and the construction of refineries and power stations, thus encouraging recipient countries to develop economies dependent on fossil fuels. The Bank invested heavily in India's coal industry, from mining operations to power plants, including the large Singrauli complex of twelve open-pit coal mines and eleven coal-fired power plants in the state of Madhya

Pradesh. The complex, known as "the inferno," emitted 10 million tons of carbon into the atmosphere each year and denuded a large area that previously was lushly forested and home to indigenous peoples and numerous plant and animal species. China, Indonesia, Pakistan, the Philippines, and Poland are among other countries that constructed large coal- or oil-fired power plants with loans from the World Bank. Projects that led to the destruction of forest cover, such as those in Indonesia and Brazil (described above) have also contributed to rising atmospheric greenhouse gas levels.[49]

In 1987 World Bank president Barber Conable acknowledged that not enough scrutiny was being given to the environmental consequences of the projects the Bank funded. To address the problem, environmental divisions were established for each of the Bank's four regional operational offices—Sub-Saharan Africa, Asia, the Middle East, and Latin America—and were charged with assessing the environmental impacts of all loan applications. The Bank's 1992 annual report stressed the importance of the relationship between environment and development in line with the recommendations of the Brundtland Commission and the theme of the Rio Earth Summit. Accordingly, the Bank expanded its portfolio of "green projects" in areas such as land management, forestry, biodiversity, water resources (both freshwater and marine), pollution management, and poverty reduction through sustainable development. The Bank played a central role in the creation of the Global Environment Facility (described in the next section) and assumed responsibility for administering its grant programs. It also became an implementing agency for the Multilateral Fund for the Montreal Protocol.

Despite efforts to improve its environmental record and embrace the goal of sustainable development, questions persisted on whether the World Bank had adopted and implemented sufficient reforms. Some critics questioned whether the new environmental units and policies had had a meaningful impact on the culture of the Bank, which still appeared to be making new loans with insufficient anticipation of environmental and human impacts. For example, continuing its practice of supporting the construction of large dam projects, the Bank agreed to provide loans for the ambitious and controversial Sardar Sarovar project in India, which called for building thirty large dams on the Narmada River. The Bank withdrew from the project after an independent commission chaired by Bradford Morse issued a report in 1992 that strongly criticized the lending agency for violating its own rules on environmental impact assessment and its standards for the resettlement of displaced peoples.[50] In 1994 the fiftieth anniversary of the Bretton Woods Conference became the occasion for a campaign by a coalition of more than two hundred NGOs that argued that the World Bank had outlived its usefulness and questioned whether it could be reformed to play a more constructive role in furthering sustainable development.[51]

In 2001 the World Bank adopted an elaborate environmental strategy designed to consolidate its wide array of programs into a focused campaign to reduce poverty through sustainable forms of development. Local environmental conditions would be improved in ways that would have related regional and global ecological benefits. The Bank would address the adaptation needs of developing countries with vulnerabilities to environmental changes. Moreover, it would transfer financial resources to developing countries to cover the costs of contributing to the achievement of global environmental priorities, including fulfilling their commitments to multilateral environmental treaties.[52] In 2008 the Bank adopted a major strategy statement for furthering its long-term goals of development and poverty reduction in the face of the severe challenges posed by climate change. Toward this end, the Bank launched two Climate Investment Funds—with commitments of $6 billion from major public and private donors—that would support the development of alternative energy sources and further energy efficiency.[53]

These recent initiatives in the fields of the environment and climate change have not silenced the Bank's critics in NGO circles, who point out that the institution continues to invest heavily in fossil fuel energy projects that will generate large volumes of greenhouse gases decades into the future.[54]

The Global Environment Facility

In 1990, at the suggestion of France and Germany, the World Bank took the lead in setting up the Global Environment Facility (GEF) as an experimental fund to see whether it could be an effective mechanism for dispersing assistance to developing countries in support of major environmental treaties. At that time, developing countries were insisting that their acceptance of several of the major environmental treaties promoted by the industrialized countries was conditional upon new and additional amounts of international assistance that would enable them to comply with provisions of the treaties. The industrialized countries sponsoring the GEF saw it as a way to avoid the inefficiencies of establishing a separate fund for each major environmental treaty.[55] Without such assistance, developing countries would have little incentive to allocate their limited resources for environmental projects in view of other compelling national priorities.

During its initial phase (1991–1993), the GEF operated under the auspices of the World Bank. It distributed $750 million, with global warming and biological diversity projects each receiving approximately 40 percent of the funds, while international-waters projects received most of the remaining 20 percent. Small amounts were allocated to protecting the stratospheric ozone layer, for which there was a separate multilateral fund linked to the Montreal Protocol. The GEF quickly encountered criticism, especially from NGOs, for approving ill-conceived grants before criteria for awarding them had been established.[56]

The future of the GEF became a North-South issue at the Earth Summit in 1992 in discussions over funding for implementing Agenda 21. To developing countries, the GEF's emphasis on global environmental problems reflected the priorities of the industrialized countries with little support being given to local and national environmental initiatives they considered more pressing, such as desertification, soil loss, and urban air pollution. Developing countries also objected to having the GEF administered by the World Bank with its weighted voting procedures that gave effective control of the institution to the United States and the other industrialized countries. Thus, developing countries argued for the creation of a general purpose Green Fund that would be independent of the World Bank and would support a broader range of projects in the field of sustainable development. As the providers of funding for the GEF, the industrialized countries insisted on retaining substantial authority over GEF decision making and on keeping the program focused on preserving the global commons.[57]

The deadlock over the future of the GEF was broken at the Earth Summit when the seventy-three countries agreed that the GEF should undergo a major restructuring. It took an additional eighteen months of intense negotiations to work out the specifics on how to restructure the GEF as a permanent institution that would balance the interests of the donor and recipient countries. The GEF was moved out of the World Bank to become a permanent, independent institution with a secretariat in Washington, D.C. Under the new arrangement, the GEF would be governed by two decision-making bodies. One is the Assembly, which includes all member countries and meets every third year to review the general policies of the GEF. The second body is the smaller Governing Council, which meets much more frequently and is the GEF's primary governing organ. Of the thirty-two seats on the council, fourteen were allocated to industrialized countries, sixteen to developing countries, and two to the transitional countries of the former Soviet bloc. In the absence of a consensus, decisions of the council require simultaneous double majorities, one comprising a majority of the member states and the other the votes of countries that make at least 60 percent of all contributions to the GEF. Thus, the interests of both the developing and the donor countries are protected.[58]

Under the restructuring, the World Bank shares responsibility for operating the GEF with the United Nations Development Programme (UNDP) and UNEP, while being accountable to the facility's Governing Council. The Bank manages the facility's application process, including conducting assessments of the cost-effectiveness of proposed projects, and administers the GEF's trust fund. The UNDP oversees technical assistance projects and coordinates them with the national environment programs of the recipient countries. UNEP provides scientific and technical oversight as well as guidance in identifying and selecting projects to be funded. Implementation of many of the GEF's projects is delegated to partnering institutions, including the Inter-American Development Bank, the Food and Agriculture Organization, the Asian Development Bank, and the African Development Bank, among others.

The GEF emerged from the turmoil and contentiousness of its initial experimental phase to become a useful complement to other sources of financial assistance for environmental projects in developing countries, including various multilateral funds, UN agencies, regional development banks, NGOs, and bilateral assistance programs. The GEF now funds projects in six focal areas: biodiversity, climate change, international waters, land degradation, the ozone layer, and persistent organic pollutants. By 2008 the GEF had grown to 178 member states and since 1991 has supported more than 2,200 projects in 165 countries. As the largest source of funds to address global environment problems, it has provided more than $8 billion in grants and leveraged more than $33 billion in cofinancing from other sources.[59] The GEF has been designated the financing mechanism for several major multilateral environmental treaties, including the UN Framework Convention on Climate Change (1992), the Convention on Biological Diversity (1992), the Stockholm Convention on Persistent Organic Pollutants (2001), and the United Nations Convention to Combat Desertification (2003). Funds related to climate change have gone to projects that increase carbon-absorbing forest cover, encourage energy conservation, or promote the harnessing of solar and other renewable sources of energy. Grants directed toward preserving biological diversity have gone largely to projects for the protection of habitats, such as the establishment of parks and nature preserves and facilities for ecotourism. Among the projects to protect international waters have been initiatives to cut back on ship wastes in major trading seaports and to reduce organic and toxic pollution in the Danube River system and the Black Sea.[60]

Future Prospects

During the past several decades, international institutions have accomplished much toward facilitating cooperation among nations in addressing environmental problems that transcend their borders and affect the global commons. These include the international organizations whose missions are primarily environmental, such as UNEP and the GEF, as well as numerous other IGOs that have taken up environmental problems as part of their broadening missions, such as the UN General Assembly and several of the specialized agencies of the United Nations. Other major global organizations, most notably the World Bank, have been adopting reforms in the face of strong criticism for being insensitive to the environmental impacts of their programs and policies.

Nevertheless, the ecological predicament confronting humanity appears to be deepening, despite the monitoring networks, scientific research projects, environmental treaties, reporting mechanisms, and funding programs that have been sponsored by these international institutions. While the efforts of international institutions have been quite successful in addressing some environmental problems, most conspicuously the preservation of the stratospheric ozone layer, they have been largely ineffective in brokering effective international responses to others, including climate change, which is arguably the preeminent ecological problem confronting humanity as it enters the twenty-first century. The failure of the Johannesburg summit in 2002 to make much progress on either the environmental or sustainable development fronts did not bode well for reconciling the developed North's concerns about global environmental problems with the South's aspirations for economic development.

The question arises as to whether international institutions, as presently constituted, possess the capacity to deliver the global collective environmental benefits that they are being asked to provide. In the prevailing anarchical world order, states for the most part cannot be compelled against their will to enter into cooperative arrangements to address international problems. Thus, international agreements are the product of complex and time-consuming negotiations among disparate countries with conflicting interests that typically produce weak documents reflecting the lowest common denominator of their perceived interests. Countries tend to seek treaties that maximize the responsibilities of other nations while minimizing their own obligations, thus enabling them to play the role of a free rider on the sacrifices of others.

Concern over impending global ecological crises has prompted proposals for strengthening international institutions. One direction would be to establish a strong central organ within the United Nations system, possibly in the form of an environmental security council that would take the place of the Trusteeship Council, which has all but completed its mission of decolonization. Such a body would elevate the environment from being a peripheral, cross-sector issue to being one of the core priorities of the United Nations, along with peacekeeping and economic development. Another approach would create institutions with the power to make binding decisions that are needed to effectively address environmental problems, such as depletion of the ozone layer and climate change. Such an institution was proposed at an international conference attended by leaders from seventeen states meeting in The Hague in 1988. The absence of the United States, the Soviet Union, and China—the world's three leading emitters of carbon dioxide—did not bode well for the implementation of such a proposal.[61]

It is difficult to conceive of circumstances in which states would be willing to relinquish or pool their sovereignty in order to substantially strengthen global institutions charged with mounting a more effective response to the deepening environmental crisis confronting humanity. If anything, there is widespread public disillusionment with global institutions in both industrial and developing countries because of their perceived failure to be responsive to national needs and preferences. The best hope appears to lie in strengthening existing institutions and enhancing coordination between them. NGOs can play a significant role in mobilizing support for stronger international policies and programs and monitoring compliance with them. It remains to be seen whether such a decentralized, problem-specific approach to addressing global environmental policies will be adequate to the challenges that lie ahead. Unfortunately, at least for the present, there appears to be no viable alternative.

Too often international efforts to address environmental problems in the United Nations and other international bodies are preempted by what at the moment are perceived to be more pressing global problems, such as confronting terrorism in the aftermath of September 11, 2001, or coping with the global economic crisis of 2008. The economic downturn may be undermining the resolve of some countries to fulfill their Kyoto Protocol commitments to limit greenhouse gas emissions and to negotiate further reductions in the next climate change treaty. On the brighter side, the presidency of Barack Obama in the United States portends a more constructive role for the United States in international environmental institutions and treaty negotiations and a commitment to green technologies and sustainable development as an approach to reenergizing the global economy.

Notes

1. See J. R. McNeill, *An Environmental History of the Twentieth-Century World* (New York: W. W. Norton, 2000).
2. See Constance Mungall and Digby J. McLaren, eds., *Planet under Stress: The Challenge of Global Change* (New York: Oxford University Press, 1990).
3. Garrett Hardin, "The Tragedy of the Commons," *Science* 168 (December 13, 1968): 1243–1248. See also Marvin S. Soroos, "Garrett Hardin and Tragedies of Global Commons," in *Handbook of Global Environmental Politics*, ed. Peter Dauvergne (Cheltenham, UK: Edward Elgar, 2005), 35–40.
4. Oran Young, *International Governance: Protecting the Environment in a Stateless Society* (Ithaca, N.Y.: Cornell University Press, 1994); and Lamont C. Hempel, *Environmental Governance: The Global Challenge* (Washington, D.C.: Island Press, 1996).
5. See Stephen D. Krasner, ed., *International Regimes* (Ithaca, N.Y.: Cornell University Press, 1983).
6. See Paul Wapner, *Environmental Activism and World Civic Politics* (Albany: State University of New York Press, 1996); and Ronnie D. Lipschutz, with Judith Mayer, *Global Civil Society and Global Environmental Governance: The Politics of Nature from Place to Planet* (Albany: State University of New York Press, 1996).
7. World Commission on Environment and Development, *Our Common Future* (New York: Oxford University Press, 1987).
8. Lynton Keith Caldwell, *International Environmental Policy*, 3rd ed. (Durham, N.C.: Duke University Press, 1995), 160–161.
9. For an overview of perceptions of environmental issues during this era, see John McCormick, *Reclaiming Paradise: The Global Environmental Movement* (Bloomington: Indiana University Press, 1979), 25–46.
10. Richard A. Falk, *This Endangered Planet: Prospects and Proposals for Human Survival* (New York: Vintage Books, 1971), 284. For an account of accidents involving supertankers, see Nöel Mostert, *Supership* (New York: Warner Books, 1975).
11. See Fredrik Logevall, "The Swedish-American Conflict over Vietnam," *Diplomatic History* 17, no. 3 (1995): 421–446.
12. See Wallace W. Atwood Jr., "The International Geophysical Year in Retrospective," *Department of State Bulletin* 40 (1959): 682–689.
13. Barbara Ward, *Spaceship Earth* (New York: Columbia University Press, 1966).
14. An influential book on world population growth was Paul R. Ehrlich's *The Population Bomb* (New York: Ballantine Books, 1968).
15. See A. LeRoy Bennett, *International Organizations: Principles and Issues*, 3rd ed. (Englewood Cliffs, N.J.: Prentice Hall, 1984), 293–323.
16. Donella H. Meadows et al., *The Limits to Growth* (New York: Universe Books, 1972).
17. See Marian A. L. Miller, *The Third World in Global Environmental Politics* (Boulder: Lynn Rienner, 1995).
18. Thomas F. Malone, "Mission to Planet Earth: Integrating Studies of Global Change," *Environment* 28 (October 1986): 6–11, 39–42.

19. See World Commission on Environment and Development, *Our Common Future.*
20. For the texts of these documents see UNCED, *Earth Summit: The United Nations Conference on Environment and Development* (Boston: Trotman/Martinus Nijhoff, 1993).
21. See John Tessitore and Susan Woolfson, eds., *A Global Agenda: Issues before the 49th General Assembly of the United Nations* (New York: University Press of America, 1994), 154.
22. See International Institute for Sustainable Development, "Summary of World Summit on Sustainable Development, 26 August–4 September 2002," *Earth Negotiations Bulletin* 22 (September 6, 2002), www.iisd.ca/download/pdf/enb2251e.pdf.
23. Thomas Friedman, *Hot, Flat, and Crowded: Why We Need a Green Revolution and How It Can Renew America* (New York: Farrar, Straus and Giroux, 2008), 27.
24. See Bennett, *International Organizations.*
25. See Blaine Sloan, *United Nations General Assembly Resolutions in Our Changing World* (Ardsley-on-Hudson, N.Y.: Transnational, 1991).
26. Independent Commission on International Development Issues, *North-South: A Programme for Survival* (Cambridge: MIT Press, 1980).
27. See Marvin S. Soroos, *The Endangered Atmosphere: Preserving a Global Commons* (Columbia: University of South Carolina Press, 1997), 58–61.
28. See Marvin S. Soroos, *Beyond Sovereignty: The Challenge of Global Policy* (Columbia: University of South Carolina Press, 1986), 195–226.
29. See UN official Web site, *End Poverty 2015: Millennium Development Goals*, www.un.org/millenniumgoals.
30. Jack Shepherd, "The Earth's Keeper," *The Independent* (Spring 2007): 30–31; "About EPA," U.S. Environmental Protection Agency, www.epa.gov/epahome/aboutepa.htm.
31. United Nations Environment Programme, "Global Environment Outlook: GEO-4 Report," www.unep.org/geo/geo4/media/.
32. See Peter M. Haas, "Institutions: United Nations Environment Programme," *Environment* 36 (September 1994): 43–45.
33. See Carol Annette Petsonk, "The Role of the United Nations Environment Programme (UNEP) in the Development of International Environmental Law," *American University Journal of International Law and Policy* 5 (1990): 351–391. See also UNEP, *Organizational Profile*, n.d., www.unep.org/PDF/UNEPOrganization-Profile.pdf.
34. See Peter M. Haas, *Saving the Mediterranean: The Politics of International Environmental Cooperation* (New York: Columbia University Press, 1990).
35. United Nations Environmental Programme, "Regional Seas Programme," www.unep.org/regionalseas.
36. See Konrad von Moltke, "Why UNEP Matters," in *Green Globe Yearbook 1996*, ed. Helge Ole Bergesen and Georg Parmann (New York: Oxford University Press, 1996), 58–59.
37. Dale Boyd, "UNEP after Rio," *Our Planet* 4, no. 4 (1992): 8–11.
38. Fred Pearce, "Environmental Body Goes to Pieces," *New Scientist*, February 15, 1997, 11.
39. Shepherd, "The Earth's Keeper."
40. See Maria Ivanova, *Can the Anchor Hold? Rethinking the United Nations Environment Programme for the 21st Century* (New Haven: Yale School of Forestry and Environmental Studies, 2005).
41. Intergovernmental Panel on Climate Change Web site, "Fact Sheet," www.ipcc.ch/press/ar4-factsheet1.htm.
42. See IPCC, *Climate Change 2007: Synthesis Report, Summary for Policy Makers*, 2007, www.ipcc.ch/pdf/assessment-report/ar4/syr/ar4_syr.pdf.
43. More information on these procedures is available at IPCC, "Procedures for the Preparation, Review, Acceptance, Adoption, Approval and Publication of IPCC Reports," 2003, www.ipcc.ch/pdf/ipcc-principles/ipcc-principles-appendix-a.pdf.

44. See Juliet Eilperin, "Faster Climate Change Feared," *Washington Post,* December 26, 2008.

45. Soroos, *Beyond Sovereignty.*

46. See Catherine Caufield, *Masters of Illusion: The World Bank and the Poverty of Nations* (New York: Holt, 1996); Doug Bandow and Ian Vasquez, eds., *Perpetuating Poverty: The World Bank, the IMF, and the Developing World* (Washington, D.C.: CATO Institute, 1994).

47. World Bank Group, Independent Evaluation Group, "Transmigration in Indonesia," http://lnweb90.worldbank.org/oed/oeddoclib.nsf/DocUNIDViewForJavaSearch/4B 8B0E01445D8351852567F5005D87B8.

48. Korinna Horta, "The World Bank and the International Monetary Fund," in *Greening International Institutions,* ed. Jacob Werksman (London: Earthscan, 1996), 138–139. The most influential book on this subject is Bruce Rich, *Mortgaging the Earth: The World Bank, Environmental Impoverishment, and the Crisis of Development* (Boston: Beacon Press, 1994).

49. See Christopher Flavin, "Banking against Global Warming," *World Watch* 10 (November/December 1997): 25–35.

50. See Hilary F. French, "The World Bank: Now Fifty, But How Fit?" *World Watch* 7 (July-August 1994): 10–18.

51. David R. Francis, "IMF and World Bank 50th Birthday Bash: Critics Crash Parties," *Christian Science Monitor,* October 3, 1994, 4.

52. World Bank, *Making Sustainable Commitments: An Environment Strategy for the World Bank* (Washington, D.C.: World Bank, 2001).

53. World Bank, *Strategic Framework for Development and Climate Change* (Washington, D.C.: World Bank, 2008).

54. Ramest Jaura, "Don't Leave Climate Change to the World Bank," Inter Press Service, December 10, 2008.

55. "The Global Environmental Facility," *Our Planet* 3, no. 3 (1991): 10–13.

56. See Andrew Jordan, "Paying the Incremental Costs of Global Environmental Protection: The Evolving Role of the GEF," *Environment* 36 (July/August 1994): 12–20, 31–36.

57. David Fairman, "The Global Environment Facility: Haunted by the Shadow of the Future," in *Institutions for Environmental Aid,* ed. Robert O. Keohane and Marc A. Levy (Cambridge: MIT Press, 1996), 57–58. See also Helen Sjoberg, "The Global Environmental Facility," in *Greening International Institutions,* ed. Jacob Werksman, 148–162.

58. Ibid.

59. Global Environment Facility, "What Is the GEF?" n.d., www.gefweb.org/interior. aspx?id=50.

60. Ibid.

61. See Hilary F. French, "An Environmental Security Council," *World Watch* 2 (September/October 1989): 6–7. For a collection of essays on global environmental governance, see Frank Biermann and Steffan Bauer, eds., *A World Environmental Organization: Solution or Threat for Effective International Environmental Governance?* (Burlington, Vt.: Ashgate, 2005).

3

Environmental Protection in the Twenty-first Century: The Role of International Law

*Jacqueline Peel**

This chapter examines the historical development, central principles, and current implementation of international environmental law. Half a century ago discussion of this topic would probably have begun with a question as to whether the subject of international environmental law even existed: there were no treatises or journals specifically on the subject, only a very small number of law school seminars were taught, and most public international law texts avoided addressing the environment, with little risk of being criticized for incompleteness.

Today the situation is entirely different. The International Court of Justice has confirmed the "obligations of States to respect and protect the natural environment."[1] Moreover, it has declared that states' "general obligation . . . to ensure that activities within their jurisdiction or control respect the environment of other States or of areas beyond national control is now part of the corpus of international law relating to the environment."[2] This latter obligation, it is now clear, is applicable at all times and to all activities, even the use of nuclear weapons.[3] These general obligations have been further developed in the context of the international community's commitment to "integrate environment and development in pursuance of the overall goal of sustainable development."[4]

This chapter is divided into three sections. The first section describes the historical development of international environmental law and the institutional context within which that development has taken place. The second section examines certain general principles of international law that have emerged in relation to environmental matters. The last section sets out basic rules of international environmental law in fields such as protection of flora and fauna, protection of freshwater resources and the marine environment, air quality, waste, and hazardous substances.

International Environmental Law: Context, History, and Sources

International legal efforts to protect the environment go back at least to the 1890s, when a dispute was submitted to international arbitration as a consequence of U.S. efforts to prevent British vessels from exploiting fur seals in the international waters of the Bering Sea. Although the Pacific

---

* This chapter is based on the earlier version coauthored with Philippe Sands, which was published in the second edition of this text.

Fur Seal Arbitral Tribunal did not find in favor of a unilateral U.S. approach to conservation, it did adopt regulations for the "proper protection and preservation" of fur seals.[5] These regulations have served as an important precedent for the subsequent development of international environmental law, reflecting an acknowledgment that environmental problems transcend national boundaries.

In the twenty-first century, as we face problems like climate change, there is even greater recognition of the inherent and fundamental interdependence of the global environment and the challenge of reconciling this with the fact that many land, sea, and air spaces are part of the sovereign areas of independent states.[6] To understand how international rules of environmental protection have developed in this context, it is first necessary to know something of the nature of international society and the structure of the international legal order, as well as the sources of international environmental law.

The International Legal Order

International law and international organizations provide the basis for cooperation between the various members of the international community in their efforts to protect the global environment. At each level the task becomes progressively more complex as new actors and interests are drawn into the process. Whereas just two states, representing the interests of local fishing communities, negotiated the early fisheries conventions in the middle of the nineteenth century, more than 150 states were involved in negotiations sponsored by the United Nations General Assembly that led to the 1992 UN Framework Convention on Climate Change (FCCC) and its 1997 Kyoto Protocol. In the current round of negotiations for a treaty to replace the Kyoto Protocol there are more than 190 participating states (see Chapter 6).

Whether negotiations are bilateral or multilateral in nature, the principles and rules of public international law are intended to serve similar functions. The overall objective of the international legal order is to provide a framework within which the various members of the international community may cooperate, establish norms of behavior, and resolve their differences. Accordingly, as with national law, the functions of international law are legislative, administrative, and adjudicative. The legal principles and rules that impose binding obligations requiring states and other members of the international community to conform to certain norms of behavior are accomplished through the legislative function. These obligations place limits on the activities that may be conducted or permitted because of their actual or potential impact on the environment. Such impact may be entirely within national borders, across territorial boundaries, or in areas beyond national jurisdiction.

The administrative function of international law allocates tasks to the various actors to ensure that standards imposed by the principles and rules of international environmental law are carried out. The adjudicative function of international law aims, in a limited way, to provide mechanisms or forums for the pacific settlement of differences or disputes that arise between members of the international community involving the use of natural resources or the conduct of activities affecting the environment.

Actors in International Society

Reflecting the state-centric nature of the international legal order, states remain far and away the most important actors shaping international environmental law. As with the human rights field, however, international environmental law provides clear evidence of an evolution from the view that international society comprises only a community of states to one that encompasses individuals, groups, and corporate and other entities within and among those states. This new reality is reflected in the important role played by international organizations and nongovernmental actors in virtually all aspects of the international legal process relating to environment and development.[7]

Different actors have different roles and functions, both as subjects and objects of international environmental law. These functions and roles include participating in the law-making process; monitoring implementation, including reporting; and ensuring enforcement of obligations. The nature of each actor's contribution turns upon the extent of its international legal personality and the rights and obligations granted to it by general international law, as well as the rules established by particular treaties and other instruments.

States. States continue to play the primary and dominant role in the international legal order. It is still states that create, adopt, and implement international legal principles and rules, establish international organizations, and permit other actors to participate in the process. In 2009 there were 192 member states of the UN, and several others with observer status.[8] The members encompass both developed and developing countries. Developed countries include the industrialized member states of the Organization for Economic Cooperation and Development (OECD)[9] as well as states that previously formed part of the Soviet bloc. The latter are commonly referred to as "economies in transition." Some 130 member states are the developing countries that form an association referred to as the Group of 77, which often works as a single negotiating bloc within the UN.[10] Fifty of the most vulnerable developing countries are designated "least developed countries," or LDCs. Within the UN system states are also grouped regionally, usually for the purpose of elections to UN bodies. The five groupings are Latin America and the Caribbean, Africa, Asia, western Europe and others, and central and eastern Europe.

In environmental negotiations these rather simple distinctions tend to break down as states pursue what they perceive to be vital national interests, including their strategic alliances. However, the divide between industrialized nations of the OECD and the developing countries of the Group of 77 remains a prominent part of most environmental negotiations at the international level. The current post-2012 climate change negotiations, for instance, illustrate the extent of the differences that exist between developed and developing countries on the contentious issue of responsibility for controlling greenhouse gas emissions in order to avoid dangerous global warming.

International Organizations. The international organizations involved in environmental matters make up a complex and unwieldy network at the global, regional, subregional, and bilateral levels. It is unlikely that any international organization today will not have some responsibility for environmental matters. Indeed, emerging as among the most significant international organizations for environmental purposes are those with an economic or development mandate, including the World Bank, the International Monetary Fund, and the World Trade Organization (WTO).

The lack of coordination between international organizations in the environmental field makes it difficult to assess their role by reference to any functional, sectoral, or geographic criteria. To help understand their activities and interests, they can, however, be divided into three general categories: (1) global organizations under the auspices of, or related to, the UN and its specialized agencies, such as the United Nations Environmental Programme (UNEP), the Food and Agriculture Organization, and the International Maritime Organization; (2) regional organizations outside the UN system, including the OECD, the Council of Europe, the African Union, the Organization of American States, and the Association of Southeast Asian Nations; and (3) organizations established by environmental and other international agreements, such as the Intergovernmental Panel on Climate Change and the numerous administrative and subsidiary bodies set up under environmental treaties.

International organizations perform a variety of different functions and roles in the development and management of international legal responses to environmental issues and problems. These range from simply providing a forum for general cooperation and consultation between states on environmental matters, to the creation of international legal obligations and standards, to the provision of independent mechanisms for the resolution of disputes. The actual functions of each institution depend to a great extent on the powers granted to it as subsequently interpreted and applied by the parties and the practice of the organization.

Nongovernmental Organizations. Nongovernmental organizations (NGOs) have historically played an important role in developing international environmental law, and they continue to do so in a variety of ways (see Chapter 5). In the past few decades at least six different types of groups have emerged as actors in the development of international environmental law: the scientific community, nonprofit environmental groups and associations, private companies and business concerns, legal organizations, the academic community, and individuals. In addition, transnational corporations are more and more the object of international environmental regulation. Because they conduct activities across national boundaries in an increasingly interdependent world, the need for minimum international standards of behavior has been recognized. In line with emerging concepts of corporate social responsibility, transnational corporations have themselves begun to consider the need for further development of international environmental law governing their activities, although most of the efforts to date have produced only voluntary guidelines for corporate behavior.[11]

Sovereignty and Territory

In the traditional international legal order, states are considered sovereign and equal, imbued with equal rights and duties as members of the international community, notwithstanding differences of an economic, social, or political nature. The sovereignty and equality of states means that each has prima facie exclusive jurisdiction over its territory and the natural resources found there. States also have a duty not to intervene in the area of exclusive jurisdiction of other states. In principle, this means that each state has competence to develop policies and laws in regard to the natural resources and environment of its own territory. That territory comprises

- the state's landmass and subsoil
- internal waters, such as lakes, rivers, and canals
- the territorial sea adjacent to the coast, including its seabed, subsoil, and the resources thereof
- the airspace above a state's land, internal waters, and territorial sea, up to the point at which the legal regime of outer space begins

States may also have more limited sovereign rights and jurisdiction over other areas, including a contiguous zone adjacent to their territorial seas; the continental shelf, its seabed and subsoil; and "exclusive economic zones" important for fishing rights.

As a result of these arrangements, certain areas fall outside the territory and exclusive jurisdiction of any state. These areas, sometimes referred to as the global commons, include the high seas and their seabed and subsoil, the atmosphere, outer space, and, according to a majority of states, the Antarctic.

This apparently straightforward international legal order was a satisfactory organizing structure until technological developments, and their environmental effects, permeated national boundaries. The traditional structure does not coexist comfortably with an environmental order that consists of a biosphere of interdependent ecosystems that do not respect artificial territorial boundaries between states.[12] As an ecological matter, if not a legal one, many natural resources and their environmental components are shared, and the use by any one state of the natural resources within its territory will invariably have consequences for the use of natural resources and their environmental components in other states. Ecological interdependence therefore poses a fundamental challenge for international law, as no one state, acting within its territorial boundaries, can adequately address global environmental problems. International cooperation and the development of shared norms of behavior are indispensable.

Historical Development

The deficiencies of the traditional international legal order in responding to environmental challenges led to the rapid development of new, "greener" rules of international law. The process of "greening" international law occurred over four periods, responding to particular factors that influenced legal developments.[13] In the early stages of the development of international environmental law, the field lacked a coordinated legal and institutional framework. Attempts to create such a framework came with two global environmental conferences: the 1972 Stockholm Conference and the Rio Earth Summit in 1992.

To 1945. The first distinct period in the greening process began with nineteenth-century bilateral fisheries treaties and the Pacific Fur Seal arbitration. It concluded with the creation of the new UN family of international institutions in 1945. This period might be characterized as one in which states first acted internationally upon their understanding that the process of industrialization and the rapid expansion of economic activities relying on natural resources required limits on the exploitation of flora and fauna and the adoption of appropriate legal instruments.

Until the establishment of the UN in 1945, no international forum existed in which to raise environmental concerns, and most of the agreements adopted in this initial period did not create arrangements to ensure that legal obligations were complied with or enforced. Many initiatives grew from activities by private citizens, an early harbinger of the more intensive activism of NGOs that marks international negotiations today.

1945–1972. The establishment of the UN in 1945 introduced a second period in the development of international environmental law, culminating in the 1972 Stockholm Conference on the Human Environment. During this period many international organizations with competence in environmental matters were created, and legal instruments were adopted to address particular sources of pollution and the conservation of general and particular environmental resources. These included rules governing oil pollution, nuclear testing, wetlands, the marine environment and its living resources, freshwaters, and the dumping of waste at sea.[14]

The UN provided a forum for discussing the consequences of technological progress and introduced a period characterized by proliferation of international organizations, engagement with environmental issues, and action to address the causes of pollution and environmental degradation. The relationship between economic development and environmental protection began to be understood. However, the UN Charter did not, and still does not, explicitly address environmental protection or the conservation of natural resources.

Stockholm to Rio. The third period began with the 1972 Stockholm Conference and concluded with the Earth Summit in 1992. In this twenty-year span the UN attempted to put in place a system to address a growing range of environmental issues in a more coordinated and coherent way. A raft of regional and global conventions addressed new issues, and new techniques of regulation were employed.

The 1972 Stockholm Conference, convened by the UN General Assembly, adopted several nonbinding instruments, including a Declaration of Twenty-six Guiding Principles.[15] The conference represented the international community's first effort at constructing a coherent strategy for the development of international policy and institutions to protect the environment, and the Stockholm Declaration is generally regarded as the foundation of international environmental law.[16]

One of the most significant contributions of the Stockholm Conference has proved to be the creation of UNEP. UNEP has subsequently been instrumental in the establishment and implementation of important global and regional treaties addressing ozone depletion, trade in hazardous waste, biodiversity, and marine protection.

In addition, the Stockholm Conference catalyzed other global treaties adopted under the UN's auspices, such as the 1982 United Nations Convention on the Law of the Sea (UNCLOS).[17] This treaty establishes a unique, comprehensive framework of global rules for protection of the marine environment and marine living resources, including detailed institutional arrangements and provisions on environmental impact assessment, technology transfer, and liability. These provisions have provided an influential basis for the language and approach of many other environmental agreements.

By 1990, when preparations for the Earth Summit formally began, there existed a solid body of rules of international environmental law. States were increasingly subject to limits on the right to allow or carry out activities that harmed the environment. New standards were in place, and a range of techniques sought to implement those standards. Environmental issues, moreover, had begun to intersect with economic matters, especially trade and development lending. But in spite of these relatively impressive achievements, environmental matters remained on the periphery of the international community's agenda and the activities of most institutions.

Earth Summit and Beyond. The 1992 Earth Summit launched a fourth period in the development of international environmental law, requiring that environmental concerns be integrated into all international activities. International environmental law merged with international law in the new field of sustainable development.

The origins of the Earth Summit lay in the UN General Assembly's endorsement of the Brundtland Report in December 1987, and its call the following year for a global conference on environment and development.[18] The Earth Summit, held in Rio de Janeiro, saw participation in environmental negotiations by an unprecedented number of states (176 in total), together with several dozen international organizations, and several thousand NGOs. Three nonbinding instruments were adopted at the Summit: the Rio Declaration on Environment and Development (the Rio Declaration), the Non-Legally Binding Authoritative Statement of Principles for a Global Consensus on the Management, Conservation, and Sustainable Development of All Types of Forests (the Forest Principles), and Agenda 21.[19] Two treaties were also opened for signature: the Convention on Biological Diversity and the FCCC.[20] These two treaties have since formed the basis for further elaboration of international environmental law in their respective fields through the adoption of protocols and implementing arrangements. For example, the Marrakesh Accords adopted in 2001 elaborate emission reduction obligations under the 1997 Kyoto Protocol.[21] The parties to the FCCC have also launched a further round of negotiations for a new treaty to replace the Kyoto Protocol when it expires in 2012.[22]

Since the Earth Summit, progress in developing and implementing the international concept of sustainable development has not been as promising.[23] The 2002 World Summit on Sustainable Development (WSSD) held in Johannesburg produced a plan of implementation, but in fact it contained few new commitments.[24] This may have been a result of the breadth of the negotiating agenda, which included poverty eradication, agricultural practices, and public health issues. The WSSD's failure to agree on concrete actions for implementing sustainable development suggests that the concept may function best as an overall policy goal, rather than as the basis for prescriptive rules constraining state conduct with respect to the environment.

Sources of International Environmental Law

International law consists of rules, rights, and obligations that are legally binding on states and other members of the international community in their relations with each other. As a branch of general international law, international environmental law relies on the same legal sources, including:

- bilateral or multilateral treaties
- binding acts of international organizations
- rules of customary international law
- judgments of an international court or tribunal

Treaties. The most important binding source of international environmental law is treaties—formal international agreements also referred to by such names as conventions or protocols. These can be adopted bilaterally, regionally, or globally. With more than 192 states now in existence, the number of bilateral environmental agreements runs into the thousands, supplemented by dozens of regional agreements and a smaller but increasing number of global treaties. Countries of the European Union (EU) and other industrial nations have adopted a large body of regional environmental rules that frequently provide a basis for measures adopted in other parts of the world. Regional treaties are less well developed in Africa, the Caribbean, and Oceania and are even more limited in Asia and parts of the Americas. Industrial activity is prohibited by treaty in Antarctica.

Acts of International Organizations. The second principal source of international law in the environmental field is acts of international organizations. Almost all international environmental agreements establish institutional organs with the power to adopt certain rules, make decisions, or take other measures. Such acts, sometimes referred to as secondary legislation, can provide an important source of international law. Some of the more far-reaching international measures affecting the use of natural resources have been adopted in the form of acts of international organizations rather than by treaty.

Many environmental treaties allow the institutions they create to have a choice of adopting acts with or without binding legal effects. Binding acts of international organizations derive their legal authority from the treaty on which their adoption was based and can therefore be considered part of treaty law. Those acts that do not have binding legal consequences could, however, subsequently be relied on as reflecting a rule of customary international law.

Customary International Law. The primary place of treaties and acts of international organizations as sources of international environmental law should not obscure the important, albeit secondary, role played by customary international law. Customary law fulfills a number of functions by creating binding obligations and contributing to the codification of obligations in the form of treaty rules and other binding acts. The significance of customary law lies in the fact that, as a general matter, it establishes obligations for all states (or all states within a particular region) except those that have persistently objected to a practice and its legal consequences. Article 38(1)(b) of the statute establishing the International Court of Justice identifies the two elements of customary international law: state practice and *opinio juris*—the belief that the practice is required as a matter of law. Establishing the existence of a rule of customary international law requires evidence of consistent state practice. Such practice will rarely provide clear guidance as to the precise content of any particular rule.

International Case Law. The case law of international courts and tribunals and arguments presented to such bodies identify some general principles and rules of international environmental law. The significance of arbitral awards in the development of international environmental law should not be understated. Important principles were elaborated by arbitral tribunals in the previously mentioned Pacific Fur Seal case, in the Lac Lanoux arbitration between France and Spain (concerning the use of a shared river), and more recently in the Iron Rhine Railway arbitration between Belgium and the Netherlands (clarifying the nature of the concept of sustainable development). Another important arbitral decision is the much-cited Trail Smelter case between the United States and Canada concerning transboundary air pollution from a zinc smelter in British Columbia. This case famously articulated the principle that "no state has the right to use or permit the use of its territory in such a manner as to cause injury by fumes in or to the territory of another or the properties or persons therein, when the case is of serious consequence and the injury is established by clear and convincing evidence."[25]

Judgments of the International Court of Justice have also contributed to the development of international environmental law, particularly in the Icelandic fisheries cases (on fisheries conservation), the nuclear test cases of 1974 and 1995 (on the legality of atmospheric and underground nuclear tests), the 1997 Danube dam case (concerning a large hydroelectric project with potential impacts on biodiversity), and the opinions on the legality of the use of nuclear weapons. More recently the Court has ruled against the issue of provisional measures to restrain potential environmental harm from a proposed pulp mill in a case between Argentina and Uruguay. Its forthcoming decision on the merits of this case promises to make a significant contribution to international law regarding the protection of freshwater ecosystems. Another current case, brought by Ecuador against Colombia over aerial spraying of toxic herbicides near the countries' shared border, may offer the Court an opportunity to develop further transboundary pollution law.

Soft Law. Sources of binding obligation with respect to environmental matters are supplemented by nonbinding sources of "soft law," reflected in guidelines, recommendations, and other nonbinding acts adopted by states and international institutions. Both the 1972 Stockholm Declaration and the 1992 Rio Declaration fall into the category of international environmental soft law. So too do newer instruments like the WSSD Plan of Implementation (elaborating guidelines for the pursuit of sustainable development in various sectors) and the 2007 Bali Road Map that charts a course for future climate change negotiations designed to culminate in a new international agreement by the end of 2009. Although not formally binding on states, rules of soft law can still be politically influential and play an important role by pointing to the likely future direction of legal development, by informally establishing acceptable norms of behavior, and by "codifying" rules of customary law.

International Environmental Law: General Principles

Several general principles of international law have emerged specifically in relation to environmental matters. They are general in the sense that they potentially apply to all members of the international community, span every range of activities, and address the protection of all aspects of the environment. They are principles in the sense that they usually operate as broad, overarching objectives rather than prescriptive rules for state conduct, although if sufficiently well subscribed they may amount to customary international law.[26] In international environmental law, general principles serve an important structural function, providing the common scaffolding upon which more specific rules affecting different environmental resources are built and implemented.

Sovereignty and Responsibility for the Environment

The rules of international environmental law have developed in pursuit of two principles that pull in opposing directions: that states have sovereign rights over their natural resources and that states must not cause damage to the environment. These objectives are reflected in Principle 21 of the Stockholm Declaration and Principle 2 of the Rio Declaration and provide the foundation of international environmental law.

The first element (sovereignty) reflects the preeminent position of states as primary members of the international legal community. It is tempered by the second element (environmental protection), which places limits on the exercise of sovereign rights. In an environmentally interdependent world, activities in one state almost inevitably produce effects in other states or in areas beyond national jurisdiction (such as the high seas).

In the form presented by Principle 21 and Principle 2, the responsibility to prevent damage to the environment of other states or of areas beyond national jurisdiction has been accepted as an obligation by all states.[27] As indicated in the introduction, the International Court of Justice has now confirmed that the second element reflects customary international law.[28]

The emergence of this responsibility has historical roots that predate the Stockholm Conference. These relate to the obligation of all states "to protect within the territory the rights of other states, in particular their right to integrity and inviolability in peace and war" and the principle endorsed by the arbitral tribunal in the Trail Smelter case.[29]

Good Neighborliness and International Cooperation

The principle of "good neighborliness," as enunciated in Article 74 of the UN Charter, concerning social, economic, and commercial matters, has been extended to environmental matters by rules promoting international cooperation. It applies particularly to activities carried out in one state that might have adverse effects on the environment of another state or in areas beyond national jurisdiction. The commitment to environmental cooperation is reflected in many international agreements and is supported by state practice. In general, the obligation includes commitments to implement treaty objectives or to improve relations outside a treaty or in relation to certain tasks. Specifically, the obligation can require information sharing, notification, consultation or participation rights in certain decisions, the conduct of environmental impact assessments, and cooperative emergency procedures, particularly where activities might be ultrahazardous. The construction of nuclear power plants on borders is an example of an area where cooperative obligations are reasonably well developed, although, as examples like the Austria-Czech Republic dispute over the Temelin nuclear power plant illustrate (see Chapter 14), their implementation in practice is often more problematic.

The required extent of cooperation was one of the central issues in the Danube Dam case between Hungary and Slovakia over construction of the Gabcikovo Dam, referred to the International Court of Justice in 1993.[30] Construction of the dam, as well as a second dam at Nagymaros, required the diversion of the Danube River, which Hungary claimed would produce dire environmental consequences. Hungary alleged that Slovakia violated its obligation to cooperate in good faith in the implementation of principles affecting transboundary resources. In its 1997 judgment, the Court found that Hungary had not been entitled to terminate construction work on the dams or to terminate the treaty, and that Slovakia was undertaking work on an alternative dam, known as "Variant C," illegally. The parties subsequently undertook negotiations to implement the judgment, but in the absence of agreement, Slovakia returned to the Court in September 1998 with a further request that the Court lay down guidelines on the conduct of the negotiations. The international dispute remains unresolved, but, in the meantime, Slovakia has completed Variant C, apparently without the occurrence of detrimental ecological impacts.

More recently, the International Tribunal for the Law of the Sea (ITLOS) considered Ireland's allegation that the United Kingdom failed to cooperate in protecting the Irish Sea by refusing to share information and failing to carry out a proper environmental impact assessment of the proposed operation of a nuclear fuel recycling plant at Sellafield in England. ITLOS affirmed that "the duty to cooperate is a fundamental principle in the prevention of pollution of the marine environment" under UNCLOS and general international law. In the interests of "prudence and caution," the tribunal ordered the parties to cooperate in exchanging information about the environmental risks and effects of the operation of the plant and in devising appropriate measures to prevent pollution of the marine environment.[31]

Sustainable Development

The International Court of Justice in the Gabcikovo-Nagymaros case described this principle as expressing the "need to reconcile economic development with protection of the environment."[32] The ideas underlying the concept of sustainable development have a long history in international law, dating back at least to the Pacific Fur Seal arbitration in 1893. The concept came of age with the Earth Summit and the international agreements that it spawned. It now seems that the principle has acquired a harder legal edge. For instance, in 2005 an arbitral tribunal of the Permanent Court of Arbitration in the Iron Rhine Railway case declared:

> Environmental law and the law on development stand not as alternatives but as mutually reinforcing, integral concepts, which require that where development may cause significant harm to the environment there is a duty to prevent, or at least mitigate, such harm . . . This duty, in the opinion of the Tribunal, has now become a principle of general international law.[33]

What sustainable development means in international law today is a more complicated matter. Where it has been used, it appears to refer to at least four separate but related objectives that, taken together, might constitute the legal elements of the concept of sustainable development as used in the Brundtland Report.[34] First, as invoked in some agreements such as the FCCC, it refers to the commitment to preserve natural resources for the benefit of present and future generations (the principles of intragenerational and intergenerational equity). Second, in other agreements, sustainable development refers to appropriate standards for the exploitation of natural resources like fisheries based upon sustainable harvest or wise use (the principle of conservation of resources). Third, yet other agreements require an equitable use of natural resources such as international watercourses, suggesting that a state must consider the needs of other states and people (the equitable-use principle). A fourth category of agreements requires that environmental considerations be integrated with economic and other development plans, programs, and projects and that development needs be taken into account in applying environmental objectives (the integration principle).

Common but Differentiated Responsibility

This principle has emerged from applying the broader principle of equity in general international law and recognizing that the special needs of developing countries must be considered if these countries are to be encouraged to participate in global environmental agreements. The principle includes two important elements. First, states have a common responsibility to protect certain environmental resources. Second, it is necessary to take account of differing circumstances, particularly in relation to each state's contribution to causing a particular environmental problem and its ability to respond to the threat.

Application of the principle of common but differentiated responsibility has important, practical consequences. It leads to the adoption and implementation of environmental standards that impose different commitments for states, and it provides a basis for providing financial and technical assistance to developing countries and LDCs to assist them in implementing their commitments. To date the principle is reflected in a mere handful of agreements, although these include the treaties dealing with climate change that require parties to protect the climate system "on the basis of equity and in accordance with their common but differentiated responsibilities and respective capabilities" and place the burden of reducing greenhouse gas emissions primarily on developed countries.[35] In the negotiations for a post-2012 agreement, continuing adherence to the principle of common but differentiated responsibilities is coming under challenge from some developed countries that stress the need for large emitters in the developing world, such as China and India, to accept greenhouse emissions reduction targets.

Precautionary Principle

This principle emerged in international legal instruments only in the mid-1980s, although it had previously been relied upon in some domestic legal systems. The core of this legal principle, which some believe reflects customary international law,[36] is reflected in Principle 15 of the Rio Declaration, one part of which provides that "[w]here there are threats of serious or irreversible damage, lack of full scientific certainty shall not be used as a reason for postponing cost-effective measures to prevent environmental degradation." The precautionary principle aims to provide guidance to states and the international community in the development of international environmental law and policy in the face of scientific uncertainty and is, potentially, the most radical of environmental principles. Some invoke it to justify preemptive international legal measures to address potentially catastrophic environmental threats such as climate change. Opponents, however, have decried the principle, arguing that it promotes overregulation of a range of human activities.

Notwithstanding the controversy, the principle has been endorsed in a large number of international agreements. Among these is the Biosafety Protocol to the Convention on Biological Diversity, which permits parties to ban imports of genetically modified organisms where there is a "lack of scientific certainty due to insufficient relevant scientific information and knowledge" concerning health or environmental impacts.[37] Similar language is found in the provisions of the 2001 Stockholm Convention on Persistent Organic Pollutants regarding placing controls on additional chemicals in the future,[38] although the words "precautionary principle" are not used on account of objections raised by the United States, Australia, and other countries.[39]

International judicial acceptance of the precautionary principle has been more cautious. The principle was not mentioned in the majority decision in the Gabcikovo-Nagymaros case, despite considerable scientific uncertainty over the environmental impact of the project.[40] Likewise, the Appellate Body of the WTO, in the Beef Hormones and Apples cases, declined to take a position on whether the principle amounts to customary international law, commenting that the international status of the principle is "less than clear."[41] ITLOS was more forthcoming in the Southern Bluefin Tuna case, citing "prudence and caution" as a basis for its decision requiring Japan to cease an experimental fishing program despite scientific uncertainty as to the impacts of fishing on stocks of the migratory tuna species.[42]

Polluter-Pays Principle

This principle states that the costs of pollution should be borne by those responsible for causing the pollution. The precise meaning, international legal status, and effect of the principle remain open to question because international practice based upon the principle is limited. It is doubtful whether it has achieved the status of a generally applicable rule of international law, except perhaps in relation to states in the EU, the UN Economic Commission for Europe (UNECE), and the OECD. It has nevertheless attracted broad support and underlies rules on civil and state liability for environmental damage (for example, the Liability Protocol to the Basel Hazardous Wastes Convention) and on the permissibility of state subsidies. Developed countries increasingly are acknowledging the "responsibility that they bear in the international pursuit of sustainable development in view of the pressures their societies place on the global environment" as well as the financial and other consequences that flow from this acknowledgment.[43] Supporting instruments include Principle 16 of the Rio Declaration, OECD Council Recommendations, the Treaty of Rome (as amended) and related instruments, and the 1992 agreement establishing the European Economic Area.

Basic Rules of International Environmental Law

As international environmental law has developed, standards have been adopted to address a widening range of environmental resources. Integrated concepts of the environment have become prevalent in recent years, but these standards still tend to address particular resources or sectors of the environment, such as flora and fauna, water quality, air quality, hazardous substances, and waste. Hence wide-ranging problems like climate change, which encompasses aspects of biodiversity conservation and water management along with atmospheric pollution, pose significant (and largely unresolved) challenges for the coordination of different bodies of international environmental rules.

Protection of Flora and Fauna

The protection of flora and fauna was the subject of the earliest international environmental regulation, and there are now widely accepted standards that prohibit interference with endangered species in particular. Important global instruments regulate wetlands, trade in endangered species, the conservation of biodiversity generally, and transboundary movement of genetically modified organisms.[44] However, efforts to adopt a convention on forests, initiated at the Earth Summit, have proved to be fruitless in the face of sustained opposition from many developing countries. A more likely avenue for promoting forest conservation may be negotiations under the international climate change regime to allow tradeable credits to be earned for "avoided deforestation."

Protection of the Marine Environment

International law to prevent pollution of oceans and seas is now relatively well developed at the global and regional levels. At the global level the 1982 UN Convention on the Law of the Sea, which entered into force in November 1994, establishes a comprehensive framework to address marine pollution from various sources, including dumping at sea, land-based sources, vessels, and offshore installations such as oil rigs.[45] In addition there are detailed international agreements on the dumping of waste at sea, protection of the environment during salvage operations, hazardous substances, ballast management, and oil pollution preparedness and response.[46] However, no global agreement specifically regulates pollution from land-based sources, which is particularly consequential because this accounts for more than 70 percent of total marine pollution.

Acts adopted by international organizations have also contributed significantly to the development of this area of international law. Notable examples include the 1982 decision by the International Whaling Commission to adopt a moratorium on commercial whaling and the 1985 decision of the parties to the 1972 London Dumping Convention to adopt a moratorium on the dumping of radioactive waste at sea.

At the regional level, early agreements addressed dumping from ships and pollution from land-based sources.[47] These have since been supplemented by an extensive network of conventions adopted under the UNEP Regional Seas Programme. Initiated in 1975, this now includes programs covering thirteen regional seas with more than 140 coastal state participants.[48] Framework conventions and supplementary protocols are in force for the Caribbean, Kuwait, the Mediterranean, the Red Sea and Gulf of Aden, the Southeast Pacific, the South Pacific, the Northeast Pacific, West and Central Africa, the Indian Ocean and East Africa, and the Black Sea.[49] Additional commitments have been adopted for the EU and Antarctic regions.

Protection of Freshwater Resources

Freshwater resources include rivers, lakes, and groundwaters. Many individual rivers and river systems are now subject to special rules governing their use and the maintenance of water quality. Noteworthy examples include the Rhine in Europe, the Zambezi in Africa, and the Plate in South America, each of which has been subject to treaty protection for many years. In addition, efforts have been made to develop rules that apply to all rivers in a particular region or to all rivers globally.[50] Lakes have also been subject to protective regimes, especially in North America and other areas where acid rain and other deposits have threatened to cause long-term damage.[51] Protection of groundwaters remains less well developed in international law.[52]

Air Quality

International law for the protection of the atmosphere addresses transboundary air pollution, ozone depletion, and climate change. Measures now place limits for many states on permissible atmospheric emissions of certain substances. This has important implications for production patterns and, particularly, energy use.

In this area of international regulation, the first instrument was the regional 1979 UNECE Convention on Long-Range Transboundary Air Pollution, which has since been supplemented with protocols on sulfur dioxide, nitrogen oxides, volatile organic compounds, heavy metals, persistent organic pollutants, and ground-level ozone.[53] The transboundary air pollution model was relied upon in global efforts to protect the ozone layer with the 1985 Framework Convention for the Protection of the Ozone Layer, as supplemented by the 1987 Montreal Protocol, subsequently amended in 1990, 1992, 1997, and 1999.[54] The 1992 FCCC and its 1997 Kyoto Protocol also have global application. The FCCC entered into force in March 1994, aiming to limit industrial countries' emissions of carbon dioxide and other greenhouse gases. It also created a framework for cooperation and commitments to ensure that greenhouse gas concentrations in the atmosphere do not lead to dangerous anthropogenic interference with the climate system.[55] These soft commitments are to be implemented by the Kyoto Protocol, which establishes emission reduction targets for certain developed countries for the commitment period 2008 to 2012.[56] Parties are permitted to use a range of innovative "flexibility mechanisms" (including emissions trading) to reach their targets, although significant domestic abatement action will still be necessary. It is likely that the flexibility mechanisms will continue operation under any post-2012 agreement, although countries are still in negotiations to determine obligations under the new treaty, including the all-important question of targets for future commitment periods.

Waste

Binding international regulation of waste management is currently limited to regulating or prohibiting trade in certain wastes, as well as provisions prohibiting the disposal at sea of certain hazardous wastes. These measures encourage waste prevention and minimization by increasing costs and are likely precursors to measures that might limit industrial waste production, including packaging and e-waste.

The principal international agreement establishing regulations and prohibitions on trade in hazardous waste is the 1989 Basel Convention, which requires that importing countries be notified of, and grant consent for, shipments before they occur (prior informed consent).[57] A proposed amendment to the convention, known as the "Basel Ban," sought to go further, prohibiting hazardous waste exports from OECD countries to non-OECD countries (see Chapter 7 for a full discussion).[58] At a regional level the 1991 African Bamako Convention prohibits imports of hazardous waste, which is defined to include all substances whose use is banned in the exporting country.[59]

Global regulation of radioactive waste movements is governed by a nonbinding 1990 International Atomic Energy Agency Code of Practice, which establishes regulatory guidelines and is far less rigorous than any of the treaty agreements.[60] More stringent regulation of transboundary movements of spent nuclear fuel was established by the Joint Convention on the Safety of Spent Fuel Management and on the Safety of Radioactive Waste Management.[61] This issue may grow in prominence in international environmental law if nuclear power is embraced by more states as a low greenhouse gas emissions technology for electricity generation.[62]

Hazardous Substances

Until the turn of the century, the management of hazardous substances other than waste, including chemicals and pesticides, was not subject to any binding global legal instruments. In 2001 the Convention on Persistent Organic Pollutants (POPs) was adopted to regulate the production, use, and transboundary movement of POPs (chemicals that remain intact in the environment for long periods and bioaccumulate in living organisms).[63] The convention establishes controls on the production, import, export, and disposal of these substances. Another new convention establishes a prior informed consent (PIC) procedure for international trade in toxic pesticides and other hazardous chemicals.[64] The PIC Convention allows countries to refuse imports of hazardous chemicals that they cannot manage safely and imposes labeling requirements on exports of these substances to promote their safe use. (See Chapter 7 for a detailed discussion of both conventions.) The two conventions supplement a large body of detailed, nonbinding regulations and other instruments dealing with the management of hazardous substances, including, in particular, international trade and chemical safety at work.[65]

Conclusion

In a relatively short space of time, a significant body of principles and rules of international law has been put in place for the protection of the environment and conservation of natural resources. These rules have been primarily developed by and are addressed to states, although increasingly international environmental law encompasses a much broader range of actors, including NGOs, treaty bodies, and corporate entities. As international environmental law has developed, its rules have become increasingly complex and technical, particularly as environmental considerations are addressed in economic and other social fields.

Compared with the frenetic treaty-making activity of the early 1970s, the pace of legal development in the twenty-first century has slowed, with the focus moving to the elaboration of existing treaties, such as those dealing with climate change, as well as to issues of implementation and enforcement. Consequently, we are seeing a shift from the legislative domain to the judicial and quasi-judicial domain, with international courts and arbitral bodies filling the gaps left by legislators. Further signs of this trend are the increasingly detailed noncompliance mechanisms adopted under treaties dealing with atmospheric pollution, including the Kyoto Protocol.[66] Nevertheless, judging by decisions of international tribunals, there is still some way to go before the more established judicial bodies will feel comfortable dealing with environmental issues and providing leadership in this next phase. Indeed, it may well be that the greatest contribution to applying the principle of sustainable development will come from bodies traditionally outside the field of international environmental law, such as the dispute settlement bodies of the WTO or the World Bank's Inspection Panel.[67]

That we now look to the WTO and other economic institutions, as much as to international environmental organizations, for rules governing environmental matters attests to the extent of integration of environmental issues into aspects of economic and development institutions and law. This is a welcome development in that it signals the potential for international environmental law to have a transformative effect on broader international society. At the same time, integration between environmental and other issues, as well as the related question of coordinating different environmental regimes, poses perhaps the greatest challenge to the future effectiveness and cohesiveness of international environmental law.

Notes

1. "Request for an Examination of the Situation in Accordance with Paragraph 63 of the Court's Judgment of 20 December 1974 in the Nuclear Tests (*New Zealand v. France*) Case," Order of September 22, 1995, *International Court of Justice Reports* (hereafter *ICJ Reports*) (1995): 306, para. 64 (hereafter "Nuclear Tests II").
2. "Legality of the Threat or Use of Nuclear Weapons, Advisory Opinion, July 8, 1996," *ICJ Reports* (1996): 226, para. 29.
3. "Legality of the Threat or Use of Nuclear Weapons," para. 33.
4. See Principle 27 of the Rio "Declaration on Environment and Development," *Report of the UN Conference on Environment and Development,* A/CONF.151/26/Rev.1, 2:3 (1993), reprinted in *International Legal Materials* (hereafter *ILM*) 31 (1992): 874.
5. "Pacific Fur Seal Arbitration (*Great Britain v. United States*)," *Moore's Report of International Arbitration Awards* 1 (1893): 755.
6. Philip Allott, *Eunomia: New Order for a New World* (New York: Oxford University Press, 1990), para. 17.52.
7. A role called for by United Nations Conference on Environment and Development, "Agenda 21," chap. 38, paras. 38.42–38.44.
8. Up-to-date membership figures for the UN can be found at www.un.org/en/members/index.shtml.
9. Up-to-date membership details for the OECD can be found at www.oecd.org/docu ment/58/0,3343,en_2649_201185_1889402_1_1_1_1,00.html.
10. Up-to-date membership details for the G-77 can be found at www.g77.org/doc/members.html.
11. For example, the OECD Guidelines for Multinational Enterprises, 2000.
12. See, generally, Philippe Sands, "The Environment, Community, and International Law," *Harvard International Law Journal* 30 (1989): 393.
13. For a general history of international environmental law, see Philippe Sands, *Principles of International Environmental Law* (Cambridge: Cambridge University Press, 2003).
14. Important treaties adopted during this period included the Geneva Conventions on the High Seas: "Convention on the High Seas," Geneva, April 29, 1958, United Nations Treaty Series [hereafter cited as UNTS], 450: 82; "Convention on Fishing and Conservation of the Living Resources of the High Seas," Geneva, April 29, 1958, UNTS, 559: 285; "Convention on the Continental Shelf," Geneva, April 29, 1958, UNTS, 499: 311. In 1963 the Nuclear Test Ban Treaty was adopted, paving the way politically for Australia and New Zealand to bring a case before the ICJ calling on France to stop all nuclear testing; see *Australia v. France, ICJ Reports* (1974): 253; *New Zealand v. France, ICJ Reports* (1974): 457.
15. *Report of the UN Conference on the Human Environment,* UN Doc. A/CONF/48/14 at 2–65, and Corr. 1 (1972), reprinted in *ILM* 11 (1972): 1416.
16. Louis B. Sohn, "The Stockholm Declaration on the Human Environment," *Harvard International Law Journal* 14 (1973): 423–515.
17. "United Nations Convention on the Law of the Sea," Montego Bay, December 10, 1982, reprinted in *ILM* 21 (1982): 1261.
18. UN General Assembly Resolution 42/187, December 11, 1987, endorsement of World Commission on Environment and Development, *Our Common Future;* UN General Assembly Resolution 43/196, December 20, 1988.

19. *ILM* 31 (1992): 881; *Report of the United Nations Conference on Environment and Development*, vol. 1.
20. *ILM* 31 (1992): 822, 849.
21. See *Report of the Conference of the Parties on its Seventh Session*, Marrakesh, October 29–November 10, 2001, FCCC/CP/2001/13. The decisions that make up the Marrakesh Accords are in four volumes: FCCC/CP/2001/13/Add.1–Add.4.
22. See "Bali Action Plan," Decision 1/CP.13, *Report of the Conference of the Parties on its Thirteenth Session*, Bali, December 3–15, 2007, FCCC/CP/2007/6/Add.1.
23. The majority of policy development in the area takes place under the auspices of the UN Commission on Sustainable Development (CSD) pursuant to its Multi-Year Programme of Work for CSD: 2004/2005 to 2016/2017; see www.un.org/esa/sustdev/csd/policy.htm. This is directed to very broad, thematic areas such as agriculture, drought, and Africa.
24. Kevin Gray, "World Summit on Sustainable Development: Accomplishments and New Directions," *International and Comparative Law Quarterly* 52 (2003): 256.
25. "*United States v. Canada*," *Reports of International Arbitral Awards* 3 (1941): 1907; citing Clyde Eagleton, *Responsibility of States* (New York: New York University Press, 1928), 80.
26. For the general distinction between rules and principles, see Ronald Dworkin, *Taking Rights Seriously* (Cambridge: Harvard University Press, 1977), 24, 26.
27. "Nuclear Tests II," *ICJ Reports* (1995): 306.
28. "Legality of the Threat or Use of Nuclear Weapons," para. 29. See also "Case Concerning the Gabcikovo-Nagymaros Project" (Hungary/Slovakia), *ICJ Reports* (1997), paras. 53 and 112.
29. Permanent Court of Arbitration, Palmas Case (1928), *HCR* 2: 93.
30. See original Hungarian Application, October 22, 1992, paras. 27, 29, and 30, in *Documents in International Environmental Law*, ed. Philippe Sands, Richard Tarasofsky, and Mary Weiss, vol. 2A (Manchester: Manchester University Press, 1995), 691, doc. 28.
31. "MOX Plant Case (*Ireland v. United Kingdom*) (Provisional Measures)," *ILM* 41 (2002): 405, paras. 82, 84, and 89.
32. "Case Concerning the Gabcikovo-Nagymaros Project," para. 140.
33. "The Iron Rhine (Ijzeren Rijn) Arbitration (Belgium-Netherlands)," *Permanent Court of Arbitration Award Series* (Cambridge: Cambridge University Press, 2005), para. 59.
34. World Commission on Environment and Development, *Our Common Future* (Oxford: Oxford University Press, 1987).
35. "Climate Change Convention," Art. 3(1), *ILM* 31 (1992): 881, and the "Kyoto Protocol," *ILM* 37 (1997): 22.
36. For a recent discussion see Arie Trouwborst, *Evolution and Status of the Precautionary Principle in International Law* (The Hague: Kluwer International, 2002).
37. "Cartagena Protocol on Biosafety," Art. 10(6), *ILM* 39 (2001): 1027.
38. "Stockholm Convention on Persistent Organic Pollutants," Art. 8.7(a) and 8.9, *ILM* 40 (2001): 532.
39. A rift has emerged in this respect between the EU, which supports the idea of the "precautionary principle" as a principle of international law, and the United States, which sees precaution merely as an approach to decision making.
40. See Afshin A-Khavari and Donald R. Rothwell, "The ICJ and the Danube Dam Case: A Missed Opportunity for International Environmental Law?" *Melbourne University Law Review* 22 (1998): 507, 530.
41. "EC Measures Concerning Meat and Meat Products (Hormones)," *Report of the Appellate Body*, WT/DS26/AB/R and WT/DS48/AB/R, January 16, 1998, para. 123; "Japan Measures Affecting the Importation of Apples (Apples)," *Report of the Appellate Body*, WT/DS245/AB/R, November 26, 2003, para. 233. See also "EC Measures Affecting the Approval and Marketing of Biotech Products," *Reports of the Panel*, WT/DS291/R, WT/DS292/R, and WT/DS293/R, September 29, 2006, para. 7.89.

42. "Southern Bluefin Tuna Cases (*New Zealand v. Japan; Australia v. Japan*) (Provisional Measures)," *ILM* 38 (1999): 1624, para, 77. Also see suggestions of Judge Weeramantry in his dissenting opinion in "Nuclear Tests II," *ICJ Reports* (1995): 342.

43. "Rio Declaration," Principle 7.

44. "Convention on Wetlands of International Importance," Ramsar, Iran, February 2, 1971, UNTS, 996: 245; "Convention on International Trade in Endangered Species of Wild Fauna and Flora," Washington, March 3, 1973, UNTS, 993: 243; "Convention on Biological Diversity," Rio de Janeiro, June 5, 1992, *ILM* 31 (1992): 822 (which also regulates the sustainable use of the components of biodiversity and the sharing of benefits arising from the use of genetic resources); "Biosafety Protocol," Montreal, January 29, 2000, *ILM* 39 (2001): 1027.

45. "United Nations Convention on the Law of the Sea," December 10, 1982, *ILM* 21 (1982): 1261.

46. "Convention on the Prevention of Marine Pollution by Dumping of Wastes and Other Matter," December 29, 1972, UNTS, 1046: 120 (in London on November 7, 1996, the parties to the Dumping Convention agreed to a protocol that will eventually replace the Convention: *ILM* 36 [1997]: 1); "International Convention Relating to Intervention on the High Seas in Cases of Oil Pollution Damage," Brussels, November 29, 1969, reprinted in *ILM* 9 (1970): 25; International Convention for the Prevention of Pollution from Ships, London, September 2, 1973, as modified by the Protocol of 1978 relating thereto, 1340 UNTS 81, 184; "International Convention on Oil Pollution Preparedness, Response, and Co-operation," London, November 30, 1990, *ILM* 30 (1991): 733; Protocol on Preparedness, Response and Co-operation to pollution Incidents by Hazardous and Noxious Substances, 2000, IMO, *OPRC-HNS Protocol*, 5; International Convention on the Control of Harmful Anti-fouling Systems on Ships, London, August 19, 2002, [2002] ATNIF 18; International Convention for the Control and Management of Ships' Ballast Water and Sediments, London, February 13, 2004, [2005] ATNIF 18.

47. The early Oslo and Paris conventions have been replaced by the "OSPAR Convention for the Protection of the Marine Environment of the North East Atlantic," Paris, September 22, 1992, *ILM* 32 (1993): 1228.

48. Up-to-date details of the UNEP Regional Seas Programme can be found at www.unep.org/regionalseas.

49. See, generally, Ellik Adler, "A World of Neighbours: UNEP's Regional Seas Programme," *Tropical Coasts* (July 2003): 4.

50. See "Convention on the Law of Non-navigational Uses of International Watercourses," reprinted in *ILM* 36 (1997): 700.

51. "Agreement between the United States and Canada Concerning the Water Quality of the Great Lakes," Ottawa, April 15, 1972, reprinted in *ILM* 11 (1972): 694.

52. See, generally, Stefano Burchi and Kerstin Mechlem, *Groundwater in International Law: Compilation of Treaties and Other Legal Instruments* (Rome: Food and Agriculture Organization, 2005).

53. "Convention on Long-Range Transboundary Air Pollution," Geneva, November 13, 1973, reprinted in *ILM* 18 (1979): 1442. Details of the protocols to the convention can be found at www.unece.org/env/lrtap/status/lrtap_s.htm.

54. "Framework Convention for the Protection of the Ozone Layer," Vienna, March 22, 1985, reprinted in *ILM* 26 (1987): 1529; "Protocol on Substances That Deplete the Ozone Layer," Montreal, September 16, 1987, reprinted in *ILM* 26 (1987): 1550.

55. *ILM* 31 (1992): 881.

56. The Kyoto Protocol entered into force on February 16, 2005. The first commitment period commenced in 2008.

57. "Convention on the Control of Transboundary Movements of Hazardous Wastes and Their Disposal," Basel, March 22, 1989, reprinted in *ILM* 28 (1989): 649.

58. Decision II/12, Report of COP-2, UNEP/CHW.2/30, March 25, 1994. The Basel Ban is not yet in force as it has not achieved the required ratification by at least three-fourths of the parties that accepted it.
59. "Convention on the Ban of the Import into Africa and the Control of Transboundary Movement and Management of Hazardous Wastes within Africa," Bamako, January 30, 1991, reprinted in *ILM* 30 (1991): 775.
60. International Atomic Energy Agency, Doc. GC (XXXIV)/920, June 27, 1990, *Yearbook of International Environmental Law* 1 (1990): 537.
61. Joint Convention on the Safety of Spent Fuel Management and on the Safety of Radioactive Waste Management, September 5, 1997, *ILM* 36 (1997): 1436.
62. *Annual Report for 2007* (Vienna: International Atomic Energy Agency, 2008), 1.
63. Convention on Persistent Organic Pollutants, Stockholm, May 22, 2001, reprinted in *ILM* 40 (2001): 532.
64. Rotterdam Convention on the Prior Informed Consent Procedure for Certain Hazardous Chemicals and Pesticides in International Trade, Rotterdam, September 10, 1998, reprinted in ILM 38 (1999): 1.
65. 1985 UN Food and Agriculture Organization Code of Conduct on the Distribution and Use of Pesticides (as revised in 2002); 1987 UNEP London Guidelines for the Exchange of Information on Chemicals in International Trade, as amended in 1989; "Convention Concerning Safety in the Use of Chemicals at Work," Geneva, June 24, 1990, *Yearbook of International Environmental Law* 1 (1990): 295.
66. See Decision 24/CP.7, Procedures and Mechanisms Relating to Compliance under the Kyoto Protocol, in *Marrakesh Accords,* Report of the Conference of the Parties on its Seventh Session, Marrakesh, October 29–10 November 10, 2001, FCCC/CP/2001/13/Add.2.
67. Of particular significance are two decisions of the Appellate Body in the Shrimp-Turtle dispute. See "United States–Import Prohibition of Certain Shrimp and Shrimp Products," *Report of the Appellate Body,* WT/DS58/AB/R, reprinted in *ILM* 38 (1999): 118, and "United States–Import Prohibition on Certain Shrimp and Shrimp Products," Recourse to Article 21.5 of the DSU by Malaysia, *Report of the Appellate Body,* October 22, 2001, WT/DS58/AB/RW.

4

Global Environmental Policy: Governance through Regimes

David Leonard Downie

As diplomats gathered in Copenhagen in December 2009 for the global climate negotiations, many around the world hoped the meeting would yield the framework for a new global climate treaty—a successor to the Kyoto Protocol that would lead humankind on a path away from very dangerous climate change. These moments—the creation of new environmental treaties—are rightly seen as significant achievements. Indeed, countries must agree to specific goals and policies if real progress is going to be made. However, students and scholars would fail to understand global environmental policy in a given issue area if they focused only on a single treaty rather than the entire evolving set of principles, norms, rules, procedures, and institutions—the "international regime"—that countries and other actors create and implement for a specific issue.

This chapter provides an introduction to "regimes" in the context of global environmental policy. It provides a detailed definition of the term, delineates prominent examples in global environmental politics, and outlines obstacles to creating and implementing effective global environmental regimes.[1]

International Regimes

International regimes are dynamic, sector-specific, international regulatory and administrative systems. A useful formal definition is: a system of principles, norms, rules, operating procedures, and institutions that actors create or accept to regulate and coordinate action in a particular issue area of international relations. Principles are beliefs of fact, causation, and rectitude. Norms are standards of behavior. Rules are specific prescriptions or proscriptions for action. Operating procedures are prevailing practices for work within the regime, including those for making and implementing collective choice. Institutions are mechanisms and organizations for implementing, operating, evaluating, and expanding the regime and regime policy.[2]

These five regime elements are created, structured, and implemented through formal agreements, international organizations, private international law, soft law, accepted norms of international behavior, or a combination of these structures among actors involved in the issue area (governments, international organizations, nongovernmental organizations [NGOs], multinational corporations, and others). States, as the dominant actors in the international system, are the primary and most important creators of international regimes, but they are not the only source, and the involvement of other actors often proves critical. Similarly, while formal, legally binding treaties often form the core of a regime, a regime can also be based on private international law, soft law, or other arrangements, provided that these are accepted by the actors in the issue areas as creating principles, rules, and procedures that guide their behavior. Examples include certification programs that identify wood and wood products harvested from sustainable forests (rather than clear-cutting old-growth forests or rain forests)[3] and the international management and manufacturing standards, such as the ISO frameworks developed under the rubric of the International Organization for Standardization.[4]

A regime is more than patterned interaction, a single international agreement, or a single organization, although each of these is usually part of one. Rather, an international regime consists of the principles, norms, rules, and procedures contained in one or more interrelated agreements, organizations, standard practices, and shared understandings that together regulate international action in a particular issue area. The nuclear nonproliferation regime, for example, consists of the principles, norms, rules, and procedures contained or included in the Partial Test Ban Treaty, the Nuclear Non-Proliferation Treaty, and the relevant activities of the International Atomic Energy Agency. When effective, regimes, through their principles, help to sharpen international goals in an issue area, shape international behavior toward a common goal through their rules and norms, manage state interactions, augment policy coordination and collaboration, reduce conflict, and facilitate the making of further agreements.

The regime that seeks to protect stratospheric ozone—the ozone layer that in turn protects the Earth from ultraviolet radiation—is one of the best-developed and most effective global environmental regimes and can be used to illustrate the definition and its components. Many students and scholars correctly understand the famous Montreal Protocol as a ground-breaking environmental treaty, but global ozone policy consists of much more.[5]

Beginning in the 1970s, scientists discovered that certain man-made chemicals posed a serious threat to stratospheric ozone. Ozone is a gas composed of three oxygen atoms (O_3). While anthropogenic ozone is a harmful air pollutant at ground level, 90 percent of naturally occurring ozone resides in the stratosphere, far above the Earth. This ozone layer helps to shield the Earth from ultraviolet radiation produced by the sun. Because large increases in certain types of this radiation would seriously harm many plants, animals, and humans, the ozone layer is considered an essential component of the Earth's natural systems. Chemicals that threaten the ozone layer include chlorofluorocarbons (CFCs), once very widely used as refrigerants, industrial solvents, aerosol propellants, and in the manufacture of rigid and flexible foam; hydrochlorofluorocarbons (HCFCs), less ozone-depleting CFC substitutes; halons, widely used for fire control; methyl bromide, an inexpensive, widely used, and very toxic soil and structural fumigant used to kill pests across a wide range of agricultural and shipping sectors; as well as other substances such carbon tetrachloride and methyl chloroform. What these chemicals share is the ability to release into the stratosphere chlorine or bromine atoms that then act as a catalyst in the destruction of ozone molecules.

The ozone regime is the set of integrated principles, norms, rules, and procedures that nation-states have created to regulate and coordinate action in an attempt to protect stratospheric ozone from human-made chemicals such as CFCs and methyl bromide. The international agreements that delineate the main elements of the regime include the 1985 Vienna Convention for the Protection of the Ozone Layer, the 1987 Montreal Protocol on Substances That Deplete the Ozone Layer, and the binding amendments and adjustments to the Montreal Protocol agreed to during more than twenty meetings of the parties to the protocol. Of these, the most important agreements are the 1987 Montreal Protocol, the 1990 London Amendment and Adjustment, the 1992 Copenhagen Amendment and Adjustment, the 1995 Vienna Adjustment, the 1999 Beijing Amendment and Adjustment, and the 2007 Montreal Adjustment.[6] The 1987 Montreal Protocol established the mechanism to control ozone-depleting substances (ODSs) and placed binding controls on the production and use of certain CFCs and halons. Subsequent amendments and adjustments to the protocol added restrictions on additional chemicals, such as HCFCs and methyl bromide, and increased the level of controls so that the regime now mandates that countries eliminate the production and use of most of these chemicals. As a result, the production and use of CFCs and several other ozone-depleting chemicals have declined dramatically and have been essentially eliminated in the United States and other industrialized countries.

Also central to the ozone regime are operations of its constituent institutions. The Meeting of the Parties (MOP) is the supreme decision-making authority and can negotiate amendments and adjustments to the protocol as well as make binding decisions on issues related to its implementation. The MOP meets annually and includes representatives of all governments that have ratified the protocol as well as observers (who can participate but do not take part in the decision-making procedures) from nonparty governments, international organizations, environmental NGOs and industry groups; most other environmental regimes call this MOP body the Conference of Parties or COP. The Open-Ended Working Group (OEWG) holds discussions in preparation for the MOP. Three independent assessment panels—the Scientific, Environmental Effects, and Technology and Economic assessment panels—provide the parties and the general public with periodic, comprehensive, and authoritative reviews of key issues, under instructions from the parties.[7] The Implementation Committee provides a forum for discussing issues of noncompliance and offers recommendations to the MOP. The Ozone Secretariat provides day-to-day administration of the regime and supports the MOP, OEWG, assessment panels, and Implementation Committee. The Multilateral Fund, created in a landmark agreement as part of the 1990 London Amendment and Adjustment, provides financial assistance to developing countries to aid their transition from using ozone-depleting chemicals—under rules established by the protocol and decisions by the parties.[8] The Executive Committee, composed of representatives from fourteen governments—seven industrialized-country donor parties and seven developing-country recipient parties—is the decision body for the Multilateral Fund. The World Bank, United Nations Development Programme (UNDP), United Nations Environment Programme (UNEP), and United Nations Industrial Development Organization (UNIDO) have been designated as the official implementing agencies that execute work plans approved and funded by the Multilateral Fund. The Multilateral Fund Secretariat performs day-to-day administration functions for the Multilateral Fund and its Executive Committee.

The major principles (beliefs of fact, causation, and rectitude) of the ozone regime are enunciated in the Vienna Convention and the Montreal Protocol, particularly in their preambles. These include statements that the ozone layer is a critical component of the Earth's natural systems and should be protected; that certain human-made chemicals have the capacity to deplete the ozone layer and have already done so; that political action should be based on the best scientific and technical information available; that regulations should be guided, in general, by precaution; and that all states have a common responsibility to help protect the ozone layer but have different responsibilities in doing so.

The norms of the ozone regime include all standards of behavior enunciated in the Vienna Convention, the Montreal Protocol, amendments to the protocol, and decisions by the parties or Executive Committee that do not carry the binding nature of rules. The telling difference is the verb used to proscribe the action. For example, "Parties shall" indicates a rule. "Parties should" or "are requested to" indicates attempts to create norms.

The rules (specific prescriptions or proscriptions for action) of the ozone regime constitute the binding international law of global ozone policy. The rules are enunciated most prominently in the binding provisions of the Montreal Protocol and the amendments and adjustments to the protocol. The most important regime rules establish specific targets and timetables for countries to reduce and eventually eliminate the production and use of nearly all ODSs. They also include a variety of requirements regarding assistance to developing countries, implementation of the treaty, reviews of the efficacy of the regime, and requirements for country reporting on annual production and use of ODSs and efforts to implement the protocol. Rules on a variety of policy and procedural issues are also created by binding decisions of the MOP and the Executive Committee of the Multilateral Fund—decisions that are within the jurisdiction of these bodies and that are established by the protocol.

Finally, the procedures of the ozone regime are the prevailing practices. These include provisions for amending the treaty; deliberating on, agreeing to, and implementing other types of binding and nonbinding decisions made by the MOP and Executive Committee of the Multilateral Fund; as well as the standard operating procedures of the regime's institutions: the MOP, OEWG, Ozone Secretariat, Executive Committee, Fund Secretariat, assessment panels, Implementation Committee, and implementing agencies.

Moreover, because the ozone regime is nearly twenty-five years old, many operating procedures are fully entrenched and provide clear and well-regarded precedents for considering, developing, deciding upon, mandating, and implementing global ozone policy.

International Regimes in Global Environmental Policy

Regimes are found in most areas of international relations, including trade (the World Trade Organization, for example), finance, environment, human rights, managing such global commons as the oceans and Antarctica, communications, travel, and even security.[9] As a result, regimes have received a good deal of theoretical and empirical attention within the international organization subfield of international relations.[10] Of course, comparative levels of regime development and impact vary significantly across issue areas.

Although some wildlife treaties date from early in the twentieth century, the prominence of transnational environmental politics has risen significantly since the UN Conference on the Human Environment in 1972 in Stockholm. Today, global environmental policy—of varying specificity, effectiveness, and importance—exists for stratospheric ozone climate change, global biodiversity, migratory species, trade in endangered species, protection of individual species such as whales, wetlands protection, ocean dumping, desertification, hazardous waste, toxic chemicals, and other issues. Funding for several of these issues is provided by the Global Environment Facility (GEF), an international organization that distributes funds to developing countries for projects that address biodiversity, climate change, international waters, land degradation, the ozone layer, and persistent organic pollutants (POPs). Negotiations on these and other global issues continue, as do talks on numerous regional and bilateral issues. The section below lists several notable international environmental regimes and their constituent agreements and organizations. This is by no means an exhaustive list, and information on all these regimes and treaties can be found on the treaty Web sites.):[11]

• The climate change regime seeks to mitigate human-induced climate change by limiting anthropogenic emissions of greenhouse gases such as carbon dioxide and methane and protecting associated sinks. Components of the climate regime include the principles, norms, rules, and procedures contained in the 1992 UN Framework Convention on Climate Change and the 1997 Kyoto Protocol as well as the international organizations interconnected with these agreements, including the Climate Secretariat, which, like the ozone and other secretariats, runs the day-to-day operations of the regime; Intergovernmental Panel on Climate Change; GEF's climate program; and the Conference of Parties and its numerous subsidiary bodies.

• The hazardous waste regime seeks to protect human health and the environment from wastes that are toxic, poisonous, explosive, corrosive, ecotoxic, or infectious. The hazardous waste regime centers on the global 1989

Basel Convention on the Control of Transboundary Movements of Hazardous Wastes and Their Disposal, and related agreements, which requires or urges parties to minimize the generation of hazardous wastes; work to ensure their environmentally sound management and disposal; and control, reduce, or ban their transnational movement, including taking measures to prevent and punish illegal traffic (see Chapter 7).

• The toxic chemicals regime seeks to protect human health and the environment from certain types of toxic chemicals. It consists of several agreements that exist independently but are also increasingly interconnected. The 2001 Stockholm Convention on Persistent Organic Pollutants (POPs) eliminates or restricts the production, use, trade and release of certain chemicals. The original 2001 treaty covered nine extremely toxic substances. A 2009 expansion of the treaty added nine more chemicals, and the treaty's review process will consider adding additional toxic substances in the future. The 1998 Rotterdam Convention on the Prior Informed Consent Procedure for Certain Hazardous Chemicals and Pesticides in International Trade (PIC) facilitates information exchanged regarding hazardous chemicals, promotes shared responsibility among exporting and importing nations regarding their trade, and allows countries to restrict imports of certain substances unless they provide explicit prior informed consent that such imports are allowed. As noted above, the 1989 Basel Convention seeks to protect human health and the environment from wastes that are toxic, poisonous, explosive, corrosive, eco-toxic, or infectious. The Strategic Approach to International Chemicals Management initiative (SAICM) is a policy framework that promotes the sound management of chemicals throughout their life cycle, with the objective that by 2020 chemicals around the world will be produced and used in ways that minimize significant adverse impacts on human health and the environment. The chemicals regime includes several other international organizations and networks—such as the treaty secretariats, UNEP Chemicals, and the Intergovernmental Forum on Chemical Safety—that promote and assist efforts to manage chemicals in an environmentally sound manner.

The Stockholm, Rotterdam, and Basel conventions can be considered to exist as centerpieces of distinct POPs, PIC, and hazardous waste regimes, respectively, but they are closely related; and parties to these regimes have agreed to coordinate their continuing development and implementation in pursuit of more effective global management of toxic chemicals and wastes.[12] Along with related activities in the SAICM process, those supporting this process seek to create a broader global chemicals regime that seeks to reduce the harmful impacts of toxic chemicals at all points in their life cycles, including production, use, trade, management of stockpiles and wastes, and disposal.[13]

• The global biodiversity regime seeks to protect the global diversity of species, ecosystems, and genes. The regime centers on the 1992 Convention on Biological Diversity (CBD), the Biodiversity Secretariat, and associated funding activities by the GEF. The CBD has three core objectives: to conserve biological diversity, to use biological diversity in a sustainable fashion, and to share the benefits of biological diversity fairly and equitably.

• Several endangered species and habitat protection regimes exist that seek to protect specific species from extinction or specific types of ecosystems. In its broadest sense, the biodiversity regime could be considered to include the species and habitat regimes, as they are crucial to preserving biodiversity. However, unlike the toxic chemicals regime, the various wildlife and habitat regimes engage in far less official coordination, so it is useful to consider them as individual but mutually supporting entities. They include:

  • The 1973 Convention on International Trade in Endangered Species of Wild Fauna and Flora (CITES), which seeks to ensure that international trade in specimens of wild animals and plants does not threaten their survival; it currently seeks to protect more than 30,000 species;
  • The 1979 Bonn Convention on the Conservation of Migratory Species of Wild Animals, which seeks to protect a variety of marine, bird, and land-based species that migrate across international borders;
  • The 1991 Ramsar Wetlands Convention, which provides the framework for national action and international cooperation for the conservation and wise use of wetlands, which are important and diverse natural resources that provide unique habitats and ecosystem services; and
  • The 1946 International Convention for the Regulation of Whaling, which originally sought to protect whale stocks and thus make possible an orderly whaling industry but has come to focus primarily on prohibiting whaling except for particular species.

• The ocean pollution regime seeks to reduce the amount of pollution dumped from ships. It includes the London Dumping Convention (which regulates waste disposal in the oceans); the 1973, 1978, and 1990 International Conventions for the Prevention of Marine Pollution from Ships (which regulate discharges from ships); and relevant activities of the International Maritime Organization (IMO). The IMO is a small, specialized agency of the United Nations that addresses various aspects of international shipping, encourages cooperation among governments, supports high standards of safety, and encourages the control and prevention of marine pollution. The IMO is unusual in that it has some power to enforce and administer matters relating to these issues.

• The Mediterranean Sea regime consists of more than a dozen individual agreements designed to protect and improve the water quality and general environmental condition in the Mediterranean Sea.[14] Several other regional sea regimes have also been created.[15]

• The desertification regime seeks to reduce land degradation and desertification. It includes the 1994 UN Convention to Combat Desertification, its constituent institutions, and the associated funding activities of the GEF.

• The Antarctic Treaty regime arose from broader political and economic issues but includes important environmental components, including the 1972 Convention for the Conservation of Antarctic Seals, the 1980 Convention on the Conservation of Antarctic Marine Living Resources, the 1988 Wellington Convention on the Regulation of Antarctic Mineral Resource Activities, and the 1991 Protocol on Environmental Protection.

• The pan-European air pollution regime, which also includes Canada, Russia, and the United States, has built upon the 1979 Geneva Convention on Long-Range Transboundary Air Pollution (CLRTAP).[16] CLRTAP has provided the forum for creation of eight issue-specific protocols, including the 1984 Protocol for Long-Term Financing of Monitoring; the 1985 Sulfur Protocol; the 1988 Nitrogen Oxides Protocol; the 1991 Volatile Organic Compounds Protocol; the 1998 Heavy Metals Protocol; and the 1998 POPs Protocol.

Obstacles to Effective Global Environmental Policy

The existence of international regimes in many environmental issue areas should not obscure the fact that creating and implementing effective global environmental policy are not easy tasks. It took many years to create each of the environmental regimes listed in the first section of this chapter, and several of them remain weak and rather ineffective (for example, the climate change, desertification, and global biodiversity regimes). It is important, therefore, to understand the obstacles to effective global environmental policy.

This section outlines factors that make it difficult for governments to create and implement effective international environmental policy and regimes. Four types of factors stand out: (1) systemic obstacles, (2) procedural obstacles, (3) lack of necessary and sufficient conditions, and (4) obstacles characteristic of international environmental issues. These broad categories are obviously interrelated, and the individual and relative impact of each characteristic varies across countries and issue areas. Nevertheless, they are a useful starting point for discussing why governments have not created more effective global policy for many environmental issues despite increasingly compelling evidence of serious and dangerous environmental problems.

Systemic Obstacles

Several significant impediments to creating and implementing effective global environmental policy can be traced to core elements of the global political, ecological, and legal systems.[17]

The International Political System: Effective Cooperation Is Difficult. Anarchy is one defining characteristic of the structure of the international system. Anarchy in this sense does not mean chaos but rather the absence of hierarchy. In international politics, the absence of a world government with recognized authority to create common rules, maintain order, and punish violators demands that states ultimately rely on self-help to ensure their safety. Many theorists and national leaders argue that the exigencies of this situation and the resulting security dilemma that states face have broad consequences for international relations.[18] Among the most familiar are that states tend to balance the power of others through alliances and armaments, states prefer and strive for independence over interdependence, and effective cooperation among states is difficult to achieve.[19]

It is the last of these consequences that concerns us here. Even without fully ascribing to strict interpretations of classic or structural "realist" international theory, one can make strong theoretical arguments and cite a history of unfortunate examples that support the proposition that the structure of the international system can make it difficult for states to follow cooperative paths.[20] For example, states sometime do not cooperate successfully, or they fail to develop effective rules to govern their behavior in a particular issue area productively, because they fear another state might not follow the rules and then double-cross them.[21] States sometimes fail to cooperate if they fear that another country might benefit more from the arrangement, even if they themselves benefit, because this would erode their relative economic, military, or political position in relation to that country.[22] At other times, a country might be tempted to free ride or gain benefits without paying a fair share of the costs (for example, it might continue to emit a certain pollutant when others agree to stop), or it will fear others might free ride, thereby destroying the ability to create and implement effective rules.[23] Anarchic situations also produce incentives that cause actors to pursue actions that might be rational individually but result in destruction of a collective good or common-pool resource[24] (think about the destruction of certain stocks of ocean fish as certain countries and fishing fleets try to get as much fish as they can even as the resource runs out for all). In international relations, it is also easy to misperceive the motives, intentions, or actions of other governments,[25] which can contribute to states missing the opportunity to make mutually beneficial deals (a type of situation known as market failure)[26] or in extreme cases contribute to actual conflict.

Environmental politics takes place within the international arena. The fact that governments are discussing the environment does not divorce these interactions from the pressures that system structure places on state actors. Even in environmental politics, cooperative international solutions do not arise without concerns for comparative costs. The national negotiating positions of many countries on climate change provide numerous examples. States do engage in distributive bargaining—they often try to pay less than the other side and to get more benefits. They do compromise possible solutions by linking them to extraneous political, security, and economic issues. They do fail to locate mutually advantageous policies (market failure). In short, international environmental politics is still international politics, and, therefore, creating and implementing effective global policy and regimes remain difficult.

Global Political and Ecological Systems. Ecological systems have their own logic and laws and exist independent of the international political and legal systems. Simply put, the causes, consequences, and geographic scope of environmental problems do not respect national boundaries. Maps of the two systems do not match up. This somewhat simplistic observation nevertheless captures an important truth: the structure of the global political system, composed of independent sovereign states, is not structurally well suited to address complex, interdependent, international environmental problems whose causes, impacts, and solutions transcend unrelated political boundaries.

Global Legal Systems and the Requirements for Effective International Environmental Policy. Principle 21 from the 1972 UN Conference on the Human Environment in Stockholm is often cited as one of the most important foundations of modern international law. It reads: "States have, in accordance with the Charter of the United Nations and the principles of international law, the sovereign right to exploit their own resources pursuant to their own environmental policies, and the responsibility to ensure that activities within their jurisdiction or control do not cause damage to the environment of other states or of areas beyond the limits of national jurisdiction"[27] (such as the atmosphere or oceans). Note the profound contradiction between the two halves of this sentence. The fundamental principle of international law is sovereignty. States have, to a significant extent, unique and unfettered legal control over activities within their borders. This has been, and continues to be, particularly true when it comes to economic development and the use of natural resources (as both raw materials and as sinks for pollution).

At the same time, actions taken within a country—from emitting greenhouse gases to clearing rain forests to discharging pollutants into the air or water—can have international environmental implications. Legitimate actions within one country can create environmental problems for another. Effective international policy, therefore, often requires limiting what a state does within its own borders. Climate change presents the classic example. Both China and the United States possess enough coal within their borders to meet their energy needs for two hundred years or more. Blessed with this natural resource, each country has the sovereign right to exploit it for the benefit of its citizens. Burning so much coal, however, would produce massive amounts of carbon dioxide, producing climate change that would have dangerous global impacts. Thus, the structure of international law, in the form of sovereign legal control of resources within one country's borders, conflicts with the requirements for effective international environmental policy.

Procedural Obstacles

The structural obstacles outlined above give rise to specific procedural problems when nation-states actually attempt to address an international environmental issue. Two problems stand out: the lowest-common-denominator problem and the time-lag problem.

Lowest Common Denominator. Because, states are sovereign entities, they can choose to join or not join international environmental agreements. At the same time, the active participation of many countries is usually necessary to address a regional or global problem. This often means that the countries most interested in addressing a problem must gain the cooperation of countries with less, little, or even no interest. Thus international and global environmental policy often represents, at least at the start, the lowest-common-denominator measures that the relevant countries are willing to accept.

During the early stages of negotiations on protecting the ozone layer, from 1983 to 1985, for example, there were two major coalitions. The United States, the Nordic states, Canada, and Switzerland supported creating international controls on CFCs and other ODSs, while the European Community and its Member States, supported quietly by Japan and the Soviet Union, largely opposed them. (Most other countries were either undecided or, as in the cases of China and India, uninterested in regulation and largely uninvolved in the negotiations.) In March 1985, representatives of forty-three states and dozens of international governmental and nongovernmental organizations met in Vienna to review and adopt a framework treaty that affirmed the importance of protecting the ozone layer but did not include specific measures on potential threats. Until the last moments, the United States, Canada, and the Nordic countries considered forcing delegates to vote on adding a protocol mandating binding controls on certain uses of CFCs. They abandoned this strategy, however, understanding that such controls without participation by the European Community, and probably without Japan and the Soviet bloc, would not significantly impact the global problem and probably threaten the ability of the planned framework treaty, the Vienna Convention, to produce a binding protocol in the future. The most reluctant, necessary actor, Europe, set the lowest common denominator for global policy.

We see this today in climate change politics as well. The world cannot prevent dangerous climate change without concerted efforts by all the major emitters of greenhouse gases, including China, Europe, India, and the United States. The greenhouse gases from any one of these countries could eventually lead to significant global climate change, so all must eventually participate for the world to address this issue successfully. However, the United States, China, and India have been very reluctant, at least until 2009, to even discuss substantive actions to curb their domestic emissions. This has limited the ability of Europe and other countries to move forward with aggressive global policies. They could create an agreement without U.S., Chinese, and Indian participation, or act on their own domestically, as the European Union has done, but effective global policy will require the eventual participation of the least willing but necessary actors. Such actors, the necessary but least willing, are thus in position to have a lowest-common-denominator impact on global policy.

As a result, proposals to increase emissions reductions for industrialized nations were significantly impeded by opposition to such efforts by the United States during the George W. Bush administration. The U.S. position acts as a lowest common denominator in these negotiations. India and China have consistently refused to begin action until the United States and other industrialized countries initiate steps beyond the Kyoto Protocol, a position that has made it difficult for other developing countries, even those that have supported more aggressive climate policy, to initiate greenhouse gas reduction efforts. China's and India's positions act as a lowest common denominator in talks among developing countries.

This obstacle also impacts the chemical regime. Many countries wanted the complete elimination of all production and use of most chemicals addressed in the 2001 Stockholm Convention and its 2009 expansion, but many states also made claims that particular uses of certain chemicals were essential. The need to create a treaty with global participation necessitated accepting the lowest common denominator in the form of a series of different official exemptions that allowed the continued use of certain chemicals by particular countries.

Slow Development and Implementation: Time Lags. The sovereignty of states and the fact that each can choose to join or not join an international environmental agreement also contribute to a significant time lag between the identification of an international environmental problem and the impact of international policy. In short, it is neither an easy nor a quick process to create and implement global policy. Negotiations must be convened, policies agreed to, and treaties formally ratified by governments—and by enough governments so that the treaty can enter into force and be effective, treaty implementation initiated, and policy implemented effectively over a long enough period of time to impact the environmental problem.

Yet during this process the issue at hand does not wait. While the policy process drags on, greenhouse gases continue to pour into the atmosphere, biodiversity continues to decline, and toxic pollutants continue to accumulate. To prevent very serious and perhaps irreversible environmental damage requires addressing such issues before they pass particular tipping points. Those timelines follow the laws of nature, not politics. Thus, the years, even decades, required by the global policymaking process, even when it reaches a successful conclusion in a new agreement, present a significant procedural obstacle to effective global environmental policy and regimes because by the time the policy is put into place, the situation is often far worse.

The Absence of Necessary Conditions: Concern, Contractual Environment, and Capacity

As Peter Haas, Robert Keohane, and Marc Levy argue, effective international environmental policy, when reduced to its most basic and obvious elements, requires three fundamental conditions.[28] First, government "concern must be sufficiently high." States do not have infinite resources of time, money, and diplomatic attention. For international environmental policy to be successful, many governments must decide to devote resources to addressing a particular problem, resources they could use on other competing political or economic issues. Second, a sufficiently "hospitable contractual environment" must exist. Because of the obstacles (outlined above) associated with the international system, international environmental cooperation requires that states "be able to make credible commitments, to enact joint rules with reasonable ease, and to monitor each other's behavior at moderate costs . . . without debilitating fear of free riding or cheating by others." This can be difficult. Third, states must possess the scientific, political, and administrative "capacity" to understand the issue, to negotiate international policies that can address it successfully, and then to implement the policies within their own countries effectively and within the necessary time frame.

Capacity in this context is a broad term that encompasses the bureaucratic, scientific, and economic resources a country possesses to address a particular issue as well as the physical and political ability to deploy those resources effectively. Understanding the many aspects of capacity and the role it plays is an increasingly important issue in the study and practice of international environmental politics. It is often discussed in terms of the importance of building economic, political, and governmental capacity within developing countries to address particular issues, including by officials from those developing countries who regularly argue at international negotiations that increased financial and technical assistance is necessary to build capacity in their countries and otherwise assist them to implement particular international environmental regimes. Capacity can be considered more broadly, however, to include, from different perspectives, the political capacity or political will of industrialized states to enact environmental policies even when they run counter to the economic interests of key political and economic constituencies, the ability to make difficult decisions in the presence of considerable uncertainty about future events, or the ability of human society to address very complex, long-term environmental issues through collective decision making and action.

These conditions can be considered necessary (but not sufficient) for effective international environmental policy. Although it is easy to oversimplify the terms, it is a fact that concern, contractual environment, and capacity encapsulate important, even critical, requirements for successful environmental policy. Thus, while they are not obstacles themselves, the absence of any one of them presents significant obstacles to the creation and implementation of effective environmental regimes.

General Characteristics of International Environmental Issues

International environmental issues also possess inherent characteristics that make effective cooperation difficult. These characteristics are not unique to environmental issues, but they are prominent in, and common to, environmental issues. Individually or in combination, these characteristics can exacerbate systemic or procedural constraints on international cooperation as well as inhibit the creation of sufficient concern, a hospitable contractual environment, and sufficient capacity. Of course, the individual and relative impact of each characteristic in obstructing effective environmental policies varies across countries and issue areas.

This section delineates these obstacles and illustrates their impact with the use of examples from the development of the ozone regime. Note that the categories represent somewhat artificial but useful heuristic divisions. Thus their components and impacts are interrelated rather than mutually exclusive.

Scientific Complexity and Uncertainty. Environmental issues often involve both complex scientific issues and significant uncertainty about their ultimate impact. New environmental issues often exist, almost by definition, at the edge of current knowledge of chemistry, biology, physics, and natural systems.

Scientific complexity can create uncertainty concerning the content, scope, severity, and time frame of individual problems. In such situations, reaching agreement on international policy can be difficult. It can be difficult to understand the extent of the threat, to determine all cause-and-effect relationships, and to design solutions. Lack of firm knowledge can undermine concern as uncertainty allows other, more certain economic or political interests to maintain priority in the policy hierarchy. Complexity can challenge the capacity of government bureaucracies to understand the problem or to implement common solutions properly. Uncertainty and complexity can lead different states to perceive the payoff matrix differently, perhaps reducing incentives to risk cooperation and increasing incentives to free ride, thereby harming the contractual environment.

Climate change, biodiversity loss, ocean fish stocks, and toxic chemicals are examples of issues in which complexity and uncertainty continue to hamper international negotiations despite general agreement that complete inaction could lead to significant if not disastrous outcomes. Scientific complexity and uncertainty also affected the development of the global ozone regime. The initial claim that a relatively small number of inert molecules released near ground level would threaten stratospheric ozone in the next century through a complex set of chemical reactions appeared to many an unlikely proposition.[29] For many years, scientists investigated and debated many issues surrounding the CFC-ozone theory, including reaction rates, secondary reactions, feedback mechanisms, CFC sinks, and related points of atmospheric chemistry and physics—all with no actual depletion being observed in the stratosphere and during a period when atmospheric science was far less developed than it is today. The complexities and uncertainties provided opponents of CFC controls with significant leverage to argue that national and international regulations were unnecessary and that further discussion should wait for atmospheric chemistry to become better understood and for scientists to provide proof that CFCs had caused measurable ozone depletion.[30]

Debates on climate change, particularly in the United States, proceeded along obviously similar lines.

Linked Economic and Political Interests. A second and equally critical obstacle is that environmental problems are inextricably linked to important economic and political interests. Environmental issues, and therefore environmental negotiations, do not exist independent of other economic and political activities and interests. Rather, environmental issues exist *because* of these activities and interests. Environmental problems are produced as externalities of individuals, corporations, and nations pursuing other important interests such as energy production, mining, manufacturing, farming, fishing, transportation, resource consumption, livestock husbandry, urbanization, weapons production, territorial expansion, and military conflict. The fact that many of these activities could be pursued successfully while producing less environmental degradation does not erase the links between the issues.

Thus international cooperation on environmental issues must also entail de facto cooperation on important economic and even security concerns. Addressing climate change requires controlling fossil fuel consumption. Preventing more serious declines in stocks of ocean fish requires limiting fishing economies. Safeguarding biodiversity requires addressing the economic pressures that lead to habitat destruction. Protecting or restoring regional seas and waterways, such as the Mediterranean, Baltic, and Red seas, the Nile, and the Danube, requires cooperative agreements and coordinated regulatory policy among large numbers of states with very different economic interests concerning the use of these waters.

Such issue linkage also affects concern, contractual environment, and capacity. For example, governments and their constituencies often express greater concern for the underlying economic and political interests than for the environmental consequences. In addition, as high economic costs become associated with collaborative action, actors face fears that others might try to free ride, thus harming the contractual environment. Many governments lack the capacity to negotiate, enact, and enforce environmental regulations in the face of significant economic or political costs.

Cooperation to protect stratospheric ozone first appeared to be an extremely difficult case for exactly these reasons. Many of the world's largest and most influential corporations produced or used CFCs.[31] Many believed CFCs were technically or economically essential to products and processes intimately associated with modern life, including refrigeration, air conditioning, flexible and rigid foam, aerosol sprays, and the manufacture of transistors and computer chips.[32] In addition, production of CFCs and many of the products that make use of them had become standardized, creating new actors that valued their continued availability. Production and use in the developing world were rising rapidly, particularly in China, India, Argentina, Brazil, and the newly industrialized countries of the Pacific Rim.[33] Many observers were convinced that very large production increases in developing countries were inevitable without further international agreements and, thus, that the success of global ozone policy depended on addressing the associated economic and political interests of developing countries.[34]

Unequal Adjustment Costs. Addressing the underlying economic activity that caused an environmental problem can produce broad benefits to the environment, human health, and even the economy. For example, replacing fossil fuel power plants with wind, solar, and geothermal energy reduces carbon dioxide emissions that cause climate change; cleans the air of other air pollutants that impact human health; reduces energy imports from other countries, which improves countries' balances of trade; and creates new, sustainable jobs in the alternative-energy industry.

At the same time, however, those with economic interests attached to the old, polluting energy industries will incur economic costs, sometimes very significant costs. Thus, solving a common problem might produce many common benefits, but that does not mean there will be equal costs. The costs of change—of adjusting to the new policies and practices—can vary significantly within a country and across different countries, and this can produce obstacles to effective policy.

Solutions to international environmental problems thus frequently involve unequal adjustment costs. This accentuates the difficulties inherent in international cooperation and significantly impacts the contractual environment. Because states can be concerned with relative or positional advantages, they may reject solutions that ask them to bear a relatively larger burden than other states.[35] Alternatively, they may demand special compensation for joining the regime. Such difficulties are common in the creation of trading regimes but their importance in environmental issues must also be recognized.

Comparative costs vary depending on the environmental issue area, level of industrialization, method of energy production, resource base, transportation policy, and other factors. For example, Saudi Arabia will bear a much greater burden than Japan in global attempts to combat climate change. Indeed, one could argue that Saudi Arabia would be put out of business, while Japan could sell energy-efficient technology. The severe adjustment costs that Saudi Arabia would face if the world were to convert to electric vehicles to address climate change is one reason Saudi Arabia works so diligently at the global climate negotiations to slow the process down. Brazilian cattle and farming interests that convert forests to farmland or Indonesian companies that clear-cut old forests would be impacted far more than sustainable tree farms if the world were to succeed in creating policy that truly protected forests or critical biodiversity habitats. Western societies, particularly the United States, would bear a higher burden in any systematic global attempt to reduce or equalize energy and resource consumption. The industries that rely on toxic chemicals face more severe adjustment costs than does the expanding organic industry as the POPs, PIC, and Basel regimes continue to expand. Managing the impacts of these and other unequal adjustment costs is a critical and difficult part of global environmental negotiations.

Extended Time Horizons and Time Horizon Conflicts. For many environmental problems, the most serious impacts will not occur for many years. This extended time horizon can make it difficult for societies and policymakers to bear short-term costs to fix such a problem, despite the fact that it would often be most effective and least costly to take significant action to address the problem before the most serious consequences occur.

In addition, the elected officials and government bureaucrats who are responsible for making decisions on when and how to address environmental problems often operate in a much shorter time frame—a two-, four-, or six-year election cycle and a one- or two-year budget cycle—than do global environmental problems. This is not to cast aspersions on these individuals, their abilities, or their priorities, but rather to acknowledge that even the most enlightened officials usually face time pressures and perspectives far different from those required to address a problem with a fifty- or a one-hundred-year horizon.

These conflicts present political difficulties, especially if the threat is not well defined or the costs of abatement measures are very high. Policymakers can find it difficult to enact policies that entail significant short-term costs in order to achieve long-term benefits. They and the electorate will definitely bear the short-term costs (perhaps threatening the policymaker's reelection), but they may not be around to enjoy the long-term benefits. This can reduce concern and harm the contractual environment. In the late 1970s and 1980s, for example, many corporations and governments, facing the prospect of incurring high short- and medium-term costs if they had to reduce CFC use to prevent ozone depletion from emerging sometime in the next century, came out against CFC controls and instead proposed further study. Currently, some opponents of climate change policy still argue that rather than transition to clean energy now, we should save money by delaying action until the most serious impacts begin and then adapt.

Nonlinear Patterns of Change. Many environmental problems do not develop in a linear, predictable pattern. Sudden declines in fish stocks, the surprise appearance of the ozone hole above Antarctica, and the recent, rapid acceleration of melting of northern sea ice owing to climate change are but a few examples. Nonlinear change makes it difficult to predict the timing and impact of environmental problems. This, in turn, can make it difficult to develop and implement effective policy. This is particularly true if the proposed policy is controversial or expensive, as opponents can cite the uncertainty of the impact and its timing as reasons to forgo action.

Large-Number Problems. Solutions to international environmental problems often require the participation of a large number of state and private actors. The problems associated with creating cooperation in such situations are well known. Large numbers present significant incentives for free riding—not participating in the policy, and thereby avoiding the costs, while hoping to enjoy the benefits. This can be particularly dangerous when the environmental policy aims to manage and protect a common pool resource—such as oceans or the atmosphere, which all can use but no one controls—if fears that others will cheat can lead actors to believe they face a use-it-or-lose-it situation.[36] Large numbers can also harm the contractual environment and decrease the possibility of effective environmental cooperation because of increased transaction costs, difficulties in identifying and reaching consensus, increased likelihood of free riding, and problems in detecting and sanctioning violators. Large numbers also increase the likelihood of significant differences in culture, environmental values, and economic and institutional development among the states. Again, the logic tempting states to cheat (and continue to pollute) is exacerbated if the benefits of cooperation are suspect or the adjustment costs high or uneven.

Global issues such as biodiversity, climate change, ozone depletion, ocean issues, and population expansion present special problems. Solutions must not only involve a large number of state and private actors but also overcome North-South divisions. Although neither group is uniformly cohesive, many global negotiations exhibit strong differences between industrialized and developing nations on issues such as the targets and timetables required for different types of parties, financial assistance, technology transfer, and the relative importance of environmental protection versus other issues (see Chapter 12 for a detailed discussion).

Different Core Beliefs. States and groups within states (including cultural, religious, regional, economic, and political groups) sometimes possess different core beliefs and values relevant to environmental cooperation. Religions differ. Cultural beliefs differ. Values differ. Opinions differ regarding the environment and the relative importance of precaution in setting public policy. These differences matter and can create obstacles to effective global environmental policy. Some individuals in certain Asian societies, for example, believe products from certain endangered animal or plant species have significant medicinal, psychological, or sexual properties. This creates a market for these animals and undercuts international controls designed to protect them. Many Catholics and members of other religious groups oppose certain policies designed to control human population growth. Some countries or groups within them have no ethical concerns with hunting whales; others have very strong concerns. Some groups have strong cultural links to fishing, timbering, or hunting certain animals. Some political ideologies treat economic development and freedom from government regulations as higher priorities than environmental protection. Others contend the reverse.

Core beliefs, values, and cultures are clearly important in international environmental negotiations, perhaps to a degree greater than most discussions acknowledge. They not only can inhibit the identification and implementation of cooperative solutions but also can obstruct attempts to begin discussions by limiting concern for particular environmental issues.

Intersecting Obstacles. In addition to their individual impact, the characteristics of global environmental issues outlined above can also create intersecting or crosscutting obstacles to effective cooperation. For example, complexity, uncertainty, issue linkages, and the possibility of unequal adjustment costs offer opportunities for aggressive or less risk-averse states to seek positional advantages while enhancing fears of positional disadvantages (sucker's payoff) among risk-averse or less-well-informed states. Long time horizons and scientific complexity offer policymakers opportunities to postpone economically and politically expensive solutions. Complex, lengthy, and expensive remedies, involvement by many actors, and disparate state interests and capacities reduce the likelihood of agreement and increase the opportunity for, and attractiveness of, free riding (should an agreement be created).

Conclusion

International environmental regimes are dynamic and sector-specific international regulatory and administrative systems that states create to manage policy on particular issues. They comprise sets of integrated principles, norms, rules, procedures, and institutions. Some environmental regimes, like those for protecting stratospheric ozone, are of long standing, are well developed, and are increasingly successful. Most, however, face significant challenges, and it is unclear whether they will meet their objectives.

It is important to understand the obstacles to effective global environmental policy—systemic obstacles, procedural obstacles, a lack of necessary and sufficient conditions, and characteristic obstacles—so that we can better understand the successes as well as the significant challenges that remain. It is also important to look at global environmental policy, particularly the type of policy created and implemented by states and international organizations, not as a single, static international treaty but as a complex regime. By examining and understanding the comparative creation, content, evolution, and impact of these regimes, students and policymakers can gain insight into the sources of effective global environmental policy.

Effective global environmental policy is not easy to design or implement, but it does exist. Protection of the ozone layer, reducing trade in endangered species, and addressing pollution in regional seas are three increasingly successful examples. These and other global regimes prove that the international community has the ability to address complex global environmental problems with innovative and successful policies. These lessons will have to be learned if humankind is to be successful in addressing long-standing issues such as climate change and new issues such as endocrine-disrupting toxic chemicals.

Notes

1. This chapter draws extensively on previous work by the author. See, in particular, Chapter 3 in Pamela Chasek, David Downie, and Janet Welsh Brown, *Global Environmental Politics*, 4th ed. (Boulder: Westview, 2006), sections of which this chapter follows closely; David Downie, "Understanding International Environmental Regimes: Lessons of the Ozone" (PhD dissertation, University of North Carolina, 1996); "Opportunities and Obstacles to Effective International Environmental Cooperation" (paper presented to Institute for Defense Analyses conference on environmental issues, Washington D.C., July 28, 1995); David Downie, "Road Map or False Trail:

Evaluating the Precedence of the Ozone Regime as Model and Strategy for Global Climate Change," *International Environmental Affairs* 7 (Fall 1995): 321–345; and Pamela Chasek, David Downie, and Janet Welsh Brown, *Global Environmental Politics*, 5th ed. (Boulder: Westview, 2010).

2. Chasek, Downie, and Brown, *Global Environmental Politics*, 4th ed., 17. As noted in that volume, and previous writing by the author, it can be useful to compare definitions and the use of the term "regime" in John Gerard Ruggie, "International Responses to Technology: Concepts and Trends," *International Organization* 29 (1975): 557–583; Ernst Haas, "On Systems and International Regimes," *World Politics* 27 (1975): 147–174; Robert Keohane and Joseph Nye Jr., *Power and Interdependence: World Politics in Transition* (Boston: Little, Brown, 1977); Oran Young, "International Regimes: Problems of Concept Formation," *International Organization* 32 (1980): 331–356; Stephen Krasner, *International Regimes* (Ithaca, N.Y.: Cornell University Press, 1983); Robert Keohane, *After Hegemony* (Princeton: Princeton University Press, 1984); Jack Donnelly, "International Human Rights: A Regime Analysis," *International Organization* 40 (1986): 599–642; Stephan Haggard and Beth Simmons, "Theories of International Regimes," *International Organization* 41 (1987): 491–517; Thomas Gehring, "International Environmental Regimes: Dynamic Sectoral Legal Systems," in *Yearbook of International Environmental Law*, vol. 1, ed. G. Handl (London: Graham & Trotman, 1990); and Downie, "Road Map or False Trail.

3. See, for example, the Forest Stewardship Council at www.fsc.org/about-fsc.html.

4. See the homepage for the International Organization for Standardization at www .iso.org/iso/home.htm.

5. For discussions of the Montreal Protocol and the ozone regime, see Downie, "Understanding International Environmental Regimes: Lessons of the Ozone"; David Downie, "UNEP and the Montreal Protocol: New Roles for International Organizations in Regime Creation and Change," in *International Organizations and Environmental Policy*, ed. Robert V. Bartlett, Priya A. Kurian, and Madhu Malik (Westport, Conn.: Greenwood Press, 1995); Richard Benedick, *Ozone Diplomacy*, 2nd ed. (Cambridge: Harvard University Press, 1998); David Downie, "The Power to Destroy: Understanding Stratospheric Ozone Politics as a Common Pool Resource Problem," in *Anarchy and the Environment: The International Relations of Common Pool Resources*, ed. J. Samuel Barkin and George Shambaugh (Albany: State University of New York Press, 1999); Downie, "Road Map or False Trail"; and Stephen O. Andersen and K. Madhava Sarma, *Protecting the Ozone Layer: The United Nations History* (Sterling, Va.: Earthscan, 2004).

6. Texts of the ozone treaties, amendments, and adjustments as well as reports from each Meeting of the Parties, OEWG meeting, and Implementation Committee meeting are available online from the UNEP Ozone Secretariat, at www.unep.org/ozone/ index.shtml.

7. For more information on the panels as well as recent reports, see www.unep.ch/ ozone/Assessment_Panels/index.shtml.

8. See the Multilateral Fund home page at http://www.multilateralfund.org/.

9. See Krasner, *International Regimes*.

10. Influential early discussions of regimes in international relations include Ernst Haas, "Why Collaborate? Issue-Linkage and International Relations," *World Politics* 32 (1980): 357–405; Robert Keohane, "The Theory of Hegemonic Stability and Changes in International Economic Regimes," in *Changes in the International System*, ed. Ole Holsti (Boulder: Westview, 1980); Krasner, *International Regimes*; Keohane, *After Hegemony*; Friedrich Kratochwil and John Gerard Ruggie, "International Organization: A State of the Art on an Art of the State," *International Organization* 40 (1986): 753–776; and Haggard and Simmons, "Theories of International Regimes."

11. Chasek, Downie, and Brown, *Global Environmental Politics*, 5th ed., provides detailed summaries of the development and content of these and other environmental regimes.

12. For details, see the relevant decisions by the COPs for the Rotterdam and Basel conventions in 2008 and the COP for the Stockholm Convention in May 2009 as well as the extraordinary combined COP of all three conventions held in February 2010.

13. Delegates attending recent meetings associated with the Stockholm, Rotterdam, and Basel conventions, communications with the author; author's observations. In addition, see the relevant sections of the official meeting reports from the COPs for the Rotterdam and Basel conventions in 2008 and the COP for the Stockholm Convention in 2009 as well as the extraordinary combined COP of all three conventions held in 2010.

14. These include the 1976 Barcelona Convention for the Protection of the Mediterranean Sea against Pollution; the 1976 Protocol Concerning Cooperation in Combating Pollution of the Mediterranean Sea by Oil and Other Harmful Substances in Cases of Emergency; the 1976 Protocol for the Prevention of Pollution of the Mediterranean Sea by Dumping from Ships and Aircraft; and the 1980 Protocol for the Protection of the Mediterranean Sea from Land-Based Sources.

15. Examples include the Baltic Sea regime, which emerged from the 1974 Helsinki Convention on the Protection of the Marine Environment of the Baltic Sea Area.

16. For updated and detailed information, see the Web site for the Convention on Long-Range Transboundary Air Pollution, www.unece.org/env/lrtap.

17. Some would also argue that the current structure of the international economic system—particularly a global capitalism that emphasizes consumerism, lowest-cost production, globalization, and resource extraction while largely failing to cost in environmental degradation—also presents a structural impediment to effective global environmental policy. Although these characteristics can present obstacles to effective policy, I believe that they are not as structurally inherent as the other factors. Indeed, at times, such as in the expansion of the ozone regime, they have supported global environmental policy by helping to speed the introduction of environmentally friendly technology.

18. Classic examples include Thucydides, Machiavelli, and Hobbes. Influential modern examples include Hans Morgenthau, *Politics among Nations,* 5th ed. (New York: Knopf, 1973); Robert Jervis, "Cooperation under the Security Dilemma," *World Politics* 30 (1978): 167–186; Kenneth Waltz, *Theory of International Politics* (Reading, Mass: Addison-Wesley, 1979); and Glenn Snyder, "The Security Dilemma in Alliance Politics," *World Politics* 36 (1984):461–495.

19. Waltz, *Theory of International Politics.*

20. For example, Reinhold Niebuhr, *Moral Man and Immoral Society* (1932; repr., New York: Scribner, 1960); and Morgenthau, *Politics among Nations.*

21. Glenn Snyder and Paul Diesing, *Conflict among Nations: Bargaining, Decision Making, and System Structure in International Crises* (Princeton: Princeton University Press, 1977); Jervis, "Cooperation under the Security Dilemma"; and Kenneth Oye, ed., *Cooperation under Anarchy* (Princeton: Princeton University Press, 1986), 1–22.

22. Joseph M. Grieco, "Anarchy and the Limits of Cooperation," *International Organization* 42 (Summer 1988): 485–507.

23. Mancur Olson, *The Logic of Collective Action* (Cambridge: Harvard University Press, 1965).

24. J. Samuel Barkin and George Shambaugh, eds., *Anarchy and the Environment: The International Relations of Common Pool Resources* (Albany: State University of New York Press, 1999).

25. Robert Jervis, *Perception and Misperception in International Politics* (Princeton: Princeton University Press, 1976).

26. Keohane, *After Hegemony.*

27. *Report of the United Nations Conference on the Human Environment,* UN Document no. A/CONF.48/14, June 1972, 118. This principle later became Principle 2 of the Rio Declaration, but with the words "and developmental" inserted before "policies," thus making it even more self-contradictory.

28. Peter Haas, Robert Keohane, and Marc Levy, eds., *Institutions for the Earth: Sources of Effective International Environmental Protection* (Cambridge: MIT Press, 1993). All quotations in this paragraph are from pages 19–20.

29. Mario Molina and F. Sherwood Rowland, "Stratospheric Sink for Chlorofluoromethanes: Chlorine Atomic Catalyzed Destruction of Ozone," *Nature* 249 (June 28, 1974): 810–812.

30. The best secondary literature on the interplay of scientific and technical debates in the early development of the ozone regime includes Lydia Dotto and Harold Schiff, *The Ozone War* (New York: Doubleday, 1978); Paul Brodeur, "Annals of Chemistry: In the Face of Doubt," *New Yorker,* June 9, 1986, 70–87; and Karen Litfin, *Ozone Discourses: Science and Politics in Global Environmental Cooperation* (New York: Columbia University Press, 1994).

31. These corporations include, for example, DuPont, ICI, Atochem, General Motors, Toyota, General Electric, and Procter and Gamble.

32. Estimates of specific figures vary widely.

33. As far back as 1976, ODSs were produced in Argentina, Brazil, Czechoslovakia, East Germany, Mexico, and India, although the United States, the United Kingdom, West Germany, France, Japan, the Soviet Union, and the Netherlands accounted for more than 90 percent of total production. For discussion, see David Downie, "Comparative Public Policy of Ozone Layer Protection," *Political Science* 45 (1993): 186–197.

34. Based on personal communications, global ozone negotiations, London, June 1990; see also Benedick, *Ozone Diplomacy.*

35. Grieco, "Anarchy and the Limits of Cooperation."

36. Downie, "The Power to Destroy."

5

The Role of Environmental NGOs
in International Regimes

John McCormick

Since the 1960s, environmental issues have been moving steadily up the
political agenda. As we have learned more about the damaging effects of
human activity on the environment, opinion polls have found new levels of
public support for political action. Policies have been developed and fine-
tuned, laws and regulations have been agreed, and international treaties have
been signed. But the record of governments in addressing the causes and
consequences of threats to the environment has been mixed at best. Political
leaders talk in general terms about the urgency of environmental management, but practical action has often fallen short of what governments have
promised and of what majority public opinion has usually demanded. And
where the demands of economic and environmental policy compete, economic priorities usually win.

At the national level, the development of effective environmental policies
has been undermined by a lack of political will, by questions about the science
of environmental problems, by a conflict between political and economic priorities, and by a failure (or unwillingness) to understand and quantify the costs
and benefits of preventive or remedial action. At the international level, the
handicaps to effective action have been even greater, for several reasons. First,
although there is an expanding global legal system in the form of international
treaties, the terms of those treaties are often weak, they typically lack meaningful enforcement mechanisms, and there is no global authority that might
work to coordinate action. Second, national governments and corporations are
less motivated to act on transboundary or global issues than on national issues
because they face few legal obligations, face few direct political pressures from
voters and other constituencies outside their own borders, and find it easier to
ignore the costs of inaction or transfer them to another party. Finally, because
many environmental problems are shared by multiple states, or are common
to multiple states, state governments lack the motivation to act unless they can
be sure that their neighbors will take similar action.

Frustrated at the lack of political action, private citizens have stepped
into the breach by creating nongovernmental organizations (NGOs) designed
to increase the pressure for change or even to take the necessary action themselves. As private organizations that are neither formed by governments
nor speak on behalf of governments, NGOs have employed multiple tools
to achieve their goals, including undertaking research into environmental
problems, lobbying local and national governments, exerting pressure on

international organizations and multinational corporations, raising and spending the funds needed to implement practical management measures, monitoring the actions of governments and corporations, building political coalitions in support of public policy, and promoting public awareness of environmental problems.

Most work at the local or national level, but the need to address international problems has led to the creation of transnational NGOs (or networks of NGOs), formed to bring together the collective interests of national groups and lobbies so as to influence multiple governments and publics and to draw attention to the many environmental problems that are international, regional, or global in nature. For some, the creation of these NGOs has helped compensate for the structural weakness of states and has brought a wider range of views to bear on the environmental debate. They have been active and effective in many other areas as well, and it is revealing that in the thirty-five years between 1974 and 2008, NGOs or individuals associated with NGOs won the Nobel Peace Prize sixteen times. But they also have their critics, who raise questions about whose interests and opinions are represented by NGOs and, therefore, about how much their work promotes democracy rather than the more limited views of their particular constituencies. It is also not always clear exactly how NGOs have used their influence, and certainly their powers fall far short of those of governments and corporations.

This chapter examines the roots, the structure, the work, and the effects of environmental NGOs. It argues that they have collectively played a critical role in influencing the nature of international regimes and have become important sources of pressure for international action on environmental management. As such, they have often done much of the work that we might have expected of governments, were the environment to occupy a higher position on political agendas. In addition, they have contributed to the development of a global civil society within which humans have increasingly come to appreciate that most economic and social problems—and environmental problems in particular—are not limited by national boundaries but are part of the common experience of humanity and must be addressed as such.[1]

The Rise of International Regimes

The earliest attempts to build cooperation among state governments date back to the nineteenth and early twentieth centuries, but it has been only since 1945 that internationalism has come into its own. The key motivation has been the desire to avoid conflict, but cooperation was also encouraged among the protagonists in the Cold War, and then by the growth of aid programs to the newly independent states of Africa and Asia. Further cooperation has been generated by the dynamics of international trade, by a revolution in communications, and by the need to deal with problems such as terrorism, the drug trade, the spread of disease, and the collapse of failed or failing states. As a result, governments have found themselves drawn into greater cooperation on issues of mutual interest.

That cooperation has also obliged us to rethink the way we try to understand global politics. Most of us still see the world in terms of states, and
the study of international relations since the end of World War II has been
heavily influenced by realist theory, which argues that sovereign states are the
key actors in the international system. That system is anarchic in the sense
that there are no higher authorities capable of resolving conflict between
states, states are more interested in accumulating power and maintaining
security than in promoting values or ethics, and global politics is best understood by studying relations among states: forming alliances, going to war,
imposing sanctions, and protecting and promoting state interests. Realism
was, for example, at the heart of the neoconservative philosophy championed
by President George W. Bush.

An alternative approach is offered by idealist theory, which emphasizes
justice rather than power and focuses on individuals, groups, and communities rather than the state. Idealism argues that values predominate over military strength and strategic resources and that humans can place higher causes
above self-interest, can pursue ideals in the interest of improving the quality
of life, and can thus work to avoid conflict. Idealists support the development
of international organizations as a means to bridging differences among states
and avoiding destructive competition. Idealism is also based on a belief in the
notion of globalism, where institutions and ideals other than the state attract
the loyalty of humans, and on multilateralism, where states work together
rather than in isolation on shared concerns and problems.

The idealist view has been encouraged in part by increased doubts
about the health of the modern state system, which has been pummeled by
numerous forces, including globalization, the rise of international institutions and law, changes in technology and communications, the power of
multinational corporations, the growth of international markets and more
complex trade regimes, new levels of personal mobility, new patterns of
migration, global culture, and the need to respond to shared or common
problems such as terrorism and illegal immigration.[2] The state is also criticized for four key failings:

• During the Cold War (1945–1990), the superpowers were apparently
unable to guarantee global peace through anything less than mutually assured
nuclear destruction.

• States have failed to respond effectively to demands for self-determination
from national minorities or groups divided by state lines (such as the Kurds,
the Basques, and the Hutus) and have promoted the kind of national
ism that has encouraged conflict and war rather than cooperation and
compromise.

• States have failed to resolve pressing economic and social issues, so that the
rich industrialized world has become richer, while one in every three people—
according to World Bank calculations—remains poor.

- States have failed to develop an effective response to issues that transcend state lines and have instead encouraged people to think of themselves as competing citizens of individual states rather than as cooperating members of the human race.

Weaknesses in the state system since World War II—combined with growing support for the principle of international cooperation—have contributed to a growth in the number and activities of international organizations (IOs). As Tarrow puts it, transnational activism has been shaped "by changes in the opportunity structure of international politics."[3] In their attempts to address and remove the causes of interstate conflict and to address matters of shared interest collectively, national governments have created and joined IOs dealing with everything from defense, trade, and economic development to humanitarian issues, education, environmental management, and consumer safety. According to the Union of International Associations, there were just over 200 international organizations in existence in the early twentieth century; by 1964 the number had grown to nearly 2,000, by 1987 it had risen to 27,000, and by 2009 it stood at more than 62,000.[4]

IOs mainly take the form of intergovernmental organizations (IGOs), international nongovernmental organizations (INGOs), or multinational corporations (profit-making organizations that function in more than one country). IGOs are made up of states or national government bodies, generally lack autonomy in decision making, have few assets, lack the power to impose taxes or enforce their rulings, and are normally used as forums within which states can negotiate or cooperate with one another. The most influential IGOs are those in the network of United Nations specialized agencies, such as the World Bank, the Food and Agriculture Organization (FAO), and the United Nations Development Programme. Others have been created to deal with defense issues (the North Atlantic Treaty Organization, or NATO), global trade (the World Trade Organization, or WTO), and regional economic development (the Organization for Economic Cooperation and Development, or OECD).

For their part, INGOs normally have memberships consisting of individuals or private associations rather than states, and they are rarely in the position to create or supervise the implementation of rules other than those relating to their own operations or those of their members. The most important rules are made by governments and by agreement among governments, so INGOs function outside the rule-making process, offering expert advice, undertaking research, and monitoring the application of these rules. Some are made up of delegations from participating national and local NGOs (examples include the International Chamber of Commerce and the World Federation of Trade Unions), while others work to rise above national identity and to become truly global in their memberships and interests.

IOs have been critical actors in the rise of international regimes. If national regimes are defined as the common expectations, principles, norms, laws, objectives, and organizations that bind a national government and its citizens, then international regimes can be defined as the same factors applied to a group of states. An international regime is a set of principles, rules, norms, and decision-making procedures that govern the behavior of states and drive the expectations of participants in a particular issue area (whether it is the environment, arms control, or international trade) and that facilitate extensive reciprocity in a given issue area.[5] It might be argued that we live in a single global regime driven by the balance of power and expectations among the more than 190 independent states of the world, but regime theory has also been applied to specific issue areas, such as trade (as influenced by decisions taken within the auspices of the WTO), monetary relations (the International Monetary Fund), and transportation (the International Civil Aviation Organization).

International regimes emerge when states need to reach agreement on common problems in a fashion that goes beyond ad hoc action but does not extend to obliging them to relinquish sovereignty to a more permanent decision-making system. At one end of the scale, the ad hoc multilateral Western responses to problems such as the crises in the Balkans and the Middle East could not be defined as regimes, while—at the other end—the pooling of national sovereignty that has occurred during the development of the European Union has taken its twenty-seven Member States far beyond the creation of a regime.

Environmental issues have become the subject of several different international regimes. This reflects the difficulty of compartmentalizing environmental issues and divorcing them from other issues (such as international trade) as well as the fact that the international response to environmental problems has often demanded managing what are known as "common-pool resources." These are resources whose size or characteristics make it costly or impossible to control access; they include fisheries, forests, lakes, and rivers, and—at the global level—the atmosphere, Antarctica, deep seabed minerals, and oceans outside territorial waters.[6] It has also been suggested that the tropical rain forests of the Amazon basin, central Africa, and Southeast Asia—because of their role in global weather patterns—are also part of the global commons.

The weaknesses of states have contributed to the pressures that have led to the rise of an international environmental regime. First, there has been a lack of scientific agreement about the causes and effects of environmental problems, which has encouraged states—out of self-interest—to err on the side of caution in making their policy calculations. Scientific debate, for example, has encouraged the United States to drag its feet during negotiations over addressing climate change, mainly because many American political and corporate leaders have been concerned about the loss of comparative economic advantage arising from the costs of the United States controlling its emissions of greenhouse gases such as carbon dioxide while China and India have no such obligations.

Second, states have worried about the economic costs of environmental regulation. The United States, for example, was slow to take action on acid pollution in the 1980s in part because of the potential costs to auto-manufac-turing and coal-producing states (mainly Michigan and West Virginia) and the lack of political concern for Canada, which received many of the emissions generated by power stations in upwind U.S. states. Similarly, Britain was largely unmoved during the same period by the appeals of downwind Scandinavian states to reduce its pollution emissions; it took action only when it discovered forest damage within its own borders and was obliged to do so by European Union law.[7]

Third, while states are members of international organizations and signatories of international treaties, there is no authority or executive in the environmental field that has significant powers of coercion over states or—like the WTO on issues of trade—that can help settle disputes over obligations under the terms of international treaties. Furthermore, the signature of treaties often commits governments to adhere to principles rather than to meet specific objectives, and they use language that is carefully crafted to provide opt-outs. Consider, for example, the 1979 Convention on Long-Range Transboundary Air Pollution, which committed signatories to "endeavour to limit, and as far as possible, gradually reduce and prevent air pollution . . . [using] the best available technology *which is economically feasible*" (italics added). Governments may have obligations as signatories of international treaties and conventions, but they are not obliged to sign, will do so only when acceptable compromises have been reached, and during negotiations may work to ensure that the obligations are as weak as possible. Signature itself is not an obligation to act; that only comes with ratification. And even then, states may be ratifying general principles rather than making real commitments. And even if they commit themselves to specific targets, there is usually no monitoring body with the ability to enforce the terms of the treaty.

One of the consequences of the weakness of state responses to environmental problems has been the growth—particularly since World War II—in the number, reach, and activities of NGOs with a focus on the environment.[8] Known also as interest groups or pressure groups, NGOs are legally constituted bodies made up of individuals, corporations, or other groups that come together outside the formal structures of government in an institutionalized and regularized manner in order to achieve social, economic, or political change. They may try to effect change just among their own members, mobilizing citizens or member organizations to act in their collective interests, but they will often try to influence public opinion, the media, elected officials, and bureaucrats with a view to influencing the actions of government.

The Growth of the Environmental Movement

To the extent that they were identified and understood, environmental problems were approached for much of the nineteenth and early twentieth centuries mainly as a local matter, to which national governments paid little or no attention. Driven by the findings of the scientific revolution of the nineteenth century, by concerns about the effects on urban life of the spread of industry, and the effects on nature of agricultural intensification, local and national NGOs were created in the United States, Canada, and several European countries. Among the first NGOs with a focus on the environment were the (now Royal) Society for the Protection of Birds (founded in Britain in 1889) and the Sierra Club (founded in the United States in 1892).

Their work was important, but it soon became clear that a broader perspective was needed if environmental problems were to be addressed effectively. First, private citizens and scientists began to realize that many problems were common to two or more countries and began communicating with each other and sharing ideas about how best to respond. Second, these communications led to the realization that many problems could not be addressed by individual countries acting alone, especially if governments were not engaged. Finally, it was clear that the science of environmental problems was not fully understood and that only a marshaling of resources could support the research needed to understand the causes, effects, and interrelationships of those problems.

The Europeans were the first to begin looking outside their borders, both to their colonies and to their immediate neighbors. The protection of colonial wildlife was the motivation for the creation in Britain in 1903 of the world's first international protective NGO, the Society for the Preservation of the Wild Fauna of the Empire. Meetings among European nature protectionists led in 1913 to the creation of the Commission for the International Protection of Nature (CIPN). The growth in the number and reach of environmental IGOs and INGOs accelerated following World War II. Some IGOs predated the war—for example, the International Joint Commission was created in 1909 to encourage cooperation between the United States and Canada on the management of the Great Lakes—but postwar IGOs were more ambitious in their scope and objectives. The UN Food and Agriculture Organization, for example, was created in 1945 not only to deal with an immediate food supply crisis but also to look at long-term supply, and its founders quickly realized that a more globalized approach was needed for the effective management of natural resources.

In 1947 the CIPN was reorganized as the International Union for the Protection of Nature, becoming the first INGO with a global interest in environmental problems. Renamed the International Union for the Conservation of Nature (IUCN) in 1956, it became the precursor to many more environmental INGOs, notably the World Wildlife Fund (WWF, later renamed the World Wide Fund for Nature outside the United States), created in 1961 to raise funds for IUCN projects. But the focus on nature and wildlife was not enough because the threats they faced came mainly from industry and economic development. That link was given stark illustration in 1962 with the publication of Rachel Carson's book *Silent Spring*, which drew attention to the use of chemicals in agriculture but also had broader lessons to tell about threats to the environment. Public opinion was also alarmed by the threat of fallout from nuclear testing, by a series of well-publicized environmental disasters (including several major marine oil spills), and by advances in scientific knowledge.

The changing dynamics of NGO interests and methods were illustrated by the origins of Friends of the Earth (FoE) and Greenpeace, two of the best-known environmental NGOs in industrial countries because of their focus on generating publicity for their causes. FoE was founded in the United States in 1969 after a disagreement between the Sierra Club and its executive director, David Brower, who felt that the Sierra Club had become too conservative. He argued that the solution to environmental problems lay not in temporary remedies but in fundamental social change and that vigorous campaigning was needed to achieve maximum publicity.[9] Similar motivations led to the creation of Greenpeace, which was born in 1971 as the Don't Make a Wave Committee, a group that sailed a ship into northern Pacific waters to protest nuclear weapons tests. It has since used a combination of public protests and political lobbying to draw attention to issues such as deforestation in Russia, Canada, and Brazil; the dangers of nuclear energy and toxic wastes; and the problem of overfishing.

A new political focus was given to environmental issues by the convening in 1972 in Stockholm, Sweden, of the United Nations Conference on the Human Environment. Attended by representatives from 113 countries and more than 400 intergovernmental and nongovernmental organizations, the Stockholm conference was the first meeting at which a combination of governments and NGOs from around the world sat down to address the global aspects of the emerging environmental crisis.

Among the many consequences of the Stockholm conference, three in particular stand out. First, the presence of so many national and international NGOs drew new public and political attention to their work and encouraged them to be more persistent in their efforts to work with one another and to influence public policy. Second, the presence of many newly independent African and Asian governments encouraged the industrial countries—for the first time—to acknowledge that poorer and emerging countries had a different set of priorities and that underdevelopment was as much a cause of environmental problems as overdevelopment. Americans and Europeans might be worrying about the effects of industrialization and the accelerated exploitation of resources, and air and water pollution in particular, but for Africans and Asians the major problems were deforestation and soil erosion created by the dual pressures of poverty and population growth. The key issue, then, was not curbing consumption or development, but making sure that it was sustainable. Third, the conference resulted in the creation in 1973 of the United Nations Environment Programme (UNEP), which gave the UN a stake in environmental issues and offered NGOs and INGOs a new forum in which they could attempt to influence public policy.

In contrast with the priorities and methods of NGOs in the richer countries, those in poorer countries must often focus on mobilizing grassroots support for their objectives. Such groups are most common in rural and urban communities in poorer countries and have been active, for example, in mobilizing forest dwellers in Brazil, India, and Malaysia to block the activities of lumber companies. The most famous of these was Chipko Andalan, the movement to "hug trees" in India in 1973–1974, which encouraged local villagers (mainly women) to band together to physically block the felling of trees by timber companies. In Kenya, the Green Belt Movement encourages people (again, mainly women) to find public areas and plant seedlings to form tree belts. Founder Wangari Maathai won the Nobel Peace Prize in 2004, becoming the first African woman (and the first environmentalist) to be so recognized. Local community mobilization has also been effective in stopping the building of nuclear power stations, new highways, and toxic waste dumps in industrial countries.[10]

Although they might at first seem all but powerless to act, NGOs in poorer countries have been active in drawing attention to the issue of environmental justice, the challenge of ensuring that the costs of exposure to environmental threats are equally borne rather than allowing low-income or disadvantaged populations to bear more of the burden. Of particular concern has been the international trade in toxic and hazardous wastes. As the production of such wastes has increased and as the cost of disposing of them in industrialized countries has grown (thanks in part, ironically, to the success of Northern NGOs in encouraging a tightening of environmental regulations at home), the governments of Southern countries have been encouraged by financial incentives to accept much of that waste, including garbage, chemical wastes, and used electronic products. Several transnational networks have grown in response, including Global Response (a network of activists, students, attorneys, doctors, and educators that works to oppose development projects that threaten public health), Health Care Without Harm (a network of about four hundred organizations in fifty-two countries that works to reduce the impact of the health care industry), and the International Campaign for Responsible Technology (which promotes a sustainable high-technology industry).[11]

Discussions that opened in 1982 as a ten-year review of the Stockholm Conference involved NGOs and led to the creation in 1983 of the World Commission on Environment and Development (known more commonly as the Brundtland Commission after its chair, former Norwegian prime minister Gro Harlem Brundtland). Charged with reporting on progress in achieving the objectives of sustainable development, the commission finished its work in October 1987 and was replaced by a new body called the Center for Our Common Future (COCF). NGOs influenced the Brundtland Commission through the testimony they provided, but they played a more active role in the work of COCF. COCF's mission was to publicize the goals of the Brundtland Commission, which it did in part through establishing contacts with partners, including NGOs and INGOs.

In 1989 it was announced that the United Nations Conference on Environment and Development (UNCED, or the Earth Summit) would be held in Rio de Janeiro in 1992. NGOs played an active role in preparatory hearings, working through COCF and the Environment Liaison Centre International, which was a conduit for contacts between NGOs and UNEP. NGOs also directly lobbied negotiators at the preparatory meetings for UNCED and had further influence as members of national delegations involved in those meetings.[12] More than 1,000 NGOs attended negotiations held in Geneva and New York in preparation for the 1992 Earth Summit, and more than 1,400 NGOs were accredited to the summit itself.[13] Since Rio, NGOs have played a central role in publicizing the extent to which the goals and objectives of the conference have found (or failed to find) their way into public policy. Another opportunity to make their case came with the September 2002 World Summit on Sustainable Development, held in Johannesburg, South Africa, at which more than 3,200 NGOs were accredited. The meeting took a critical look at UNCED, its deliberations significantly influenced by the presence once again of so many NGOs.

The Global NGO Network

Although the environmental movement has evolved into one of the most influential and widespread of what are called transnational advocacy networks,[14] there is no authoritative source on its size and reach despite the fact that the number of groups has grown at least in concert with the growth of NGOs more generally, and probably even faster. The *World Directory of Environmental Organizations* listed 2,500 environmental organizations in its 2001 edition.[15] These are the bigger NGOs, however, and many are themselves umbrella bodies for smaller local and grassroots organizations, whose numbers are constantly changing. The European Environmental Bureau, for example, which acts as a conduit for contacts between NGOs and the major bodies of the European Union, has 143 NGO members and associate members from thirty-three countries.[16] If we extrapolate from cases such as these, and take into account national and regional umbrella bodies around the world, the total number of environmental NGOs in the world probably runs well into six figures.

It would be wrong to suggest that there is a homogeneous global community of environmental NGOs that is driven by complementary goals and uses similar methods. Although they share the common goal of encouraging a workable relationship between humans and their environment, NGOs use many different methods, often have different priorities and objectives, and vary substantially in size, goals, durability, stability, credibility, and ideological orientations (see Table 5–1).[17] The core division is the philosophical gap between groups based in the wealthy industrial states of the North and those based in the emerging and poorer states of the South. The NGOs of the North focus on the environmental consequences of industrial development and argue that we need to curb the free market through greater regulation of industry, changes in the nature of consumerism, and investment in pollution control. Meanwhile, Southern NGOs argue that many environmental problems result from poverty, the shift of polluting industries from the North to the South, and the demands of wealthy consumers and that we need to

Table 5-1 Philosophies, Structures, and Methods of
Environmental NGOs

Philosophy	Structure	Method
Northern NGOs focusing on the environmental consequences of industrial development and consumerism	Federations of national or international groups; created to facilitate communication and cooperation among member bodies	Working with elected officials, bureaucrats, and employees of corporations
Southern NGOs focusing on the environmental consequences of poverty and inequalities in the global economic system	Universal membership groups	Raising and spending money
Conservative, pragmatic groups working to achieve change within established political processes	Intercontinental membership groups; interests go beyond a particular region, but are not necessarily global	Campaigning and organizing public protests
Green organizations seeking fundamental changes in the relationship among humans, and between humans and the environment	Regionally defined membership groups; interests restricted to one continent or region	Promoting media coverage of environmental issues
Radical organizations that use confrontation to draw attention to the problems of the environment and argue that conventional political processes are part of the problem	Internationally oriented national groups; national NGOs partly or wholly focused on international issues	Litigating and monitoring the implementation of environmental law
NGOs representing the views of socioeconomic groups with an interest in the environmental debate, such as women, minorities, and business		Exchanging information Undertaking research Acquiring and managing property Generating grassroots involvement

address inequalities in the global economic system. The philosophical difference was clear to one of the participants at UNCED in 1992: "While the North set the agenda with high profile statements on the need to tackle population growth and deforestation, without committing substantial new funds to do so, the South's insistence on the need for justice, relief of crippling international debt, new financial resources for sustainable development including environmental protection, and technology transfer went unheeded."[18]

But even among Northern NGOs there are different styles and priorities. In his review of the NGO community in the United States, for example, Rosenbaum identifies three "ideological enclaves": the mainstream of pragmatic reformist organizations, the more philosophical deep ecologists, and the radicals.[19] The pragmatists consist of the largest and most politically active and publicly visible groups, which prefer to work within established political processes to influence public policy. In the United States, these include members of what is sometimes informally known as the Group of Ten, the biggest and most visible mainline NGOs, such as the National Wildlife Federation, the Sierra Club, and the National Audubon Society. (They have their counterparts in Europe in the form of the Royal Society for the Protection of Birds in Britain, Bund für Vogelschutz in Germany, and WWF.)

The deep ecologists include groups that emphasize the place of humans as a part of nature, believe that all forms of life have an equal right to exist, challenge the underlying institutional structures and social values upon which governments are based and economies function, and argue the need for fundamental social change as a prerequisite for effective environmental management. While other groups generally accept the existing sociopolitical order and do not question the dominant values of society, ecologists reject those values; they criticize existing political structures, consumerism, and materialism and propose the development of a new environmental paradigm more compatible with the realities of environmental limits.[20] In several countries, these views have combined with grassroots movements to produce green political parties that see themselves as the vanguard of a new society in which humans take a holistic approach to their relationship with one another and their environment. Those parties have been particularly influential in Germany, Finland, Belgium, and France, where they have participated in government. Supporters see green politics as a clarion call for good sense in a world driven by consumption and acquisition, where greed threatens to undermine the foundations of life on Earth. But critics of the greens see them as a threat to economic development, jobs, and livelihoods and as a brake on human progress.

The third of Rosenbaum's enclaves—the radicals—consists of groups that have become disenchanted with the methods and goals of mainstream environmentalism and believe in the use of direct action as a means to bring about urgently needed political and social change. Radicalism is apparently difficult to sustain. Notable among such groups in the 1970s were Friends of the Earth and Greenpeace, which had a reputation for headline-grabbing tactics such as interfering with whaling activities and having their members tie themselves to bridges to protest shipments of nuclear waste; since then, they have become less confrontational and more willing to work within established political procedures. Greenpeace still believes in using "non-violent confrontation to raise the level and quality of public debate,"[21] but it has been replaced at the radical end of the spectrum by groups such as Earth First! and the Earth Liberation Front (ELF). Earth First! was founded in the United States in

1980 and argues that mainstream environmental groups have become too soft and corporate and that extreme methods are needed to deal with urgent problems. Variously termed ecotage or monkey wrenching,[22] those methods include hammering metal spikes into trees to discourage lumber companies from cutting them down. ELF was founded in Britain in 1992 and has been implicated in acts of arson, property destruction, and economic sabotage and was declared a terrorist organization in the United States in 2001.

Within these broad philosophical groupings, NGOs also vary in the way they are structured. The Belgian-based Union of International Associations has developed a structural typology that focuses on INGOs in particular and divides them into five major groups:

Federations of International and National Organizations. These are bodies set up to facilitate communication and cooperation among their member bodies. They can be global networks of national offices of the same NGO, such as WWF, Friends of the Earth, or Greenpeace, which—respectively— have national offices in ninety-two, seventy-seven, and thirty-nine countries, but the national offices are autonomous and have their own funding and strategic priorities. Cooperation is promoted by international secretariats in Amsterdam and, for WWF, Switzerland. Federations also take the form of umbrella bodies, bringing together different organizations that act either as conduits for contacts between those NGOs and an IGO (for example, the Environment Liaison Centre International, with NGO members in 104 countries, provides a point of contact between NGOs and UNEP),[23] or as a channel for contacts among NGOs, as is the case with the NGO members of the African NGOs Environment Network.

Universal Membership Organizations. These are bodies that have a widespread, geographically balanced membership, the prime example of which is the International Union for Conservation of Nature (IUCN). Tracing its origins back to 1947, IUCN is headquartered in Switzerland and is an unusual hybrid of governmental and nongovernmental members. Its membership in 2009 consisted of eighty-six governments (the United States, for example, is a state member), 120 government agencies (including the U.S. Environmental Protection Agency, the Indian Ministry of Environment and Forests, the Kenyan Ministry of Tourism and Wildlife, the Russian Ministry of Natural Resources, and so on), and 902 national and international NGOs.[24] This arrangement not only brings together equivalent organizations from different states but also allows national NGOs to take part in the work of an organization that includes their own governments and government agencies.

IUCN provides governments and NGOs with information, acts as a clearinghouse for the exchange of ideas, and carries out its own environmental management projects, notably the creation of national parks and other protected areas and the gathering of information on the status of threatened species and ecosystems. It has also been active in the drafting of international treaties, such as the Convention on Biological Diversity and the Convention on International Trade in Endangered Species. It is one of the more conservative INGOs, shying away from controversy and—unlike FoE or Greenpeace—doing little to draw media attention to itself. This is because it is not a campaigning organization so much as a meeting place for government bodies and NGOs, less engaged in changing policy and public opinion than in facilitating the exchange of ideas and information.

Intercontinental Membership Organizations. These are bodies whose interests go beyond a particular region but not to the point where they become universal membership groups. Among these are environmental INGOs with more focused interests, such as BirdLife International and Wetlands International. BirdLife International is a network of partner organizations in 105 countries that works collectively to gather and share information and to build strong national bodies working to protect birds and their natural habitats. It has a global secretariat in Britain and regional offices in Kenya, Ecuador, Japan, Belgium, Fiji, and Jordan.[25] Wetlands International is a federation headquartered in the Netherlands that brings together government agencies and NGOs in thirty-two countries, promotes research and information exchange, and has played an active role in the development and application of the 1971 Ramsar Convention on Wetlands of International Importance.[26]

Regionally Defined Membership Organizations. These are bodies whose interests are restricted to a particular continent or region, such as the African Wildlife Foundation (Kenya), the Caribbean Conservation Association (Barbados), and the European Environmental Bureau (Belgium). As noted earlier, the latter facilitates contacts between groups in the Member States of the European Union (EU) and the main policymaking bodies of the EU.

Internationally Oriented National Organizations and National NGOs That Are Partly or Wholly Focused on International Issues. The former include (in the United States) the Sierra Club and the Natural Resources Defense Council, and the latter include environmental think tanks such as the World Resources Institute and the Worldwatch Institute. The Sierra Club is mainly active on the domestic political front in the United States but also campaigns on issues such as human rights and the environment, environmentally compatible trade policies, global warming, and population growth control. The World Resources Institute, meanwhile, focuses on policy research and publishing, among other things, the well-respected annual World Resources series.

In addition, it is important to appreciate that NGOs also have different interests and priorities as well as different constituencies. At one end of the scale are the single-issue groups, which pursue a specific, focused objective, such as clean water, opposition to toxic waste storage sites, or even the welfare of a single species of wildlife (as is the case with the U.S.-based Mountain Lion Foundation and Bat Conservation International). At the other end of the scale are environmental organizations that take a broader view of the place of humans in their environment, quality-of-life issues, and the damaging consequences of human activities. Many of these groups grew out of the expansion of environmental consciousness during the 1960s and address issues as broad as nuclear power, acid pollution, toxic waste disposal, chemicals in the environment, oil spills, and climate change.

A phenomenon that has emerged in large part since the mid-1970s has been the creation of groups with an interest in promoting sustainable development. This is a term that replaced conservation in the dictionary of environmentalism and means development that takes place within the carrying capacity of the natural environment. The sustainable development lobby focuses on managing resources for continued use. For example, it supports the management of forests and fisheries with a view to preventing clear-cutting and overfishing, arguing that sustainable use will allow them to be a constant source of resources. Although the term is usually applied to African, Asian, and Latin American states, it has been a central factor in environmentalism in industrial states for decades.

Environmental Groups and International Regimes

The environmental debate has been impacted significantly in recent decades by the work and contributions of a large and varied community of NGOs that has lobbied governments and intergovernmental organizations and has influenced negotiations on international environmental agreements. As suggested in this chapter, these NGOs have goals, philosophies, styles, structures, and methods that are often very different from one another. In some respects, this has been their strength, enabling them to develop a variety of methods to deal with a variety of problems at a variety of levels. It has also been a weakness, however, because the fragmentation of the environmental NGO community has prevented it from presenting a united front to policymakers and has thus impeded its policy impact.[27]

At the national level, NGOs have government institutions and bodies of law that they can monitor, influence, lobby, and attempt to change. They can appeal to elected officials; use their members and funds to exert influence on the electoral process; and work through the media, elected officials, the courts, and the bureaucracy to influence the policy process. They can also take direct action by owning and managing land and natural resources such as forests, wetlands, and areas of ecological importance. They exist within a civil society, an organized society over which a state rules and in which citizens participate. But the same cannot be said for NGOs working at the international level, where they face at least three major handicaps.

First, there is no central authority to which NGOs can appeal, other than the United Nations and its specialized agencies, which lack the powers and authority needed to play a significant role in resolving disputes. The United Nations Environment Programme comes closest to being an international environmental authority, but it suffers from several critical handicaps: it is a junior member of the UN system, it has no executive powers, it has little scope for carrying out its own projects, and it was intended from the outset to be an agent of cross-cutting policy coordination, working through the other UN specialized agencies.[28] UNEP has achieved the most when it has been a facilitator, bringing together governments and institutions with shared interests and encouraging them to negotiate and reach agreement on those interests. It cannot compel governments to act against their will.

Second, there is no body of voters or of public opinion at the international level to which NGOs can appeal. At the national level, NGOs can make a political case that can influence the way in which elected leaders craft their arguments and the way in which voters decide to cast their ballots. The rise of environmental NGOs has also merged into the rise of green political parties and has also influenced the platforms of mainstream parties. At the international level it is more difficult for NGOs to make an impact on political platforms, in part because they must deal with the reality of divided national priorities and in part because it is more difficult to influence either public opinion or voter choices across state borders.

Finally, international treaties and organizations are the result of agreements among states, and citizens of those states can influence such compacts only indirectly through their own national governments. It is true that NGOs have worked around this handicap and have played an active role in, for example, the development of international treaties and the discussions at international conferences such as Stockholm, Rio de Janeiro, and Johannesburg. However, there is no formal provision in international treaties for public review and comment, nor is there a formal mechanism by which citizens or NGOs can bring suit before international tribunals such as the International Court of Justice against IGOs or states failing to meet their obligations.[29]

NGOs have nevertheless been able to exploit their strengths in several ways to overcome the handicaps inherent in exerting influence over an international regime:

• They have acted as information brokers, becoming the source of much of the research upon which policy decisions are taken. Reports to the Stockholm, Rio, and Johannesburg conferences as well as the intergovernmental discussions leading up to many of the most important international environmental treaties have been heavily influenced by research generated by NGOs and by NGO influence over media coverage of these events.

• They have been whistle-blowers, helping IGOs keep track of progress (or the lack thereof) in the implementation of international treaties in signatory states. Indeed, it is arguable that without NGO pressure there would be little obligation upon states to agree to substantial goals, and there would be little transparency in the process of agreeing and implementing international treaties.

• They have promoted democracy (albeit in limited form) in the work of IGOs and the deliberations preceding agreement of international treaties by ensuring that the views of their members have been taken into consideration.

• They have played a valuable role as opponents of national government policy, drawing attention to the failures of domestic policies and exerting international pressure to change those policies.

- They have provided models for new government programs, using their resources and links with other NGOs to develop and offer solutions to environmental problems. In many instances, NGOs have themselves carried out the work of government by undertaking necessary research, raising funds, and carrying out practical environmental management projects.

- They have built international coalitions that have occasionally bypassed states and helped make up for some of the weaknesses of IGOs.

But have they always been a positive force? At least until the 1990s, their work was generally welcomed, in part because their impact was relatively limited and so posed no threat to governments. But as their role and influence grew, questions began to be asked about their authority to lobby. Did they in fact represent a legitimate and discernible constituency, or were they only the representatives of narrower interests and more limited philosophies? Who did they claim to be working for: a public concerned about environmental problems, or a smaller group of activists with a narrower agenda? The methods and goals of NGOs have always been questioned by those who stand to be most negatively impacted by NGO activities, hence industry and environmental NGOs have long had a conflictual relationship, as have repressive governments and human rights groups. But there is a broader issue of accountability, which has drawn more political attention in recent years as a debate has emerged over how best to balance the rights and responsibilities of NGOs, and how to certify and manage groups while not impinging upon their right to express themselves.[30]

There are also questions about exactly when and how NGOs have been able to exert influence. It has long been taken for granted that they have had an important role in influencing the outcomes of policies and lawmaking, but there have been relatively few structured analyses of that influence. Betsill and Corell have developed an analytical framework in which they differentiate between three levels of influence:[31]

- Low influence, where NGOs actively participate in international environmental negotiations but have almost no observable effect on the negotiation process or outcome. An example is offered by the limited input of NGOs into the United Nations Forum on Forests, founded in 2000 to promote sustainable forestry on the basis of principles agreed at Rio.

- Moderate influence, where NGOs have observable effects on the negotiating process but not on the final outcome. An example is offered by the Kyoto Protocol to the international convention on climate change, where NGOs influenced the negotiating agenda, but the final protocol did not reflect any of their positions.

- High influence, where NGO activities impact both the negotiating process and the outcome. An example is offered by their participation in the negotiations in 1993–1994 over the UN Convention to Combat Desertification, in which NGOs—most of them representing grassroots interests—played a key role and saw their views reflected in the outcome.

Betsill and Corell conclude that several critical factors affect the influence that NGOs bring to bear on negotiations, including the extent to which they are coordinated, the rules of access to the negotiations (NGO influence is obviously greater if steps are taken to facilitate their participation), the political stakes involved in the outcome (NGO influence is lowest when the political stakes are lowest), the extent to which competition is posed by other NGOs with different agendas, and the extent to which NGOs are able to form alliances with key states involved in the negotiations.[32]

In the absence of an international body of environmental law backed up by a global governmental authority with responsibility for—and powers of—enforcing that law, much of the responsibility for promoting environmental concern at the international level since World War II has fallen to—or been adopted by—an increasingly complex network of nongovernmental organizations. These organizations operate at several different levels, use many different methods, and have multiple objectives and underlying principles. As well as identifying problems, proposing solutions, and monitoring the responses of states and the international community, environmental NGOs have contributed to the promotion of international regimes and a global civil society within which states and their citizens have redefined their relationships to one another and have helped us better understand the nature of global society. Although the dynamics of NGO participation are not yet fully understood, their role in the development of an international environmental regime has been undeniable.

Notes

1. For a review of the debate over global civil society, see Ronnie D. Lipschutz, *Civil Societies and Social Movements: Domestic, Transnational, Global* (Aldershot, UK: Ashgate, 2006).
2. See discussion, for example, in Susan Strange, *The Retreat of the State: The Diffusion of Power in the World Economy* (Cambridge: Cambridge University Press, 1996); and Kenichi Ohmae, *The Next Global Stage: Challenges and Opportunities in Our Borderless World* (Upper Saddle River, N.J.: Wharton School Publishing, 2005).
3. Sidney Tarrow, *The New Transnational Activism* (New York: Cambridge University Press, 2006), 3.
4. Union of International Associations Web site, www.uia.be.
5. Andreas Hasenclever, Peter Mayer, and Volker Rittberger, *Theories of International Regimes* (Cambridge: Cambridge University Press, 1997).
6. For a discussion of this concept, see Susan J. Buck, *The Global Commons: An Introduction* (Washington, D.C.: Island Press, 1998).
7. John McCormick, *Acid Earth: The Politics of Acid Pollution*, 3rd ed. (London: Earthscan, 1997).
8. For more details on the emergence of the international environmental movement, see John McCormick, *The Global Environmental Movement*, 2nd ed. (New York: John Wiley, 1995).
9. Ibid., 170–172.

10. For more details on citizen action movements, see Michael Edwards and John Gaventa, eds., *Global Citizen Action* (London: Earthscan, 2001).
11. For details, see David Naguib Pellow, *Resisting Global Toxics: Transnational Movements for Environmental Justice* (Cambridge: MIT Press, 2007), particularly chap. 3.
12. For more details on the role of NGOs in UNCED, see Matthias Finger, "Environmental NGOs in the UNCED Process," in *Environmental NGOs in World Politics,* ed. Thomas Princen and Matthias Finger (London: Routledge, 1994).
13. Princen and Finger, eds., *Environmental NGOs in World Politics,* 4; Michele M. Betsill and Elisabeth Corell, "Introduction," in *NGO Diplomacy: The Influence of Nongovernmental Organizations in International Environmental Negotiations,* ed. Michele M. Betsill and Elisabeth Corell (Cambridge: MIT Press, 2008), 1.
14. See discussion in Margaret E. Keck and Kathryn Sikkink, *Activists beyond Borders: Advocacy Networks in International Politics* (Ithaca, N.Y.: Cornell University Press, 1998), chap. 4.
15. Thaddeus C. Trzyna, ed., *World Directory of Environmental Organizations,* 6th ed. (London: Earthscan, 2001); see also National Wildlife Federation, *Conservation Directory 2003: The Guide to Worldwide Environmental Organizations* (Washington, D.C.: Island Press, 2003).
16. See European Environmental Bureau Web site, www.eeb.org.
17. For further discussion, see Princen and Finger, eds., *Environmental NGOs in World Politics,* 6–9.
18. Andrew Simms, "If Not, Then When? Non-Governmental Organizations and the Earth Summit Process," *Environmental Politics* 2, no. 1 (Spring 1993): 94–100.
19. Walter A. Rosenbaum, *Environmental Politics and Policy,* 7th ed. (Washington, D.C.: CQ Press, 2008), 40–46.
20. Riley E. Dunlap and Kent D. Van Liere, "The 'New Environmental Paradigm': A Proposed Measuring Instrument and Preliminary Results," in *Journal of Environmental Education* 9, no. 4 (Summer 1978): 10–19.
21. See Greenpeace Web site, www.greenpeace.org/international.
22. This term was inspired by Edward Abbey's book, *The Monkey Wrench Gang* (Philadelphia: Lippincott, 1975).
23. See Environment Liaison Center International Web site, www.elci.org.
24. See the IUCN Web site, www.iucn.org.
25. See the BirdLife Web site, www.birdlife.org.
26. See the Wetlands International Web site, www.wetlands.org.
27. Lynton K. Caldwell, *Between Two Worlds: Science, the Environmental Movement, and Policy Choice* (Cambridge: Cambridge University Press, 1990), 89–97.
28. McCormick, *The Global Environmental Movement,* chap. 6.
29. Hilary French, "The Role of Non-State Actors," in *Greening International Institutions,* ed. Jacob Werksman (London: Earthscan, 1996).
30. See Lisa Jordan and Peter Van Tuijl, eds., *NGO Accountability: Politics, Principles and Innovations* (London: Earthscan, 2006).
31. Betsill and Corell, eds., *NGO Diplomacy,* particularly concluding chapter.
32. Ibid.

6

International Climate Change Policy: Toward the Multilevel Governance of Global Warming

Michele M. Betsill

Global climate change presents a significant challenge to the international community. Anthropogenic emissions of greenhouse gases (GHGs) are causing a warming of the Earth's surface at an unprecedented rate.[1] Scientists predict that, if left unchecked, climate changes produced by this warming could include disruptions in rainfall and temperature patterns, a global rise in sea level, and an increased frequency of severe weather events such as droughts, hurricanes, and floods.[2] In turn, these and other impacts of climate change could have serious implications for food security, freshwater supplies, human health, and species survival.

Climate change is a *global* environmental problem. Its causes, effects, and potential solutions transcend state boundaries, creating a need for international cooperation. Achieving such cooperation has proven difficult, however. Indeed, several factors create incentives for states and other actors to avoid taking meaningful steps to control their GHG emissions. For example, political and ethical questions remain regarding who bears responsibility for mitigating the threat. Although industrialized countries emitted the vast majority of GHGs in the past, some developing countries are among the largest emitters today. In 2007 China surpassed the United States as the world's leading emitter of GHGs. Second, because most GHGs remain in the atmosphere for a long time, the benefits of reducing emissions today will go to future generations rather than to those who must bear the cost of achieving such reductions. Third, the issue of climate change remains intimately linked with the global energy system. Any requirement to reduce emissions will likely impact the cost and availability of energy, a central component of the global economy.

This chapter examines the development of the international climate change regime, from the agenda-setting phase through the negotiation and operationalization phases.[3] Therefore, the chapter begins with a discussion of how the problem of climate change emerged on the international agenda through a gradual buildup of scientific concern and then the transfer of that concern to the political arena. The subsequent section examines the negotiation of the two multilateral environmental agreements that make up the international climate change regime: the 1992 United Nations Framework Convention on Climate Change (FCCC) and its 1997 Kyoto Protocol. The discussion emphasizes those aspects of the negotiations and agreements that are relevant to understanding contemporary climate change politics. The third section examines efforts by parties to the Kyoto Protocol to operationalize their commitments to reduce GHG emissions and evaluates the effectiveness of the international climate change regime to date. Its significance goes beyond the direct effects of the FCCC and the Kyoto Protocol on state behavior. These agreements have indirectly inspired activities carried out by both state and nonstate actors at a variety of levels, all aimed at mitigating or adapting to the risk of global climate change. These multilevel governance initiatives are increasingly central components of global climate change governance.

The final section examines current debates and future challenges in international climate change policy. Members of the international community continue to negotiate the future of the climate change regime for the years after 2012, focusing on developing country commitments for GHG reductions and additional reduction commitments by industrialized countries. There is also a great deal of anticipation about how the election of Barack Obama as president may change the role of the United States in the negotiations. Finally, it is essential that the multilateral treaty-making process be integrated into the emerging complex multilevel system of global climate change governance.

Agenda Setting: From the Scientific to the Political Arena

The agenda-setting phase of the international climate change regime saw the expansion of concern about the problem from the scientific to the political arena (see Table 6–1). The threat of global warming is rooted in what is commonly referred to as the "greenhouse effect." Molecules of particular gases that exist naturally in the atmosphere (GHGs) trap heat like the panes of a greenhouse. This "natural" greenhouse effect keeps the Earth's surface temperature 30 degrees Celsius warmer than would otherwise be the case and is thus essential to preserving life on Earth. Global climate policy—the climate change regime—is concerned with the "enhanced" greenhouse effect, first identified in 1896 by Swedish chemist Svante Arrhenius. Arrhenius claimed that humans were altering the makeup of the atmosphere through the burning of coal, which would increase carbon dioxide (CO_2) concentrations.[4] He speculated that a doubling of CO_2 could lead to a 4-degree to 6-degree Celsius warming of the Earth's surface temperature.

International Scientific Cooperation

The scientific community generally ignored Arrhenius's claim of an enhanced greenhouse effect until the 1950s. In 1957 Roger Revelle and H. E. Seuss raised concern that the oceans would not be capable of absorbing the high levels of CO_2 being emitted through industrialization processes and that these emissions would thus alter the composition of the global atmosphere. They concluded, "Human beings are now carrying out a large scale geophysical experiment of a kind that could not have happened in the past nor

Table 6-1 Key Events in the International Climate Change Regime

Agenda-setting phase	1896	• Arrhenius identifies enhanced greenhouse effect
	1957–1958	• Revelle and Seuss study
		• International Geophysical Year
		• Regular monitoring of atmospheric CO_2 levels begins at Mauna Loa
	1979	• First World Climate Conference
	1980–1985	• Villach scientific conferences
	1987	• Villach and Bellagio policy conferences
	1988	• Toronto Conference
		• IPCC created
	1988–1992	• All industrialized states (except United States) adopt domestic targets and timetables for controlling GHG emissions
	1990	• IPCC First Assessment Report
Negotiation phase	1991–1992	• UN FCCC negotiations
	1994	• FCCC enters into force
	1995–1997	• Kyoto Protocol negotiations on commitments
	1996	• IPCC Second Assessment Report
	1998–2001	• Kyoto Protocol negotiations on rules for flexible mechanisms (Marrakesh Accords)
	2001	• IPCC Third Assessment Report
		• United States withdraws from Kyoto Protocol
Operationalization phase	2005	• Kyoto Protocol enters into force
		• European Union Emissions Trading Scheme begins
	2007	• IPCC Fourth Assessment Report
		• Agreement at COP-13 on Bali Road Map for post-2012 negotiations
	2008–2012	• First commitment period under the Kyoto Protocol
	2009	• Copenhagen Accord

be reproduced in the future."[5] Later that same year, the International Council of Scientific Unions launched the 1957–1958 International Geophysical Year (IGY). One of the research activities initiated as part of the IGY was the establishment of an observatory at Mauna Loa, Hawaii, to monitor atmospheric CO_2 concentrations. These observations, along with other types of data, soon revealed that CO_2 levels had risen significantly since the industrial revolution.[6] Observations of higher atmospheric CO_2 concentrations were accompanied by findings of increased mean global surface temperature, as had been predicted by Arrhenius.

Based on these emergent findings, delegates and scientists attending the 1979 First World Climate Conference, which had been organized by the World Meteorological Organization, established the World Climate Program and called on the world's governments "to foresee and prevent potential man-made changes in climate that might be adverse to the well-being of humanity."[7] In collaboration with the United Nations Environment Programme and the International Council of Scientific Unions, the World Climate Program organized a series of scientific conferences in Villach, Austria, in the early 1980s. By 1985 these meetings had produced an emerging scientific consensus that climate change posed a legitimate threat to the international community.[8] Two follow-up conferences were held in 1987—one in Villach (September 28 to October 2) and one in Bellagio, Italy (November 9–13)—to consider what policy steps might be appropriate given the state of scientific knowledge on climate change. As a result, scientists participating in the Bellagio conference recommended that governments "immediately begin to reexamine their long-term energy strategies with the goals of achieving high end-use efficiency, reducing multiple forms of air pollution and reducing CO_2 emissions."[9]

The process of placing climate change on the international political agenda culminated in the World Conference on the Changing Atmosphere, held in Toronto, Canada, in June 1988. Although the Toronto Conference, as it came to be known, was sponsored by the Canadian government, it was organized by individuals who had participated in the Villach and Bellagio conferences and thus built directly on the outcomes of those meetings. Participants, including scientists, policymakers, industry representatives, and environmentalists, suggested the first concrete target and timetable for controlling GHG emissions. The "Toronto target," which continues to figure prominently in international debates, called upon states to reduce their CO_2 emissions 20 percent below 1988 levels by 2005.[10]

In the aftermath of the Toronto Conference, the United Nations convened formal international negotiations. The first session, held in 1991, marked the beginning of the "negotiation phase" of the climate regime (see below). During this period, a number of industrialized countries adopted domestic targets and policies for limiting GHG emissions. By 1992 all but the United States had adopted such targets, with members of the European Union (EU) committing to stabilizing their emissions at 1990 levels by 2000.[11] The United States had initiated a domestic debate and a significant research program but had not yet developed an action plan for controlling emissions.[12]

Scientific research continues to play an important role in the climate change regime. In November 1988 the World Meteorological Organization and the United Nations Environment Programme created the Intergovernmental Panel on Climate Change (IPCC) to synthesize and assess the state of scientific knowledge on climate change and evaluate response strategies. (The IPCC does not conduct original scientific research.) The IPCC has completed four major assessments (1990, 1996, 2001, and 2007) as well as numerous technical reports and is generally viewed as the authoritative scientific body on the issue of climate change, giving the IPCC a privileged position in the policy process (see Chapter 2).

Negotiating an International Climate Policy

The process of developing a coordinated international response to climate change has focused on negotiation of the FCCC and the Kyoto Protocol. As a "framework" convention, the FCCC establishes the basic architecture within which international efforts to address global climate change take place. The Kyoto Protocol outlines specific obligations consistent with the guiding principles set forth in the FCCC. Together, these documents form the core of the international climate change regime, setting forth the principles, norms, rules, and decision-making procedures that govern interactions among members of the international community on this issue. More than 190 countries have participated in international climate negotiations, along with hundreds of nongovernmental organizations (NGOs). In the UN context, countries have primary decision-making authority, but NGO representatives can participate as observers, allowing them to provide input into the diplomatic process. In the climate change negotiations, NGOs frequently comment on proposals under consideration, provide technical expertise, and make formal statements in plenary sessions.

To make the negotiating process more efficient, many states have organized themselves into negotiating blocs (Table 6–2), a common strategy in the UN system. These blocs allow groups of states with relatively common interests to share information and coordinate their positions on issues under consideration. The Group of 77 (G-77) and China and the Africa Group are standing coalitions throughout the UN, while others, such as the Umbrella Group and the Environmental Integrity Group, have been organized on an ad hoc basis specifically for the climate change negotiations.[13] Similarly, NGOs have created "observer constituencies" (Table 6–3) to facilitate their participation in the negotiation process.[14] In many instances, state negotiating blocs and NGO observer constituencies work together to pursue common interests.

Negotiating the United Nations Framework Convention on Climate Change

Under a United Nations General Assembly mandate, the Intergovernmental Negotiating Committee for a Framework Convention on Climate Change met six times between February 1991 and May 1992. The negotiations took place as part of the preparations for the 1992 United Nations Conference on Environment and Development (the Earth Summit), held in

Table 6-2 State Negotiating Blocs

Group Name	Members	Interests
EU	27 Member States of the European Union	Support strict targets and timetables for emissions reductions
Umbrella Group	Russia, Iceland, Ukraine, Japan, United States, Canada, Australia, Norway, and New Zealand	Seek to minimize the negative economic impact of emissions reduction measures through widespread use of market mechanisms
OPEC	Members of the Organization of Petroleum Exporting Countries	Concerned about the negative impact of emissions reduction regulations on export markets for oil and natural gas upon which their economies are heavily dependent
AOSIS	Alliance of Small Island States—43 low-lying or island developing states that are particularly vulnerable to the impacts of climate change, especially sea level rise	Support strict targets and timetables for emissions reductions as a matter of survival
G-77 and China	Developing countries	Priority on social and economic development and securing new financial resources for developing countries
Least-developed countries	49 countries identified as least developed by the United Nations	Seek to secure resources to reduce vulnerability to impacts of climate change.
Environmental Integrity Group	Mexico, the Republic of Korea, and Switzerland	Promote the environmental integrity of the climate change regime
Africa Group	53 members of the African regional group in the United Nations	Seek to secure resources to reduce vulnerability to impacts of climate change and enhance capacity building
CACAM	Central Asia, Caucasus, Albania, and Moldova	Concerned about clarifying the status of its members in the climate regime because several of them did not exist when the negotiations began

Sources: UN FCCC, "Party Groupings" (Bonn, Germany: FCCC Secretariat, 2009), http://unfccc .int/parties_and_observers/parties/negotiating_groups/items/2714.php; Farhana Yamin and Joanna Depledge, *The International Climate Change Regime: A Guide to Rules, Institutions and Procedures* (Cambridge: Cambridge University Press, 2004).

Rio de Janeiro. The FCCC entered into force in March 1994 and had been ratified by 194 countries as of October 2009. Key elements of the FCCC, and thus of international climate policy, include its objective, principles, and commitments and the creation of an organizational structure for the regime.

Table 6-3 NGO Observer Constituencies

Constituency name	Description and interests
Environmental NGOs	Loosely organized under the umbrella of the Climate Action Network; united in desire to set strict emissions reduction targets and timetables and to hold states accountable for their commitments
Business and industry NGOs	Includes a range of organizations with interests based in the public sector; considerable variation in support of strict emissions reduction targets but united in support for the use of market mechanisms
Local government and municipal authorities	Represented by ICLEI-Local Governments for Sustainability; seek to gain recognition for the role of local authorities in controlling GHG emissions
Indigenous peoples organizations	Seek to ensure that rules for the use of forests in achieving emissions reductions do not infringe on the rights of indigenous peoples
Research-oriented and independent organizations	Organizations engaged in research and analysis focused on developing solutions to the causes and consequences of climate change
Other	Trade unions, farmers organizations, women and gender organizations, and youth

Source: UN FCCC, "Non-Governmental Organization Observer Constituencies" (Bonn, Germany: FCCC Secretariat 2004), http://unfccc.int/files/parties_and_observers/ngo/application/pdf/const.pdf.

Objective. Article 2 of the FCCC establishes the objective of the climate change regime as:

> stabilization of greenhouse gas concentrations in the atmosphere at a level that would prevent dangerous anthropogenic interference with the climate system. Such a level should be achieved within a time-frame sufficient to allow ecosystems to adapt naturally to climate change, to ensure that food production is not threatened and to enable economic development to proceed in a sustainable manner.[15]

Note that the FCCC does not state what constitutes "dangerous" interference with the climate system or at what level atmospheric GHG concentrations must be stabilized to avoid such interference. During the FCCC negotiations, countries could not agree on more specific language owing to significant differences on the need for action. Despite more widespread agreement on the need for action, this remains a central area of debate in the negotiations today.[16]

Principles. Article 3 of the FCCC sets forth principles to guide the international community in its efforts to address climate change. Many of the current political debates discussed below revolve around the interpretation of these principles. The principle of common but differentiated responsibilities acknowledges that, although all members of the international community have an obligation to protect the climate for present and future generations, industrialized countries and formerly communist countries with economies in transition have a responsibility to take the lead in addressing climate change. This stems from their historical responsibility for emitting GHGs as well as the assumption that they possess the financial and technological capabilities to control those emissions. This principle has been a source of U.S. objections to the climate change regime because it is seen to give large developing country emitters, such as China, a free ride.

The FCCC also states that *equity* should be a guiding principle in the development of a global response to climate change. Equity has been interpreted in a variety of ways, however, and remains an unsettled matter. Many developing countries argue, for example, that equity would be best achieved through a per capita allocation of GHG emissions rights, noting their low historical contribution to the climate problem, current low levels of per capita GHG emissions compared with industrialized countries, and lack of resources. Per capita emissions allocations would enable developing countries to raise their living standards, thereby reducing their vulnerability to the impacts of climate change.[17] However, achieving a convergence of per capita emissions would require even more significant reductions on the part of industrialized countries than have been adopted thus far.

The FCCC also recognizes the specific needs and special circumstances of developing countries that may be particularly vulnerable to climate change, either to adverse impacts, such as drought, or because their economies are dependent on the production and export of fossil fuels (states belonging to the Organization of Petroleum Exporting Countries [OPEC]). In addition, the FCCC embraces the *precautionary principle*, stating that the absence of full scientific certainty should not be used as an excuse to avoid taking action to mitigate the threat or impact of climate change.

The principles of the FCCC also reflect the relationship between climate change and economic conditions. Measures taken to deal with climate change should be *cost-effective*, ensuring the greatest benefit at the lowest cost. This has been a particularly important point for members of the Umbrella Group as well as some of the EU Member States. In addition, all countries are seen to have a right to *sustainable development*, and measures to address climate change should promote that objective. This was a particularly important issue for the G-77 and China during the FCCC negotiations and continues to be a central part of their negotiating position today.[18] Finally, the FCCC emphasizes the importance of *maintaining an open international economic system*.

Commitments. The FCCC imposes three types of obligations on parties. First, all Annex I parties (industrialized countries and formerly communist countries with economies in transition) were required to adopt policies and measures aimed at returning their GHG emissions to 1990 levels by 2000 (Article 4.2). Second, Annex I parties must provide "new and additional financial resources" as well as technology to help developing countries meet their commitments under the Convention (Article 4(3)). Note that consistent with the principles outlined above, the FCCC differentiates between industrialized and developing countries, placing the primary burden for addressing global climate change on the industrialized countries. Despite repeated efforts to establish new financial mechanisms, funding for developing countries remains inadequate. Third, under Articles 4 and 12, all parties must regularly report on their national emissions inventories and programs to mitigate climate change. Thus, under these and other articles, developing countries do have a general obligation to address global climate change.

Organizational Structure. The FCCC creates the central institutional architecture for international climate policy. Article 7 establishes the Conference of the Parties (COP) as the supreme body, with responsibility for reviewing the implementation of the FCCC (and any related legal instruments) and making decisions to promote its effective implementation. The COP usually meets annually. The Secretariat (Article 8), located in Bonn, Germany, administers the convention, making meeting arrangements and compiling and transmitting information. The FCCC also established two other important subsidiary bodies—the Subsidiary Body for Scientific and Technological Advice (SBSTA, Article 9) and the Subsidiary Body for Implementation (SBI, Article 10), which meet at least twice a year and assist the COP with assessing the state of scientific and technological knowledge related to climate change as well as the effects of measures taken under the convention and subsequent legal decisions. The FCCC designated the Global Environment Facility (GEF) as the financial mechanism for the treaty on an interim basis (Articles 11 and 21). Developing countries had argued for the creation of an independent financial mechanism because they feared that industrialized states, as the principal donors to the GEF, would use their leverage to control the allocation of resources.[19]

Negotiating the Kyoto Protocol

At the first Conference of the Parties to the FCCC (COP-1), held in Berlin in 1995, delegates adopted the Berlin Mandate, which stated that commitments contained in the convention were insufficient to meet its long-term objective, and they initiated a process of negotiating a protocol to the FCCC that would contain binding targets and timetables for reducing GHG emissions beyond 2000. Following two years of extremely complex and intense negotiations, parties adopted the Kyoto Protocol to the FCCC at COP-3, held in Kyoto, Japan, in December 1997.[20] Building on the principle of common but differentiated responsibilities, the Kyoto Protocol set specific targets for industrialized countries to reduce their GHG emissions (see below) but left the specific rules and operational details for how countries could achieve those reductions unresolved. These issues were debated in several formal and informal negotiating sessions between 1998 and 2001. The future of the Kyoto Protocol was called into question in spring 2001 when the United States withdrew from the negotiations. Newly elected president George W. Bush viewed the treaty as "fatally flawed" on the grounds that it failed to include emissions reduction commitments for developing countries and would damage the U.S. economy. Owing in large part to leadership from the European Union, the rest of the international community agreed to go forward without the United States and reached final agreement at COP-7 in Marrakesh, Morocco (the Marrakesh Accords). The Kyoto Protocol entered into force in 2005, and 189 countries have ratified the protocol as of November 2009. While the FCCC laid out the general architecture of the climate change regime, the Kyoto Protocol identified mechanisms to be used to achieve its overall objective. The central elements include commitments, rules on flexible mechanisms and compliance, and the creation of new organizations.[21]

Commitments. Article 3 of the Kyoto Protocol requires industrialized countries to reduce their aggregate GHG emissions 5.2 percent below 1990 levels by the period 2008–2012. These commitments are differentiated in that each country has an individual target (see Table 6–4). In addition, some countries with economies in transition were permitted to select a year other than 1990 as a baseline. These differentiated targets are widely recognized as "purely political," the result of tough bargaining in closed-door sessions involving the EU leadership, the United States, and Japan during the final days (and ultimately hours) of the Kyoto negotiations. They are not based on scientific or economic analysis and are far below what the IPCC says is necessary to stabilize atmospheric concentrations of GHGs.

Flexible Mechanisms. Consistent with the principle of cost-effectiveness, the Kyoto Protocol gives parties considerable flexibility in choosing how to achieve their emissions reduction commitments. The "Kyoto mechanisms" or "flexible mechanisms" include emissions trading (Article 17), joint implementation (Article 6), and the Clean Development Mechanism (CDM; Article 12). Emissions trading permits countries that exceed their allowed emissions to purchase emissions credits from countries whose emissions are below their allotted amount. Industrialized countries may also invest in emissions reduction activities in other industrialized countries under the rules of joint implementation. The investing country receives emissions reduction units (ERUs) that can be applied toward its target (the ERUs are subtracted from the host country's assigned amount). The CDM allows industrialized countries to invest in emissions-reducing activities in developing countries in return for certified emissions reductions that may then be used toward meeting Kyoto targets.[22]

During the initial negotiation of the Kyoto Protocol, the United States, supported by other members of the Umbrella Group and industry representatives, pushed strongly for a broad set of flexibility measures. The EU, most developing countries, and environmental groups objected, arguing that extensive reliance on such mechanisms would allow rich countries to buy their way out of making any meaningful commitments domestically, thereby violating the polluter-pays principle. In the final hours of the COP-3 in Kyoto, the flexible mechanisms were included in the protocol in exchange for U.S. support of

Table 6-4 Emissions Reduction Targets and Progress

Country	Emissions reduction target in Kyoto Protocol (% below 1990 levels)[1]	2005 emissions (relative to 1990 levels)
Australia	+8	+25.6
Austria	−8 (−13)	+18
Belgium	−8 (−7.5)	−1.3
Bulgaria	−8	−40
Canada	−6	+25.3
Croatia	−5	−3.4
Czech Republic	−8	−25.8
Denmark	−8 (−21)	−7
Estonia	−8	−52.6
European Community	−8	−1.5
Finland	−8 (0)	−2.7
Germany	−8 (−21)	−18.4
Greece	−8 (+25)	+28
Hungary	−6	−18.2
Iceland	+10	+10.5
Ireland	−8 (+13)	+26.3
Italy	−8 (−6.5)	+12.1
Japan	−6	+6.9
Latvia	−8	−58.9
Liechtenstein	−8	+17.4
Lithuania	−8	−53
Luxembourg	−8 (−28)	−0.4
Monaco	−8	−3.1
Netherlands	−8 (−6)	−0.4
New Zealand	0	+24.7
Norway	+1	+8.8
Poland	−6	−17.8
Portugal	−8 (+27)	+42.8
Romania	−8	−38.2
Russia	0	−28.7
Slovakia	−8	−33.3
Slovenia	−8	+10.2
Spain	−8 (+15)	+53.3
Sweden	−8 (+4)	−7.3
Switzerland	−8	+1.7
Ukraine	0	−55.4
United Kingdom	−8 (−12.5)	−14.8
United States	−7	+16.3

Sources: Climate Analysis Indicators Tool (CAIT UNFCCC), version 2.0 (Washington, D.C.: World Resources Institute, 2009), http://cait.wri.org; European Environment Agency, *Annual European Community Greenhouse Gas Inventory 1990–2007 and Inventory Report 2009* (Copenhagen: European Environment Agency, 2009), www.eea.europa.eu/publications/european-community-greenhouse-gas-inventory-2009; UN FCCC, *The Kyoto Protocol to the Convention on Climate Change* (Bonn, Germany: FCCC Secretariat, 1997), Annex B.

[1]EU member countries further differentiated their Kyoto Protocol target under a burden-sharing agreement, as indicated in parentheses.

reduction, rather than stabilization, targets. As noted, negotiations to finalize the rules about how these mechanisms could be used were extremely contentious. Of particular concern was the issue of "additionality." While the Marrakesh Accords do not place a specific limit on the use of flexible mechanisms, they clearly state that countries should achieve a significant portion of their emissions reductions through domestic measures. The use of the mechanisms should be in addition to, not instead of, such measures.

Compliance. While the issue of compliance was largely ignored in the Kyoto Protocol, the subsequent Marrakesh Accords set forth a compliance system consisting of a Compliance Committee with two branches—the facilitative and enforcement branches—each having ten members. The facilitative branch helps parties fulfill their commitments under the protocol. The enforcement branch determines whether parties are in compliance with their commitments. Parties that are found to be in noncompliance with their reporting obligations become ineligible to use the flexible mechanisms. Parties that fail to meet their emissions reduction targets in the first commitment period are required to make up the difference during the second commitment period, with a 30 percent penalty.[23]

Organizational Structure. The Kyoto Protocol and Marrakesh Accords added several new institutions to the organizational structure of the international climate change regime. The CDM Executive Board supervises the operation of the CDM.[24] It consists of ten representatives from the various state blocs that participate in the climate change negotiations (see Table 6–2). As of January 2009, the CDM Executive Board has certified 1,324 projects (of the more than 4,000 projects in the pipeline), which are expected to produce 1.4 billion tons of emissions reductions by 2012.[25]

For developing countries, one of the major objectives has been to secure financial resources to assist in meeting current and future commitments under the climate change regime. To that end, the Marrakesh Accords call for an increase in funds to the GEF as well as the creation of three new funds.[26] The Special Climate Change Fund is designed to finance activities related to adaptation, technology transfer, development of policies and measures in a number of different sectors, and diversification of economies. The Least-Developed-Country Fund assists these countries in the preparation and implementation of national action plans as required under the FCCC, while the Adaptation Fund provides resources for activities related to adaptation. Unfortunately, progress in mobilizing new resources for developing countries has been slow. As of March 2008, the Special Climate Change Fund had received pledges from thirteen countries for a total of $90.3 million and had approved $36.14 million for projects. Nineteen countries had pledged $172.84 million for the Least-Developed-Country Fund, with $13.52 million allocated for approved projects. Delegates were still finalizing the operational details for the Adaptation Fund.[27]

From Commitments to Action: Operationalizing the International Climate Change Regime

The first step in operationalizing the Kyoto Protocol involved ratification and entry into force. Under Article 25, the protocol would enter into force upon ratification by at least fifty-five countries, including parties accounting for 55 percent of 1990 emissions. Meeting this standard was difficult without the United States, which accounted for 36 percent of industrialized country 1990 emissions. Russia, which accounted for 17 percent of 1990 emissions, used its leverage to secure concessions from the EU regarding entry into the World Trade Organization before ratifying the Kyoto Protocol in 2004. The treaty entered into force six months later.

With the completion of the ratification process, industrialized countries began the task of developing policies and programs to meet their emissions reduction commitments. In most cases, this task has proven more difficult than originally anticipated. For example, the European Union embraced the idea of emissions trading in 2003 (despite strong earlier objections) when it became clear that Member States could not meet their Kyoto targets through traditional policies and measures. Since 2005 the EU Emissions Trading Scheme has become the central element in EU climate policy and is currently the world's largest cap and trade system for GHGs.[28] In addition to the practical challenges of reducing GHG emissions, several countries have had to contend with powerful political opposition. Canadian climate policy has fallen victim to a shift from a Liberal to Conservative government, with the latter reluctant to impose regulations on large emitters such as the oil industry.[29] Similarly, Japan has had to rely on voluntary action because of opposition from the industrial sector.[30]

Evaluating the effectiveness of international environmental regimes is difficult as it raises a host of methodological challenges.[31] Of particular import is whether one chooses to focus solely on the direct impacts of a particular cooperative arrangement, such as the FCCC and the Kyoto Protocol, or on targeted actors and ultimately the environment, or if one also includes consideration of more indirect effects that may be generated as a result of the negotiation process and reflected in society more broadly. This section contends that, although the direct effects of the FCCC and the Kyoto Protocol may be limited, the indirect effects have prompted a shift in the governance of climate change beyond nation-states, opening up greater possibilities for meaningful action in the future to address the problem.

Effects on Targeted Actors and GHG Emissions

A legalistic definition of effectiveness focuses on whether states are complying with the rules of the regime.[32] The vast majority of countries in the world have ratified the FCCC and submitted national communications containing emissions inventories and an overview of policies and measures taken to address climate change. Thus, compliance with this basic requirement is quite high. Critics argue, however, that much of the information in these communications is not useful, is incomplete, and often cannot be compared across states.[33]

In terms of commitments to control GHGs, the performance to date is less encouraging. Only the United Kingdom, Germany, and Russia achieved the goal of stabilizing their GHG emissions at 1990 levels by 2000. In each case, however, such progress had little to do with adopting innovative climate policies and more to do with economic circumstances.[34] In 2006 aggregate emissions from industrialized parties to the Kyoto Protocol were 17 percent below 1990 levels; however, most of that can be attributed to the fact that emissions from countries with economies in transition were 37 percent below the Kyoto baseline (Table 6–4).[35] Emissions from other industrialized country parties were above the 1990 baseline, and overall emissions from all industrialized parties have grown in the period 2000–2006.

In some cases compliance may be a misleading measure of regime effectiveness. Where standards set in an international treaty are low, high levels of compliance may be meaningless.[36] Alternatively, analysts can consider whether agreements prompt changes in behavior among targeted actors by comparing their behavior with business-as-usual scenarios.[37] For example, although U.S. GHG emissions in 1999 were 11 percent above 1990 levels, the Clinton administration argued that they would have been even higher were it not for its 1993 Climate Change Action Plan, developed in compliance with the FCCC, which consisted of more than fifty voluntary measures designed to stabilize emissions.[38]

Assessments of regime effectiveness might also consider "the degree to which the degrading or polluting processes and consequences are arrested or reversed."[39] In other words, does the regime actually help ameliorate the problem that gave rise to its creation? On this basis, the short-term effectiveness of the international climate change regime must be called into question. Global GHG emissions continue to increase, and although the precise meaning of "dangerous anthropogenic interferences with the climate system" has yet to be defined, preventing such interference is generally expected to involve emissions reductions well beyond the level called for in the Kyoto Protocol. In its Fourth Assessment Report, the IPCC estimates that industrialized countries would need to reduce emissions 25–40 percent below 1990 levels by 2020 to keep atmospheric concentrations from rising above 450 parts per million.[40] Moreover, even if the Kyoto targets were achieved, atmospheric concentrations would continue to rise as emissions from developing countries increase.

Broader Effects

Despite the regime's shortcoming in the near term, it is possible to argue that the processes and institutions created under the FCCC and the Kyoto Protocol will facilitate international action to address climate change in the long term. This optimistic perspective stems from viewing international regimes as catalysts for learning and generating shared understandings rather than simply as a set of specific rules and obligations.[41] As Underdal argues,

> International negotiation processes are often large-scale exercises in *learning*, through which at least some parties modify their perceptions of the problem and of alternative policy options and perhaps see their incentives change as well. As a consequence, the process itself may lead governments as well as nongovernmental actors to make unilateral adjustments in behavior—even in the absence of any legal obligation to do so. The aggregate impact of such side effects may well be more important than the impact of any formal convention or declaration signed in the end.[42]

Through the negotiation of the FCCC and the Kyoto Protocol, the international community has come to view the problem of climate change as a legitimate threat. Together, these agreements send a clear message to states as well as industry that business as usual (for example, unregulated emission of GHGs) is no longer acceptable.[43] Moreover, the climate change regime has given rise to new actors, institutions, and interests that are likely to play a significant role in addressing the threat of climate change over the long term.[44]

Nation-states increasingly behave in ways that suggest they have accepted a responsibility to address climate change by limiting their GHG emissions. During the past decade, all industrialized countries have institutionalized responsibility for addressing climate change within their respective governments and adopted policies for controlling emissions. This is true even in some oil-producing countries, which are attempting to secure resources to protect their economies, as well as in laggard countries, such as the United States. Despite the Bush administration's objection to the Kyoto Protocol, the United States remained engaged on the issue of climate change by continuing to participate in ongoing negotiations related to the FCCC and adopting a goal of reducing the GHG intensity of the American economy.[45] Many developing countries have also institutionalized the need to address climate change and are taking steps to limit their emissions even though they are not formally required to do so under the FCCC and the Kyoto Protocol.[46]

The international climate change regime has given rise to a new discourse linking economic growth with the achievement of emissions reductions, illustrated in the striking shift in the position of many business and industry groups since the early 1990s.[47] During the FCCC negotiations, the business groups that participated in the process primarily consisted of members of the fossil-fuel industry that organized themselves under the umbrella of the Global Climate Coalition (GCC). Members of the GCC were united in their opposition to international regulations on GHG emissions. During the Kyoto Protocol negotiations, the business and industry community diversified, with groups representing members of the renewable energy industry as well as the insurance industry coming out in support of international GHG regulations. In addition, a number of companies whose profits derive from the production and consumption of fossil fuels left the GCC (which disbanded in December 2001) and began working to find economically viable ways to control GHG emissions. For example, the Business Environmental Leadership Council, an initiative of the Pew Center on Global Climate Change in Washington, D.C., works with forty-four major corporations including British Petroleum, DuPont, Boeing, Toyota, and Weyerhaeuser. In the late 1990s, British Petroleum and DuPont voluntarily pledged to reduce GHG emissions within their operations by 10 percent and 65 percent, respectively. In 2002 each company announced that it had met its target eight years ahead of schedule.[48] Today, a growing number of companies, large and small, are following their example.

Perhaps most striking, the international climate change regime has mobilized actors beyond national governments, giving rise to a complex system of multilevel governance.[49] More than eight hundred municipal governments around the world (accounting for more than 8 percent of global GHG emissions) participate in the Cities for Climate Protection campaign sponsored by the International Council for Local Environmental Initiatives (ICLEI).[50] These communities have committed to developing policies and programs to reduce GHG emissions and in the process have recognized linkages between environmental protection and economic growth. In federal systems, many state and provincial governments have become leaders in developing climate change policies. This has been particularly striking in the United States, where state and local governments have stepped in to fill the void left by weak federal action.[51] As noted above, the private sector has become an important site of climate change governance as companies, large and small, seek to control their own emissions. Transnational networks linking public and private actors across national borders often promote innovation in ideas and technology development.

This trend toward multilevel governance challenges the centrality of the international regime in the governance of global climate change and presents new opportunities for developing effective responses. This is not to suggest the multilateral treaty negotiation process is irrelevant. Instead, it highlights the fact that actors at other levels of social organization are not sitting around waiting for negotiators to reach agreement on the next multilateral treaty. This is readily apparent when one attends the international climate change negotiations. While country delegates tediously pore over complicated technical language, many of these actors meet in side events where they showcase the innovative policies and measures they are working on. The energy and enthusiasm in these events are palpable and often stand in stark contrast to the mood in the formal halls of international diplomacy.

Current Debates and Future Challenges

Many members of the international community are now considering the future of the climate change regime after 2012 (the end of the first Kyoto commitment period). The contemporary debate focuses on two main issues: developing country commitments to reduce GHG emissions and future reductions by industrialized countries under the Kyoto Protocol. It is clear that controlling global GHG emissions requires action by large developing country emitters such as China, India, and Brazil. In recent years, the international community has made several efforts to engage these countries outside of the formal climate regime institutions. In 2005 the United States spearheaded the creation of the Asia-Pacific Partnership on Clean Development and Climate, which also involves Australia, Canada, Japan, China, South Korea, and India. Members cooperate in promoting the deployment of clean energy technologies to achieve the goals of energy security and climate protection.[52] Also in 2005, the Group of Eight—a forum of the eight largest industrialized country economies—initiated the "Gleneagles Dialogue" involving the twenty largest GHG emitting countries. Leaders have used this venue to discuss the post-2012 international framework. These discussions appear to have laid the foundation for moving this issue forward within the international negotiations. At COP-13 in Bali, Indonesia, in 2007, parties agreed to pursue negotiations on long-term cooperative action under the FCCC, including commitments for mitigation actions by developing countries. Under the Bali Road Map, these negotiations were to conclude at COP-15 in Copenhagen in December 2009. The Bali Road Map also created an ad hoc working group to negotiate future commitments for industrialized countries under the Kyoto Protocol by COP-15.

Despite unprecedented levels of public, media, and political attention, COP-15 did not proceed as planned.[53] In the months leading up to the Copenhagen meeting, diplomats debated over several hundred pages of draft text but reached a stalemate on several substantive and procedural issues. In the final hours of COP-15, a small group of heads of state, led by U.S. president Barack Obama, jettisoned the draft text and negotiated a compromise "Copenhagen Accord." The Copenhagen Accord acknowledges the goal of limiting the increase in global temperature to 2 degrees Celsius to avoid dangerous interference with the climate system and commits industrialized countries to providing $30 billion for adaptation and mitigation activities in developing countries by 2012 and $100 billion a year by 2020. However, the Copenhagen Accord does not contain quantified emissions reduction goals. Rather, industrialized countries are required to set their own 2020 emissions targets (countries may choose their baseline year), and developing countries are required to implement and report on mitigation actions. In the closing plenary, delegates requested that both of the ad hoc working groups continue their work on developing more concrete emissions reduction commitments, but it is unclear what progress can be made in the face of the deep cleavages between industrialized and developing countries as well as between developing countries that were revealed in the Copenhagen talks.

Ultimately, confronting the challenge of climate change will require a global transition to a low-carbon economy. Achieving this transition will require the mobilization of resources and creativity at all levels of social organization from the global level the local level. The international climate change regime likely will continue to define the core principles and objectives of the global effort to address climate change, but it is increasingly clear that these agreements alone will not solve the problem. Many subnational governments, companies, and transnational networks are working hard to find solutions to the threat of global climate change. It is essential that the multilateral treaty-making process be integrated into the complex multilevel process of global climate change governance. As additional actors engage in efforts to address climate change, new opportunities emerge to enhance the effectiveness of the global response through public-private partnerships, bottom-up pressure, and transnational networks.[54] The key challenge is to ensure that all of these pieces work together.

Notes

1. The major greenhouse gases are carbon dioxide (CO_2), methane (CH_4), nitrous oxide (N_2O), chlorofluorocarbons (CFCs), and water vapor. Regulations within the climate change regime focus on a "basket" of six gases: CO_2, CH_4, N_2O, hydrofluorocarbons (HFCs), perfluorocarbons (PFCs), and sulfur hexafluoride (SF_6).
2. Intergovernmental Panel on Climate Change (hereafter IPCC), *Summary for Policy Makers: Climate Change 2007: Synthesis Report* (Cambridge: Cambridge University Press, 2007). Available from www.ipcc.ch.
3. Oran R. Young, "Rights, Rules and Resources in World Affairs," in *Global Governance: Drawing Insights from the Environmental Experience*, ed. Oran R. Young (Cambridge: MIT Press, 1997). Note that these phases are for analytical purposes only and that in practice there are considerable overlaps and feedbacks.
4. Svante Arrhenius, "On the Influence of Carbonic Acid in the Air on the Temperature on the Ground," *Philosophical Magazine* 251 (1896): 236–276.
5. Quoted in Michael Oppenheimer and Robert H. Boyle, *Dead Heat: The Race against the Greenhouse Effect* (New York: Basic Books, 1990), 36.
6. Robert T. Watson and Core Writing Team, eds., *Climate Change 2001: Synthesis Report* (Cambridge: Cambridge University Press, 2001), 4–8.
7. World Meteorological Organization, *Proceedings of the First World Climate Conference— A Conference of Experts on Climate and Mankind, 12–23 February 1979* (Geneva: World Meteorological Organization, 1979), 709.
8. World Climate Program, *Report of the International Conference on the Assessment of the Role of Carbon Dioxide and of Other Greenhouse Gases on Climate Variations and Associated Impacts* (Geneva: World Meteorological Organization, 1986).
9. Jill Jaeger, *Developing Policies for Responding to Climatic Change: A Summary of the Discussions and Recommendations of the Workshops Held in Villach (28 September–2 October 1987) and Bellagio (9–13 November 1987), under the Auspices of the Beijer Institute, Stockholm* (Geneva: World Meteorological Organization, 1988), 37.
10. World Meteorological Organization, *Proceedings of the World Conference on the Changing Atmosphere: Implications for Global Security* (Geneva: World Meteorological Organization, 1988), 296.
11. International Energy Agency, *Climate Change Policy Initiatives*, vol. 1: *OECD Countries* (Paris: International Energy Agency, 1994).
12. Loren Cass. *The Failures of American and European Climate Policy* (Albany: SUNY Press, 2006), chap. 2.
13. For a more detailed treatment of the state negotiating blocs, see Joyeeta Gupta, *Our Simmering Planet: What to Do about Global Warming?* (New York: Palgrave Macmillan,

2000); Sebastian Oberthür and Hermann E. Ott, *The Kyoto Protocol: International Climate Policy for the 21st Century* (New York: Springer, 1999); Farhana Yamin and Joanna Depledge, *The International Climate Change Regime: A Guide to Rules, Institutions and Procedures* (Cambridge: Cambridge University Press, 2004).

14. On the different NGO constituencies, see Michele M. Betsill, "Environmental NGOs and the Kyoto Protocol Negotiations," in *NGO Diplomacy: The Influence of Nongovernmental Organizations in International Environmental Negotiations*, ed. Michele M. Betsill and Elisabeth Corell (Cambridge: MIT Press, 2008), 44–66; Peter Newell, *Climate for Change: Non-state Actors and the Global Politics of the Greenhouse* (Cambridge: Cambridge University Press, 2001); Kal Raustiala, "Nonstate Actors in the Global Climate Regime," in *International Relations and Global Climate Change*, ed. Urs Luterbacher and Detlef F. Sprinz (Cambridge: MIT Press, 2001), 95–118; Yamin and Depledge, *The International Climate Change Regime*.

15. United Nations, *United Nations Framework Convention on Climate Change* (Bonn: FCCC Secretariat, 1992), art 2, www.unfccc.int.

16. The European Union has established a goal of limiting warming to 2 degrees Celsius, which in turn guides development of energy and climate policies in Member States. However, other countries have not embraced this goal. See Commission of the European Communities, "Limiting Global Climate Change to 2° Celsius: The Way Ahead for 2020 and Beyond," Communication from the Commission to the Council, the European Parliament, the European Economic and Social Committee and the Committee of the Regions, document no. COM(2007)2, Brussels, January 10, 2007, http://ec.europa.eu/development/icenter/repository/env_cc_com_2007_2_en.pdf.

17. Ambuj Sagar, "Wealth, Responsibility, and Equity: Exploring an Allocation Framework for Global GHG Emissions," *Climatic Change* 45 (2000): 511–527; P. R. Shukla, "Justice, Equity and Efficiency in Climate Change: A Developing Country Perspective," in *Fair Weather? Equity Concerns in Climate Change*, ed. F. L. Toth (London: Earthscan, 1999), 150–155; Gary W. Yohe, David Montgomery, and Ed Balistreri, "Equity and the Kyoto Protocol: Measuring the Distributional Effects of Alternative Emissions Trading Regimes," *Global Environmental Change* 10 (2000): 121–132.

18. Tariq Osman Hyder, "Looking Back to See Forward," in *Negotiating Climate Change: The Inside Story of the Rio Convention*, ed. I. M. Mintzer and J. A. Leonard (Cambridge: Cambridge University Press, 1994).

19. Joyeeta Gupta, *Our Simmering Planet: What to Do about Global Warming?* (London: Zed Books, 2001), 75–76.

20. For a detailed discussion of the negotiating process, see Oberthür and Ott, *The Kyoto Protocol*.

21. For a more detailed analysis of these elements, see Michael Grubb, Christian Vrolijk, and Duncan Brack, *The Kyoto Protocol: A Guide and Assessment* (London: Royal Institute of International Affairs, 1999); and Oberthür and Ott, *The Kyoto Protocol*. For a more critical review, see David G. Victor, *The Collapse of the Kyoto Protocol and the Struggle to Slow Global Warming* (Princeton: Princeton University Press, 2001).

22. Oberthür and Ott, *The Kyoto Protocol*, 165–186.

23. Climate Change Secretariat, *A Guide to the Climate Change Convention and Its Kyoto Protocol: Preliminary Version* (Bonn: FCCC Secretariat, 2002), http://unfccc.int/resource/process/guideprocess-p.pdf.

24. FCCC, *Kyoto Protocol Mechanisms* (Bonn: FCCC Secretariat, 2003), http://unfccc.int/issues/mechanisms.html.

25. FCCC, *CDM Statistics* (Bonn: FCC Secretariat, 2009), http://cdm.unfccc.int/Statistics/index.html.

26. Davis A. Wirth, "The Sixth Session (Part Two) and the Seventh Session of the Conference of the Parties to the Framework Convention on Climate Change," *American Journal of International Law* 96, no. 3 (2002): 648–660.

27. Global Environment Facility, "Status Report on the Climate Change Funds as of March 4, 2008" document no. GEF/LDCF.SCCF.4/Inf.2, March 20, 2008.

28. Jon Birger Skjærseth and Jørgen Wettestad, *EU Emissions Trading* (Aldershot, UK: Ashgate, 2008). There were several smaller-scale experiments with emissions trading prior to the European system, and today there are several other markets being developed in other jurisdictions, including at the subnational level; see Michele M. Betsill and Matthew Hoffman, "The Evolution of Emissions Trading Systems for Greenhouse Gases" (paper presented at the annual meeting of the International Studies Association, March 26–29, 2008).

29. Peter Stoett, "Canada, Kyoto, and the Conservatives: Thinking/Moving Ahead," in *Changing Climates in North American Politics: Institutions, Policy Making and Multilevel Governance,* ed. H. Selin and S. D. VanDeveer (Cambridge: MIT Press, 2009).

30. Yves Tiberghien and Miranda A. Schreurs, "High Noon in Japan: Embedded Symbolism and Post-2001 Kyoto Protocol Politics," *Global Environmental Politics* 7, no. 4 (2007): 70–91.

31. See Edward Miles, Arild Underdal, Steinar Andresen, Jørgen Wettestad, Jon B. Skjærseth, and Elaine Carlin, *Environmental Regime Effectiveness: Confronting Theory with Evidence* (Cambridge: MIT Press, 2001); David G. Victor, Kal Raustiala, and Eugene B. Skolnikoff, eds., *The Implementation and Effectiveness of International Environmental Commitments* (Cambridge: MIT Press, 1998); Oran R. Young, ed., *The Effectiveness of International Environmental Regimes: Causal Connections and Behavioral Mechanisms* (Cambridge: MIT Press, 1999).

32. Edith Brown Weiss and Harold K. Jacobson, eds., *Engaging Countries: Strengthening Compliance with International Environmental Accords* (Cambridge: MIT Press, 1998), 4–5.

33. Victor, *Collapse of the Kyoto Protocol,* 112–113.

34. Grubb et al., *Kyoto Protocol,* 81; Matthew Paterson, *Global Warming and Global Politics* (London: Routledge, 1996), 69.

35. FCCC Secretariat, "Rising Industrialized Country Emissions Underscore Urgent Need for Political Action on Climate Change at Poznan Meeting," press release, Bonn, November 17, 2008, http://unfccc.int/files/press/news_room/press_releases_and_advisories/application/pdf/081117_ghg_press_release.pdf.

36. Marvin S. Soroos, "Global Climate Change and the Futility of the Kyoto Process," *Global Environmental Politics* 1, no. 2 (2001): 1–9.

37. Victor, Raustiala, and Skolnikoff, eds., *Implementation and Effectiveness of International Environmental Commitments,* 7.

38. EPA, *Inventory of U.S. Greenhouse Gas Emissions and Sinks: 1990–1999* (Washington, D.C.: Environmental Protection Agency, 2001).

39. Gabriela Kütting, *Environment, Society and International Relations: Towards More Effective International Environmental Agreements* (London: Routledge, 2000), 36.

40. IPCC, "Policies, Instruments and Co-operative Arrangements," in *Climate Change 2007: Mitigation of Climate Change,* Contribution of Working Group III to the Fourth Assessment Report of the IPCC (Cambridge: Cambridge University Press, 2007), 776. The current carbon dioxide concentration in the atmosphere is 383 parts per million.

41. Oran R. Young, *The Institutional Dimensions of Environmental Change: Fit, Interplay and Scale* (Cambridge: MIT Press, 2002), 31.

42. Arild Underdal, "One Question, Two Answers," in *Environmental Regime Effectiveness: Confronting Theory with Evidence,* ed. Edward L. Miles, Arild Underdal, Steinar Andresen, Jørgen Wettestad, Jon. B. Skjærseth, and Elaine M. Carlin (Cambridge: MIT Press, 2002), 5 (emphasis in original).

43. Michele M. Betsill, "The United States and the Evolution of International Climate Change Norms," in *Climate Change and American Foreign Policy,* ed. P. G. Harris (New York: St. Martin's, 2000), 205–224; Oberthür and Ott, *The Kyoto Protocol,* 287–300; Hermann E. Ott, *The Kyoto Protocol to the UN Framework Convention on Climate Change: Finished and Unfinished Business* (Wuppertal, Germany: Wuppertal Institute for Climate, Environment and Energy, 1999).

44. Harriet Bulkeley and Susanne C. Moser, "Responding to Climate Change: Governance and Social Action beyond Kyoto," *Global Environmental Politics* 7, no. 2 (2007): 1–10.
45. George W. Bush, quoted in "Clear Skies Initiative: Executive Summary," White House press release, February 14, 2002, http://georgewbush-whitehouse.archives.gov/news/releases/2002/02/clearskies.html.
46. Bonizella Biagini, *Confronting Climate Change: Economic Priorities and Climate Protection in Developing Countries* (Washington, D.C.: National Environmental Trust, 2000); William Chandler, Roberto Schaeffer, Zhou Dadi, P. R. Shukla, Fernando Tudela, Ogunlade Davidson, and Alpan-Atamer Sema, *Climate Change Mitigation in Developing Countries: Brazil, China, India, Mexico, South Africa, and Turkey* (Arlington, Va.: Pew Center on Climate Change, 2002).
47. Ans Kolk, "Developments in Corporate Responses to Climate Change in the Past Decade," in *Climate Change, Sustainable Development and Risk: An Economic and Business View*, ed. B. Hansjurgens and R. Antes (New York, Physica Publishers, 2008); David L. Levy and Ans Kolk, "Strategic Responses to Global Climate Change: Conflicting Pressures on Multinationals in the Oil Industry," *Business and Politics* 4, no. 3 (2002): 275–399.
48. Eileen Claussen, "Solving the Climate Equation: Mandatory and Practical Steps for Real Reductions" (remarks to Alliant Energy conference, Madison, Wisconsin, April 15, 2003), www.pewclimate.org/press_room/speech_transcripts/speech_april15.cfm.
49. Michele M. Betsill and Harriet Bulkeley, "Cities and the Multilevel Governance of Global Climate Change," *Global Governance* 12, no. 2 (2006): 141–159; Barry G. Rabe, "Beyond Kyoto: Climate Change Policy in Multilevel Governance Systems," *Governance–An International Journal of Policy and Administration* 20, no. 3 (2007): 423–444; Henrik Selin and Stacy D. VanDeveer, "North American Climate Governance: Policy Making and Institutions in the Multilevel Greenhouse," in *Changing Climates in North American Politics*, ed. Selin and VanDeveer.
50. ICLEI, Cities for Climate Protection (CCP), www.iclei.org/index.php?id=800; see also Harriet Bulkeley and Michele M. Betsill, *Cities and Climate Change: Urban Sustainability and Global Environmental Governance* (London: Routledge, 2003); Harriet Bulkeley and Kristine Kern, "Local Government and the Governing of Climate Change in Germany and the UK," *Urban Studies* 43, no. 12 (2006): 2237–2259.
51. Barry G. Rabe, "States on Steroids: The Intergovernmental Odyssey of American Climate Policy," *Review of Policy Research* 25, no. 2 (2008): 105–128.
52. Asia-Pacific Partnership on Clean Development and Climate, "About the Asia-Pacific Partnership on Clean Development and Climate," www.asiapacificpartnership.org/about.aspx.
53. More than 40,000 individuals representing governments, media, and nongovernmental organizations were accredited to attend the meeting, and thousands more descended on Copenhagen to participate in public protests. One hundred fifteen heads of state assembled for the high-level segment in the closing days of the meeting. Tomilola "Tomi" Akanle et al., "Summary of the Copenhagen Climate Change Conference: 7–19 2009," *Earth Negotiations Bulletin* 12, no. 459 (2009), www.iisd.ca/download/pdf/enb12459e.pdf.
54. Michele M. Betsill and Harriet Bulkeley, "Transnational Networks and Global Environmental Governance: The Cities for Climate Protection Program," *International Studies Quarterly* 48, no. 2 (2004): 471–493; Philipp Pattberg and Johannes Stripple, "Beyond the Public and Private Divide: Remapping Transnational Climate Governance in the 21st Century," *International Environmental Agreements: Politics, Law and Economics* 8, no. 4 (2008): 367–388; Henrik Selin and Stacy VanDeveer, "Canadian-U.S. Environmental Cooperation: Climate Change Networks and Regional Action," *American Review of Canadian Studies* (Summer 2004): 353–378.

7

Global Politics and Policy of Hazardous Chemicals

Henrik Selin

The chemicals regime, designed to mitigate environmental and human health problems caused by hazardous chemicals, is one of the oldest environmental regimes.[1] Chemicals management concerns fundamental issues of how societies apply pesticides for food production and public health protection against vector-borne diseases, use industrial chemicals to produce countless goods from satellites to cell phones, and target emissions of combustion and production processes. There is no precise figure for chemical use worldwide, but it may be approximately 500 million metric tons yearly. While some chemicals are manufactured in volumes of millions of metric tons per year, most are produced in quantities of fewer than 1,000 metric tons annually. Global chemical sales are worth approximately $2 trillion, constituting roughly 10 percent of all trade. Asia (mainly Japan, China, and India) is the leading chemical-producing region in monetary terms, followed by the European Union (EU) and the United States.[2]

The first multilateral instrument addressing hazardous chemicals may have been the St. Petersburg Declaration from 1868. This agreement, which is part of humanitarian law, banned the use of "fulminating or inflammable substances" in military projectiles weighing less than 400 grams.[3] A few discrete actions to limit workers' exposure to hazardous substances, including lead and white phosphorus, were taken by the International Labour Organization (ILO) starting in 1919. After the end of World War II, states, intergovernmental organizations (IGOs), and nongovernmental organizations (NGOs) began expanding the chemicals regime based on broader environmental and human health concerns. Continuing central political debates concern how to design and fund multilevel governance systems across global, regional, national, and local scales, and how to regulate and manage risks under conditions of scientific uncertainty.

At the World Summit on Sustainable Development (WSSD) in Johannesburg in 2002, states adopted several policy goals on hazardous chemicals.[4] Among others, they agreed that chemicals worldwide should be "used and produced in ways that lead to the minimization of significant adverse effects on human health and the environment" no later than the year 2020. Many chemicals also pose significant waste problems, both on their own and as components in discarded goods. Consequently, governments at the WSSD stressed the importance of sustainable consumption and production and set the goal to "prevent and minimize waste and maximize reuse, recycling and use of environmentally friendly alternative materials." Societies are, however, still a long way from realizing these policy goals agreed to at the WSSD, which remain important sustainable development issues on a global scale.

Many international environmental regimes are structured around a framework convention outlining general policy goals. These framework conventions are then followed by subsequent protocols that spell out more detailed controls and requirements. The ozone regime, the biodiversity regime, and the climate change regime, among others, all follow this structure. In contrast, the chemicals regime is structured around four main, independent multilateral agreements addressing overlapping policy issues. This includes separate agreements on persistent organic pollutants (POPs), which are a category of particularly toxic chemicals that remain in the environment for a long time. Furthermore, concentrations of POPs build up in individuals over time (this is called bioaccumulation) and increase as they are moved up food webs through consumption (called biomagnification). The four main chemicals treaties are:

- The 1989 Basel Convention on the Control of Transboundary Movements of Hazardous Wastes and Their Disposal (regulating international shipments and generation of hazardous wastes);
- The 1998 Rotterdam Convention on the Prior Informed Consent Procedure for Certain Hazardous Chemicals and Pesticides in International Trade (defining procedures managing exports and imports of hazardous chemicals);
- The 1998 Protocol on Persistent Organic Pollutants to the Convention on Long-Range Transboundary Air Pollution (CLRTAP) (controlling production, use, disposal, and release of POPs); and
- The 2001 Stockholm Convention on Persistent Organic Pollutants (regulating production, use, trade, disposal, and release of POPs).

Under the chemicals regime, collaborative political and scientific efforts, including the development of the four major treaties, have established controls of the full life cycle of production, use, trade, and disposal of a limited number of industrial chemicals and pesticides, as well as emission controls on by-products of production and combustion processes. Treaties also contain mechanisms to assess and regulate additional chemicals, increase and harmonize information about commercial and discarded chemicals traded across national borders, and build regional and domestic management capacities. In addition, regime participants have established organizational structures to aid implementation of treaty commitments. Furthermore, the fact that many of the same countries, IGOs, and NGOs collaborate on similar sets of chemicals under multiple treaties creates specific challenges in ensuring the effectiveness of the chemicals regime.

This chapter examines the creation and implementation of the chemicals regime. The next section gives a brief introduction to the challenges of managing hazardous chemicals. This is followed by an examination of the creation and implementation of the main chemical treaties, including their roles in life-cycle management. This is continued by a discussion about four critical governance challenges for improving environmental and human health protection, focusing on treaty ratification and implementation, risk assessments and controls, management capacity and awareness, and the generation of hazardous substances and waste. Next, the importance of developing more proactive and precautionary approaches to assessing and regulating hazardous chemicals is discussed, noting the role of the EU as a policy leader on these issues. The chapter ends with a few concluding remarks on the future of multilevel chemical governance.

Managing Hazardous Chemicals

The famous DuPont slogan "Better Things for Better Living . . . Through Chemistry" from the 1930s captured early optimism in the "chemicals revolution" as chemical production has increased steadily since World War II.[5] Modern societies routinely use many tens of thousands of chemicals in varying quantities. Most of these are not classified as dangerous and provide numerous benefits, but societies' reliance on a multitude of chemicals also poses significant environmental and human health risks. Hazardous chemicals are released through normal use of pesticides, common industrial and manufacturing practices involving the use of industrial chemicals, combustion processes, leakages from a large number of wastes, and industrial and household accidents. Policymakers and regulators are tasked to develop and implement socially appropriate chemical policies in the face of a host of scientific uncertainties. Regulatory decisions routinely must be made on the basis of limited scientific information in situations of competing political and economic interests.

Many problems are related to the persistence, toxicity, bioaccumulation, and biomagnification characteristics of chemicals. The more persistent a substance is, the longer it remains in the environment before it is biodegraded. Persistence per se is not dangerous, but there is cause for concern if a substance exhibits other undesirable qualities with respect to toxicity, bioaccumulation, and biomagnification. Common concerns about toxic substances include their ability to cause cancer, act as endocrine disrupters, and hinder human development in early developmental stages. Through bioaccumulation, hazardous substances may build up in fatty tissues of organisms over time. Hazardous substances that have bioaccumulated in organisms at a lower trophic level can also be passed up food webs in a process known as biomagnification. As a result, species (including humans) at the top of food webs have higher concentrations of many hazardous substances in their bodies than species lower down the same food web.

With her book *Silent Spring*, published in 1962, Rachel Carson drew attention to the indiscriminate use of DDT (dichlorodiphenyl trichloroethane) and other similar pesticides. Nevertheless, as many as three million people may still be hospitalized every year as a result of pesticide poisoning, resulting in close to 300,000 deaths, with 99 percent of these cases occurring in developing countries.[6] Many industrial chemicals, including PCBs (polychlorinated biphenyls) and by-products such as dioxins and furans, are also major environmental pollutants and dangerous to human health. This has been evident in major disasters in, for example, Yusho, Japan in 1962 (PCBs), Seveso, Italy in 1976 (dioxins), and Bhopal, India in 1984 (methyl isocyanate gas). More recently since the opening of a chemical park with twenty-five industries in Wuli Village in eastern China in 1992, Wuli has become one of possibly several hundreds of Chinese "cancer villages," with a rapid surge in cancer-related illnesses and deaths.[7]

Emissions of many hazardous chemicals can travel long distances from their point of origin, predominantly through the atmosphere. Global wind current patterns carry emissions from the tropics toward the poles in what has been described as a series of "grasshopper" movements, in which compounds volatilize and condense with seasonal temperature changes at mid-latitudes as they move toward the polar regions. This causes contamination problems in remote parts of Antarctica and the Arctic where there is no local chemical use.[8] Another way in which hazardous chemicals may reach countries where they are not (any longer) in use is through the so-called circle of poison. This refers to the process by which a hazardous pesticide that has been banned for use in one country is still lawfully produced and exported, then it is used in agricultural production in another country, and then it returns to the exporting country in the form of residues in imported vegetables, fruits, and other food products.[9]

Discarded chemicals and waste products containing hazardous substances can cause critical waste problems. For example, toxic chemicals dumped in Love Canal in upstate New York between the 1930s and the 1950s leaked through to buildings built on the old dump site. This caused high rates of birth defects, miscarriages, and liver cancer and an elevated incidence of seizure-inducing nerve disease in children.[10] Hazardous substances also leak from the unsafe handling of rapidly growing levels of electronic wastes (e-wastes; for example, old refrigerators, televisions, computers, and media players). Much e-waste is shipped legally and illegally from industrialized countries to developing countries where workers in recycling and disposal businesses are exposed to significant risks. One policy advocate working to stop the e-waste trade from the United States to China noted: "You know, it's a hell of a choice between poverty and poison. We should never make people make that choice."[11]

The Chemicals Regime

Under the chemicals regime, states, IGOs, and NGOs have developed four major treaties covering overlapping policy issues: the 1989 Basel Convention; the 1998 Rotterdam Convention; the 1998 CLRTAP POPs Protocol; and the 2001 Stockholm Convention. Table 7-1 contains a brief

Table 7-1 Summary of the Four Main Treaties on Chemicals Management

Basel Convention *Adopted in 1989* *Entry into force in 1992* *172 parties as of 2009*	• Regulates the transboundary movement and disposal of hazardous wastes; covers chemicals if they fall under the treaty's definition of hazardous wastes • Hazardous waste transfers subject to a prior informed consent (PIC) procedure in which a party must give explicit consent before a shipment can take place • Exports of hazardous wastes prohibited to Antarctica and to parties that have taken domestic measures banning imports • Exports of hazardous wastes to nonparties must be subject to an agreement at least as stringent as the Basel Convention • 1995 Ban Amendment (not yet in force) bans export of hazardous wastes from parties that are members of the OECD or the EU, as well as Liechtenstein, to other parties • 1999 Protocol on Liability and Compensation (not yet in force) identifies financial responsibilities in cases of waste transfer accidents • Basel Convention regional centers address management and capacity building issues
Rotterdam Convention *Adopted in 1998* *Entry into force in 2004* *131 parties as of 2009*	• Regulates international trade in commercial chemicals using a PIC scheme • Forty chemicals covered by 2009 • Exporting party must receive prior consent from importing party before the export of a regulated chemical can take place • Parties are obligated to notify the Secretariat when they ban or severely restrict a chemical • Contains mechanism for evaluating and regulating additional chemicals under the treaty
CLRTAP POPs Protocol *Adopted in 1998* *Entry into force in 2003* *29 parties as of 2009*	• Regulates production and use of persistent organic pollutants (POPs) pesticides and industrial chemicals listed in the treaty • Outlines provisions regarding environmentally sound transport and disposal of POPs pesticides and industrial chemicals, consistent with Basel Convention • Sets technical standards for controlling emissions of unintentionally produced by-product POPs • Sixteen chemicals regulated by 2009 • Contains mechanism for evaluating and regulating additional chemicals under the treaty
Stockholm Convention *Adopted in 2001* *Entry into force in 2004* *168 parties as of 2009*	• Regulates production, use, trade, and disposal of POPs pesticides and industrial chemicals listed under the treaty • Sets technical standards for controlling release of by-product POPs listed under the treaty

(continued)

- Parties required to ban import or export of controlled POPs except for purposes of environmentally sound disposal
- Contains mechanism for evaluating and regulating additional chemicals under the treaty
- Twenty-one chemicals regulated by 2009
- Stockholm Convention regional centers support capacity building and implementation

---

description of the major components of each of these agreements. Although the treaties are formally independent, their creation and implementation are legally, politically, and practically connected in multiple ways because of their overlapping controls and membership. Other regional treaties covering shared seas, lakes, and rivers also address hazardous substances and wastes. The adoption of many of these global and regional treaties was possible only after long assessments and contentious negotiations on which specific chemicals were to be controlled, how they were to be regulated, and what kind of management structures were to be created.

Basel Convention on the Control of Transboundary Movements of Hazardous Wastes and Their Disposal

The Basel Convention targets the generation and trade in hazardous wastes, which have increased sharply since the 1960s. Industrialized, high-consumption societies generate the vast majority of hazardous waste, and most waste trade takes place between industrialized countries. However, it was primarily the growing North-South waste trade between industrialized and developing countries that led to the creation of the Basel Convention, and many continuing controversies surrounding the development and implementation of the Basel Convention also involve North-South politics and disagreements. Several high-profile cases of firms located in industrialized countries illegally dumping hazardous wastes in developing countries in the 1980s drew much attention to issues of hazardous wastes.

Many early cases of illegal North-South waste disposal involved the dumping of banned and discarded chemicals as well as wastes that contained high levels of hazardous substances.[12] This is not just a historical problem, however. For example, during the night of August 19, 2006, the Greek-owned and Panama-registered vessel *Probo Koala*, chartered by the Dutch-based company Trafigura, dumped near the city of Abidjan in the Ivory Coast an estimated 500 tons of "a fuming mix of petrochemicals and caustic soda" originating in the Mediterranean region.[13] This illegal dumping resulted in several deaths and severe health problems for tens of thousands of people living close to the dump site. In response to this environmental and human health disaster, local civil servants were fired, and the Dutch firm agreed to pay $200 million in compensation to the Ivorian government amid allegations that the dumped waste was not cleaned up quickly enough to prevent the exposure of local residents to great risks.[14]

The Organization for Economic Cooperation and Development (OECD) in the 1980s developed guidelines for managing the trade in hazardous wastes among its members that included a prior informed consent (PIC) mechanism. Under this PIC scheme, an exporting country needed permission from the importing country prior to shipment. The Governing Council of the United Nations Environment Programme (UNEP) in 1987 adopted the first global standards, the Cairo Guidelines and Principles for the Environmentally Sound Management of Hazardous Wastes. These guidelines introduced a voluntary PIC scheme for all transnational transport of hazardous wastes. Many developing countries and environmental NGOs, however, did not think that these guidelines were stringent enough, and pushed for mandatory controls. The resultant Basel Convention, which seeks to minimize the generation of hazardous wastes and to control and reduce their transboundary movement, was adopted in 1989.[15]

The Basel Convention prohibits exports of hazardous wastes to Antarctica and to parties that have taken domestic measures to ban imports. Waste transfers to other parties are subject to a mandatory PIC procedure; a party cannot export hazardous wastes to another party without the prior consent of the importing state. Waste exports to nonparties are prohibited unless subject to an agreement between the exporter and importer that is at least as stringent as the requirements under the Basel Convention. Discarded chemicals are covered by the treaty if they meet definitions of "hazardous." Wastes are designated as hazardous if they come from certain waste streams (for example, wood preserving chemicals), belong to certain categories (for example, mercury compounds), or exhibit certain characteristics (for example, are poisonous or toxic). The Basel Convention relies on domestic legislation to define "waste," which typically includes substances or objects that are intended or are required to be disposed of by law.

Many developing countries, supported by NGOs such as Greenpeace and the Basel Action Network as well as the Nordic countries, were disappointed that the Basel Convention did not include a North-South trade ban. Following some minor policy developments in the early 1990s, the ban supporters convinced the parties in 1995 to adopt the Ban Amendment despite opposition from some industrialized countries and industry organizations.[16] The Ban Amendment prohibits the export of hazardous wastes for final disposal and recycling from countries listed in Annex VII (members of the OECD and the EU as well as Liechtenstein) to all other parties (primarily developing countries). However, because of a desire by several industrialized and developing countries to maintain the economically valuable trade in hazardous wastes, the amendment has yet to enter into force. The Basel Action Network hosts a Ban Amendment "hall of shame" on its Web site to draw attention to countries and organizations opposing the Ban Amendment.[17]

The parties in 1999 adopted the Basel Protocol on Liability and Compensation based on developing country concerns that they lack sufficient funds and technologies for coping with illegal dumping or accidental spills. This agreement identifies who is financially responsible in the event of an incident during the transboundary movement of hazardous wastes. The Basel Protocol on Liability and Compensation, however, has not yet entered into force. In addition, Basel Convention parties have created several regional centers; as of 2009, fourteen regional centers had been set up in Latin and South America, Africa, Asia, and Europe.[18] The regional centers focus on issues such as training for customs officials, staff of local municipalities, and other stakeholders in identifying and handling hazardous wastes; promoting environmentally sound waste management in each region; facilitating the transfer of cleaner production technologies to their member countries; aiding in data collection and reporting to the Basel Secretariat; and engaging in public education and awareness raising.

Rotterdam Convention on Prior Informed Consent

The Rotterdam Convention regulates the international trade in commercial chemicals. Despite the fact that most industrial chemicals and pesticides are traded among industrialized countries, it was the largely unregulated North-South trade that acted as the main stimulus for the development of international regulations (similar to the hazardous wastes case). North-South politics is also shaping much of the implementation of the Rotterdam Convention. Concerns about the mishandling and unsafe use of pesticides were validated by emerging scientific data on high levels of pesticide poisonings among farmers and other handlers, particularly in many developing countries. Even if some risks have been reduced, many problems remain. A study of one hospital in the Indian state of Andhra Pradesh found that approximately 8,000 patients were admitted with severe pesticide poisoning between 1997 and 2002—more than 20 percent (more than 1,800 people) died as a result of this exposure.[19]

Developing countries, working with IGOs, led attempts to regulate the trade in hazardous chemicals.[20] In 1977, the UNEP Governing Council adopted a resolution stating that hazardous chemicals should not be exported without the knowledge and consent of the importing country. In 1982, a UN General Assembly resolution called for the establishment of a PIC procedure governing the export of domestically banned chemicals. The OECD Council in 1984 adopted a recommendation that member states implement a PIC system for trade in chemicals. In 1985, the United Nations Food and Agriculture Organization (FAO) adopted a Code of Conduct on the Distribution and Use of Pesticides. Similarly, the UNEP Governing Council in 1987 adopted the London Guidelines for the Exchange of Information on Chemicals in International Trade. None of these initiatives, however, included formal PIC requirements, which were rejected by major chemical-producing countries and industry organizations.

Nevertheless, as pressure from developing countries increased, the UNEP Governing Council in 1989 adopted the Amended London Guidelines to create a first voluntary global PIC procedure. The same year, the FAO Council made similar changes to the FAO Code of Conduct. The PIC scheme was managed jointly by the FAO in Rome for pesticides and by UNEP Chemicals in Geneva for industrial chemicals. The PIC procedure operated in three sequential steps. First, the government of an exporting country on behalf of a domestic firm had to notify an importing country of any control action that it had taken to ban or severely restrict a chemical for human health or environmental reasons. Second, the government of the importing country was obligated to respond to this notification, stating whether or not it accepted the import. Third, the exporting country government was responsible for communicating this response to the firm seeking export permission and for ensuring that the company complied with the decision of the importing country's government.

In the 1990s, many developing countries and environmental NGOs, as well as a growing number of industrialized countries, argued that it was necessary to convert the voluntary PIC scheme into a treaty to further strengthen environmental and human health protection from hazardous chemicals. Chapter 19 of Agenda 21—adopted at the United Nations Conference on Environment and Development in 1992—called on states to create a legally binding PIC instrument. The FAO Council (in 1994) and the UNEP Governing Council (in 1995) approved the start of treaty negotiations, which began in 1996. The Rotterdam Convention was adopted in 1998. During the negotiations, some developing countries proposed a ban on the export of nationally prohibited chemicals from OECD countries (in other words, from industrialized countries) to other countries (to developing countries), but such a ban received little support. As a result, the negotiations largely transformed the voluntary procedure into a similar legally binding mechanism.[21]

Consequently, the Rotterdam Convention stipulates that a party through the national government can respond in three different ways after having received a formal request to accept the importation of a particular chemical on the PIC list. First, the government can declare that it consents to receive the import of the chemical and any other shipments within the same calendar year; second, the government may reject the request; or third, the government may consent to the import, but only if specific conditions are met by the exporting party. The government of the potential exporter must abide by any decision made by the potentially receiving country. The Secretariat, which is divided between UNEP Chemicals and FAO, acts as facilitator and communicator throughout this process and distributes all the responses between the parties. National governments are responsible for communicating all information and decisions from the other party to all relevant domestic firms.

A party that has domestically banned or severely restricted the use of a chemical is required to notify the Secretariat about this action.[22] When the Secretariat has received notification from parties from at least two different geographical regions—or a single party that is a developing country or a country with an economy in transition experiencing domestic problems—it forwards all this information to the Chemical Review Committee, made up of thirty-one government-appointed experts. Based on its assessment according to procedures outlined in the Rotterdam Convention, the Chemical Review Committee submits a recommendation to the conference of the party making the final decision regarding inclusion on the PIC list by consensus.[23] However, the PIC procedure applies only to Rotterdam Convention parties, and the PIC scheme is not mandatory in trade with nonparties. As such, a party may avoid PIC requirements by using a nonparty country as an intermediary, which does not formally violate any treaty rules.[24]

The PIC procedure operated on a voluntary basis between 1998 and 2006, two years after the Rotterdam Convention entered into force in 2004. Originally, twenty-seven substances were listed in the Rotterdam Convention based on their inclusion under the voluntary procedure. Following multiple additions, the Rotterdam Convention as of 2009 covered forty chemicals. Several of these chemicals are also covered by the two POPs agreements. Many other substances are lined up for review by the Chemical Review Committee. There are, however, indications that the PIC procedure is becoming increasingly politicized.[25] For example, the addition of two substances—chrysotile asbestos and endosulfan—has been blocked by a minority of parties despite recommendations for listing by the Chemical Review Committee. This suggests that future debates on at least some economically important chemicals will be contentious, as the same chemical is also assessed and discussed under more than one treaty.

CLRTAP Protocol on Persistent Organic Pollutants

The CLRTAP POPs Protocol was the first international treaty that specifically targeted POPs as a category of particularly hazardous chemicals. It is a regional agreement that operates under the auspices of the United Nations Economic Commission for Europe (UNECE), which comprises North America and Europe as far east as Russia and Kazakhstan. The CLRTAP POPs Protocol was born out of a concern with the long-range atmospheric transport of emissions to northern latitudes, and in particular the Arctic. Reports by the Arctic Monitoring and Assessment Programme (AMAP) state that the majority of many chemicals found in the Arctic environment and wildlife come from distant sources. AMAP assessments have also concluded that subtle health effects are occurring in human population in the Arctic as a result of chemical contamination of food sources. Reports express the greatest concern for fetal and neonatal development risks.[26]

CLRTAP actions on POPs are closely linked with scientific and political concerns about Arctic pollution, as identified by the AMAP assessments. The Arctic was long viewed as too remote from industrial societies to be at serious environmental risk. Studies in the 1980s, however, established three interrelated issues: systematic long-range atmospheric transport of emissions to the Arctic, high environmental contamination levels throughout the Arctic region, and actual and potential environmental and human health implications.[27] It is now recognized that the sensitive Arctic environment functions as a window to the future, as the first to react to environmental hazards. Indigenous peoples' exposure to POPs is mainly a result of dietary intake of contaminated wildlife. Taking into consideration the physiological and nutritional benefits of traditional food systems, as well as their social and cultural importance, dietary recommendations have been developed by public health authorities to minimize POPs exposures.

In Canada more than any other country, the POPs issue became integrated with more general scientific and political concerns about Arctic environmental contamination and health risks of indigenous peoples.[28] Indigenous peoples' rights became a hot political issue in Canada in the 1980s, and the inclusion of indigenous groups in scientific and political work on chemicals increased the sensitivity and status of the chemicals issue in Canada. Indigenous groups were active participants in Canadian and circumpolar research programs, producing results that prompted Canada and other Arctic countries to push for international policy responses. Indigenous groups also lobbied successfully for the Arctic region to be recognized as particularly sensitive to POPs. As a result of their lobbying, the preamble of the CLRTAP POPs Protocol gives special recognition to the exposed situation of the Arctic environment and human populations.

CLRTAP POPs assessments in the 1990s identified a set of priority POPs that was found extensively in the environment throughout the northern hemisphere. Following the start of treaty negotiations in 1997, the CLRTAP POPs Protocol was adopted in 1998 (the same year the Rotterdam Convention was finalized). It entered into force in 2003. The CLRTAP POPs Protocol is designed to reduce the release and long-range transport of POPs emissions. Chemicals are divided into three annexes. The production and use of pesticides and industrial chemicals listed in Annex I are banned. Annex II lists pesticides and industrial chemicals for which some uses are permitted. Parties are required to apply best available techniques and best environmental practices for controlling emissions of POPs by-products listed in Annex III. The CLRTAP POPs Protocol also mandates the environmentally sound transport and disposal of POPs, consistent with the Basel Convention.

Following a long assessment process and tough political negotiations where countries disagreed on which chemicals should be included and how they should be regulated, sixteen POPs were originally covered by the CLRTAP POPs Protocol.[29] Similar to the Rotterdam Convention, the CLRTAP POPs Protocol contains a mechanism for reviewing additional chemicals (as well as granted exemptions of chemicals already regulated). By 2009, twelve more chemicals were subject to assessments; many of these chemicals were put forward by the EU or individual European countries. It is likely that these and other chemicals will be regulated by the CLRTAP POPs Protocol in the future, even if only after protracted negotiations. Furthermore, there are many legal, political, regulatory, and management overlaps between the CLRTAP POPs Protocol and the Stockholm Convention, as parties expand the list of regulated chemicals simultaneously under the two agreements.

Stockholm Convention on Persistent Organic Pollutants

The Stockholm Convention, which was adopted in 2001 and entered into force in 2004, seeks to protect human health and the environment from POPs. In comparison with the CLRTAP POPs Protocol, which includes only countries located in the Northern Hemisphere, the Stockholm Convention also includes developing countries often facing difficult management problems. For example, the government of Tanzania reported in a 2005 national assessment that POPs waste management facilities, including those for storage, transportation, and disposal, were basically nonexistent. Staff working with equipment possibly containing PCBs did not use any kind of protective gear. Tanzanian government officials also noted that spillage of transformer oil likely to contain PCBs was frequent and that waste transformer oil was usually kept in open areas or was burned or discharged "haphazardly into the environment."[30]

In 1995, the UNEP Governing Council called for global assessments of twelve POPs (known as "the dirty dozen").[31] Based on these assessments, treaty negotiations began only three months after the adoption of the Rotterdam Convention. Many issues during the assessments and negotiations concerned the situations of developing countries with respect to domestic chemicals use and local management problems. The International POPs Elimination Network, a network founded in 1998 of more than four hundred NGOs, lobbied in support of the global elimination of POPs. The same Arctic indigenous peoples' groups that influenced the CLRTAP negotiations again advocated for controls on the long-range transport of POPs to mitigate human health risks from POPs.[32] Their concerns are also reflected in the preamble of Stockholm Convention, which recognizes that Arctic ecosystems and indigenous communities are particularly at risk because of the biomagnification of POPs and the contamination of traditional foods.

The Stockholm Convention covers all of the dirty dozen, which by the time the treaty was adopted were also regulated by the CLRTAP POPs Protocol. The Stockholm Convention divides POPs into three annexes (like the CLRTAP POPs agreement). The production and use of pesticides and industrial chemicals listed in Annex A are generally prohibited, but parties may apply for country-specific and time-limited exemptions. Annex B lists pesticides and industrial chemicals subject to restrictions where only specified uses are allowed. Annex C lists by-products regulated through the setting of best available techniques and best environmental practices for their minimization. The import and export of pesticides and industrial chemicals are permitted only for substances subject to use exemptions or for the environmentally sound management and disposal of discarded chemicals. On these issues, the

Stockholm Convention is designed to be legally compatiable with the Rotterdam Convention and the Basel Convention.

The Stockholm Convention includes a mechanism for evaluating and regulating additional chemicals, similar to the one under CLRTAP. Evaluations are carried out by a POPs Review Committee consisting of thirty-one government-designated experts. Any party can submit a proposal to regulate a new chemical. The POPs Review Committee examines the proposal according to a set of scientific criteria.[33] The POPs Review Committee conducts a management evaluation, which is submitted to the next conference of the parties making the regulatory decision. In 2009 the parties added nine more POPs to the Stockholm Convention, making a total of twenty-one POPs that are covered by the treaty. More are likely to be added in the future, but as under other treaties these discussions may be controversial on chemicals that are still in extensive production and use and are therefore economically important to some firms and countries.

One divisive issue concerns DDT. In 1955 the World Health Organization (WHO) launched the Global Malaria Eradication Programme, which relied heavily on the use of DDT. Because eradication turned out to be difficult in large parts of the tropics, the WHO in 1992 shifted focus from eradication to management through the Global Malaria Control Strategy. Building on this effort, the WHO, UNICEF (United Nations Children's Fund), the UN Development Programme, and the World Bank in 1998 launched the Roll Back Malaria Partnership to fight malaria. Consistent with the Roll Back Malaria Partnership, the Stockholm Convention allows for the use of DDT for disease vector control against malaria mosquitoes. The WHO estimates that more than one million people die from malaria every year, with 90 percent of these deaths occurring in Africa.[34] If indirect effects of the disease (such as malaria-induced anemia, maternal pathology, and hypoglycemia) are taken into consideration, as many as three million people may die annually from malaria in Africa alone.[35]

By 2009 sixteen countries had issued formal notifications for continuing DDT production, use, or both.[36] However, other countries also use DDT. Three countries were known to still produce DDT by the early 2000s. India was the largest producer, followed by China and South Korea. Although the use of DDT has been politically and scientifically controversial since the 1960s and it is becoming clear that malaria-carrying mosquitoes in many areas are developing resistance to DDT, parties in 2009 concluded that countries that still use DDT for disease vector control may need to continue doing so until better, cost-effective, local alternatives become available. Thus, issues relating to the ongoing use of DDT and the advancement of alternatives will be discussed under the Stockholm Convention in the future. These discussions are further linked to DDT debates under the CLRTAP POPs Protocol and by the WHO, as the global community works to support both chemical and nonchemical alternatives to DDT use.

Parties are working to establish a monitoring program to evaluate implementation progress. Countries are also developing technical guidelines for the environmentally sound management of stockpiles and wastes. This work is carried out in collaboration with the Basel Convention Secretariat, as Basel Convention parties are simultaneously formulating technical guidance documents on handling POPs wastes. Parties are furthermore establishing guidelines for best available techniques and best environmental practices for controlling by-products. In 2009, parties established eight Stockholm Convention regional centers to aid capacity building.[37] Of these, two were already operating as Basel Convention regional centers. Other Stockholm Convention regional centers, which may or may not also be Basel Convention regional centers, are likely to be created in the future. In addition, parties are engaged in discussion with the Rotterdam Convention Secretariat on issues relating to the legal and illegal trade in POPs.

Other Regional Treaties

In addition to the four main treaties, many other agreements address region-specific problems with hazardous chemicals. Under the UNEP's Regional Seas Programme, thirteen action plans targeting pollution problems were created by 2009; they involved more than 140 countries.[38] There are also several other regional seas agreements. For example, the 1972 Convention for the Prevention of Marine Pollution by Dumping from Ships and Aircraft and the 1974 Convention for the Prevention of Marine Pollution from Land-based Sources cover the Northeast Atlantic. In 1974, the Convention on the Protection of the Marine Environment of the Baltic Sea Area was adopted. Canada and the United States signed the Great Lakes Water Quality Agreement in 1972. Updated in 1978, Canada and the United States pledged the virtual elimination of discharges of all persistent and toxic substances. Many shared rivers are also covered by pollution-related legal provisions.

In addition, several regional waste trade treaties operate alongside the global agreements. Reacting to the lack of a North-South trade ban under the Basel Convention, African countries negotiated the 1991 Convention on the Ban of the Import into Africa and the Control of Transboundary Movements and Management of Hazardous Wastes within Africa, the so-called Bamako Convention. The Bamako Convention seeks to prevent dumping of hazardous wastes in Africa by banning the import of hazardous wastes from any outside country. Additional regional measures initiated by developing countries linked to the Basel Convention include the adoption of the Lomé IV Convention 1991. This treaty bans the trade in hazardous wastes between members of the EU and former colonies in Asia, the Caribbean, and the Pacific. The 1995 Waigani Convention bans the import of hazardous and radioactive wastes to the island countries in the South Pacific region.

Multilevel Challenges for Improved Management

Multilevel governance, involving many levels of social organization and policy forums, is needed to manage hazardous chemicals. To improve coordination and implementation of treaties and other policy instruments, governments adopted the Strategic Approach to International Chemicals

Management (SAICM) in 2006. SAICM outlines a plan of action to fulfill the 2020 goal formulated at the WSSD by, for example, increasing information on hazardous chemicals and enhancing domestic enforcement and management capabilities. Although some important progress can be noted, several multilevel governance issues are critical for improved management of hazardous chemicals. Four governance challenges in particular stand out: enhance treaty ratification and implementation, expand risk assessments and controls, improve management capacity and raise awareness, and minimize generation of hazardous chemicals and waste.[39]

First, enhanced ratification of the main treaties would increase the number of states that take on formal responsibilities to address problems with hazardous chemicals as well as strengthen the treaties' position under international law. Although more than 170 countries have ratified the Basel Convention, the United States—one of the world's largest exporters of discarded goods and e-waste for recycling and disposal—is not a party. The Basel Convention Ban Amendment also has not received sufficient ratification to enter into force, while even fewer countries have ratified the Protocol on Liability and Compensation. More than 160 countries are parties to the Stockholm Convention, while 130 countries have ratified the Rotterdam Convention, however, the United States and many developing countries are not parties to either of these agreements. The United States is also not a party to the CLRTAP POPs Protocol.

As recognized by SAICM, better coordination of the development of regulations and management programs across treaties would make it easier for parties to more than one agreement to meet their commitments. Each treaty is administered by a secretariat providing legal and managerial support. There would be obvious benefits if cooperation between different secretariats and conferences of parties were closer; this could not only help save limited resources, for example, but could also make it easier to improve regulatory and management consistency across agreements and minimize (if not eliminate) the possibility that important issues fall into regulatory or administrative "cracks" between treaties.[40] This, however, is made difficult by the fact that there is uneven membership across treaties—which is another reason to promote increased ratification to minimize membership gaps (there will, of course, always be differences in membership between regional and global treaties).

Regimes that use a monitoring mechanism and periodically review parties' compliance records and publish compliance reports tend to perform better than those that do not. Although it is rare to find strong monitoring and compliance programs in environmental regimes, states have sometimes been willing to accept such mechanisms to improve transparency and treaty implementation. Statements and actions by many industrialized and developing countries under all major chemical treaties, however, demonstrate that so far they have been unwilling to cede sovereignty and give much independent authority to secretariats and regional centers on data collection and monitoring, and even less so to give them the right to initiate political or legal actions against a state that does not fulfill its treaty obligations and commitments.[41] Continuing debates on these issues, which are central to regime effectiveness, are set to be contentious.

Second, parties need to expand risk assessments and regulations using appropriate treaty mechanisms. For most commercial chemicals, there are only scant data on emissions, environmental dispersion, and ecosystem and human health effects. This hinders the ability to conduct adequate risk assessments. Nevertheless, several at least partially unregulated POP-like chemicals have already been detected in remote areas. Many pesticides that may not meet the POPs criteria still fall under WHO class I (extremely and highly hazardous) and class II (moderately hazardous) of toxic pesticides that are strong candidates for inclusion under the Rotterdam Convention. There is also a need to increase participation by IGOs such as FAO, WHO, and the United Nations Institute for Training and Research on integrated pest management. This involves using a combination of environmentally friendly methods designed to significantly reduce and, where possible, eliminate the use of pesticides.

Despite important legal and organizational developments since the 1990s, hazardous waste management, including management of e-wastes, also suffers from important shortcomings. To better manage hazardous wastes, it is necessary to tackle the growing generation of hazardous wastes, develop more extensive management guidelines for more waste streams, and continue to minimize human health and environmental risks from the transport, reuse, recycling, and disposal of hazardous wastes. There is also a need to monitor the transport and disposal of hazardous wastes and stimulate improvements in management techniques and technology. To that end, the Basel Convention in collaboration with other treaties can be an important mechanism for monitoring waste transport and disposal, setting sound management standards, raising awareness and increasing training, and disseminating the latest waste disposal techniques and technology.

Third, better connections among global, regional, national, and local efforts to build management capacities are required to improve environmental and human health protection. In particular, many developing countries have difficulties ensuring safe handling of hazardous chemicals and wastes in the face of both legal and illegal trade. The release of by-products also poses a major management challenge. Working with treaty secretariats, the Basel Convention and Stockholm Convention regional centers can aid information generation and sharing, human training and public education, technology transfer, and building of domestic management capabilities for emission prevention and remediation of contaminated sites. The regional centers could also operate more ambitious mechanisms for monitoring and enforcement, which would increase opportunities to enhance compliance across major treaties.

Many management issues are linked with critical disagreements over funding issues between developing and industrialized countries common in much North-South politics. While developing countries are pushing for mandatory financing mechanisms to support domestic capacity building, the chemical treaties only contain provisions for voluntary contributions because of resistance from industrialized countries to compulsory financial contributions. Effective operation of the Basel Convention and Stockholm Convention regional centers also requires human, financial, and technical resources, and acquiring such resources from the Global Environment Facility, Northern donor countries, and developing countries in each region continues to be a problem. Nevertheless, multilevel management of hazardous chemicals and wastes in many regions of the world would benefit from stronger financial support of the regional centers.

Better management of hazardous substances and wastes also requires raising public awareness. This involves expanding education about environmental and human health hazards among local populations exposed to chemical risks, and better training for handlers and users of hazardous chemicals in selecting safe control strategies based on which specific substances are used and their intended purpose. Key issues for improving local handling include the appropriate application of pesticides for public health purposes targeting vector-borne diseases, effective use of pesticides in agriculture, and the wearing of proper and workable protective gear such as overalls, boots, hats, gloves, and face masks. Increasing awareness about integrated pest management approaches would also help reduce risks from pesticides. Similar education efforts are also needed for many workers handling industrial chemicals and heavy metals.

Fourth, efforts to minimize the generation of hazardous substances and wastes should be intensified, and such efforts need to involve expanded collaboration between public and private sector actors. The most effective way to protect human health and the environment from risks posed by hazardous substances is, of course, to avoid producing and using them in the first place. However, global political efforts to date have focused on the management of known or suspected hazardous substances rather than finding effective ways to reduce demand. The same is true for hazardous wastes: although the best long-term hazardous waste management policy is waste reduction, parties under the Basel Convention have focused largely on developing controls on the transboundary movement of wastes and technical guidelines for waste management. They have paid very little attention to treaty stipulations on waste minimization.

Rapidly increasing global levels of e-waste—and the development of associated policy and management efforts—further connect the management of hazardous substances and hazardous wastes. The introduction of market-based incentives and different kinds of supportive governmental regulations making firms increasingly responsible for their products—including electronic and electrical goods—throughout their entire life cycles could play a significant role in stimulating more effective waste management and minimization efforts. E-waste is also attracting more attention under the Basel Convention. The Mobile Phone Partnership Initiative, for example, was launched in 2002. Through this initiative, leading multinational mobile phone manufacturers committed to recover used mobile phones. This and other global corporate responsibility efforts remain limited in scope, however; and they are entirely voluntary.

More Proactive and Precautionary Approaches Needed

Although many legal and political actions on hazardous chemicals have been taken since the 1960s, more fundamental changes are ultimately needed to effectively minimize the risks posed by hazardous chemicals.[42] Typical regulatory frameworks have assumed that a particular chemical is harmless until scientifically proven dangerous. Furthermore, the burden of proof is on regulators to prove that a chemical is not safe rather than on producers or sellers to produce data demonstrating that a substance is not likely to cause adverse environmental and human health effects. Regulators also have often been unable to restrict or ban a chemical until harm has been documented. Such a reactionary approach has resulted in much damage as it has often taken authorities a long time to regulate hazardous substances (if any regulations have been introduced at all).[43] It also creates few incentives for phasing out the use of hazardous substances and focusing on waste minimization.

In designing a more proactive approach for managing chemical risks, the EU has taken on a regional and global leadership role since the early 2000s. EU actions aim to better incorporate a precautionary approach to risk assessment and regulation. A regulatory approach based on the precautionary principle is defined in Principle 15 of the 1992 Rio Declaration on Environment and Development. It is based on the idea that "where there are threats of serious or irreversible damage, lack of full scientific certainty shall not be used as a reason for postponing cost-effective measures to prevent environmental degradation." In the early 1970s, Germany and Sweden were among the first countries to introduce the precautionary principle in domestic legislation and regulation of risk, and EU treaties since the 1990s state that precaution should guide all EU environmental policy making.[44] The EU is often a strong supporter of the precautionary principle under different chemical treaties.

To implement a more precaution-based approach, the EU in 2007 adopted the Registration, Evaluation, Authorisation and Restriction of Chemicals (REACH) regulation.[45] REACH puts the burden on producers and sellers to provide authorities with risk assessment data to show that there is no cause for concern. Commercial handling of any chemical covered by REACH is prohibited unless it is proven to be harmless, adequately controlled, or that societal benefits outweigh costs. Instead of waiting until harm can be documented, REACH targets chemicals that are CMR (carcinogenetic, mutagenic, and toxic for reproduction), PBT (persistent, biological accumulating, and toxic), or vPvB (very persistent and very biological accumulating) based on these characteristics. All such chemicals have to be individually authorized before they can be sold on the EU market. REACH also contains guidelines for substituting less harmful substances or nonchemical alternatives for hazardous chemicals.

The EU is also leading in banning the use of specific hazardous sub-stances in electronic goods and improving management of e-wastes.[46] EU directives adopted in the early 2000s on the restriction of the use of certain hazardous substances in electrical and electronic equipment (RoHS) and waste electrical and electronic equipment (WEEE) are designed to phase out several hazardous substances, including mercury and brominated flame-retardants, from most kinds of electronic goods and increase recycling of such goods. European consumers are required to return a large number of dis-carded electronic` goods to the producers (rather than municipal authorities); the producers are responsible for establishing management systems for their safe recycling, reprocessing, and disposal. In this respect, the WEEE and RoHS directives—together with the REACH regulation—increase producer responsibility and take a more preventive approach to managing hazardous substances and e-wastes.

As the EU pushes for the adoption of similar policy ideas and approaches in international forums, REACH, RoHS, and WEEE are attracting the atten-tion of politicians and policymakers around the globe.[47] Major producers and users of chemicals and electronic goods such as China, Japan, and South Korea are adopting similar policies and regulations, in effect helping to raise global standards. A growing number of U.S. states, including California, are also copying European policy ideas. EU leadership in these policy developments is engendering changes in the private sector that help drive changes worldwide. Firms that are adjusting to comply with new product and waste standards in the EU and elsewhere are changing their production processes and also the goods they sell in other markets. Similarly, advocacy organizations use policy innovations regarding chemicals and wastes in other jurisdictions to advocate for similar regulatory changes within their own jurisdictions.

Still a Long Way to Go

Improving global, regional, national, and local management of hazard-ous chemicals remains a critical sustainable development issue. Working together under SAICM and multiple treaties, states, IGOs, and NGOs over several decades have taken important implementation steps toward enhanced environmental and human health protection from hazardous chemicals. This includes the creation of expanded legal and organizational structures for risk assessment and policymaking, leading to controls on a small set of hazardous chemicals (the same chemicals are often regulated under several treaties). The establishment of regional centers under the Basel Convention and the Stock-holm Convention seeking to better connect global policymaking with regional and domestic management needs represents an important step forward to address a host of capacity building issues and challenges.

Although there is a need to expand treaty ratification and controls, there have been—and continue to be—notable disagreements among states over the possible regulation of specific chemicals, expressed during meetings of chemical review committees and conferences of the parties. Furthermore, many countries protective of national sovereignty remain opposed to the establishment of strong and independent treaty mechanisms for monitoring and enforcement, even though many studies show that such mechanisms are important to treaty implementation and effectiveness. While all countries struggle to reduce environmental and human health risks of hazardous substances, many developing countries face particular problems. Building management capacities and increasing awareness in developing countries are consequently important environmental justice and human security issues.

As hazardous substances continue to cause significant environmental and human health harm all over the world, the adoption of more proactive and precautionary policies and management approaches is needed. This includes strengthening and expanding existing controls, shifting data generation tasks away from public authorities to firms and industry organizations, and increasing producer responsibilities for phasing out the use of hazardous substances and managing waste streams. While some industry organizations and firms express great concern about the financial burden of recent EU policies, one study estimated that the total cost for implementing REACH over eleven years would be less than 0.1 percent of the industry's sales revenues.[48] Any short-term costs from strengthening controls should also, of course, be judged against the many environmental and human health benefits of better management.

Precaution-based regulations furthermore reduce long-term financial costs of cleaning up contaminated areas. The U.S. Comprehensive Environmental Response, Compensation, and Liability Act (the so-called Superfund Act) was passed in 1980 to deal with contaminated sites like Love Canal. In 2007 the Comprehensive Environmental Response, Compensation, and Liability Act listed 275 priority chemicals and heavy metals commonly found at contaminated sites. The U.S. government spent $1.2 billion on Superfund projects in 2006 alone.[49] Although 24 sites were completed in 2007, there are more than 1,250 unaddressed sites on the Superfund national priority list (and more will be added). Global cleanup costs are unknown but enormous—and they will keep on growing as long as societies continue to allow large-scale production and use of hazardous substances coupled with inadequate waste management capabilities.

Finally, societies need to rethink the way that chemicals are made. Green chemistry—the utilization of principles that reduce or eliminate the use or generation of hazardous substances in the design, manufacture, and application of chemicals—is an effort to incorporate environment and health concerns into the development of chemicals.[50] To target the chemical problem at its source, green chemistry proponents stress the importance of synthesizing substances with little or no environmental toxicity. Chemicals should also be designed so that at the end of their functional lives they break down into innocuous degradation products, as part of a broader effort to create a more sustainable use of materials.[51] Public and private sector acceptance of green chemistry is a critical step toward ensuring chemical safety. Both voluntary industry-led programs and mandates set by governments can play important roles in switching to a world where hazardous chemicals pose less risk.

Notes

1. Henrik Selin, *Global Governance of Hazardous Chemicals: Challenges of Multilevel Management* (Cambridge: MIT Press, 2010).
2. European Chemical Industry Council, "Facts and Figures: The European Chemical Industry in a Worldwide Perspective," December 2006, 2; *OECD Environmental Outlook for the Chemicals Industry* (Paris: OECD, 2001), 10.
3. Malcolm Shaw, "The United Nations Convention on Prohibitions or Restrictions on the Use of Certain Conventional Weapons, 1981," *Review of International Studies* 9, no. 1 (1983): 109–121.
4. WSSD, *Plan of Implementation of the World Summit on Sustainable Development* (Johannesburg: World Summit on Sustainable Development, 2002), paras. 22 and 23.
5. John Kenly Smith, "DuPont: The Enlightened Organization," n.d., http://www2.dupont.com/Heritage/en_US/Enlightened/Enlightened.html.
6. C. H. Srinivas Rao et al., "Pesticide Poisoning in South India: Opportunities for Prevention and Improved Medical Treatment," *Tropical Medicine and International Health* 10, no. 6 (2005): 581–588.
7. Jean-François Tremblay, "China's Cancer Villages," *Chemical & Engineering News* 85, no. 44 (2007): 18–21.
8. Frank Wania and Donald Mackay, "Tracking the Distribution of Persistent Organic Pollutants: Control Strategies for These Contaminants Will Require a Better Understanding of How They Move around the Globe," *Environmental Science and Technology* 30, no. 9 (1996): 390A–396A.
9. Richard W. Emory, "Probing the Protections in the Rotterdam Convention on Prior Informed Consent," *Colorado Journal of International Environmental Law and Policy* 12 (2001): 47–69.
10. Judith A. Layzer, *The Environmental Case: Translating Values into Policy*, 2nd ed. (Washington, D.C.: CQ Press, 2006), 54–80.
11. "The Electronic Wasteland," *60 Minutes*, November 10, 2008.
12. Kate O'Neill, *Waste Trading among Rich Nations: Building a New Theory of Environmental Regulation* (Cambridge: MIT Press, 2000); Jennifer Clapp, *Toxic Exports: The Transfer of Hazardous Wastes from Rich to Poor Countries* (Ithaca: Cornell University Press, 2001).
13. "Cote D'Ivoire: Dumping Ground," *Africa Research Bulletin: Economic, Financial and Technical Series* 43, no. 9 (2006): 17107–17108.
14. Lisa Bryant, "Ivory Coast Still Suffering from Toxic Spill," Voice of America, December 15, 2007.
15. Katharina Kummer, *International Management of Hazardous Wastes: The Basel Convention and Related Legal Rules* (Oxford: Clarendon Press, 1995); Berndt H. Brikell, "Negotiating the International Waste Trade: A Discourse Analysis" (PhD dissertation, Örebro University, 2000), *Örebro Studies in Political Science* 2.
16. Jonathan Krueger, *International Trade and the Basel Convention* (London: Royal Institute for International Affairs, 1999), 32–35; Brikell, "Negotiating the International Waste Trade," 181–189.
17. See Basel Action Network, "Hall of Shame," www.ban.org/main/hall_of_shame.html.
18. The fourteen regional centers are located in Argentina, China, Egypt, El Salvador, Indonesia, Iran, Nigeria, Senegal, Slovak Republic, Russian Federation, Samoa, South Africa, Trinidad & Tobago, and Uruguay.
19. Srinivas Rao et al., "Pesticide Poisoning in South India."
20. Robert L. Paarlberg, "Managing Pesticide Use in Developing Countries," in *Institutions for the Earth: Sources of Effective International Environmental Protection*, ed. Peter

M. Haas, Robert O. Keohane, and Marc A. Levy (Cambridge: MIT Press, 1993), 309–350; David G. Victor, "Learning by Doing in the Nonbinding International Regime to Manage Trade in Hazardous Chemicals and Pesticides," in *The Implementation and Effectiveness of International Environmental Commitments: Theory and Practice,* ed. David G. Victor, Kal Raustiala, and Eugene B. Skolnikoff (Cambridge: MIT Press, 1998), 221–281; Marc Pallemaerts, *Toxics and Transnational Law: International and European Regulation of Toxic Substances as Legal Symbolism* (Portland, Ore.: Hart Publishing, 2003).

21. Katharina Kummer, "Prior Informed Consent for Chemicals in International Trade: The 1998 Rotterdam Convention," *Review of European Community & International Environmental Law* 8, no. 3 (1999): 323–330.

22. The Rotterdam Convention explicitly excludes, among others, pharmaceuticals, narcotic drugs, food additives, radioactive materials, wastes, chemical weapons, and chemicals used in research (Article 3). Some of these are covered by other treaties, whereas others were left out because it is believed that they are not likely to be subject to any significant environmental releases.

23. Kummer, "Prior Informed Consent for Chemicals in International Trade"; Pia M. Kohler, "Science, PIC and POPs: Negotiating the Membership of Chemical Review Committees under the Stockholm and Rotterdam Conventions," *Review of European Community & International Environmental Law* 15, no. 3 (2006): 293–303.

24. Ted L. McDorman, "The Rotterdam Convention on the Prior Informed Consent Procedure for Certain Hazardous Chemicals and Pesticides in International Trade: Some Legal Notes," *Review of European Community & International Environmental Law* 13, no. 2 (2004): 187–200.

25. "Summary of the Third Meeting of the Conference of the Parties to the Rotterdam Convention on the Prior Informed Consent Procedure for Certain Hazardous Chemicals and Pesticides in International Trade: 9–13 October 2006," *Earth Negotiations Bulletin,* October 16, 2006.

26. AMAP, "Arctic Pollution 2009" (Oslo: Arctic Monitoring and Assessment Programme, 2009).

27. Henrik Selin, "Regional POPs Policy: The UNECE/CLRTAP POPs Agreement," in *Northern Lights Against POPs: Combatting Toxic Threats in the Arctic,* ed. D. L. Downie and T. Fenge (Montreal: McGill-Queen's University Press, 2003), 111–132.

28. Henrik Selin and Noelle Eckley Selin, "Indigenous Peoples in International Environmental Cooperation: Arctic Management of Hazardous Substances," *Review of European Community & International Environmental Law* 17, no. 1 (2008): 72–83.

29. Selin, "Regional POPs Policy."

30. Government of Tanzania National Implementation Plan (NIP) for the Stockholm Convention on Persistent Organic Pollutants (POPs), 2005.

31. David Leonard Downie, "Global POPs Policy: The 2001 Stockholm Convention on Persistent Organic Pollutants," in *Northern Lights against POPs.*

32. Sheila Watt-Cloutier, "The Inuit Journey towards a POPs-Free World," in *Northern Lights Against POPs;* Selin and Selin, "Indigenous Peoples in International Environmental Cooperation."

33. Annex D contains basic scientific criteria for persistence, bioaccumulation, potential for long-range transport, and adverse effects that a substance has to meet in order to qualify as a POP.

34. World Health Organization, "Malaria," January 2009, www.who.int/mediacentre/factsheets/fs094/en/index.html.

35. Joel Breman, Martin S. Alilio, and Anne Mills, "Conquering the Intolerable Burden of Malaria: What's New, What's Needed: A Summary," *American Journal of Tropical Medicine and Hygiene* 71, no. 2 (2004): 1–15 (supplement).

36. The sixteen countries were Botswana, China, Ethiopia, India, Madagascar, Marshall Islands, Mauritius, Morocco, Mozambique, Myanmar, Senegal, South Africa, Swaziland, Uganda, Yemen, and Zambia.

37. The eight Stockholm Convention regional centers approved by COP-4 are located in Brazil, China (also a Basel Convention regional center), Czech Republic, Kuwait, Mexico, Panama, Spain, and Uruguay (also a Basel Convention regional center).

38. The thirteen action plans are: 1) Mediterranean Action Plan (adopted in 1975); 2) Red Sea and Gulf of Aden Action Plan (adopted in 1976, revised in 1982); 3) Kuwait Action Plan (adopted in 1978); 4) West and Central African Action Plan (adopted in 1981); 5) Caribbean Action Plan (adopted in 1981); 6) East Asian Seas Action Plan (adopted in 1981); 7) South-East Pacific Action Plan (adopted in 1981); 8) South Pacific Action Plan (adopted in 1982); 9) Eastern Africa Action Plan (adopted in 1985); 10) Black Sea Strategic Action Plan (adopted in 1993); 11) North-West Pacific Action Plan (adopted in 1994); 12) South Asian Seas Action Plan (adopted in 1995); 13) North-East Pacific Action Plan (adopted in 2001).

39. Henrik Selin, *Managing Hazardous Chemicals: Long-Range Challenges*, The Pardee Papers, no. 5 (Boston: Boston University, The Frederick S. Pardee Center for the Study of the Longer-Range Future, 2009).

40. David L. Downie, Jonathan Krueger, and Henrik Selin, "Global Policy for Hazardous Chemicals," in *The Global Environment: Institutions, Law and Policy*, ed. R. S. Axelrod, D. L. Downie, and N. J. Vig (Washington, D.C.: CQ Press, 2005), 125–145.

41. Selin, *Global Governance of Hazardous Chemicals*.

42. Selin, *Managing Hazardous Chemicals*.

43. P. Harremöes et al., *The Precautionary Principle in the 20th Century* (London: Earthscan, 2002).

44. Noelle Eckley and Henrik Selin, "All Talk, Little Action: Precaution and European Chemicals Regulation," *Journal of European Public Policy* 11, no. 1 (2004): 78–105.

45. Henrik Selin, "Coalition Politics and Chemicals Management in a Regulatory Ambitious Europe," *Global Environmental Politics* 7, no. 3 (2007): 63–93.

46. Henrik Selin and Stacy D. VanDeveer, "Raising Global Standards: Hazardous Substances and E-Waste Management in the European Union," *Environment* 48, no. 10 (2006): 6–18.

47. Henrik Selin, "Transatlantic Politics of Chemicals Management," in *Enlarging Transatlantic Environment and Energy Politics: Comparative and International Perspectives*, ed. M. A. Schreurs, H. Selin, and S. D. VanDeveer (Ashgate, UK: Aldershot, 2009).

48. Frank Ackerman and Rachel Massey, *The True Costs of REACH* (Copenhagen: Nordic Council of Ministers, 2004).

49. Kara Sissell, "Hinchey Renews Push for Corporate Superfund Tax," *Chemical Week* 169, no. 15 (2007): 35.

50. Paul T. Anastas and John C. Warner, *Green Chemistry: Theory and Practice* (Oxford: Oxford University Press, 1998).

51. Kenneth Geiser, *Materials Matter: Towards a Sustainable Materials Policy* (Cambridge: MIT Press, 2001).

8

Economic Integration and Environmental Protection

Daniel C. Esty

No mention was made of the word *environment* in the original General Agreement on Tariffs and Trade (GATT)—the central pillar of the international trading system—put into place just after World War II. At that time, no one saw much connection between trade liberalization and environmental protection. For the next forty years, trade and environmental policymakers pursued their respective agendas on parallel tracks that rarely, if ever, intersected. In recent years, however, trade and environmental policy making have increasingly appeared to be linked, and the two realms have often seemed to collide. Environmental advocates have come to fear that freer trade means increased pollution and resource depletion. Free traders worry that protectionism in the guise of environmental policy will obstruct efforts to open markets and integrate economies around the world.

This chapter explores the trade-environment relationship. It traces the origins of the tension between trade liberalization and environmental protection and identifies the events that triggered the conflict. It examines why environmentalists worry about free trade and why free traders worry about unrestrained environmentalism. Ways to reconcile trade and environmental goals are highlighted, and the North American Free Trade Agreement (NAFTA) is explored as a model in this regard.

Freer trade and economic integration more broadly offer the promise of improved social welfare, as do programs aimed at pollution abatement and improved natural resource management. While not theoretically inconsistent, in practice, these goals are often not in perfect alignment. Only through concerted policy attention and efforts to overcome conflicts and tensions can both aims be addressed simultaneously and progress be made toward sustainable development.

Origins of the Trade and Environment "Conflict"

The trade and environmental policy agendas have been driven together by a number of factors. First, environmental issues have taken on increased salience in the last several decades. Climate change, drinking-water safety, chemical exposures, and other pollution problems have become a major focus of public concern. Trying to accommodate new issues on the public agenda often creates strain.[1] The precise focus of the public's environmental interest varies from nation to nation, and particularly from industrialized to developing countries. But almost every corner of the world has experienced a marked increase in the attention paid to environmental problems in recent years.

Second, recognition of a set of inherently global pollution and resource problems has further propelled environmental issues up the international policy agenda. Scientific advances have transformed the environmental policy landscape. From the threat of global climate change arising from a buildup of greenhouse gases in the atmosphere to ozone layer destruction, from emissions of chlorofluorocarbons (CFCs) and other related chemicals to the depletion of fisheries in most of the world's oceans, overexploitation of the "global commons" has added to the sense of priority given to the environment on the international scene.[2]

Third, a policy focus on "sustainable development" has led to an appreciation that environmental progress is easier to achieve under conditions of prosperity—and long-term economic growth depends on careful stewardship of the natural environment. The 1992 Earth Summit in Rio de Janeiro (formally known as the United Nations Conference on Environment and Development) highlighted the link between economic development and environmental protection generally, and trade and the environment more specifically.[3] When a new round of global trade negotiations was launched in 2001 in Doha, the trade-environment relationship was made an explicit element of the negotiating agenda.[4] The 2002 World Summit on Sustainable Development in Johannesburg consolidated the focus on the trade-environment linkage.

Finally, economic integration has also helped to transform environmental protection from a clearly domestic, highly localized issue into one of inherently international scope. In a world of liberalized trade, where the competition for market share is global, the stringency of environmental regulations in each nation, state, or province becomes an important determinant of the competitiveness of the enterprises located within that territory. Thus, for example, while hazardous waste management requirements have long been viewed as simply a function of local pollution control priorities and risk tolerances, today these policy choices are understood to have important consequences for the production costs of the enterprises that must meet the standards.[5] Concerns about competitiveness transform even the most local environmental issue into a matter of international significance. These worries take on added significance in the context of efforts to open markets and promote economic integration.

Triggering Events

Recent free trade initiatives and commitments to liberalized investment regimes have sharpened the trade-environment debate. President George H. W. Bush's 1989 announcement that he intended to negotiate a free trade agreement with Mexico first brought "trade and environment" issues to the fore. The prospect of a free flow of goods across the U.S.-Mexico border struck fear in the hearts of environmentalists. They worried that a trade agreement with Mexico might mean an expansion of the highly polluted "maquiladora" (duty-free) zone along the border, lowering U.S. environmental standards ("harmonized" to match lax Mexican regulatory requirements), or worse, a downward spiral in environmental standards on both sides of the border as industry claims of competitive disadvantage induced governments to relax their environmental rules. Pressed by Congress, the Bush administration committed to a program of environmental efforts in parallel with the trade negotiations with Mexico and Canada that led to NAFTA.[6]

While NAFTA set the environmental pot on the trade fire, the decision of a GATT dispute resolution panel in the 1991 "tuna/dolphin" case caused a simmering issue to boil over. The GATT declared the U.S. law requiring an embargo on Mexican tuna that were caught in nets that killed dolphins to be illegal under the rules of international trade.[7] U.S. environmentalists saw the decision as an affront to American environmental "sovereignty."[8] How could an obscure set of trade experts sitting in Geneva judge a U.S. law (the Marine Mammal Protection Act) to be unacceptable? The environmental community saw this decision as proof that, in a conflict between trade and environmental goals, the trade liberalization principles would trump environmental values. Outraged environmentalists decried "GATTzilla" and began a campaign to "green" trade law and policymaking.[9]

Interest in the trade and environment relationship has now widened and evolved. Protesters concerned about the effects of globalization, including the environmental impacts of economic integration, helped cause the collapse of the World Trade Organization (WTO) ministerial meeting in Seattle in 1999. Similar protests are now a fixture at almost every meeting of international economic officials. In fact, the push for further free trade agreements, including a Free Trade Area of the Americas and new commitments to multilateral trade liberalization through the WTO, has continued to make "trade and environment" a hot issue on the international agenda.[10]

Some success has been achieved in making trade and environmental policy making more mutually supportive.[11] For example, through the Dominican Republic–Central America–United States Free Trade Agreement (CAFTA-DR), the United States has initiated $20 million toward cooperative environmental projects in the region.[12] Policymakers have furthermore learned that they ignore the trade-environment link at some peril. For example, negotiations within the Organization for Economic Cooperation and Development (OECD) to establish a Multilateral Agreement on Investment (MAI) faltered in the face of environmentalists' outcries over the lack of attention to pollution control and resource management issues in the draft treaty.

Efforts to make trade and environmental policies more compatible continue to face significant obstacles. The trade and environmental communities have distinct goals, traditions, operating procedures, and even languages. The ultimate good for environmentalists—"protection"—sounds a lot like the consummate bad—"protectionism"—that free traders seek to avoid. In both terminology and substance, bringing these two worlds together continues to be a challenge.[13]

Core Environmental Concerns about Free Trade

Environmentalists worry that economic integration and more globalized markets will make environmental protection harder to achieve. Their concerns can be boiled down to a few key propositions.[14]

Expanded trade will cause environmental harm by promoting economic growth that, without environmental safeguards, will result in increased pollution and the unsustainable consumption of natural resources. Environmentalists who adhere to a traditional "limits to growth" perspective would reject the possibility that environmental safeguards might make trade liberalization environmentally acceptable. They see free trade inescapably resulting in environmentally damaging economic growth. Of course, many environmentalists today adhere to the "sustainable development" paradigm, which would accept the possibility that environmental improvements might arise from economic growth so long as pollution control and natural resource consumption issues are expressly addressed.[15] They also recognize that poverty leads to short-term decision making that is often environmentally harmful. Thus, to the extent that trade promotes growth and alleviates poverty, it can yield environmental benefits.

Many environmentalists fear that the "disciplines" to which countries bind themselves as part of a trade agreement will result in a loss of regulatory sovereignty. Specifically, they worry that the market access obligations and other trade principles designed to permit the free flow of imports and exports will override environmental policies and goals, resulting in the harmonization of environmental standards at or below baseline levels.[16] This outcome might arise, they believe, through negotiated commitments to common regulatory rules. Alternatively, they fear that a free trade zone might make it hard for high-standard countries to keep their strict environmental requirements in the face of industry claims of competitive disadvantage from producers in low-standard jurisdictions whose environmental compliance costs are lower.

Even where pollution does not spill across national borders, countries with lax environmental standards will have a competitive advantage in a global marketplace, putting pressures on countries with high environmental standards to reduce the rigor of their environmental requirements. Fear that the United States would be competitively disadvantaged in an integrated North American marketplace was the central trade and environment issue in NAFTA. Ross Perot's memorable suggestion that low labor costs and lax environmental standards in Mexico would result in a "giant sucking sound" of U.S. factories and jobs going down the drain to Mexico resonated broadly.[17] Similar concerns have been an issue in virtually all of the recent trade agreement ratification debates.[18]

Although there is little empirical evidence of companies moving to "pollution havens," academics continue to debate the seriousness of fears about a "race toward the bottom" in setting environmental standards.[19] Variations in the stringency of regulations are not necessarily a problem. Differences in environmental standards can be seen as an important component of comparative advantage. Indeed, the fact that countries have different levels of commitment to environmental protection—and thus different pollution control costs—makes gains from economic exchange and trade possible. Competitiveness pressures may also induce "regulatory competition" among jurisdictions as governments work to make their location attractive to industry. In some circumstances, these pressures will induce governments to provide services and regulate efficiently. Competition of this sort enhances social welfare.[20] But in other circumstances, competition among horizontally arrayed jurisdictions (national governments versus national governments) may precipitate a welfare-reducing cycle of weakening environmental commitments as political leaders seek to relax their environmental standards to attract investment and jobs.[21] In practice, governments rarely lower their environmental standards to improve their competitive position. They may, however, relax the enforcement of their standards or fail to raise standards to optimal levels for fear of exposing their industries to higher costs than foreign competitors face.[22]

The critical issue, therefore, is why environmental standards diverge. If the stringency of the rules varies because of differences in climate, weather, population density, risk preferences, level of development, or other "natural" factors, the variations in regulatory vigor should be considered legitimate and appropriate. Any competitive pressure created is simply the playing out of socially beneficial market forces. In contrast, divergent standards may also arise from regulatory authorities' failure to monitor fully the harms that spill across their borders into other jurisdictions. These spillovers may result in "externalizing" part of the costs of pollution control. In addition, regulatory "incapacity" may lead to suboptimal environmental standards or lax enforcement of environmental requirements. And special interest manipulation of the regulatory process or other distortions in environmental policy making may result in regulations that deviate from what would be the optimal environmental policies (what academics call "public choice" problems).

Underregulation that permits pollution to spill over into neighboring jurisdictions or into a global commons represents an unfair (and economically inefficient) basis on which to establish a competitive advantage. Likewise, suboptimal standards that arise from regulatory failures—including results driven by weak government performance and inadequate environmental decision making or outcomes manipulated by special interests through lobbying, campaign contributions, or outright corruption of public officials—break the promise of improved social welfare through interjurisdictional competition. And where competitors have selected, for whatever reason, suboptimal environmental policies, governments often respond strategically and set their standards with an eye on those adopted by their competition. In each of these circumstances, international cooperation in response to environmental challenges promises to improve policy outcomes. Insofar as trade negotiations generate the competitive pressures that trigger a "race toward the bottom," they also provide an occasion to advance the collective action required to avoid a welfare-reducing regulatory chill.

The likelihood of a "race" dynamic increases as economic integration deepens. If Jurisdiction A is a comparatively unimportant destination of Jurisdiction B's exports, or if Jurisdiction A is an insignificant international competitor, then differentiated environmental standards matter very little. B will be relatively unaffected by environmental policy choices in A. But if the level of interaction grows, so does B's exposure to "economic externalities" arising from suboptimal environmental policies in A. For example, in 1985 U.S. exports to China totaled $7 billion, and imports from China stood at $3 billion. In 2008 Chinese exports to the United States topped $337 billion, and U.S. exports to China amounted to $71 billion.[23] This extraordinary growth in U.S.-China trade makes U.S. industries much more sensitive to cost disadvantages that they suffer in relation to Chinese competitors—and will focus increasing attention on whether any such disadvantages that arise from environmental conditions are appropriate and legitimate.

If countries fail to carry out their international environmental obligations, trade restrictions may need to be used to limit "free riding." Yet the market-opening commitments made in the course of trade agreements may reduce the availability of trade measures as an environmental enforcement tool. Environmentalists fear that commitments to trade liberalization will limit the international community's leverage over countries that are refusing to sign on to or are not living up to international environmental agreements. This issue, prominent in the early 1990s, has returned to salience in the context of climate change as well as efforts to ensure that countries sign on to (and uphold) obligations to limit greenhouse gas emissions.

While recognizing the need to discipline free riders (those who are benefiting from but not paying for pollution control or shared resource management), trade officials argue that it is not appropriate to use trade measures as a way of achieving environmental goals. They reason that it is hard enough to keep markets open without trying to carry environmental burdens at the same time. Environmentalists respond that there are very few ways of exerting pressure in the international domain and that trade measures must be available as an enforcement tool.

The Free Trade Response

Free traders worry that the environmentalists' critiques of trade are misplaced and could result in the disruption of efforts to promote trade liberalization and to obtain the benefits promised by more open markets around the world. Trade advocates note, in particular, that trade and environmental policy goals can be made compatible. As the members of the World Trade Organization declared at the launch of the WTO in 1994:

> There should not be, nor need be, any policy contradiction between upholding and safeguarding an open, nondiscriminatory and equitable multilateral trading system on the one hand, and acting for the protection of the environment and promotion of sustainable development on the other.[24]

Free traders note that both trade liberalization and environmental protection efforts are aimed at promoting efficiency and reducing waste. They posit that, to the extent that environmental policies seem to be in tension with freer trade, the conflict generally arises from poorly constructed environmental policies rather than any inherently anti-environmental bias embedded in the trading system. Trade experts further observe that environmental policies that seek to internalize externalities through the application of the polluter-pays principle represent virtually no conflict with freer trade.[25]

Trade supporters also maintain that, as an empirical matter, as the wealth of the society increases, its spending on environmental protection almost always goes up. Thus they contend that environmentalists should support freer trade as a way of achieving economic growth and greater wealth, some part of which can be devoted to expanded pollution control and resource conservation programs. More dramatically, trade advocates observe that poverty is the source of a great many environmental harms. And indeed, poor people often make bad environmental choices because of the short-term time frame forced upon them. For example, those who lack modern conveniences must cut down nearby trees to cook their evening meal. They are unable to focus on the longer-term consequences of deforestation, such as soil erosion and pollution of nearby bodies of water.

Professors Gene M. Grossman and Alan B. Krueger have demonstrated that some environmental problems seem to worsen during the early stages of development, peak at a per capita gross domestic product of about $8,000, and improve as countries become wealthier beyond that point.[26] Some problems are so localized and pressing that even the poorest countries will be under pressure to address them as economic growth begins and incomes start to rise. Governments, for example, seek to provide drinking water to their people at even the lowest levels of development. Other problems appear to follow the inverted-U "Kuznets" curve that Grossman and Krueger hypothesize, rising in the initial stages of industrialization but falling as wealth increases. Local air pollution problems seem to fall into this category. But other environmental problems continue to worsen even as incomes rise.[27] For instance, greenhouse gas emissions may go up at a less rapid rate, but they do not fall even when high income levels are achieved. Other scholars have argued that the relationship between environmental harms and income is somewhat more complicated.[28]

A more nuanced understanding of the relationship between economic growth and environmental protection leads to the conclusion that trade can be a mechanism for advancing economic growth and social welfare, but this result is not guaranteed. Economic gains *can* permit resources to be made available for investments in environmental protection. But welfare losses from trade-exacerbated environmental harms could outweigh the benefits of freer trade. To maximize the chances of net welfare gains, environmental policy must evolve in tandem with commitments to trade liberalization.[29]

NAFTA—First Steps

The need to address environmental issues in the NAFTA context led to a commitment to a set of environmental negotiations alongside the trade negotiations—a "parallel track." These talks generated a joint U.S.-Mexican commitment to address pollution issues along their shared border. The "integrated border environmental plan" cataloged comprehensively for the first time the spectrum of environmental concerns arising along the 2,000-mile border between the two countries. The initiative also produced a game plan for addressing the issues identified and a set of priorities to be undertaken jointly by Mexican and U.S. environmental officials.

In addition to the border plan, the parallel track negotiations led to an Environmental Side Agreement to NAFTA. The Side Agreement, concluded during the Clinton administration, set up a "development bank" to promote environmental infrastructure investments along the U.S.-Mexico border and established a Commission for Environmental Cooperation (CEC) to oversee the environmental issues associated with closer trade links across North America.[30] The CEC provides a mechanism for facilitating cooperation among the NAFTA countries on the full range of environmental issues and resource challenges facing them. It serves as a forum for regular high-level meetings, provides an independent secretariat to report on significant environmental issues confronting the NAFTA parties, ensures that environmental enforcement remains a priority in all three countries, and offers opportunities for public participation in the development and implementation of environmental laws and programs in Mexico, the United States, and Canada.

In addition to the parallel track environmental negotiations, environmental officials were included, for the first time, in the trade negotiations themselves. EPA negotiators participated in several of the issue-specific working groups. A senior EPA official served on the high-level negotiating team of the U.S. Trade Representative (USTR). Likewise, nongovernmental organizations (NGOs), including environmental groups, were considered an important constituency in the course of the NAFTA debate—a role they had never played before. In addition, trade representative Carla Hills placed four environmental group leaders on her public advisory committees on various aspects of trade policymaking.[31]

Perhaps the most important procedural advance associated with NAFTA was the decision to undertake an environmental review of issues associated with freer trade across North America. This analysis helped to focus the negotiators on both large and small issues, ranging from the benefits of broadening Mexico's economic development beyond the maquiladora zone to finding ways to reduce the traffic jams (and resulting air pollution) caused by backups at customs in Texas, New Mexico, Arizona, and California. The value of this type of analysis is now widely recognized. In fact, the Clinton administration issued an executive order in 1999 requiring the USTR to carry out environmental reviews in advance of all future trade agreements.[32]

Substantive advances in the integration of environmental sensitivity into the trade system were also made in the course of the NAFTA process. The preamble to the agreement makes environmental considerations a central focus of the effort to promote freer trade. It calls on the parties to pursue their program of trade liberalization so as to promote "sustainable development" and to "strengthen the development and enforcement of environmental laws and regulations."[33]

The NAFTA parties further agreed that major environmental agreements with trade provisions should be given precedence if a conflict were to develop between the party's obligations under the environmental agreement and under NAFTA. Similarly, NAFTA makes clear in its chapter on "sanitary and phytosanitary" provisions that each party to the agreement retains an unrestricted right to set and maintain environmental health and safety standards at its own chosen level of protection. By clarifying that the NAFTA parties are free to make their own risk assessments and apply their own risk policies, NAFTA acknowledges that some legitimate national environmental policies will have impacts on trade but should still be permitted.

NAFTA's investment chapter also breaks new ground in addressing environmental issues.[34] Specifically, the investment provisions assure each country the right to adopt and enforce any pollution control or resource management measure it deems necessary to protect its environment. This language prevents trade commitments from trumping environmental policies and programs as long as the policies are based on scientific foundations and are not disguised barriers to trade. The treaty also contains a "pollution haven" proviso that declares that a NAFTA party cannot seek to attract investments by relaxing environmental standards or cutting back on enforcement. A structure of binding arbitration and the possibility of trade penalties being imposed for noncompliance back this provision.

NAFTA also establishes more environmentally sensitive dispute resolution procedures. Specifically, where environmental issues are in question in a trade dispute, the agreement provides procedures for convening a board of scientific or technical experts to advise the dispute settlement panel. It also forbids countries to take disputes out of NAFTA and into the WTO to obtain less environmentally protective ground rules.

The NAFTA efforts to make trade liberalization and environmental protection mutually compatible have generally worked quite well.[35] Fears of industrial migration to Mexico based on a promise of lax environmental standards have not been realized. Rather, NAFTA's broadly based program of environmental cooperation has greatly increased the focus on pollution control in Mexico. While many problems remain, and the attempt to finance new environmental projects on the U.S.-Mexico border has gotten off to a slow start, environmental conditions across large parts of Mexico are beginning to improve.

Some environmentalists remain concerned that environmental issues are still not being taken seriously in the trade context. In the 1997–1998 debate over "fast track" legislation to authorize negotiations to extend NAFTA to all of the Western Hemisphere, these complaints rang true. The Clinton administration proposals for a Free Trade Area of the Americas (FTAA), devoid of any environmental provisions, represented a significant step back from NAFTA. And, ironically, the president failed to win the trade negotiating authority he sought.

In 2002 the George W. Bush administration won approval for "trade promotion authority," the new name for "fast track authority." As part of the package approved by Congress, the Bush administration agreed to binding negotiating objectives related to the environment, including assurances that any new trade agreement would:

- require U.S. trading partners to enforce their own environmental laws
- promote the sale of U.S. environmental goods and services
- support environmental capacity building
- address governmental practices that threaten sustainable development
- strengthen consultative mechanisms aimed at enhancing implementation of environmental and human health protection standards
- include an environmental review consistent with the procedures established under the Clinton administration
- protect multilateral environmental agreements[36]

In addition, the recent U.S.-Jordanian, U.S.-Singaporean, U.S.-Chilean, U.S.-Moroccan, U.S.-Omanian, and CAFTA free trade agreements have included express environmental commitments.[37]

In all of these recent agreements, the NAFTA environmental provisions have provided a template. But none of the agreements includes a strong institutional structure such as that found in the U.S.-Mexico-Canada context. Of course, the NAFTA Side Agreement's Commission for Environmental Cooperation has not been an unmitigated success. The CEC has undertaken several studies designed to ensure that environmental considerations are factored into trade policy across North America. But the CEC has also faced pressure not to pursue its environmental goals too aggressively. The lack of clear political support has driven the CEC to back away from several controversial trade and environment issues, including questions about a Mexican cruise ship pier in Cozumel and efforts to address clear-cutting in the U.S. Northwest and British Columbia. Whether the CEC will mature into an effective mechanism for environmental coordination among the United States, Mexico, and Canada remains to be seen.[38]

The Broader Policy Response

The World Trade Organization (WTO), the international body set up in 1994 to implement the General Agreement on Tariffs and Trade (GATT) and to manage international trade relations, has come under considerable criticism for its lack of environmental sensitivity. Although the WTO has a Committee on Trade and the Environment (CTE), little substantive progress has been made toward the goal of more mutually supportive trade and environmental policies.

New disputes have increased the trade and environment tension. Notably, the European Union (EU) challenged U.S. efforts to block wine imports containing procymidone, an unregistered fungicide used on grapes.[39] The EU also challenged the U.S. Corporate Average Fuel Economy (CAFE) car mileage standards, arguing that this policy tool unfairly penalized European automobile manufacturers (for example, BMW, Mercedes, and Volvo) that sell only at the upper (low-gas-mileage) end of the car market. The United States brought a successful WTO claim against the EU for obstructing exports to Europe of U.S. beef found to contain growth hormones.[40] Canada forced the EU to back off on plans to forbid fur imports if the animal had been caught through the use of a leghold trap. Brazil and Venezuela won a case against the United States based on a claim of discrimination against foreign refiners in the EPA's implementation of the reformulated gasoline regulations under the 1990 Clean Air Act. And Thailand and several other countries in Southeast Asia got a WTO panel to agree that U.S. trade limitations imposed on shrimp fishermen who refused to use turtle excluder devices (TEDs) to protect endangered sea turtles were illegal under the GATT, although the WTO Appellate Body decision in this case endorsed the use of trade measures as a last resort to reinforce internationally agreed environmental standards.[41]

As the pace of economic integration increases, so does the number of trade-environment conflicts. The pressure for a more systematic commitment to building environmental considerations into the international trading system shows little sign of abating. In fact, the WTO has been criticized generally for failing to advance trade-environment harmony and specifically for focusing almost exclusively on the trade effects of environmental policy while paying little attention to the environmental consequences of trade policy.

At the 2001 launch of a new round of multilateral trade talks—the Doha Development Round—the European Union insisted that environmental issues be added to the agenda.[42] Although the identified issues are carefully circumscribed, the fact that the environment is on the global trade agenda represents a break with the past. As of 2008 the Doha Round had broken down, however, so "greening" of the WTO remains doubtful.

Strengthening the Global Environmental Regime

Many observers of the trade and environment debate have concluded that part of the explanation for the ongoing conflict lies in the weakness of the international environmental regime. The centerpiece of international environmental protection efforts, the United Nations Environment Programme (UNEP), is in serious disarray.[43] Moreover, global environmental responsibilities are spread across a half-dozen other UN agencies (including the United Nations Development Programme, the United Nations Commission on Sustainable Development, and the World Meteorological Organization), the secretariats to various international environmental treaties (including the Climate Change Convention, the Montreal Protocol, the Desertification Treaty, and the Basel Convention), as well as the Bretton Woods institutions (the World Bank, the regional development banks, and the WTO). This fragmented institutional structure results in disjointed responses to global pollution and resource challenges, difficulty in clarifying policy and budget priorities, little coordination across related problems, and lost opportunities for synergistic responses.

The presence of a global environmental organization, able to operate in tandem with the WTO and to provide some counterbalance to the WTO's trade emphasis, would be advantageous.[44] But fears of lost national sovereignty and concerns about creating a new UN bureaucracy make the prospect of establishing a comprehensive and coherent international umbrella environmental institution any time soon seem remote. In the absence of a functioning global environmental management system capable of addressing trade and environment issues, much of the responsibility for integrating these two policy realms will continue to fall to the WTO. A serious effort to make the international trading system more environmentally sensitive would require action on many fronts.

First, the activities of the WTO must become more transparent—that is, more open and easily followed by average people. Currently, most of the activities of the international trading system occur behind closed doors. This secrecy generates hostility from those who feel excluded from WTO processes or who are simply put off by the prospect that important decisions are being made without public input or understanding. What's more, the WTO's legitimacy and authoritativeness would be broadly enhanced by allowing representatives of NGOs to participate in or at least observe its proceedings.[45] This logic has been advanced by the United States with a series of proposals to open up the WTO. But to date, the efforts to promote transparency have been blocked by representatives from various developing countries.

This opposition reflects many concerns. Most notably, many free traders fear that the presence of environmentalists and others within the walls of the WTO would result in special interest manipulation of trade policymaking. It seems unlikely, however, that the presence of outside observers would really distort the decision processes of the international trading system. The system is not free of special interest manipulation now, and inviting environmental groups might produce some influence to counteract that of the existing producer and business lobbying and other activities. Allowing NGOs to make submissions when they have a position on issues being addressed by dispute settlement panels, or more broadly by the WTO governing council, would improve the knowledge base of the WTO and might assist the organization's decision making, especially in relation to environmental policy outcomes, which are so fraught with uncertainty.[46]

Over the longer term, the WTO must find a more refined way of balancing trade and environmental goals. The current mechanism (found in Article XX of the GATT) requires a country whose environmental policies have been challenged as an obstacle to free trade to demonstrate that it has selected the "least GATT-inconsistent" policy tool available. This standard sets an almost impossibly high hurdle for environmental policies because, in almost every case, there is some environmental strategy or approach that would intrude less on trade. A variety of proposals has been advanced that would amend Article XX and make it easier for legitimate environmental policies to be maintained in the face of trade challenges.[47]

In addition, while the trade system permits restrictions on imports when the product itself fails to meet national environmental standards, current GATT rules forbid discrimination against imports based on the environmental conditions associated with their production process or method (PPM). This means that imports of cars without the requisite pollution control devices can be banned. Similarly, imports of strawberries containing chemical residues can be barred. But GATT rules do not permit a country to block imports of cars because the steel that goes into them was made in polluting mills. Nor do the rules allow imported strawberries to be turned back just because the farmers polluted nearby rivers with pesticides and fertilizers. The prohibition against PPM-based environmental requirements is, however, untenable in a world of ecological interdependence.

Today the issue of *how* things are made is just as important as *what* is traded. If a semiconductor is produced using chlorofluorocarbons in violation of the ozone-layer-protection provisions of the Montreal Protocol, GATT rules would not permit an importing nation to bar the offending chip.[48] Even if the current blanket prohibition on PPM-based regulation were swept aside, the WTO would face lingering questions at the trade-environment interface.[49] Whose regulatory standards should be adopted? Who should determine compliance with agreed-upon standards? And who should assess penalties or takes other enforcement actions when a violation is uncovered?

These questions persist even if the standards in question arise from an international agreement. The WTO remains vulnerable to challenges arising from the imposition of trade measures under multilateral environmental agreements. This is especially true in those cases where a WTO member is not a party to the environmental accord. A strong possibility exists that, under current interpretations of the GATT, a country facing trade penalties for failing to sign or adhere to a multilateral environmental agreement would be able to argue that those imposing the trade sanctions for environmental reasons are in violation of their GATT obligations. Thus a nation that failed to join the Montreal Protocol banning the use of ozone-layer-depleting chemicals might be able to free ride on the environmental protection efforts of others and dodge trade sanctions imposed by parties to the protocol. In response to this issue, the WTO could adopt a provision, such as that found in NAFTA, that declares that trade measures taken in accordance with multilateral environmental agreements are not NAFTA violations. Beyond finding ways to balance conflicting trade and environmental goals more effectively, those seeking to make trade and environmental policies more mutually reinforcing could identify many places where trade and environmental policy aims dovetail.

Notably, the elimination of subsidies for timber, water, agriculture, and energy and the more careful regulation of fisheries would yield both substantial trade benefits and environmental improvements. Agricultural price supports, for instance, encourage farmers to plant on marginal lands, which often require heavy doses of chemicals to be productive. Reduced agricultural subsidies would diminish the incentives to farm marginal lands and reduce trade distortions, thus providing new agricultural export opportunities for many developing countries.

Managing Interdependence

Despite the breadth of activities linking trade and environment policies in recent years and the reasonably favorable results arising on this score from NAFTA, some policymakers continue to dismiss the significance of the trade-environment relationship. The call for separation of economic and environmental interests is, however, not just normatively wrong but practically impossible. The relationship between environmental and trade issues in the context of deepening economic integration is inescapable and multilayered. Ignoring these linkages threatens to reduce social welfare, limit the gains from trade, and cause unnecessary environmental degradation. Ignoring the environmental implications of trade policymaking poses an acute threat to current and future economic integration efforts, not to mention environmental programs.

The fundamental challenge is to manage interdependence on multiple levels, representing both shared natural resources and a common economic destiny. Governance in this context requires working across divergent priorities— North versus South, economic growth versus environmental protection, and present interests versus future ones. Sustainable development has emerged as the shorthand way of refining a systems-oriented policy approach that considers these conflicting needs simultaneously. Making trade and environmental policies work together, therefore, stands as a classic example of the on-the-ground challenge of sustainable development.

Notes

1. Kym Anderson and Richard Blackhurst, "Trade, the Environment, and Public Policy," in *The Greening of World Trade Issues*, ed. Kym Anderson and Richard Blackhurst (Ann Arbor: University of Michigan Press, 1992), 3.
2. Daniel C. Esty, *Greening the GATT: Trade, Environment, and the Future* (Washington, D.C.: Institute for International Economics, 1994), 17–20; Andrew Hurrell and Benedict Kingsbury, *The International Politics of the Environment* (Oxford, England: Clarendon Press, 1992).
3. Richard N. Gardner, *Negotiating Survival: Four Priorities after Rio* (New York: Council on Foreign Relations, 1992); "Rio Declaration on Environment and Development," UNCED, UN Doc. A/Conf. 151/5/Rev. 1, reprinted in *International Legal Materials* 31 (1992): 874, 878; "Agenda 21," UNCED, UN Doc. A/Conf. 151/26/Rev. 1 (1992).
4. Doha WTO Ministerial Declaration, WT/MIN(01)/DEC/1, November 14, 2001, paragraphs 31–33.

5. For a discussion of the far-reaching repercussions of the improper management of hazardous waste, see André Dua and Daniel C. Esty, *Sustaining the Asia Pacific Miracle* (Washington, D.C.: Institute for International Economics, 1997), 41–42.

6. John J. Audley, *Green Politics and Global Trade: NAFTA and the Future of Environmental Politics* (Washington, D.C.: Georgetown University Press, 1997); "Binational Statement on Environmental Safeguards That Should Be Included in the North American Free Trade Agreement," issued by Canadian Nature Federation, Canadian Environmental Law Association, Sierra Club-Canada, Rawson Survival-Canada, Pollution Probe-Canada, National Audubon Society, National Wildlife Federation, Community Nutrition Institute, and Environmental Defense Fund, May 28, 1992.

7. Robert Housman and Durwood Zaelke, "The Collision of the Environment and Trade: The GATT Tuna/Dolphin Decision," *Environmental Law Reporter* 22 (April 1992): 10268.

8. Steve Charnovitz, "Environmentalism Confronts GATT Rules," *Journal of World Trade* 28 (January 1993): 37.

9. For an entertaining depiction of how GATTzilla might devour cities and leave destruction in its wake, see Esty, *Greening the GATT,* 34.

10. Dua and Esty, *Sustaining the Asia Pacific Miracle;* Yoichi Funabashi, *Asia–Pacific Fusion: Japan's Role in APEC* (Washington, D.C.: Institute for International Economics, 1995).

11. For a discussion of NAFTA's environmental dimensions and effects, see Carolyn Deere and Daniel C. Esty, eds., *Greening the Americas: NAFTA's Lessons for Hemispheric Trade* (Cambridge: MIT Press, 2002).

12. J. F. Hornbeck, "The Dominican Republic-Central America-United States Free Trade Agreement (CAFTA-DR)," Report no. RL31870 (Washington, D.C.: Congressional Research Service, January 16, 2008), www.nationalaglawcenter.org/assets/crs/RL31870.pdf.

13. Daniel C. Esty, "Bridging the Trade-Environment Divide," *Journal of Economic Perspectives* 15 (Summer 2001): 113–130.

14. Esty, *Greening the GATT,* 42–55.

15. It is interesting to see how "trade and environment" issues have split the environmental community, separating those who accept the promise of sustainable development from those who believe that economic growth is inherently environmentally harmful. See Audley, *Green Politics and Global Trade.*

16. For instance, in the debate over NAFTA, some environmentalists expressed concerns regarding the likelihood of a deterioration in meat inspection standards along the U.S.-Mexico border. See Lori Wallach, *The Consumer and Environmental Case against Fast Track* (Washington, D.C.: Public Citizen, 1991), 16. But some scholars instead contend that trade can uplift product standards. See Alan O. Sykes, *Product Standards for Internationally Integrated Goods Markets* (Washington, D.C.: Brookings Institution, 1995); David Vogel, *Trading Up: Consumer and Environmental Regulation in a Global Economy* (Cambridge: Harvard University Press, 1995). Further excellent considerations of harmonization issues are provided in Jagdish Bhagwati and Robert E. Hudec, eds., *Fair Trade and Harmonization: Prerequisites for Free Trade?* (Cambridge: MIT Press, 1996).

17. Ross Perot, *Save Your Job, Save Our Country: Why NAFTA Must Be Stopped—Now!* (New York: Hyperion, 1993); Daniel C. Esty, *Greening the GATT.*

18. This includes the U.S. Free Trade Agreements with Chile, Singapore, Jordan, Morocco, Bahrain, and Oman.

19. Various aspects of this debate are reviewed in Daniel C. Esty and Damien Geradin, *Regulatory Competition and Economic Integration: Comparative Perspectives* (Oxford: Oxford University Press, 2001) as well as in Esty, "Governing at the Trade-Environment Interface."

20. Charles M. Tiebout, "A Pure Theory of Local Expenditures," *Journal of Political Economy* (October 1956): 416; Wallace E. Oates and Robert M. Schwab, "Economic Competition among Jurisdictions: Efficiency Enhancing or Distortion Inducing,"

Journal of Public Economy 27 (April 1988): 333; Richard L. Revesz, "Rehabilitating Interstate Competition: Rethinking the 'Race to the Bottom' Rationale for Federal Environmental Regulation," *New York University Law Review* 67 (December 1992): 1210.

21. Daniel C. Esty, "Revitalizing Environmental Federalism," *Michigan Law Review* 95 (December 1996): 629–634.

22. Lyuba Zarsky and Jason Hunter, "Environmental Cooperation at APEC: The First Five Years," *Journal of Environment and Development* (September 1997): 222–252.

23. U.S. Census Bureau, "Foreign Trade Statistics: Trade with China: 2008," www.census .gov/foreign-trade/balance/c5700.html#2008.

24. Marrakesh Decisions Concurrent to Establishing the WTO, "Decision on Trade and Environment," April 14, 1994, reprinted in *International Legal Materials* 33 (1994): 1255.

25. Steve Charnovitz, "Free Trade, Fair Trade, Green Trade: Defogging the Debate," *Cornell International Law Journal* 27 (1994): 459–525; Sanford Gaines, "The Polluter-Pays Principle: From Economic Equity to Environmental Ethos," *Texas International Law Journal* 26 (Summer 1991): 463.

26. Gene M. Grossman and Alan B. Krueger, "Economic Growth and the Environment," *Quarterly Journal of Economics* 110 (May 1995): 353, 369.

27. Dua and Esty, *Sustaining the Asia Pacific Miracle*, 73–77.

28. Theo Panayotou, "Demystifying the Environmental Kuznets Curve: Turning a Black Box into a Policy Tool," *Environment and Development Economics* 2 (1997): 4, 465–484; M. A. Cole et al., "The Environmental Kuznets Curve: An Empirical Analysis," *Environment and Development Economics* 2 (1997): 4, 401–416; S. M. DeBruyn et al., "Economic Growth and Emissions: Reconsidering the Empirical Basis of Environmental Kuznets Curves," *Ecological Economics* 25 (1998): 2, 161–175.

29. Esty, "Bridging the Trade-Environment Divide," 119.

30. NAFTA Supplemental Agreements, "North American Agreement on Environmental Cooperation," September 13, 1993, reprinted in *International Legal Materials* 32 (1993): 1480.

31. *Inside U.S. Trade*, August 23, 1991, 7; Trade and Environment Committee of the National Advisory Council for Environmental Policy and Technology, *The Greening of World Trade*, Report to the EPA (Washington, D.C.: EPA, 1993).

32. Executive Order 13141—Environmental Reviews of Trade Agreements, November 16, 1999.

33. NAFTA Preamble, December 17, 1992, reprinted in *International Legal Materials* 32 (1993): 296 and 605.

34. NAFTA Chapter 11, however, became a source of controversy because its loose drafting seemed to create a risk that legitimate environmental regulation might trigger compensation requirements. For further discussion on this point, see Howard Mann and Monica Araya, "An Investment Regime for the Americas: Challenges and Opportunities for Environmental Sustainability," in *Greening the Americas: NAFTA's Lessons for Hemispheric Trade*, ed. Carolyn L. Deere and Daniel C. Esty (Cambridge: MIT Press, 2002).

35. Gary C. Hufbauer et al., *NAFTA and the Environment* (Washington, D.C.: Institute for International Economics, 2001); Deere and Esty, "Trade and the Environment: Reflections on the NAFTA and Recommendations for the Americas," in Deere and Esty, *Greening the Americas: NAFTA's Lessons for Hemispheric Trade*, 329.

36. John Audley, "Environment's New Role in U.S. Trade Policy," Trade, Equity, and Development Policy Brief no. 3, Carnegie Endowment for International Peace, September 2002.

37. John Audley, "Evaluating Environmental Issues in the US-Singapore Free Trade Agreement," Trade, Equity, and Development Issue Brief, Carnegie Endowment for International Peace, April 2003; John Audley, "Opportunities and Challenges to Advance Environmental Protection in the US-Central America Free Trade Negotiations," Trade,

Equity, and Development Issue Brief, Carnegie Endowment for International Peace, February 2003.

38. Gary C. Hufbauer et al., *NAFTA and the Environment: Seven Years Later* (Washington, D.C.: Institute for International Economics, 2000); Laura Carlsen and Hilda Salazar, "Limits to Cooperation: A Mexican Perspective on the NAFTA's Environmental Side Agreement and Institutions," in Deere and Esty, *Greening the Americas: NAFTA's Lessons for Hemispheric Trade.*

39. An "unregistered" fungicide is one that has not gone through EPA safety testing to establish a safe residue level under the Federal Insecticide, Fungicide, and Rodenticide Act, 7 U.S.C. §136 et seq. (1996).

40. Michael B. Froman, "International Trade: The United States–European Community Hormone Treated Beef Conflict," *Harvard International Law Journal* 30 (Spring 1989): 549–556.

41. For a compilation of many important and interesting trade disputes, see Esty, *Greening the GATT,* app. C, 257–274. See also Carrie Wofford, "A Greener Future at the WTO: The Refinement of WTO Jurisprudence on Environmental Exceptions to the GATT," *Harvard Environmental Law Review* 24, no. 2 (2000): 563–592.

42. Doha WTO Ministerial Declaration, WT/MIN(01)/DEC/1, November 14, 2001, paragraphs 31–33.

43. Even UNEP acknowledges that "global governance structures and global environmental solidarity remain too weak to make progress a world-wide reality. . . . The gap between what has been done thus far and what is realistically needed is widening." See UNEP, *Global Environment Outlook* (New York: Oxford University Press, 1997).

44. For a review of global environmental governance issues, see Daniel C. Esty and Maria Ivanova, eds., *Global Environmental Governance: Options & Opportunities* (New Haven: Yale School of Forestry and Environmental Studies, 2002).

45. Steve Charnovitz, "Two Centuries of Participation: NGOs and International Governance," *Michigan Journal of International Trade* 18 (Winter 1997): 183–286; Daniel C. Esty, "Non-governmental Organizations at the World Trade Organization: Cooperation, Competition, or Exclusion," *Journal of International Economic Law* 1 (1998): 123–147; James Cameron and Ross Ramsey, "Participation by NGOs in the WTO," Working Paper, Global Environment and Trade Study (GETS), New Haven, 1995.

46. Christophe Bellmann and Richard Gerster, "Accountability in the WTO," *Journal of World Trade* 30 (December 1996): 31–74. On the advantages of NGO "co-opetition," see Daniel C. Esty and Damien Geradin, "Regulatory Co-opetition," in *Regulatory Competition and Economic Integration: Comparative Perspectives,* ed. Daniel C. Esty and Damien Geradin (Oxford: Oxford University Press, 2001).

47. Daniel C. Esty, "Making Trade and Environmental Policies Work Together: Lessons from NAFTA," in *Trade and Environment: The Search for Balance,* ed. Damien Geradin et al. (London: Cameron, 1994), 382.

48. Duncan Brack, *International Trade and the Montreal Protocol* (London: Royal Institute of International Affairs, 1996).

49. Some softening of the WTO rules has begun to emerge, especially in the Appellate Body decision in the Shrimp/Turtle case. See Wofford, "A Greener Future at the WTO."

9

Compliance with Global Environmental Policy

Michael G. Faure and Jürgen Lefevere

The United Nations Conference on the Human Environment, held in Stockholm in 1972, set off an unprecedented development of new international environmental treaties. Before 1972 only a dozen international treaties with relevance to the environment were in force; twenty-five years later more than a thousand such instruments can be counted.

With the intensified use of international treaties as a means to combat environmental degradation, concerns have arisen regarding the compliance of states with the commitments to which they have agreed. Even within relatively strong regional organizations such as the European Union (EU), compliance problems regularly overshadow successes in the adoption of new instruments. In a hearing on the subject conducted in 1992 by the UK's House of Lords, a member of the European Parliament even warned that "we have now reached the point in the EC where, if we do not tackle implementation and enforcement properly, there seems very little point in producing new environmental law."[1]

In recent decades international actors have tried new approaches to drafting, implementation, and enforcement in an attempt to improve compliance with international environmental treaties. This activity has been mirrored by advances in the scholarly study of factors that affect state compliance and increased discussion of such factors in both academic and policymaking circles.

This chapter examines the theory and practice of national compliance with international environmental treaties. In doing so, the chapter uses as its primary examples the United Nations Framework Convention on Climate Change (FCCC) and its Kyoto Protocol, the EU environmental regime, and the Montreal Protocol on Substances that Deplete the Ozone Layer. We begin by discussing the theory of compliance as it has been developed in both the academic literature and in practice.[2] We then provide an overview of sources for compliance and noncompliance. Finally, we examine methods developed to date that seek to improve compliance with international environmental treaties.

Theory of Compliance

The term *compliance* is often used inconsistently and confused with related terminology such as *implementation, effectiveness,* or even *enforcement.* To avoid unnecessary confusion, one should be careful in using these terms.

They refer to different aspects of the process of achieving international political and legal cooperation.

Implementation refers to the specific actions (including legislative, organizational, and practical actions) that international actors and states take to make international treaties operative in their national legal systems. Implementation by relevant international actors includes, for instance, the provision of financial resources by the Global Environment Facility (GEF) in accordance with the rules adopted under the FCCC. Implementation by states establishes the link between the national legal system and the international obligations. The aim of establishing this link should be compliance.

Compliance is generally defined as the extent to which the behavior of a state—party to an international treaty—actually conforms to the conditions set out in this treaty. Some authors make a distinction between compliance with the treaty's explicit rules and compliance with the treaty's objective.[3] It is, however, difficult to assess compliance with the "spirit" of an agreement, since this evaluation can be quite subjective. The third term, *enforcement*, indicates the methods that are available to force states not only to implement but also to comply with treaty obligations. Whereas compliance and implementation concern the actions of the states themselves, *effectiveness*, as the term indicates, is more concerned with the effect of the treaty as a whole. *Effectiveness* addresses the question of whether a treaty that is correctly complied with actually achieves its stated objectives, or whether the treaty actually helped to reach the environmental goal for which it was designed.

The terms *compliance* and *effectiveness* are often used interchangeably but, in fact, have very distinct meanings. Compliance is in most cases a condition for effectiveness, if by effectiveness we mean the reaching of the treaty's goals. If a treaty is complied with, however, this does not automatically signify that it is effective in reaching the environmental goal for which it was originally designed. Effectiveness also depends on the actual treaty design, the instruments and goals contained in the treaty, as well as other external factors, such as a changing political situation or even changing environmental conditions. The Kyoto Protocol is an example: even if states fully comply with the requirements of that treaty, the protocol is still insufficient to stop climate change from occurring. Hence, compliance is only a proxy for effectiveness; greater compliance will usually lead to environmental improvement, but whether this is actually the case will to a large extent depend upon the contents of the treaty. One could even imagine a treaty that is so badly drafted that noncompliance would even contribute to its effectiveness. For example, this ironic result could be reached in a treaty that on paper protects the environment (or potential victims) but that, in fact, protects industrial operators, for example, by introducing financial caps on their liability. One could argue that potential victims would be better off with noncompliance, but this is obviously true only in cases where special interests (not primarily environmental concerns) dictated the contents of the treaty.

We will concentrate here on the issue of compliance as a requirement for an effective treaty. This issue has received increasing attention in scholarly writing and in practice since the mid-1990s. Increased attention has led to the development of a new approach to the compliance issue. The traditional view of compliance was very much connected to the principle of sovereignty of states. According to this principle, states are sovereign actors in the international arena, meaning that they are free to act as they find necessary, unrestricted by any external authority or rules. Based on this principle, one tended to believe that governments therefore accepted only those international treaties that were in their own interest. A breach of these treaties was thus seen as unlikely. If a state was in breach of its treaty obligations, it was usually considered to be intentional. Enforcement measures were thus often limited and were regarded as severe actions. Examples of these enforcement measures are procedures where states can file an official complaint against the violating state or impose trade sanctions. Because of the gravity of these sanctions, however, they are rarely applied in practice. Even in the European context, direct complaints of one state against another are still highly exceptional.[4]

Toward the end of the 1990s, the traditional view of compliance problems was criticized increasingly in scholarly writings[5]; criticism that goes hand in hand with the new approach to sovereignty. Some argue that states should no longer be seen as completely sovereign entities but as willing to accept limits on their original sovereign rights for the benefit of the environment, future generations, or the international community as a whole.[6] The international community is increasingly organized in *regimes*.[7] These regimes consist of a framework with a relatively well-developed set of rules and norms concerning a specific subject. The development of regimes can be placed between the traditional concept of sovereignty, leaving the states unbound, and a comprehensive world order, placing the states within a new world governance. Examples of important regimes are the climate change regime, constructed around the FCCC and its Kyoto Protocol, and the international trade regime, based on the agreements concluded under the World Trade Organization (WTO). With the development of these regimes, "sovereignty no longer consists in the freedom of states to act independently, in their perceived self-interest, but in membership in reasonably good standing in the regimes that make up the substance of international life."[8] States' interests are increasingly determined by their membership in, as well as good reputation under, these regimes.[9]

The new approach tries to place compliance problems in this increasingly complicated international context, with a multitude of regimes, interdependent actors, and different interests and obligations. Within this new context many factors can lead countries to conclude treaties. These factors also affect the states' willingness and, more important, their ability to comply with the obligations. In this more complex perception of compliance, the actors at the international level can no longer be seen as utilitarian decision makers weighing the benefits and costs of compliance. The compliance record of states is influenced by a large number of factors, in which the willful desire to violate rules plays only a minor role. Often it is practical obstacles, outside the direct will or control of states, that make compliance difficult.

This new concept of compliance also necessitates new solutions to problems. The traditional sanction mechanisms, based on the notion that states intentionally do not comply, have proven largely ineffective. Moreover, some of these are now often unlawful under other international arrangements. The use of military action is strictly regulated under international law, although states obviously observe such regulations unevenly, and force is now allowed in a legal sense in a limited number of situations. Certainly, military action is not seen as a legally appropriate or practical method of seeking compliance with environmental treaties.[10] Economic sanctions have become more difficult to apply since the development of an increasingly comprehensive international trade regime. It is now necessary to take into account the actual abilities of states to comply, and sanctions for noncompliance need to be developed that fit within the new international regimes. Solutions for compliance problems need to be based more on what is referred to as a "managerial approach" rather than on a more traditional "enforcement approach."[11]

Sources of Compliance and Noncompliance

The following section will address several factors that may affect compliance with environmental agreements and possible sources of noncompliance. Guzman mentions several factors that can increase the cost of violations and thus promote compliance: reputation, reciprocal noncompliance, and retaliation. Cooperative outcomes can thus be enhanced by increasing the costs of these factors.[12]

Regime Rules

The regime rules refer to the actual contents of the treaty that the parties have signed. These rules define the behavior that is required of the participating states under the terms of the treaty. The regime rules are directly related to the activity that the environmental accord is supposed to regulate. Even during the negotiations, when the primary rules are defined, the degree of treaty compliance can be determined to a large extent.

A first important aspect of the design of the regime rule system relates to whether it requires any behavioral change, what the costs of this change will be, and by whom this behavioral change is required. It is easier to achieve compliance if the degree of behavioral change and the costs of this change are low. It is therefore argued, for instance, that it might be harder to achieve compliance with the Kyoto Protocol than with the Montreal Protocol, since more people and industries must make bigger behavioral changes. The Montreal Protocol mainly requires behavioral changes by the producers and corporate users of a limited number of very important but replaceable chemicals. The greenhouse gas emission reduction targets in the Kyoto Protocol, however, require larger-scale behavioral changes, not only by industry but also by individuals, particularly with respect to the production and consumption of energy.[13]

In a number of cases treaty rules require no change in behavior of the industry in a specific country. This is often the case when industry is already meeting a specific pollution standard (for example, emissions). Those industries may even lobby in favor of treaties that will impose on their foreign competitors the standards that domestic industries already have to comply with at the national level.[14] In those cases the industries already meeting the specific standard will obviously readily comply, since the treaty merely erects a barrier to entry for the foreign competitors.

In some cases the treaties are clearly in the interest of industry for other reasons. One example is the treaties relating to liability for nuclear accidents and oil pollution. On paper these treaties serve the interests of victims, but, in fact, the contents are often such that the liability of operators is limited (for example, through financial caps). The nuclear liability conventions that originated in the late 1950s came into being as a reaction to the growing nuclear industry's fear of unlimited liability. Hence, compliance with the conventions, which included limited liability of nuclear operators, was relatively high.[15]

The amount of detail or specificity in a treaty may affect future compliance. States can facilitate their own compliance by negotiating vague and ambiguous rules. Examples include agreeing to provisions that on paper seem to be in the environmental interest but are sufficiently vague to allow business as usual. However, primary rules can often increase compliance through greater specificity. Specific obligations make compliance easier by reducing the uncertainty about what states need to do to comply. Specific treaty language will also remove the possibility of the excuse of inadvertence and misinterpretation in case of noncompliance. Moreover, the advantage of conventions with relatively precise obligations (such as the Montreal Protocol) is that it is easier to judge whether states do, in fact, comply. If the obligations are vague, assessing implementation and compliance becomes more difficult.

One obvious remedy for inadvertence as a source of noncompliance is, therefore, to draft specific, detailed obligations. These, together with an information campaign, can at least prevent states from justifying noncompliance on the basis of a lack of information or clarity with respect to their obligations. A general formulation of the obligations may, however, be unavoidable in some cases simply because political consensus may not support more precision. Article 4(2)(a) of the FCCC is an example of diplomatically formulated "obligations." The article leaves unclear whether there is any specific obligation at all.[16]

One source of noncompliance may be the incapacity of states to fulfill the treaty obligations owing to a lack of resources or technological abilities. When these problems are recognized during the drafting stage, noncompliance may be prevented by designing the primary rules in such a manner that the differing capacities of states are taken into account. Treaty obligations can be differentiated, based on the varying capacities of states, or resources or technologies can be transferred. This is, again, an example of a managerial approach; instead of blunt sanctions, instruments are developed in the treaty design stage that take into account the varying capacities and thus help to prevent noncompliance.

The idea of differentiated standards according to a state's capacities is predominant in the FCCC and its Kyoto Protocol. This treaty regime places its signatory states in different categories, imposing different obligations for each group. All signatory states commit themselves to the general obligations, such as developing national greenhouse gas inventories (albeit with different frequency) and national programs containing measures to mitigate climate change (for example, Article 4(1)(a) and (b) of the FCCC). Under the FCCC, only the developed states and states in transition that are listed in Annex I of the FCCC are required to stabilize their carbon dioxide emissions. Under the Kyoto Protocol, only the developed states and states in transition that are listed in Annex B of the protocol are required to limit their greenhouse gas emissions in accordance with the targets contained in that Annex. Annex II of the FCCC lists the developed countries that additionally need to provide financial resources to facilitate compliance by developing countries.[17] The transfer of funds from developed to developing states can also be observed in other treaties. The Montreal Protocol, for instance, provides a framework within which financial support as well as technical assistance are provided. The EU uses the instrument of structural funds to promote economic and social development of disadvantaged regions within the EU.

A new concept in the area of climate change, which also takes into account differing abilities of states, is the use of "flexible mechanisms." These mechanisms allow developed countries to meet their emission limitation targets through buying "emission rights" from countries in which the marginal costs of emission reduction are lower, thus reducing the costs of compliance. The Kyoto Protocol's flexible mechanisms are Joint Implementation (JI), the Clean Development Mechanism (CDM), and International Emissions Trading (IET). The CDM is the most interesting of these mechanisms: it allows developed countries to invest in emission reduction projects in a developing country and in return receive emission rights that can be used to comply with their emission limitation obligations. A well-implemented CDM project can thus help provide financial aid and technologies to developing countries and hence also help remedy capacity problems.[18]

The only problem with these various inducements is that they are vulnerable to "moral hazard." Moral hazard refers to the fact that incentives for the prevention of emissions may be diluted if states are subsidized through financial or technological transfers. States may indeed misrepresent their abilities in order to have others pay for their compliance costs. An example is, for instance, a developing country postponing the adoption of legislation requiring the flaring of excess methane (which is a much more powerful greenhouse gas than carbon dioxide) emissions from oil extraction rather than simply venting this methane to the atmosphere, as a result of which flaring projects can continue to be covered under the Kyoto Protocol's CDM. Any incentive system should therefore explicitly build in safeguards against such moral hazard.

The approach of using differentiated standards and financial and technological transfers is the basis of the more comprehensive noncompliance response systems that we will discuss below (see box on the Montreal Protocol as an example of the managerial approach).

Reporting and Information

The likelihood of compliance will also depend on informational issues. Information plays an important role at several stages. First, accurate information on the environmental risks increases the chances of adopting a treaty on the specific subject and also the likelihood of compliance. Second, information, through monitoring or reporting systems, serves to increase the transparency of the implementation and compliance records of states.

With regard to the first factor, it is broadly assumed that the more information there is about an environmental issue, the more effective implementation and compliance will be.[19] This understanding is rather straightforward: the clearer the presentation of the activities and risks that are the subject of the treaty, the easier it will be to build political pressure (through, among others, nongovernmental organizations [NGOs]) via public opinion to induce compliance. One of the reasons that the swift adoption of the Montreal Protocol came as a surprise to the international community was that it occurred in a time of still important scientific uncertainties about the causes and effects of the changing ozone layer.[20] These uncertainties are still significantly influencing the negotiations concerning climate change. The scientific reports of the Intergovernmental Panel on Climate Change (IPCC) play an important role in forming international consensus about the problem.[21]

With regard to the second factor, information increases the transparency of the implementation and compliance records of states. If it is known that a state does not comply, international and domestic groups can take actions aimed at improving a state's compliance. Transparency with respect to the compliance record will to a large extent depend on the complexity of the issue covered by the treaty as well as the democratic character of the complying state. Transparency can lead to public pressure to increase compliance. In this respect, one can cite the actions of NGOs to identify noncompliance, thereby giving incentives for compliance without a need for formal sanctions. Transparency is considered an almost universal element of compliance management strategy. Indeed, transparency in the form of "naming and shaming" is increasingly being used as a sanction for noncompliance, building on the desire of states and companies to satisfy an environmentally aware electorate, consumers, and shareholders.[22]

Transparency can be achieved through an effective compliance information system that is laid down in the treaty. To a large extent, treaties rely on self-reporting by states. As noted above, in a regime system with sometimes delicate political links and pressures, the status of a state is often very important. States are generally careful about losing face with other states and their own population. This fear of losing face has traditionally been used in many treaties, including those outside the environmental field, by imposing a requirement that the state report on its compliance with the treaty. This report would allow other states and citizens to hold it accountable for its compliance record. Although reporting procedures can be found in most environmental treaties, they are often vaguely formulated, and the reports are poorly drafted. Hence, the reporting procedure is often criticized for its "weak" character and the absence of sanctions in case of noncompliance with the reporting requirements.

Self-reporting is also criticized because it may lead to self-incrimination. If states take this duty seriously, they should report their own noncompliance. The hesitancy of states to incriminate themselves may be one of the reasons why the reporting requirements of environmental treaties are often violated. Moreover, governments, particularly of smaller states, are sometimes overburdened with administrative tasks, and filing reports is seen as yet another burden. Reporting can also be difficult for developing countries that often lack both financial resources and the capacity to comply with detailed reporting obligations. Reporting by states is, therefore, a first step, but obviously no guarantee of compliance.[23]

Compliance can be improved through monitoring by an independent third party. The likelihood of compliance will to a large extent be influenced by the treaty's provisions for effective monitoring. This in turn depends on the contents of the primary rules. The Montreal Protocol, for instance, regulated the production rather than the consumption of chlorofluorocarbons (CFCs) because it is easier to monitor a few producers rather than thousands of consumers. Some treaties, such as those on nuclear weapons, allow on-site monitoring. This obviously is one of the most effective instruments to control whether states not only formally adopt legislation implementing a treaty but also comply with the contents. On-site monitoring is, however, still heavily debated because it constitutes an important infringement on state sovereignty.

Even in the EU, on-site monitoring by a European authority of Member State violations of environmental directives is still not used. The compliance record will inevitably depend on the ability to monitor violations. This brought Gro Harlem Brundtland, the former Norwegian prime minister and chair of the World Commission on Environment and Development, to recommend the establishment of "an international authority with the power to verify actual emissions and to react with legal measures if there are violations of the rules" in order to ensure compliance with carbon dioxide emission targets.[24]

The problems with reporting procedures have led to the development of *compliance information systems*.[25] These systems contain elaborate procedures for the provision of information by Member States, the possible review of this information by independent experts, and the availability of this information to the general public. The development of a more elaborate and transparent system for the provision of information on the compliance of Member States automatically increases those states' accountability.

The Montreal Protocol . . .

The approach to international environmental treaty design has changed in the past decades, mainly because of the new, more realistic "managerial" approach. Prime examples of this new approach are the Vienna Convention for the Protection of the Ozone Layer and, more important, its subsequent Montreal Protocol on Substances that Deplete the Ozone Layer, adopted under this Convention.

The Vienna Convention was adopted in 1985. It did not contain any substantive commitments for the states but provided for a general framework, including the possibility of adopting protocols in the Conference of the Parties, the main institution set up under the Convention. Only two years after the adoption of the Convention, the 1987 Montreal Protocol on Substances that Deplete the Ozone Layer was adopted. The Vienna Convention and, more particularly, its Montreal Protocol surprised the international community by their swift adoption, their specific goals, their effectiveness, and the large number of states that have become parties to them (194 countries have ratified both the Vienna Convention and the Montreal Protocol as of March 2009, making its coverage virtually global). One of the main reasons given for this effectiveness is the design of the treaty system, which has several "modern" characteristics that make it very suitable for dealing with environmental problems in the current international context. In many of the more recent international environmental treaties the Vienna-Montreal system is used as a model, largely because of the flexibility of its primary rule system.

The Vienna Convention establishes the Conference of the Parties (Article 6), which is to meet "at regular intervals," in practice every three to four years. The Montreal Protocol adds a Meeting of the Parties. Montreal protocol meetings are now held annually to discuss implementation of the commitments and possible improvements to or adoption of new commitments. They are organized by the Ozone Secretariat, set up under Article 7 of the Vienna Convention and Article 12 of the Montreal Protocol. The regular convening of the Meeting of the Parties has proven very useful in keeping the treaty objectives on the political agenda and has ensured a continuous updating of its goals and standards. This updating was made possible by the framework structure chosen by the Vienna Convention. Although not a new structure (it was also used in the 1979 UN-ECE Convention on Long-Range Transboundary Air Pollution), it has been particularly effective. Whereas the Vienna Convention does no more than establish the framework for further negotiations, the real commitments are laid down in the Montreal Protocol—the first and, to date, only protocol adopted under this Convention. The provisions of the Montreal Protocol are regularly updated by means of amendments. During the two

For example, the FCCC contains, in Articles 4 and 12, elaborate provisions concerning the communication by member states of their implementation of the Convention. Although the word *reporting* is avoided in the context of the Convention—replaced by the word *communicate*—these communications have the character of national reports. The first FCCC Conference of the Parties, in 1995, promulgated the first guidelines for preparation of national communications, and, more important, procedures were adopted for the in-depth review of individual reports from developed countries by teams of experts. Developed countries now submit every four to five years their

. . . A "Managerial" Primary Rule System

decades of its existence, the Montreal Protocol has seen a total of five "adjustments" regarding the production and consumption of the controlled substances listed in the Annexes of the Protocol as well as four Amendments (the London Amendment in 1990, the Copenhagen Amendment in 1992, the Montreal Amendment in 1997, and the Beijing Amendment in 1999). This shows how compliance is likely to be influenced in the treaty design stage by creating a primary rule system that can develop over time, responding to evolving science and the capacity to deal with environmental problems.

The Montreal Protocol also provides an example of how the individual capacities of states may determine their willingness to accept treaty obligations in the first place. India and China would not become parties to the Montreal Protocol until the agreement about compensatory financing had been adopted at the London meeting in 1990. This agreement provided for financial support to developing states in order to allow them to become parties to the protocol and be financially capable of complying with its obligations.

Under the Montreal Protocol, various instruments have been developed to remedy financial incapacity. A Multilateral Fund was set up (Article 10) to provide financial assistance. The fund's implementing agencies—the International Bank for Reconstruction and Development (World Bank), the United Nations Environment Programme, and the United Nations Development Programme—have drawn up country programs and country studies that offer financial support, assistance, and training. Furthermore, the Montreal Protocol provides for the transfer of technology under its Article 10A. On the basis of this article, all states party to the protocol "shall take every practicable step" to ensure that "the best available, environmentally safe substitutes and related technologies are expeditiously transferred" to developing countries (as defined in Article 5[1] of the protocol) and that those transfers "occur under fair and most favourable conditions."

With near-universal participation of nations and energetic support from industry, the ozone regime has reduced worldwide use of ozone-depleting chemicals by 95 percent, and use is still falling.[a] The ozone regime is therefore considered the first realization of a managerial approach, using policies and institutions that promote learning about the systems being managed and that adapt in response to what is learned for any global environmental issue.

[a] Edward A. Parson, *Protecting the Ozone Layer: Science and Strategy* (New York: Oxford University Press, 2003); especially chap. 9.

national communication, which is then subjected to an in-depth review. Although written in "nonconfrontational language," the in-depth review procedure does provide an important impetus for member states to increase their efforts to comply. All national communications and the in-depth reviews are collected by the FCCC Secretariat in Bonn, Germany. Under Article 12(10) of the FCCC, the Secretariat makes these communications and their in-depth reviews publicly available. The reports may also be accessed at the Web site of the FCCC (www.unfccc.int). Under the Kyoto Protocol, this reporting procedure was further strengthened, with additional reporting requirements and a more rigorous review procedure, the results of which feed into the protocol's noncompliance procedure. Apart from strengthening the contents of the national communications, the Kyoto Protocol also strengthens the requirement for developed countries to submit annual emission inventories and provides for their review by "expert review teams." These teams consist of experts of third countries, and their work is coordinated by the FCCC Secretariat. Importantly, these teams can also raise "questions of implementation" on a specific inventory. These questions are then automatically put to the Kyoto Protocol's compliance committee.

This increased attention to information systems and reporting procedures is part of the transformation from an enforcement approach to a managerial approach to compliance. Traditionally, the incentives for states to report their own noncompliance were low because such an admission could lead only to "bad news," such as the imposition of sanctions. The situation totally changes, however, when noncompliance is not necessarily considered the intentional act of a sovereign state but may be due, for example, to incapacity. In that case, reporting the problem may lead other partners in the regime to look for remedies to overcome the difficulty, for example, through a transfer of finances or technology. In this managerial approach, reporting noncompliance should not be threatening but may well be in the state's interest. The desired result of this new approach is that in the end a higher compliance record is achieved than with traditional enforcement methods. Thus the reporting of noncompliance under the Montreal Protocol leads the Implementation Committee to investigate the possibilities of financial and technical assistance instead of threatening with sanctions.

Country Characteristics

The characteristics of the parties involved in negotiating and adopting international environmental treaties, that is, the states concerned, will have an impact on the likelihood of treaty adoption; in addition, they will have considerable influence on the probability of compliance.

There may be many reasons why states ratify treaties but nevertheless do not comply. States may ratify an agreement because of international pressure or to serve domestic interests. Domestic interests, however, may also oppose compliance. Hence, it may well be in the states' interest to ratify the agreement but not comply. Moreover, compliance with international environmental agreements is seldom a black or white situation: states may view most provisions of a treaty in their interest, complying with those provisions but violating a few others.

Other factors that may play a role include the cultural traditions, political system, administrative capacities of the country concerned, and economic factors. Compliance may also be influenced by the strength of NGOs, an issue that will be discussed below.

An important factor is whether a country has a democratic form of government. Many features of democratic governments contribute to improved implementation and compliance. There may be more transparency and hence easier monitoring by citizens who can exert pressure to improve the implementation record. Also, NGOs generally have more freedom to operate in democratic countries. A considerable role can also be played by individuals, such as the heads of state. In many cases the personal enthusiasm of a particular head of state has facilitated compliance, usually during the treaty negotiating process.[26]

As was indicated above, compliance may also fail because of incapacity. This could be due to the country's lack of administrative capacity to implement the treaty, which in turn may have to do with, for example, the level of education and training of the bureaucrats. The level of administrative capacity also depends on economic resources. In addition, compliance with treaties sometimes requires investment in technologies that countries with fewer resources simply lack.

Number of States and the International Environment

The greater the number of countries that have ratified an accord, and the greater the extent of their implementation and compliance, the greater is the probability of compliance by any individual country. Noncompliance would then run counter to international public opinion.[27] There is also a relationship between the area to be regulated in the environmental treaty and the number of countries that can be expected to comply. For example, the International Whaling Commission faces a trade-off between, on the one hand, maintaining a moratorium on commercial whaling in a treaty that fewer countries have been willing to sign, or, on the other hand, allowing some commercial whaling in order to keep a larger number of countries within the scope of the treaty and thus achieve a higher compliance record.[28] Having a large number of countries accept the contents of a treaty comes at a price, and it may lead to a lowering of the standard to be achieved.

The general "international environment" will have an influence on the willingness of a country to engage in the treaty obligations and on the subsequent compliance record as well. This can be analyzed in terms of the problems of free riding and "prisoner's dilemma."[29] Free riding refers to the fact that individual states may hope that others will take the necessary measures to reduce the sources of a transboundary pollution problem, thus free riding on their efforts. The game-theoretical prisoner's dilemma in this context refers to the fact that although mutual compliance may be in the interest of all states in order, for example, to reduce transboundary industrial pollution, the absence of enforcement may lead all parties to believe that they can violate. Because of these problems, enforcement was traditionally advocated to guarantee compliance.

Compliance also depends on the distribution of power among nations, which can influence individual states' compliance strategies. A dominant state, perceiving sufficient benefits from complying, may force compliance by other, weaker states.[30] In those cases compliance does not even require explicit enforcement. Obviously, the division of power between states may change, which will also produce changes in the incentives to comply.[31]

States sign numerous international treaties. Negotiations on treaties and compliance often involve situations in which states will encounter each other repeatedly in the context of various treaties (often referred to as "repeat-player games"). Such multiple encounters may have a beneficial influence on compliance. Thus the fear of free riding can be overcome if the record of compliance is related to potential benefits for states in existing and future international agreements.[32] In other words, states may comply because future agreements with the same partner states will be possible if they have an acceptable compliance record.

This international-environment perspective underscores the point made in the Theory of Compliance section of this chapter: that states increasingly belong to various regimes that engage them in a repeat-player game. Hence, the incentives to comply may emerge from these regimes, reducing the need for formal enforcement of one particular treaty.[33]

Role of NGOs

NGO activity can beneficially influence the compliance record of a country in various ways.[34] International environmental NGOs may influence international public opinion, shaping the agenda that determines the issues to be dealt with in a treaty. For instance, activities of environmental NGOs contributed, through increasing pressure on the international community, to the agreement on the Framework Convention on Climate Change, leading to the adoption of the Kyoto Protocol in December 1997. Once a treaty has come into being, NGOs can play a crucial role in ensuring compliance. As watchdogs, they can pressure their governments to uphold the key provisions of specific regimes. This so-called bottom-up approach to compliance is increasingly stressed in the literature.[35] The role of NGOs here also illustrates that their actions can lead to what is referred to as "compliance as self-interest," or at least not treaty-induced. Through pressure by environmental groups, public opinion may be influenced in such a manner that the country views the costs of a potential violation of treaty provisions as prohibitively high.[36]

Finally, NGOs can also provide information about activities that are addressed in international environmental treaties. Greenpeace, for instance, is an important source of information about ocean dumping.[37] Hence, NGO activity may foster transparency both at the negotiating and at the implementation and compliance stages.

These factors generally merit the conclusion that stronger and more active NGOs help increase the probability of compliance.

Responses to Noncompliance

As we have discussed, traditional treaty mechanisms for noncompliance were restricted to adversarial dispute settlement procedures. These procedures, used generally under international environmental law, mostly involve a sequence of diplomatic and legal means of dispute settlement. Diplomatic settlement procedures usually involve negotiation and consultation in a first instance. If negotiation and consultation do not lead to a solution, some form of mediation or conciliation is often prescribed. This involves third parties or international institutions. In case of deeper conflicts, parties often can have recourse to legal means of dispute settlement, either arbitration or the International Court of Justice. In July 1993 the International Court of Justice set up a special chamber for environmental matters.[38]

This standard sequence of dispute resolution—negotiation, mediation, and finally arbitration or submission to the International Court of Justice—can still be found in more recent treaties, such as the Vienna Convention for the Protection of the Ozone Layer and the FCCC. Article 11 of the Vienna Convention prescribes negotiation as the first means of dispute resolution (paragraph 1). If this fails, parties must seek mediation by a third party (paragraph 2). As an ultimate remedy, arbitration or submission to the International Court of Justice, or in absence of agreement over this remedy a conciliation committee, is prescribed (paragraphs 3–5). Article 14 of the FCCC and Article 19 of the Kyoto Protocol contain similar wording.

The number of cases brought under dispute settlement proceedings is still very limited, especially considering the compliance problems with most environmental treaties. The International Court of Justice has so far never dealt with a purely environmental conflict.[39] Conflicts under dispute settlement proceedings mostly involve either trade relationships or territorial disputes. One of the reasons for the limited use of dispute settlement instruments is that these procedures are characterized by an adversarial relationship between the parties, so they are only used as a last resort. States are rarely willing to risk their relationship with other sovereign international actors by openly challenging them. As stated above, even in a close community of states such as the EU, the state complaints procedure under Article 227 of the treaty establishing the European Community (EC Treaty)[40] has rarely been used. Not only are traditional dispute settlement procedures rarely used, they are also considered less effective and less appropriate in environmental treaties. The result of noncompliance with environmental treaties is often damage to the global commons in general, affecting all states rather than one or several well-identified parties.

The ineffectiveness of dispute settlement proceedings in international environmental agreements has led to the development of a new system for responding to noncompliance, called noncompliance procedures (NCPs). Such procedures, rather than punishing noncompliance, are aimed at finding ways to facilitate compliance by the state that is in breach of its obligations. They provide a political framework for "amicable" responses to noncompliance that cannot be considered "wrongful." This tendency to use NCPs reflects the new managerial approach, which no longer assumes that noncompliance is the result of a willful desire to violate.

One of the consequences of shifting from an adversarial approach to a more managerial approach is that sanctions play only a minor role in the noncompliance response system. Three categories of sanctions can be distinguished: treaty-based sanctions, membership sanctions, and unilateral sanctions.[41] The latter category of unilateral sanctions is now severely restricted under international law. As discussed above, resort to the use of military force is exceptional. Trade sanctions are increasingly difficult to invoke under the rapidly developing international trade regimes. Treaty-based sanctions have not proven very popular, which can be explained by the political difficulties involved in the use of such a system. The European Union is, however, an exception to this. Since November 1993, the European Commission (which supervises the application of the EC Treaty) has had the competence to ask for the imposition of a financial penalty upon a Member State that is in breach of its obligations (Article 228 of the EC Treaty).[42] After a slow start, the European Court of Justice has now imposed financial penalties for noncompliance with EC law in a number of situations, making it the "sharp end" of the EU's enforcement procedures.[43] This now also has an important preventive effect, as Member States now remedy their violation before the final court decision.

Sanctions against states party to an international treaty, including expulsion or suspension of rights and privileges, are also not considered an effective response in the case of noncompliance with an environmental treaty, since one of the aims of these treaties is to achieve global membership. (See the box on noncompliance procedures of the Montreal Protocol.)

The nonadversarial approaches to solving international environmental disputes seem to be gaining increasing popularity. For example, as far as the management of the Rivers Meuse[44] and Rhine is concerned,[45] international commissions have been installed to promote stakeholder involvement and exchange of information. The consensual approach followed in the Rhine basin has led to a substantially better water quality in the Rhine River than in the Great Lakes of the United States, despite looser regulation.[46] The politics of water protection in the Great Lakes basin has been more adversarial than in the Rhine watershed, a situation that has reduced the willingness of Great Lake firms to invest in water protection.[47]

Toward Comprehensive Noncompliance Response Systems

In this chapter we have given an overview of the new approaches to compliance with international environmental treaties that have been developed since the beginning of the 1990s. We have observed a clear shift from the old approach, including dispute settlement proceedings and sanctions in treaties, to the managerial approach, which tries to use a more comprehensive system of different methods for solving compliance problems. Increasingly, more recent treaties have included a comprehensive combination of different instruments for responding to noncompliance. These systems, also referred to as comprehensive noncompliance response systems, contain not only methods to sanction violations but also, and perhaps more important, methods to facilitate compliance, improve transparency and reporting procedures, and prevent violations.[48]

The various capacities of states can be taken into account in the design of the primary rule system by allowing financial or technology transfer

Noncompliance Procedures:
The Montreal Protocol and the Kyoto Protocol

The more recent environmental treaties have new noncompliance procedures, often side by side with the traditional dispute settlement procedures. A prime example of a well-functioning noncompliance procedure is the one set up under Article 8 of the Montreal Protocol. This article states that the parties to the protocol "shall consider and approve procedures and institutional mechanisms for determining noncompliance with the provisions of this Protocol and for treatment of Parties found to be in noncompliance."

At the Copenhagen meeting in November 1992 the Meeting of the Parties adopted the procedure under this article. An Implementation Committee was set up, consisting of ten representatives elected by the Meeting of the Parties, based on equitable geographical distribution. Although under the noncompliance procedure parties can also submit reservations regarding another party's implementation of its obligations under the protocol, this adversarial action has in practice not become the main function of the procedure. The focus has instead been on the nonadversarial functions. The procedure allows states, when they believe they are unable to comply with their obligations, to report this inability to the Secretariat and the Implementation Committee. The Implementation Committee also discusses the general quality and reliability of the data contained in the member states' reports. The Implementation Committee, meeting three to four times a year, has, in fact, assumed a very active role in improving the quality and reliability of the data reported by the member states and, in a cooperative sphere, has sought solutions for parties with administrative, structural, and financial difficulties.

The noncompliance procedure under the Montreal Protocol has served as an important source of inspiration for the development of the compliance regime under the Kyoto Protocol. This regime, which was finalized at the FCCC meeting in Marrakesh in 2001 (COP-7) and started its operation following its formal adoption after the entry into force of the Kyoto Protocol at the FCCC meeting in Montreal in December 2005, has both a facilitative and an enforcement branch. The enforcement branch will determine whether a country has met its emissions target and, as a result of this determination, apply the consequences for non-compliance that were agreed between countries at COP-7 if this is not the case. The mandate of the facilitative branch is based on the nonadversarial role that the Compliance Committee of the Montreal Protocol has assumed in practice. The facilitative branch has the task of assisting all countries in their implementation of the protocol. Of interest is that the facilitative branch has so far played only a minor role, whereas the enforcement branch has already been requested to deal with two cases (one by Greece and one by Canada). Both cases related to the eligibility of these parties to participate in the Kyoto Protocol's flexible mechanisms. Canada's case, concerning the design of its registry to track transactions under these mechanisms, was resolved before a formal finding of noncompliance. Greece was held in noncompliance for failing to set up an adequate national system to monitor and report its emissions, but its eligibility was restored following Greece's setting up of an adequate system.[a]

(continued)

Noncompliance Procedures:
The Montreal Protocol and the Kyoto Protocol (continued)

There is also evidence that other regimes are learning from the Montreal experiences and are including a more managerial approach in their treaty design as well. For example, the United Nations Economic Commission for Europe created a convention on environmental impact assessment in a transboundary context, which was signed in Espoo, Finland, in 1991 (entered into force 1997); this convention also has a structure with a secretariat and a meeting of the parties (MOP) that can facilitate implementation of the convention and resolve disputes. A similar structure was followed by the Aarhus Convention on access to information, public participation in decision making, and access to justice in environmental matters; it also makes use of MOPs that can establish "on a consensual basis, optional arrangements of a non-confrontational, non-judicial and consultative nature for reviewing compliance with the provisions of this convention" (Article 15).

The noncompliance procedures developed under the Montreal Protocol have thus strongly influenced the design of other conventions as well.

---

[a] See "Third Annual Report of the Compliance Committee to the Conference of the Parties Serving as the Meeting of the Parties to the Kyoto Protocol," document FCCC/KP/CMP/2008/5, October 31, 2008, http://unfccc.int/resource/docs/2008/cmp4/eng/05.pdf.1; see also Gilbert Bankobeza, "Compliance Regime of the Montreal Protocol," in *The Montreal Protocol: Celebrating 20 Years of Environmental Progress*, ed. Donald Kaniaru (London: UNEP/Earthprint, 2007), chap. 7, 75–106.

---

mechanisms. These differing capacities can also be taken into account in the noncompliance response system. The fact that self-reporting of noncompliance should not immediately result in negative sanctions but can lead to actual support to remedy incapacity can, in turn, also increase the reporting record. Although the managerial approach is proving successful in treaties such as the Vienna Convention and the Montreal Protocol, one should not forget that we are only at the beginning of new efforts to find solutions to compliance problems. In many other areas it remains difficult to reach any international consensus at all on the protection of our global environment.

International environmental law is increasingly moving from a phase in which the emphasis was on the adoption of standards to one in which the focus is on the implementation of and actual compliance with these standards. One should not forget, however, that it is especially in the phase of adoption that a well-designed noncompliance response system can prove decisive in getting states to agree to new commitments.

Notes

1. United Kingdom, House of Lords, Select Committee on the European Communities, "Implementation and Enforcement of Environmental Legislation," Session 1991–1992, 9th report, HL paper 53-I, March 10, 1992, sec. 39.

2. Harold K. Jacobson and Edith Brown Weiss, "Strengthening Compliance with International Environmental Accords: Preliminary Observations, from a Collaborative Project," *Global Governance* 1 (1995): 119–148. The authors rightly point to the fact that there are very few studies of compliance with international environmental treaties and even fewer studies that focus on factors at the national level that affect compliance. Their cross-treaty and cross-country evaluation of compliance is an important exception. See also Ronald B. Mitchell, "Compliance Theory: An Overview," in *Improving Compliance with International Environmental Law,* ed. James Cameron, Jacob Werksman, and Peter Roderick (London: Earthscan, 1996), 3–28; and David G. Victor, Kal Raustiala, and Eugene B. Skolnikoff, eds., *The Implementation and Effectiveness of International Environmental Commitments: Theory and Practice* (Cambridge: MIT Press, 1998).

3. Jacobson and Brown Weiss, "Strengthening Compliance," 124.

4. Article 227 of the treaty establishing the European Community, one of the treaties forming the basis of the EU, contains the possibility of one or more Member States bringing another Member State before the European Court of Justice. Since the founding of the European Community in 1958, this procedure has been rarely used. One example is the Court's judgment in the fisheries conflict between France and the United Kingdom (Case 141/78). In this case the UK was held to have breached EC law when searching a French trawler and convicting its master.

5. This new approach is, however, not followed by all scholars. See for example J. L. Goldsmith and E. A. Posner, *The Limits of International Law* (Oxford: Oxford University Press 2005), who stress that states will mainly conclude agreements and comply when this is in their self-interest. See also Andrew T. Guzman, "A Compliance-Based Theory of International Law," *California Law Review* 90 (2002): 1823–1888.

6. This new idea is probably best formulated by Abraham Chayes and Antonia Handler-Chayes, *The New Sovereignty: Compliance with International Regulatory Agreements* (Cambridge: Harvard University Press, 1995); see especially chap. 1.

7. For a review of the early literature on regimes, see Marc A. Levy, Oran R. Young, and Michael Zürn, "The Study of International Regimes," *European Journal of International Relations* (1995): 267–330. See also Oran Young, ed., *The Effectiveness of International Environmental Regimes* (Cambridge: MIT Press, 1999).

8. Chayes and Handler-Chayes, *New Sovereignty,* 27.

9. The role of reputation in complying with international agreements is strongly stressed in the work of Andrew T. Guzman: see "The Design of International Agreements," *European Journal of International Law* 16, no. 4 (2005): 579–612; and *How International Law Works: A Rational Choice Theory* (Oxford: Oxford University Press 2008), especially chap. 3.

10. Articles 2 (3) and 2 (4), in combination with Articles 42 and 51 of the UN Treaty.

11. Chayes and Handler-Chayes, *New Sovereignty,* 22–28.

12. A. Guzman, *How International Law Works,* 175.

13. For a comparison of these two cases, see David Downie, "Road Map or False Trail: Evaluating the Precedence of the Ozone Regime as Model and Strategy for Global Climate Change," *International Environmental Affairs* 7, no. 4 (fall 1995): 321–345.

14. Examples of this can be found in European environmental law. See Michael Faure and Jürgen Lefevere, "The Draft Directive on Integrated Pollution Prevention and Control: An Economic Perspective," *European Environmental Law Review* 5 (April 1996): 112–122.

15. See, with respect to nuclear accidents, Organization for Economic Cooperation and Development, *Liability and Compensation for Nuclear Damage: An International Overview* (Paris: OECD, 1994); Michael Faure and Göran Skogh, "Compensation for Damages Caused by Nuclear Accidents: A Convention as Insurance," *Geneva Papers on Risk and Insurance* 17 (October 1992): 499–513; J. Deprimoz, "Regime juridique des assurances contre les risques nucléaires," *JurisClasseur* 555 (1995): 1; with respect

to civil liability for marine oil pollution, see Michael Faure and Günter Heine, "The Insurance of Fines: The Case of Oil Pollution," *Geneva Papers on Risk and Insurance* 17 (January 1991), 39–58; and for recent developments, see E. H. P. Brans, "Liability for Ecological Damage under the 1992 Protocols to the Civil Liability Convention and the Fund Convention and the Oil Pollution Act of 1990," *Tijdschrift voor Milieuaansprakelijkheid* 94, nos. 3, 4 (1994): 61–67 and 85–91.

16. "The developed country Parties and other Parties included in Annex I commit themselves specifically as provided for in the following: (a) Each of these Parties shall adopt national policies and take corresponding measures on the mitigation of climate change, by limiting its anthropogenic emissions of greenhouse gases and protecting and enhancing its greenhouse gas sinks and reservoirs. These policies and measures will demonstrate that developed countries are taking the lead in modifying longer-term trends in anthropogenic emissions consistent with the objective of the Convention, recognizing that the return by the end of the present decade to earlier levels of anthropogenic emissions of carbon dioxide and other greenhouse gases not controlled by the Montreal Protocol would contribute to such modification, and taking into account the differences in these Parties' starting points and approaches, economic structures and resource bases, the need to maintain strong and sustainable economic growth, available technologies and other individual circumstances, as well as the need for equitable and appropriate contributions by each of these Parties to the global effort regarding that objective. These Parties may implement such policies and measures Jointly with other Parties and may assist other Parties in contributing to the achievement of the objective of the Convention."

17. For details, see Jacob Werksman, "Designing a Compliance System for the UN Framework Convention on Climate Change," in Cameron, Werksman, and Roderick, *Improving Compliance with International Environmental Law*, 85–112; and see Philippe Sands, *Principles of International Environmental Law*, vol. 1, *Frameworks, Standards and Implementation* (Manchester, England: Manchester University Press, 1995), 217–280.

18. For a more in-depth background on the Kyoto Protocol mechanisms, see Sebastian Oberthür and Hermann Ott, *The Kyoto Protocol: International Climate Policy for the 21st Century* (Berlin: Springer, 1999).

19. Jacobson and Brown Weiss, "Strengthening Compliance," 126.

20. Richard Benedick, *Ozone Diplomacy, New Directions in Safeguarding the Planet* (Cambridge: Harvard University Press, 1998); Benedick describes this process of decision making under scientific uncertainty.

21. The IPCC published its Fourth Assessment Report in 2007. This report, for which the IPCC was awarded a Nobel Peace Prize (together with former U.S. vice president Al Gore for his work on climate change), is available on the IPCC Web site, www.ipcc.ch.

22. The EU's greenhouse gas emissions trading directive (Directive 2003/87/EC) explicitly requires, for example, the publication of the names of companies that do not comply with their obligation to surrender sufficient emission allowances to compensate for their greenhouse gas emissions (Article 16(2)).

23. Several varieties of reporting and data collection are discussed by Chayes and Handler-Chayes, *New Sovereignty*, 154–173.

24. Gro Harlem Brundtland, "The Road from Rio," *Technology Review* 96 (1993): 63.

25. Mitchell, "Compliance Theory," 14; and Lynne M. Jurgielewicz, *Global Environmental Change and International Law* (Lanham, Md.: University Press of America, 1996), 113.

26. Jacobson and Brown Weiss, "Strengthening Compliance," cite the important role of the Brazilian president Fernando Collor in the UNCED conference (142). President Bill Clinton and Vice President Al Gore played an important role in Kyoto in December 1997; they contributed to the adoption of the Kyoto Protocol even though they failed to secure its subsequent ratification by the United States owing to insufficient support in the Senate.

27. Ibid., 129.
28. Mitchell, "Compliance Theory," 24.
29. Jacobson and Brown Weiss, "Strengthening Compliance," 143; and Oran Young, *International Governance: Protecting the Environment in a Stateless Society* (Ithaca, N.Y.: Cornell University Press, 1994), 110–115.
30. Young, *International Governance*, 37–39.
31. Mitchell, "Compliance Theory," 15.
32. Ibid., 11.
33. Belonging to a particular regime can thus also increase the reputational losses felt by violating parties, a point often stressed by Guzman, *How International Law Works*, chap. 3.
34. For a general discussion of the role of NGOs in international environmental law, see The Foundation for International Environmental Law and Development (FIELD) and Ecologic, *Participation of Non-Governmental Organisations in International Environmental Governance: Legal Basis and Practical Experience* (German Umweltbundesamt, June 2002), available from the Web site, www.field.org.uk/tisd_11.php. See also Chayes and Handler-Chayes, *New Sovereignty*, 250–270. See also chapter 5, "The Role of Environmental NGOs in International Regimes," in this book.
35. See, for example, James Cameron, "Compliance, Citizens and NGO's," in Cameron, Werksman, and Roderick, *Improving Compliance with International Environmental Law*, 29–42; and, more particularly, see the book review by Oran R. Young in *International Environmental Affairs* 9 (winter 1997): 84.
36. Mitchell, "Compliance Theory," 9.
37. For further details, see Jacobson and Brown Weiss, "Strengthening Compliance," 129, 140–142.
38. Patricia Birnie and Alan Boyle, *International Law and the Environment* (Oxford: Oxford University Press, 2002), 224–226.
39. A recent example of a case that does not explicitly deal with environmental issues but one in which the environment plays an important role is the one concerning the Gabcikovo-Nagymaros Dam on the Danube River, on which the International Court of Justice pronounced judgment on September 25, 1997.
40. With the implementation of the Treaty of Lisbon, Article 227 of the EC Treaty became Article 255 of the Treaty on the Functioning of the European Union 2008.
41. Chayes and Handler-Chayes, *New Sovereignty*, 30.
42. Article 260 of the Treaty on the Functioning of the European Union 2008.
43. For a full overview of the EU's noncompliance procedures, see Paul Craig and Gráinne De Búrca, *EU Law: Text, Cases and Materials* (Oxford University Press, 2008), 452–457.
44. See C. P. R. Romano, *The Peaceful Settlement of International Environmental Disputes: A Pragmatic Approach* (London: Kluwer Law International, 2000), 233–245; and M. Bouman, "A New Regime for the Meuse," *Review of European Community and International Environmental Law* 5, no. 2 (1996): 161–168.
45. See André Nollkaemper, *The Legal Regime for Transboundary Water Pollution: Between Discretion and Constraints* (Utrecht: Martinus-Nijhoff, 1993).
46. M. Verwey, "Why Is the River Rhine Cleaner Than the Great Lakes (Despite Looser Regulation)?" *Law and Society Review* 34, no. 4 (2000): 1007–1054.
47. Ibid., 1040.
48. Mitchell, "Compliance Theory," 14; Chayes and Handler-Chayes, *New Sovereignty*, 25; Werksman, "Designing a Compliance System," 115–116.

10

The United States and Global Environmental Politics: Domestic Sources of U.S. Unilateralism

Elizabeth R. DeSombre

> *"We must be very careful not to take actions that could harm consumers . . . this is especially true given the incomplete state of scientific knowledge on the causes of, and solutions to, global climate change."*

President George W. Bush in a letter
to Senator Chuck Hagel[1]

> *"The post–Kyoto climate negotiations . . . offer an important opportunity for America to re-engage with the rest of the world in taking on one of the greatest challenges of this generation. But we must start by showing the world that we are serious about tackling the climate crisis here at home."*

President-elect Barack Obama
December 10, 2008[2]

When Barack Obama was elected president of the United States in November 2008, he promised to "renew American diplomacy"[3] and to "make the U.S. a leader on climate change."[4] Environmentalists rejoiced, hoping for an end to the George W. Bush era of reduced domestic environmental regulation and rejected international environmental engagement. But in evaluating the likelihood of a return to U.S. international environmental leadership, it is essential to understand the history of the U.S. role in environmental diplomacy and the factors that underlie the positions the United States takes on international environmental issues.

The history of U.S. engagement with international environmental issues is complex. In the 1970s the United States emerged as a real leader on the development of international environmental agreements, working to negotiate agreements on international trade in endangered species, ocean pollution, and, later, to protect the ozone layer. But the decline in that leadership was evident long before George W. Bush was elected. It was most apparent at the United Nations Conference on Environment and Development in Rio de Janeiro in 1992. Of the two binding agreements signed there, the United States signed but refused to ratify the Convention on Biological Diversity (and has not signed its Biosafety Protocol) and signed and ratified the United Nations Convention on Climate Change (after working to weaken it); it refused to ratify the Kyoto Protocol to that agreement, negotiated later, which contained actual abatement obligations.

But the U.S. refusal to participate in important international environmental agreements began even earlier. Its lack of ratification of the Basel Convention on the Control of Transboundary Movements of Hazardous Wastes and Their Disposal (1989) and related treaties on transborder movement of other toxic materials suggests that it managed to avoid important global environmental obligations before Rio. Its public and sudden refusal to ratify the United Nations Convention on the Law of the Sea (1982), at least partially for reasons relating to how it addressed access to resources of the deep seabed, extends this pattern further back in time.

To be sure, the effect of the administration of George W. Bush on the U.S. role in international environmental politics should not be overlooked. Most important was his role on climate change and the stated desire of the United States to "unsign" the Kyoto Protocol.[5] U.S. unwillingness to participate delayed the protocol's entry into force and weakened the agreement because without the United States it needed the participation of almost all industrialized countries, many of which also refused to go along until their obligations were made more flexible and less onerous. It also arguably decreased the likelihood that those states that did take on obligations would meet them. Without serious action by the United States to decrease emissions, other states knew their actions could not make a serious impact on the climate system. Canada's decision to not meet its Kyoto obligations, for instance, made reference to the U.S. absence from the UN climate negotiation process.[6]

In addition, the recent unilateral behavior of the United States is not restricted to issues of environmental cooperation; even apart from broader difficulties with the United Nations over Iraq, the United States has refused to join the International Criminal Court; to sign the Convention on the Prohibition of the Use, Stockpiling, Production and Transfer of Anti-Personnel Mines and on their Destruction (1997); or to ratify the Comprehensive Test Ban Treaty (1996), to name just a few recent issues.

The recent unwillingness of the United States to lead—or even join—efforts at multilateral environmental cooperation in the post–Cold War world thus seems overdetermined: it is neither an entirely new phenomenon, nor one restricted to environmental issues, and it is certainly not one that can be attributed to the administration of George W. Bush. It is an essential trend to understand, given a U.S. history of strong domestic environmental action, previous U.S. leadership on global environmental issues, the importance of the United States for addressing global environmental issues, and a new administration that promises increased engagement with the world community. When does the United States lead in addressing global environmental problems, and when does it refuse even to go along? A variety of approaches explain U.S. action in terms of broader characteristics of the country or its ideological goals, the degree of uncertainty about the environmental problem, the ecological vulnerability of the United States or the costs of taking action on the issue in question, or the domestic political power of industrial actors likely to bear those costs.

Ultimately the most promising explanation for the pattern of U.S. unilateralism on international environmental issues involves characteristics of the domestic political system and the way in which national policymaking relates to international negotiations. The issues on which the United States leads internationally are those on which it has previously regulated domestically. The intersection between domestic politics and international relations can go a long way toward explaining what we see, and what we should expect, from U.S. environmental leadership. It also explains why, despite the particularly unilateralist bent of the George W. Bush administration, it is less the actions or the party of the president that matter, and much more the regulatory processes undertaken by Congress that provide an explanation for U.S. environmental leadership or lack thereof. If we want to understand what the United States has chosen to pursue or avoid internationally in terms of environmental policy, and predict what future leadership is likely, we need to look at what it has regulated or shunned domestically.

U.S. Environmental Leadership

The United States has traditionally had among the strictest environmental regulations on the domestic level[7] and has often been a leader internationally on environmental issues. It has a reputation for "taking environmental treaties seriously,"[8] suggesting that when it does participate in multilateral environmental efforts it tends to implement the relevant provisions domestically and comply with the obligations of the treaties. Moreover, it has been the driving force behind the negotiations to address a number of international environmental problems. This leadership can be seen in the context of U.S. actions to protect endangered species internationally and to protect the atmosphere from substances that deplete the ozone layer.

Endangered Species

The United States was one of the principal proponents of international action to protect endangered species, beginning in 1900 with the Lacey Act, which prohibited trafficking in animals taken illegally in their country of origin as well as those killed in violation of any U.S. or international law.[9] Domestically the U.S. Endangered Species Act (and its predecessors) restricted the taking, importing or exporting, and sales of species listed as endangered, and it adopted a variety of increasingly strict regulations to protect species wherever they were found. Early versions of this legislation also called on the United States to negotiate binding international agreements to protect endangered species worldwide.[10] The United States followed this concern by working for international protection of endangered species, via the creation of the Convention on International Trade in Endangered Species of Wild Fauna and Flora (CITES) (1973). U.S. participation was important in other early international negotiations to address endangered species, such as the Ramsar Convention on Wetlands of International Importance Especially as Waterfowl Habitat (1972), and in the creation of a moratorium on commercial whaling—agreed to in 1982, begun in the 1985–1986 whaling season—under the International Convention for the Regulation of Whaling (1946).[11]

Ozone Depletion

U.S. leadership on global atmospheric issues was evident in its response to ozone depletion. U.S. involvement with the issue of ozone depletion stemmed from scientific research undertaken in the early 1960s to ascertain whether a planned fleet of supersonic aircraft would harm the ozone layer. In addition, much of the other early scientific work on sources of possible harm to the ozone layer took place in the United States.[12] The United States also took the lead in domestic regulation, including in the 1977 Clean Air Act Amendments that required that U.S. industry phase out the use of chlorofluorocarbons (CFCs, the main substances implicated in ozone depletion) in nonessential aerosols, beginning in 1978.[13] The United States hosted the 1977 International Conference on the Ozone Layer, the first intergovernmental discussion of the problem of ozone depletion, which produced the World Plan of Action on the Ozone Layer. Although the United States resisted meaningful international regulation during the period shortly following that conference, by the early 1980s it had joined with the Nordic countries, Austria, Canada, and Switzerland in support of deep cuts in international production and use of ozone-depleting substances. This coalition supported such measures in the negotiation of the 1985 Vienna Convention for the Protection of the Ozone Layer.

But staunch opposition from European countries, which had not yet taken any action to regulate their domestic production of ozone-depleting substances, resulted in a framework treaty that simply supported the principle of ozone layer protection without requiring substantive abatement obligations. The United States came out as a clear leader, however, in the negotiation for binding reductions of emissions of ozone-depleting substances that resulted in the 1987 Montreal Protocol on Substances that Deplete the Ozone Layer. U.S. proposals began with a freeze on use of harmful substances and then suggested a range of further reductions. It also, along with its negotiating partners (and against the European Community), insisted that all known ozone-depleting substances be regulated under the protocol. In addition, several bills introduced into Congress in 1987 would have prohibited imports of ozone-depleting substances or products that contained them or were made from them if the exporting countries did not adopt domestic measures to protect the ozone layer. (This legislation was abandoned when the protocol was successfully negotiated.)[14]

Lack of Leadership

More recent U.S. refusals to ratify the major international initiatives to address global issues such as climate change and biodiversity protection suggest that the United States is often unwilling to exercise leadership or even participate in some multilateral environmental efforts. In addition to these two issues, it is useful to examine U.S. refusals (some earlier than the Rio conference) to accept a variety of efforts to regulate the international movement of hazardous chemicals and waste and to the ratify the Law of the Sea Convention.

Climate Change

The position of the United States on global efforts to mitigate climate change (global warming) has been the most obvious evidence of recent U.S. recalcitrance. The United States participated in the negotiation of the United Nations Framework Convention on Climate Change (FCCC) signed at the Earth Summit in Rio in 1992. Its main goals for the negotiation, however, were to avoid the creation of binding targets and timetables for reduction of greenhouse gas emissions (which European states were willing to negotiate) and to ensure that all major greenhouse gases (rather than just carbon dioxide) be included in any agreement. The United States prevailed in these goals because the other major negotiators did not want to create an agreement without U.S. participation.[15] The convention nevertheless sets out a potentially important set of principles that member states accept by ratification. The agreement's objective is to stabilize atmospheric greenhouse gas concentrations "at a level that would prevent dangerous anthropogenic interference with the climate system," although that level is not specified. The agreement acknowledges the use of the precautionary principle, indicating that lack of full certainty is not to be used to postpone taking action to address the issue, and specifies that "the developed country Parties should take the lead in combating climate change and the adverse effects thereof."[16] The Senate ratified this agreement quickly,[17] and the United States has lived up to its implementation obligations by reporting on its emissions and policies pertaining to climate change.

U.S. interaction with the Kyoto Protocol, the agreement that requires cuts in emissions of greenhouse gases from developed country parties, has been even less productive from the perspective of international environmental cooperation. The United States did take part in the negotiation of the agreement. During negotiations in 1996, Tim Wirth, the U.S. undersecretary of state for global affairs, suggested that negotiations should set "a realistic, verifiable, and medium-term emissions target," making the United States the first major FCCC party to call for binding reductions.[18] In general the United States advocated in the negotiation process that the greatest degree of flexibility (from trade in emissions, joint implementation, and the counting of sinks for greenhouse gases) be included, and most of these issues were written into the agreement in much the way the United States wanted. The one exception was the actual abatement obligations; President Bill Clinton originally set the U.S. negotiating position at a freeze at 1990 emissions levels by 2008. In the agreement as negotiated in Kyoto, the United States was persuaded to accept a reduction of its greenhouse gas emissions of 7 percent below 1990 levels.[19]

Several months before the final negotiation at which the agreement was to be signed, the U.S. Senate passed what came to be known as the Byrd-Hagel resolution, indicating the Senate's intention not to ratify any agreement that would require abatement obligations from industrialized countries unless it simultaneously "mandates new specific scheduled commitments to limit or reduce greenhouse gas emissions for developing country parties within the same compliance period." This resolution passed 95-0.[20] The Senate's resolution did not succeed in influencing the agreement's treatment of developing countries, as the entire Kyoto negotiation process had been premised on a lack of specific abatement obligations for developing countries in the first commitment period. It did, however, ensure that the Clinton administration, despite having signed the agreement, could not realistically submit it to the Senate for ratification.

Congress has also influenced the extent and content of domestic U.S. action in the absence of the Kyoto Protocol. One congressional approach was to craft provisions that would have encouraged voluntary emissions reductions by granting credit to industries that undertook emissions reductions early should there be later policies requiring them. In the absence of these types of policies, those who took early action might then have more difficulty than their competitors increasing their energy efficiency further once specific U.S. policies were passed. Several similar bills for this purpose were introduced in the 105th and 106th Congresses but were defeated. Although some argued that these efforts were not strong enough to address the climate problem, the real opposition came from those who opposed any legislative measures that would encourage the cutting of greenhouse gas emissions. Former presidential candidate Jack Kemp, for example, argued in opposition to these measures that we must "guard against a milder version of the Kyoto treaty that would serve the same purpose, offering concessions to companies that would acquiesce in creating the biggest global regulatory regime yet conceived."[21]

In reaction to efforts to encourage voluntary measures, other members of Congress introduced bills to forbid any action on climate change. Representative David McIntosh, R-Ind., proposed H.R. 2221, which not only would have prohibited the use of federal funds for advocating, developing, or implementing early credit systems for voluntary emissions reductions, but would also have mandated that federal funds not be used "to propose or issue rules, regulations, decrees, or orders or for programs designed to implement, or in preparation to implement, the Kyoto Protocol" before the Senate ratified the agreement. While this legislation did not pass, it inhibited the creation of new policies to give credit for voluntary measures.[22] The more successful effort, however, came from attaching a legislative rider to appropriations bills in 2000 and 2001. Representative Joseph Knollenberg, R-Mich., inserted language into these bills prohibiting the government from undertaking any action that would contribute to meeting the goals of the Kyoto Protocol before it had been ratified by the Senate.[23]

More recent congressional proposals, however, have proposed that the United States take domestic action, outside of the Kyoto framework, to address its emissions of greenhouse gases. Sen. Joseph Lieberman (earlier a Democrat, then later an Independent from Connecticut) has repeatedly introduced versions of legislation to cap and then reduce U.S. greenhouse gas emissions. The 2003 version (cosponsored with Sen. John McCain, R-Ariz.) would have created a cap and trade system for greenhouse gases in the United States, with the objective of returning U.S. emissions by 2010 to what they had been in 2000.[24] Subsequent versions of the proposed legislation have changed dates and targets; most have not even received a floor vote. The 2008 version, the Lieberman-Warner Climate Security Act, came closer to passing than any previous measures. Although it was subject to procedural jockeying that meant it never received a full vote in the Senate, fifty-four Senators indicated their support for cap and trade measures for greenhouse gases in the bill's process.[25] Prior to the end of George W. Bush's term as president, however, the United States did not have any governmentally supported emissions reduction plan.

In the interim, U.S. states have begun their own greenhouse gas emissions reductions mandates, many of them legally binding. California took the lead, requiring that by 2010 greenhouse gas emissions be reduced to the level of 2000, and many states since then have created state-level climate policies.[26] In addition, regional groupings of states have undertaken climate policies. The governors of six New England states created the New England Governors Climate Change Action Plan that set forth a goal of collective reduction of greenhouse gas emissions by 2010 to 1990 levels, and a further reduction by 10 percent below 1990 levels by 2020, and an ultimate reduction to a level that would not pose a threat to the climate.[27] Another effort in the Northeast, the Regional Greenhouse Gas Initiative (RGGI), began in 2005 with seven northeastern states (Connecticut, Delaware, Maine, New Hampshire, New Jersey, New York, and Vermont; joining in 2007 were Rhode Island, Massachusetts, and Maryland). RGGI caps carbon dioxide emissions from power plants (initially at 2009 levels, with a 10 percent reduction by 2019) and allows trading of emissions allowances. Six Midwestern states (Illinois, Iowa, Kansas, Michigan, Minnesota, and Wisconsin) along with the Canadian province of Manitoba created a similar cap and trade system in 2007, as did states and provinces in the North American West in the same year.[28] So individual states and regions have taken steps to create climate policy, even when a national policy proved unreachable.

It is certainly true that climate change provides an unusually difficult case for U.S. leadership; U.S. emissions of greenhouse gases on a per capita basis (and, until recently when China's emissions surpassed it, also in the aggregate)[29] are far higher than those of any other country. Certain demographic characteristics contribute to these high levels of emissions, such as the large size of the country and the long distances U.S. residents travel (particularly without access to public transportation). The large land area of the country also makes possible a number of individual choices, not only about commuting but also about the size and number of residential housing units, that increase greenhouse gas emissions. A tradition of low gasoline prices and easy access to fossil fuels has increased reliance on individual transportation and discouraged fuel efficiency and alternative energy generation. But the level of U.S. unwillingness to entertain national or international efforts to mitigate climate change, in conjunction with evidence of voluntary behavior on the part of industry, especially in the context of other reluctant environmental leadership, needs to be explained.

Biodiversity

The other main issue initiated at the 1992 Earth Summit in Rio on which the United States has resisted international action is the issue of biodiversity. In keeping with its history of concern about the protection of species, the United States helped launch the initial negotiations in the late 1980s, but the United States became apprehensive at the direction of the negotiations. In particular, the United States feared that the resulting treaty would require strengthening the U.S. Endangered Species Act and the conservation of wetlands, both of which the George H. W. Bush administration was trying to weaken. The United States was also concerned about the principle, favored by developing countries, of the importance of equitable sharing of the benefits of biodiversity. This principle as well as other fears about inadequate protection for intellectual property rights under the treaty were of concern to the biotechnology and pharmaceutical industries within the United States. It was in response to these concerns that any references to "biosafety" (or efforts to limit the trade in genetically modified organisms) were omitted from the negotiated draft.[30] The United States announced, however, before the Rio conference, that it would not sign the Convention on Biological Diversity (CBD) even in this weakened form. President Bush indicated in particular that he was concerned about the treaty's possible impact on jobs in the United States.[31]

After Bill Clinton was elected president at the end of 1992, a group of nongovernmental organizations and biotechnology and pharmaceutical firms met on their own initiative for several months to determine whether there could be advantages to U.S. participation in the treaty.[32] This group eventually proposed that the United States sign the agreement but issue an interpretive statement, providing its understanding of its obligations under the treaty. In particular, this group, which included major firms such as Merck, Genentech, and WRI, concluded that the treaty would not create major economic difficulties in the near term and that participating in the process might be better for the United States than remaining outside of it. At the same time, the United States conducted an interagency review that determined that the treaty could be implemented within the existing legal framework.[33] President Clinton signed the CBD in 1993 and sent it to the Senate for ratification, along with a letter of submittal that incorporated the interpretive language indicating that the treaty would not endanger essential patent protection or harm research or innovation by industry.

Ratification did not follow, however. Despite a 16-3 vote by the Senate Committee on Foreign Relations to support the treaty, a vote was not taken in the Senate in either 1993 or 1994, presumably because the Senate majority leader (George Mitchell, D-Maine) ascertained that the two-thirds majority needed for approval would not materialize. By the time the issue would have been considered in 1993, thirty-five Republican senators (one more than required to block ratification) had come out against the treaty. The reasons given for opposition to the treaty were varied and included claims that the text was too vague, unnecessary, would hamper U.S. business interests, or would commit the United States to transfers of funding and technology to developing countries.[34] Subsequent Republican majorities in the Senate meant the issue of ratification was not even considered, and it was not a priority in the Senate at the end of George W. Bush's term. The lack of ratification by the United States has reduced its role to that of an observer at meetings of the parties (although an observer whose interests are nevertheless influential) and in the negotiation of the protocol to the convention.

Trade in Hazardous Wastes and Other Toxic Materials

The United States generates the overwhelming majority of hazardous waste in the world, although much of it is disposed of within U.S. borders. Nevertheless, the approximately 1 percent of U.S. hazardous waste that is traded still marks it as a higher exporter of waste than many major countries.[35] The United States has signed but has refrained from ratifying the main treaty to address trade in hazardous waste, the Basel Convention on the Control of Transboundary Movements of Hazardous Wastes and Their Disposal (1989).

The United States was involved in the negotiation of the Basel Convention and used its role in the negotiation to weaken the proposed agreement. The treaty negotiation was an effort to make formal a set of nonbinding guidelines created by the United Nations Environment Programme governing council in 1987. Many states that were the recipients of hazardous wastes wanted the new binding agreement to go further and actually ban the trade in hazardous wastes; concurrent discussions outside of the specific negotiations showed many European states to be sympathetic to a stronger regulatory framework. The United States, however, served as the center of a blocking coalition of developed states that refused to participate if such stringent regulations were enacted. As a result, the eventual treaty created a system by which states needed to be notified (and given the opportunity to refuse) before hazardous waste was sent to them. It also included agreement that hazardous waste was to be disposed of in a manner that was environmentally sound, though that term was not defined.

The United States signed the agreement but did not immediately send it to the Senate for ratification. President Clinton announced his intention to submit the treaty for ratification in 1998, but the treaty has still not been ratified. One of the difficulties for the United States in terms of contemplating the implementation of this agreement is that the definition of hazardous waste under the Basel Convention is broader than under current U.S. domestic regulation, and industry groups oppose expanding current regulations.[36] Although the United States has reasonably strong existing controls on how it deals with hazardous waste, these measures are in a different format (and thus regulate a somewhat different list of substances) than would be required under the Basel agreement.

In addition, the United States actively opposes the amendment to the convention, referred to as the Basel Ban, that would end all such trade between rich and poor countries. During the negotiations on the ban the United States made a clear effort to defeat it, even though, as a nonparty to the treaty, its direct forms of influence were limited. It nevertheless worked hard to convince individual states to take leadership positions opposing the ban and allocated funding for international meetings to help persuade others of its possible negative ramifications.[37] The ban ultimately was negotiated in the form of an amendment to the convention, but it has experienced delays in entering into force. Some environmental nongovernmental organizations now actually discourage U.S. ratification of Basel if, as seems inevitable, it would happen without simultaneous ratification of the Ban amendment.[38] They fear that U.S. ratification of the agreement without the ban would then allow the United States to work to undermine the ban and enable it to trade with other Basel members that have not accepted the ban.

The United States has also been slow to take action on two other treaties on toxic substances—the Stockholm Convention on Persistent Organic Pollutants (2001) and the Rotterdam Convention on the Prior Informed Consent Procedure for Certain Hazardous Chemicals and Pesticides in International Trade (1998). Although President George W. Bush signed the Stockholm Convention and repeatedly indicated an interest in ratifying it, the United States has been reluctant to create a domestic process that could be used for deciding which chemicals would be restricted under the treaty. This unwillingness has held up the ratification process.[39]

In the negotiations on what became the Rotterdam Convention, moving from a voluntary prior informed consent (PIC) procedure to one that was mandatory for trade in hazardous chemicals and pesticides, the United States supported a proposal that increased the difficulty of including a chemical on the list. In place of a system where any chemical banned in one country would immediately trigger a PIC procedure, the chemical would need to be banned in two different countries representing two different regions, thereby preventing a chemical banned only in European countries from making the list.[40] Despite the inclusion of this U.S.-supported measure in the final version of the treaty, the United States has also not ratified this agreement. Legislation has been periodically introduced in the House of Representatives to implement the provisions that the United States would need to have in place in order to comply with the both agreements, if ratified. Although the bills have been referred to committee,[41] none have been voted on, and as of early 2010 the treaties have not been brought for ratification to the U.S. Senate.

The Law of the Sea

The United Nations Convention on the Law of the Sea is an additional international agreement on which the United States has resisted action. Negotiation on the treaty, which attempts to address in one agreement all issues relating to oceans, was completed in 1982, but President Ronald Reagan refused to sign the agreement. His administration expressed concern about the redistributive aspects of provisions in the treaty for regulating deep seabed mining and fears that the United States would not be guaranteed influence in decisions on these issues.[42] When George H. W. Bush was president, the United States worked to negotiate an annex (The Agreement Relating to the Implementation of Part XI of the Convention) that addressed these concerns, after which the United States signed the treaty in 1994 and President Clinton submitted it to Congress for ratification. The treaty received unanimous support of the Senate Committee on Foreign Relations. It was not brought to a vote in the Senate that year, however, owing to strong opposition from a group of conservative senators and the unwillingness of the White House to invest political capital in the issue.[43]

Recent developments have brought new pressure on the United States to ratify the agreement. Jockeying for newly accessible ocean resources (especially in the Arctic as climate change makes previously frozen areas accessible) has intensified. Russia made bold claims to continental shelf resources in the Arctic in 2007 by planting a flag on the seabed in an area it claims as an extension of Russia's landmass.[44] The treaty allows for states to claim mineral rights to areas of the continental shelf contiguous with their territory far beyond what had previously been accepted under international law, with the treaty's governing process responsible for adjudicating such claims. Only those states that have ratified the treaty can participate in the process.

In May 2007 President George W. Bush publicly urged the Senate to ratify the agreement. In October 2007 the Senate Foreign Relations Committee voted 17-4 in favor of ratification.[45] Opposition from some senators remained strong, however, and the full Senate did not take up the question of ratification before Bush left office.

Understanding U.S. Unilateralism

What explains the variety of U.S. actions? In an examination of only the specific cases discussed here, several possible conclusions emerge about the determinants of U.S. international environmental leadership. These include a consistent ideological approach to international regulation or other elements of U.S. exceptionalism (including a general suspicion of multilateralism), the issue of uncertainty, the severity of the environmental problem for the United States, and the degree to which U.S. industry is impacted by proposed regulations. One explanation is that the United States has become more inclined toward unilateral action in recent years, although earlier strong rejection of multilateral cooperation on environmental issues (such as the deep seabed issues in the law of the sea) and relatively recent U.S. willingness to cooperate on increasingly strict protection of the ozone layer suggest that this is not a sufficient explanation. And to the extent that recent behavior denotes a trend, ascertaining the reasons behind this trend would nonetheless be important.

Before examining a more specifically environmental hypothesis, it is worth exploring the possibility that there is a normative unity to the environmental goals the United States pursues or avoids internationally. There appear to be some ideological consistencies in the international environmental issues on which the United States has avoided serious international participation. Harold Jacobson argues that what the CBD, the Kyoto Protocol, and the Law of the Sea (three of the major international agreements that the United States has refused to ratify) have in common is specific provisions that provide a redistribution of the benefits of cooperation to developing countries.[46] The Kyoto Protocol eschews abatement obligations for developing countries but includes the promise of funding and technology transfer. The CBD requires that the profits and results from biotechnology development be shared with those states from which the biodiversity resources were obtained. The Law of the Sea created a deep seabed mining regime in which the benefits of such mining would explicitly be redistributed to developing countries.

Objections to these provisions were stated as the major impediments to U.S. participation in these agreements. These types of policies represent the approaches pursued by developing countries under the rubric of the "new international economic order" in the 1970s and 1980s. It is particularly telling that the United States participated actively in the negotiation of all of these agreements and in the case of the Law of the Sea and the CBD explicitly attempted to exclude these redistributive measures but failed. The analysis breaks down partly in the context of the Kyoto Protocol, however, since the United States did not actively push for developing country obligations under the agreement. And, as Jacobson points out, the flexibility mechanisms the United States supported so strongly for the Kyoto Protocol would likely result in some level of income redistribution to developing countries:[47] developing countries would be able to receive funding for undertaking action that reduces global emissions of greenhouse gases. Moreover, other international agreements the United States has avoided, such as the Basel Convention, do not contain these redistributive elements, and some that the United States has joined, such as the Montreal Protocol (under which the United States is the largest contributor of funding), do. If ideology does not explain recalcitrance, what does?

A related explanation points to the general U.S. reluctance to accept international norms on a wide range of issues, from human rights to international security, with environment just one additional manifestation of this approach. Some identify this issue as "exceptionalism," focusing particularly on the idea of cultural relativism.[48] If the United States is indeed exceptional, its reluctance to take on unnecessary foreign entanglements may be one side effect of this phenomenon. A related issue is the possibility that the United States, as the most powerful state internationally in the post–Cold War era, knows that it does not need international cooperation to guard its interests. This seems an unlikely explanation for issues of the global environmental commons, however, where states cannot protect themselves unilaterally. In any case, as Andrew Moravcsik points out, identifying exceptionalism, even where relevant, does not explain it.[49]

When the United States chooses not to take action on a given environmental issue such as global climate change, uncertainty is often given as a reason for inaction. U.S. reticence on climate change frequently mentions incomplete knowledge. On the face of it, this explanation for U.S. behavior seems implausible. Although genuine uncertainty may exist on many of these issues, the United States was willing to act in the face of uncertainty on ozone depletion but not climate change, and few would argue that U.S. inaction on biodiversity can be primarily attributed to lack of information. Moreover, other states have access to the same degree of information on these issues that the United States does, and they make different decisions about how to act internationally. That may not damn this explanation; some have suggested that the ways the United States handles uncertainty in the political process may be different from the way other states do.

In particular the United States has a different approach to risk than others do. Sheila Jasanoff has compared the different ways states approach risk on the domestic level, and she noted that the European policy process is more cautious about accepting risk than that of the United States.[50] This finding would not seem to explain U.S. reluctance on the international level on issues pertaining to risk (such as climate change and biodiversity or biosafety), especially when the main proponents of international cooperation on these issues are European states. Jasanoff addresses this issue with respect to U.S. responses to climate change, suggesting that because the scientific community in the country does not have a clear hierarchy, when there are political actors that gain from avoiding action, they can make use of existing uncertainty, implicitly painting the taking of action as riskier than doing nothing. Lawrence Susskind argues that the United States uses scientific evidence to support international action it prefers, but "when we prefer to take a different political course we attack the available data as insufficient regardless of the strength of the worldwide scientific consensus."[51] In this context, then, uncertainty is an excuse but not an explanation.

A common explanation for the leadership behavior of states on environmental problems is the extent to which states are likely to be harmed by them. Detlef Sprinz and Tapani Vaahtoranta argue that "the worse the state of the environment, the greater the incentives to reduce the ecological vulnerability of a state."[52] They suggest that states will be "leaders" on international environmental issues when they are particularly affected by the issue environmentally but will either resist action or simply go along when their ecological vulnerability is low. It is true that the United States is less likely to be harmed by issues such as climate change or biodiversity loss than are those states that are more generally dependent on land-based resources and less able to adapt to environmental change. However, a simple comparison of U.S. vulnerability across even the issues addressed here does not explain why the United States was more willing to act on ozone depletion than on climate change (the latter certainly has a bigger environmental and economic impact on the country than the former) or less willing to act on biodiversity protection than on trade in endangered species. Moreover, the United States is more likely to be harmed economically by its continued refusal to ratify the Law of the Sea convention.

Another plausible interpretation of U.S. decisions on environmental leadership is that decisions depend on the extent to which domestic industry bears a cost from taking action to address the issue. Sprinz and Vaahtoranta also posit that the costs of abatement play an important role in determining the extent of state leadership on the international level. Although they examine cases where restricting emissions is the abatement cost, it could be argued that the predicted costs of international action on an issue more broadly can play an important role in determining what a state—in this instance, the United States—will choose to undertake internationally.

This logic fits well with anecdotal evidence and domestic theorizing about the particularly important role U.S. businesses play in politics within the United States. It also appears consistent with U.S. avoidance of action on climate change. Sebastian Oberthür and Arthur Ott argue that the U.S. position on climate change can be understood by its status as the world's largest producer of coal, oil, and gas.[53] While estimates of the cost to the United States of implementing the Kyoto Protocol vary widely (and with some correlation to the political position of those making the estimates), it is clear that the cost and disruption, at least initially, to the U.S. way of life from addressing climate change could be large. A U.S. Department of Energy report comparing studies predicting the costs of implementing Kyoto obligations (though not accounting for emissions trading or other flexibility mechanisms) found estimates ranging from $91 billion to $311 billion.[54] (It is also worth noting that the energy intensity of the U.S. economy provides additional opportunities for behavior change not available to other states.)

A straight comparison of costliness of regulatory action does not, however, predict the U.S. pattern of international leadership on environmental issues. While some in the U.S. biotechnology and pharmaceutical industries feared the economic cost of the CBD and urged George H. W. Bush not to sign it on that basis, other similar industries had determined within the space of the year that the economic costs would not be large. Similarly, U.S. action on ozone depletion was likely at least as costly (and the costs were more clearly known in advance) as potential costs from protecting biodiversity. And if one considers the cost to the United States of implementing the provisions of CITES, which includes a set of border controls that would otherwise not be required, they are larger than might have been the case for biodiversity.

A related view is that what matters is the political power of industry within the United States on a given issue. Even if the cost to the country as a whole of an abatement measure for a given environmental problem is not enormous (or is not the main basis on which decisions about international action are made), the cost to the industry that has to adapt is meaningful to that industry. The extent to which that industry has influence within the U.S. political process should then have an impact on the willingness of the United States to take a stand internationally. Detlef Sprinz and Martin Weiß argue that industry interests in opposition to reduction of greenhouse gas emissions had a disproportionate impact on the U.S. negotiating process on the FCCC.[55] We would need to come up with a more sophisticated explanation, however, for what accounts for this disproportionate impact on policymaking and how to generalize when and how it will affect U.S. international environmental actions.

A more nuanced view about the extent to which U.S. industry will be able to marshal domestic political efforts to avoid international commitments would focus on specifying aspects of the domestic political process in the United States that allow those opposing international environmental leadership to have influence. One argument made on a different issue is that the United States has a set of decentralized political institutions that "empower small veto groups."[56] Peter Cowhey has suggested that "national politicians have been unlikely to accept any global regime that fails to reinforce the preferred domestic regime."[57] Kal Raustiala points out that states rarely create completely new domestic regulatory structures to address international issues, but rather rely on existing institutional structures domestically. That observation suggests that how domestic institutions are structured "influences what can be implemented, and often what is negotiated."[58] This explanation may help us identify either domestic structural determinants of U.S. global environmental leadership or simply content-based approaches to evaluating the likelihood of eventual U.S. international action on an issue.

The United States also has an admirable tradition of accepting only those international environmental obligations with which it intends to comply, unlike some states, including the European Union, that are more likely to see commitments as goals. Other states (such as the former Soviet Union) frequently accept obligations they have no intention of complying with or know that they will not be capable of fulfilling in the near future.[59] This propensity may influence the degree to which the United States is willing to take on obligations, limiting them to those with which it intends to comply. Structural constraints only serve to magnify this tendency.

Structurally, the separation of powers between the executive and legislative branches of government and the fact that the Senate must ratify treaties by a two-thirds majority can be seen to have the effect of hindering U.S. international environmental action under certain circumstances. Although a domestic ratification process for treaties exists in most countries, the U.S. barrier is doubly high, requiring not only a supermajority vote but also one in a completely different branch of government. Oona Hathaway notes that the United States is nearly unique in its high barrier to ratification—it is one of only six states worldwide that requires support by a supermajority of a legislative body, and it is one of only a few in which ratification involves automatic incorporation into domestic law.[60] Many other advanced industrialized democracies operate under parliamentary systems in which the head of government is a member of the majority (or largest) party; thus, treaties submitted to parliament for ratification by the prime minister are likely to be accepted. Some have noted that the willingness of Congress to reassert its control over foreign policy increased in the post–Cold War era, when the need for strong central executive leadership lessened.[61] Under this explanation, the two branches of government may be at odds about what a policy should be, resulting in a situation in which the president pushes an international approach that Congress refuses to go along with.

That it is the Senate that ratifies treaties by such a supermajority may be especially important. The U.S. Senate is particularly prone to economic pressure from special interest groups. Elections to the Senate ensure that each state is represented by two senators concerned about the issues that matter to their states to a greater degree than those that impact the country as a whole. This focus is an avenue for industry impact. And, as Hathaway points out, the ideological composition of the Senate also means that the two-thirds ratification threshold requires cooperation among senators on vastly different parts of the political spectrum. If senators serving in the 109th Congress had been lined up on an ideological spectrum, the sixty-seventh senator would have been rated more than twice as conservative as the fifty-first; the same would have been true in the liberal direction.[62] Requiring a two-thirds majority makes agreement orders of magnitude more difficult than requiring a simple majority would. This difference may serve to explain increased U.S. reluctance on international environmental issues compared with other major industrialized states, but it alone cannot explain the variations in degrees of U.S. unilateralism on different environmental issues.

What is possible, however, is that the role of the Senate intersects with some characteristics of environmental issues to influence the likelihood of U.S. international leadership on a given issue. The Senate's consideration and adoption of the Byrd-Hagel resolution is itself an indication of the important congressional role in addressing international environmental policy. The Senate took up this issue on its own, not only without direction from the executive branch, but without making President Clinton even aware, until the last minute, that such a debate would happen. At that point the White House could not hope to stop the adoption of the resolution, and it simply tried to moderate its language.[63] In the case of this particular resolution, Democratic senator Robert C. Byrd represented West Virginia, a major coal producer, and Republican senator Chuck Hagel represented Nebraska, where agriculture, the most important economic sector, is highly mechanized and thus sensitive to the price of oil.[64]

What brings these explanations together is the process of domestic congressional regulation. One notable consistency with U.S. international environmental leadership is the extent to which the United States had already undertaken domestic regulatory action—on the topic and in the form being considered internationally—at the point at which such action was being pushed internationally. Harold Jacobson's description of the U.S. experience with environmental multilateralism is telling: he points to the U.S. wave of multilateral environmental diplomacy in the 1970s with the following description: "[A]s soon as U.S. legislation designed to protect and enhance the environment was in place, the United States typically proposed that multilateral treaties be negotiated to achieve the same objective."[65] Note, for example, that a major concern in the U.S. decision about whether to sign or ratify the CBD was the question of whether it could be implemented within the existing legal framework protecting endangered species and land resources. This understanding helps explain particularly well the U.S. reluctance on climate change: the United States not only has no preexisting domestic climate change mitigation policy but also has traditionally rejected any sort of tax on energy. This reluctance has been particularly demonstrated in Congress. One analyst points out that eliminating chemicals under the Stockholm Convention on Persistent Organic Pollutants that the United States has not already banned domestically is a particular sticking point in the effort at ratification.[66]

This analysis does not imply that U.S. industry is always cheerful about adopting international environmental regulations, but it does suggest that the existence of previous domestic regulations on an industry changes its interests internationally. The example of ozone depletion, a potentially costly regulatory issue with a reasonably high degree of uncertainty at the time of international regulation, is illustrative. Although the history of U.S. regulatory efforts on the subject shows that producers and large consumers of CFCs fought initial regulatory efforts (and invoked scientific uncertainty as well as industrial cost as arguments against regulation), industry eventually acquiesced to international regulation. The process began domestically, when consumer purchasing habits and pressure from domestic environmental organizations persuaded Congress to include a ban on CFCs in nonessential aerosols in the 1977 Clean Air Act Amendments. That regulation, which the main producers of CFCs fought from the beginning (and attempted to get repealed after it had passed),[67] nevertheless put CFC producers and consumers on notice that they would have to come up with alternatives for at least some of their activities. It also fundamentally changed their incentive structure (especially when they realized that increasingly severe domestic regulations were likely). They then were more likely to support international controls on CFCs so that foreign industries with which they competed internationally would have to be bound by the same costly restrictions.

Conclusion

U.S. leadership (or even level of participation) in international environmental agreements has been mixed, and even can be seen as declining in the last decade and a half. To attribute this trend simply to U.S. unilateral urges misses the opportunity, however, to understand when and why the United States is more or less likely to lead internationally on environmental issues. Within a domestic framework that can make international participation difficult, it is nevertheless possible for the United States to exercise international leadership. It tends to do so on issues it has already addressed domestically and where the form of the domestic regulation fits the format of the international regulation being considered. Under those circumstances, domestic opposition to international action is muted or even avoided because such domestic industries, which have disproportionate influence on the senators who have to vote for ratification of any international agreements, either are not additionally disadvantaged by new international regulations or even welcome those that restrict the actions of their international competitors. To the extent that the United States returns to global environmental leadership under President Obama, it is at least as likely to be attributable to the change in the composition of the Senate as it is to executive branch leadership.

The United States took an early lead in the domestic regulation of many environmental harms in the 1960s and 1970s, and those regulations set the groundwork for many international efforts to deal with the global versions of these problems. It is thus no surprise that the United States would be both willing and able to lead globally in addressing them. To the extent that the United States has more recently ceased in many issue areas to be a domestic innovator on environmental policy, it is also no surprise that the United States resists international action on newer international environmental issues. Although issues such as uncertainty and the effect on the United States of the environmental problem or the costliness of regulatory solutions certainly contribute to the difficulty of international regulation, where they are particularly important may be at the level of domestic regulation. Those who would prefer that the United States lead internationally should perhaps focus their efforts on creating the domestic regulations that give it the incentive to do so.

The issue is rarely so clear-cut, however; and the links between domestic and international action are becoming more porous. The case of climate change particularly bears watching, as U.S. domestic industries are in some instances becoming the major proponents of U.S. action on climate change or are undertaking meaningful voluntary steps themselves to address the problem. The pattern we have traditionally seen, of U.S. action following only from domestic regulation, may be changing with the more diffuse and complex international environmental issues that are appearing on the international agenda. It may come to pass that U.S. domestic action on such issues as climate change happens in the reverse, pushed by industry impacted by international (or subnational) regulation.

Notes

1. Julian Borger and Ian Black, "Bush Drops Pledge on Cutting CO_2," *Guardian* March 15, 2001, 15.
2. Barack Obama, "Statement on Climate Change Negotiations in Bali," December 10, 2008, www.barackobama.com/2007/12/10/obama_statement_on_climate_cha.php.

210   Elizabeth R. DeSombre

3. Office of the President-Elect, "Agenda—Foreign Policy," http://change.gov/agenda/foreign_policy_agenda/2008.
4. Office of the President-Elect, "Agenda—Energy and the Environment," http://change.gov/agenda/energy_and_environment_agenda/2008.
5. Eric Planin, "U.S. Aims to Pull Out of Warming Treaty," *Washington Post*, March 28, 2001, sec. A. There is no provision under international law to "unsign" an agreement that has been signed, and withdrawal is possible only by a state bound by the treaty once the treaty has entered into force.
6. Bill Curry, "Ottawa Now Wants Kyoto Deal Scrapped," *Globe and Mail*, May 20, 2006, www.climateark.org/shared/reader/welcome.aspx?linkid=56534.
7. Richard B. Stewart, "Environmental Regulation and International Competitiveness," *Yale Law Journal* 102 (1993): 2046.
8. Michael J. Glennon and Alison L. Stewart, "The United States: Taking Environmental Treaties Seriously," in *Engaging Countries*, ed. Edith Brown Weiss and Harold K. Jacobson (Cambridge: MIT Press, 1998), 197–213.
9. 16 U.S.C. 3372(a)(1)(1988).
10. The Endangered Species Conservation Act of 1969 called on the United States to seek "the signing of a binding international convention on the conservation of endangered species." P.L. 91–135 (Section 5).
11. It should be noted, however, that the United States is not a participant in the Bonn Convention on the Conservation of Migratory Species of Wild Animals (1979).
12. William C. Clark et al., "Acid Rain, Ozone Depletion, and Climate Change: An Historical Overview," in Social Learning Group, *Learning to Manage Global Environmental Risks*, vol. 1 (Cambridge: MIT Press, 2001), 35.
13. 43 *Federal Register* 11301; 43 *Federal Register* 11318.
14. Elizabeth R. DeSombre, *Domestic Sources of International Environmental Policy: Industry, Environmentalists, and U.S. Power* (Cambridge: MIT Press, 2000), 94.
15. William A. Nitze, "A Failure of Presidential Leadership," in *Negotiating Climate Change*, ed. Irving M. Mintzer and J. A. Leonard (Cambridge: Cambridge University Press, 1994), 188.
16. United Nations Framework Convention on Climate Change (1992), Articles 2 and 3.
17. U.S. Congress, Senate, 102d Cong., 2d sess. *Senate Congressional Record*, daily ed. October 1992, S.17, 156.
18. Michael Grubb with Christiaan Vrolijk and Duncan Brack, *The Kyoto Protocol* (London: The Royal Institute of International Affairs, 1999), 54.
19. Kyoto Protocol (1997), Annex B.
20. U.S. Congress, Senate, 105th Cong., 1st sess. *Congressional Record*, daily ed. July 27, 1997, S8113–8138.
21. Jack Kemp and Fred L. Smith Jr., "Beware of the Kyoto Compromise," *New York Times*, January 13, 1999, sec. A.
22. Kai S. Anderson, "The Climate Policy Debate in the U.S. Congress," in *Climate Change Policy*, ed. Stephen H. Schneider, Armin Rosencranz, and John O. Niles (Washington: Island Press, 2002), 243.
23. Ibid., 244.
24. Joseph I. Lieberman and John McCain, "Tap U.S. Innovation to Ease Global Warming," *U.S. Department of State International Information Programs*, January 8, 2003, www.america.gov/st/washfile-english/2003/January/20030108064712bjohnson@pd.state.gov0.3441126.html.
25. Pew Center on Global Climate Change, "Analysis of the Lieberman-Warner Climate Security Act of 2008," June 6, 2008, www.pewclimate.org/analysis/l-w.
26. Pew Center on Global Climate Change, "State Legislation from Around the Country," n.d., www.pewclimate.org/what_s_being_done/in_the_states/state_legislation.cfm.
27. Henrik Selin and Stacy VanDeveer, "Political Science and Prediction: What's Next for U.S. Climate Change Policy," *Review of Policy Research* 24(1)(2007), 1–27.

28. Pew Center for Global Climate Change, "Regional Initiatives," n.d. www.pewclimate.org/what_s_being_done/in_the_states/regional_initiatives.cfm.
29. "China Surpasses U.S. Emissions," *International Herald Tribune,* June 21, 2007, 12.
30. Kal Raustiala, "The Domestic Politics of Global Biodiversity Protection in the United Kingdom and United States," in *The Internationalization of Environmental Protection,* ed. Miranda A. Schreurs and Elizabeth C. Economy (Cambridge: Cambridge University Press, 1997), 42–73. These were later included in a separate protocol.
31. Ann Devroy, "President Affirms Biodiversity Stance; Citing Jobs, Bush Firmly Rejects Treaty," *Washington Post,* June 8, 1992, sec. A.
32. Kal Raustiala, "Domestic Institutions and International Regulatory Cooperation: Comparative Responses to the Convention on Biological Diversity," *World Politics* 49, no. 4 (1997): 482–509.
33. Raustiala, "Domestic Sources," and Raustiala, "Domestic Institutions and International Regulatory Cooperation."
34. Robert L. Paarlberg, "Earth in Abeyance, Explaining Weak Leadership in U.S. International Environmental Policy," in *Eagle Adrift: American Foreign Policy at the End of the Century,* ed. Robert J. Lieber (New York: Longman, 1997), 135–160.
35. Marian A. L. Miller, *The Third World in Global Environmental Politics* (Boulder, Colo.: Lynne Reinner, 1995), 87–88.
36. Kate O'Neill, "Hazardous Waste Disposal," *Foreign Policy in Focus* 4, no. 1 (January 1999), www.fpif.org.
37. Jim Puckett, "The Basel Ban: A Triumph Over Business-As-Usual," Basel Action Network, October 1, 1997, www.ban.org/about_basel_ban/jims_article.html.
38. See, for instance, the Basel Action Network, www.ban.org.
39. Kristin S. Schafer, "Global Toxics Treaties: U.S. Leadership Opportunity Slips Away," *Foreign Policy in Focus* 7, no. 11 (September 2002), www.fpif.org/fpiftxt/1326.
40. Ibid.
41. See, for example, U.S. Congress, House of Representatives, 109th Cong., 1st sess., "Stockholm and Rotterdam Toxics Treaty Act of 2005," HR 4591; and House of Representatives, 109th Cong., 2d sess., "POPS, LRTAP POPS and PIC Implementation Act of 2006," HR 4800.
42. Don Kraus, "Time to Ratify the Law of the Sea," *Foreign Policy in Focus,* June 6, 2007, www.fpif.org/fpiftxt/4286.
43. William L. Schachte Jr., "The Unvarnished Truth: The Debate on the Law of the Sea Convention," *Naval War College Review* 61, no. 2 (Spring 2008): 119–127.
44. Paul Reynolds, "Russia Ahead in Arctic 'Gold Rush,'" BBC News, August 1, 2007, http://news.bbc.co.uk/2/hi/in_depth/6925853.stm.
45. Schachte, "The Unvarnished Truth," 119.
46. Harold K. Jacobson, "Climate Change, Unilateralism, Realism, and Two-Level Games," in *Multilateralism and U.S. Foreign Policy: Ambivalent Engagement,* ed. Shepard Forman and Stewart Patrick (Boulder, Colo.: Lynne Reinner, 2002), 428.
47. Ibid.
48. David Forsythe, *The Internationalization of Human Rights* (Lexington, Mass.: Lexington Books, 1991).
49. Andrew Moravcsik, "Why Is U.S. Human Rights Policy So Unilateralist?" in *Multilateralism and U.S. Foreign Policy,* 435–476.
50. Sheila Jasanoff, "American Exceptionalism and the Political Acknowledgment of Risk," *Daedalus* 19, no. 4 (Fall 1990): 395–406.
51. Lawrence E. Susskind, *Environmental Diplomacy: Negotiating More Effective Global Agreements* (Oxford: Oxford University Press, 1994), 65.
52. Detlef Sprinz and Tapani Vaahtoranta, "The Interest-Based Explanation of International Environmental Policy," *International Organization* 48, no. 1 (Winter 1998): 77–105.
53. Sebastian Oberthür and Arthur Ott, *The Kyoto Protocol* (Berlin: Springer, 1999), 18.

54. Department of Energy, "Comparing the Cost Estimates for the Kyoto Protocol," Report no. SR/OIA/98–03 (1998), www.eia.doe.gov/oiaf/kyoto/cost.html.
55. Detlef Sprinz and Martin Weiß, "Domestic Politics and Global Climate Policy," in *International Relations and Global Climate Change,* ed. Urs Luterbacher and Detlef F. Sprinz (Cambridge: MIT Press, 2001), 67–94.
56. Andrew Moravcsik, "Why Is U.S. Human Rights Policy So Unilateralist?" 348, lists this as one of the four characteristics he sees as explaining U.S. unilateralism on international human rights issues.
57. Peter F. Cowhey, International Telecommunications Regime: The Political Roots of Regimes for High Technology," *International Organization* 44 (Spring 1990): 171.
58. Raustiala, "Domestic Institutions," 487.
59. See, generally, Edith Brown Weiss and Harold K. Jacobson, eds., *Engaging Countries: Strengthening Compliance with International Environmental Accords* (Cambridge: MIT Press, 1998).
60. Oona A. Hathaway, "Treaties' End: The Past, Present, and Future of International Lawmaking in the United States," *Yale Law Journal* 117, no. 8 (2008): 1236–1372.
61. Stewart Patrick, "Multilateralism and Its Discontents: The Causes and Consequences of U.S. Ambivalence," in *Multilateralism and U.S. Foreign Policy,* 1–44.
62. Hathaway, "Treaties End," 1310–1311.
63. Jacobson, "Climate Change, Unilateralism, Realism, and Two-Level Games," in *Multilateralism and U.S. Foreign Policy,* 442.
64. Ibid.
65. Ibid., 415.
66. Schafer, "Global Toxics Treaties."
67. The main industry lobbying group, the Alliance for Responsible CFC Policy, did such things as draft legislation to be introduced into Congress to limit the EPA's ability to regulate ozone-depleting substance. "Congress Debates Depletion of Ozone in the Stratosphere," *Christian Science Monitor,* October 14, 1982, 19.

11

Environmental Policy Making in the European Union

Regina S. Axelrod, Miranda A. Schreurs, and Norman J. Vig

The creation of the European Union (EU), now with twenty-seven Member States, has transformed Europe. The objective of establishing a common internal economic market has contributed to the openness of national borders and the harmonization of many policies once in the exclusive domain of individual Member States. The EU also has established some of the strongest and most innovative environmental protection measures in the world. In principle, environmental protection now enjoys equal weight with economic development in EU policymaking. It is in fact quite remarkable that despite the mix of countries and cultures that form the EU—some rich, some relatively poor—the EU has managed to become an international agenda setter in relation to climate change, chemicals regulation, product standards, biosafety, and numerous other environmental matters. It is an impressive development that provides valuable lessons for other regions of the world to consider.

Political will and public support have been key factors behind EU success in approaching the environment from an integrated perspective. Over time, legal foundations were firmly established, giving the EU the right to take measures to protect the environment. This developed in part because Member States recognize that without common environmental policies, barriers to free trade develop, but also because of a growing conviction that future economic well-being is inherently tied to the quality of the environment. It may well be that the political, economic, and geographic diversity that characterize the EU has challenged policymakers to develop innovative strategies for overcoming differences and sharing burdens equitably, skills that are important at the global level as well.

The EU is therefore an important model to study, both as the most advanced regional organization of states and as a comprehensive environmental policy regime. The EU is an important actor in global environmental diplomacy, negotiating treaties on behalf of Member States. At least since the 1992 United Nations Conference on Environment and Development, the EU has played a leading role in promoting international environmental agreements. As a result of enlargement, the EU shapes environmental policy from the Baltic to the Aegean. The twelve new Member States that joined the EU between 2004 and 2007 were required to transpose into their national systems the entire body of EU laws, regulations, and directives, collectively known as the *acquis communautaire*. Enlargement has both complicated internal negotiations on environmental matters and provided opportunities to strengthen the EU's international reach on environmental issues. This chapter explores the history, institutions, current environmental policies, and future challenges of this unique supranational body.

The Political Origins of the European Union and Its Environmental Policy

The quest for political and economic union in Europe has its origins in the 1920s and 1930s, when it was recognized that some kind of supranational organization was needed to avoid brutal competition, protectionism, and war. But it was the experience of World War II that convinced statesmen to seek a new type of unity. U.S. economic assistance under the postwar Marshall Plan also called for regional cooperation.

The first step toward building a more integrated Europe was the formation of the European Coal and Steel Community (ECSC). The idea of French economic planner Jean Monnet and foreign minister Robert Schumann, the ECSC was created by the Treaty of Paris on April 18, 1951. The original members were Belgium, France, Germany, Italy, Luxembourg, and the Netherlands. Its economic goal was to pool the production of coal and steel for the benefit of all six countries. Its other purpose was to lock Germany politically and economically into a stable partnership with western Europe.

Other cooperative activities were slow to develop, but in June 1955 the six ECSC members decided to move toward closer economic integration. They saw a European free trade area or "common market" as a means to increase industrial and agricultural exports, to redistribute resources to economically depressed areas, and to encourage travel among countries. The result was the 1957 Treaty of Rome, which established the European Economic Community (EEC) and the European Atomic Energy Authority (Euratom). In the 1970s Denmark, Ireland, and the United Kingdom joined the EEC, and Greece, Portugal, and Spain followed suit by 1986. Austria, Finland, and Sweden became full members in 1995, bringing the membership to fifteen.[1] In 2004 the membership of the EU expanded to twenty-five, with the accession of Cyprus, the Czech Republic, Estonia, Hungary, Latvia, Lithuania, Malta, Poland, the Slovak Republic, and Slovenia. Bulgaria and Romania joined in 2007, bringing membership to 27 countries. Several other countries, including Croatia, the former Yugoslav republic of Macedonia, and Turkey are officially recognized as candidate countries for potential future membership; Iceland is applying for candidate status.

The European Union is built on a series of treaties. The Treaty of Rome contained no explicit provisions for protection of the environment. EEC policy on the environment dates from the 1972 Paris summit of the Community's heads of state and government, which was inspired in part by the United Nations Conference on the Human Environment held earlier that year in Stockholm. Under Article 235 of the Treaty of Rome, which permits legislation in new areas if consistent with EEC objectives, the summit proposed the

Map 11-1 European Union Member States, 2010

ICELAND

ATLANTIC
OCEAN

NORWAY

SWEDEN

FINLAND

NORTHERN
IRELAND

NORTH
SEA

ESTONIA

RUSSIA

BALTIC
SEA

LATVIA

IRELAND

UNITED
KINGDOM

DENMARK

LITHUANIA

NETHERLANDS

BELARUS

English Channel

GERMANY

POLAND

BELGIUM

LUX.

CZECH REP.

UKRAINE

FRANCE

SLOVAKIA

Bay of Biscay

SWITZERLAND

AUSTRIA HUNGARY

MOLDOVA

ROMANIA

Black Sea

PORTUGAL

ITALY

ADRIATIC SEA

BULGARIA

Corsica

SPAIN

Sardinia

MEDITERRANEAN SEA

AEGEAN SEA

TURKEY

Sicily

GREECE

CYPRUS

LEBANON

MOROCCO

ALGERIA

MALTA

1 SLOVENIA
2 CROATIA
3 BOSNIA AND HERZEGOVINA
4 SERBIA
5 KOSOVO UNDER THE UN
6 MONTENEGRO
7 ALBANIA
8 FORMER YUGOSLAV
REPUBLIC OF MACEDONIA

ISRAEL

TUNISIA

LIBYA

EGYPT

European Union members

Candidates for membership

Source: Adapted from Neal Riemer, Douglas Simon, and Joseph Romance, *The Challenge of Politics,* 3rd ed. (Washington, D.C.: CQ Press, 2011), 321.

creation of an Environmental Action Programme, in effect adding an environmental agenda to the Treaty of Rome.

During the next dozen years, the EEC adopted three environmental action plans (for 1973–1976, 1977–1981, and 1982–1986) and enacted more than twenty major environmental directives covering air and water pollution, waste management, noise reduction, protection of endangered flora and fauna, environmental impact assessment, and other topics. It took most of these actions first under Article 235 of the Treaty of Rome and later under Article 100a (added to the treaty by Article 18 of the Single European Act), which authorizes actions that directly affect "the establishment or functioning of the common market." The motivation for these laws was to avoid trade distortions caused by different environmental standards while dealing with problems that were inherently transboundary in nature.[2]

The next milestone in the development of the treaties was the Single European Act of 1986, which accelerated the integration process by calling for establishment of a single internal economic market by the end of 1992. Equally important, the act added a new section to the Treaty of Rome that formally defined the goals and procedures of EEC environmental policies and called for "balanced growth" by integrating environmental policy into all other areas of decision making. These goals and procedures can be found in Articles 174, 175, and 176 of the Consolidated Version of the Treaty Establishing the European Community (Consolidated Treaty), which was published in 2002.

The Maastricht Treaty (also called the Treaty on European Union), entered into force in 1993. It advocated closer political and monetary union and created a three "pillar" structure: Community affairs (customs union, single market, economic and monetary union, common agricultural policy, common fisheries policy, trans-European networks, environmental policy, social policy, EU competition law, consumer protection, immigration policy, asylum policy, the Schengen agreement, research, and education and culture); foreign and security policies; and cooperation in justice and home affairs. The Treaty of Lisbon has done away with this pillar structure and created a single legal entity. It also changed the name of the Treaty Establishing the European Community to the Treaty on the Functioning of the European Union.

The Maastricht Treaty also further strengthened the legal basis and procedures for environmental policy making. This trend continued upon revisions initiated by the Treaty of Amsterdam in June 1997. Article 3d of the Amsterdam Treaty (which became Article 6 of the Consolidated Treaty) states explicitly that "environmental protection requirements must be integrated into the definition and implementation of Community policies and activities . . . in particular with a view to promoting sustainable development."[3]

Expansion of the EU was addressed by the Treaty of Nice, which came into effect on February 1, 2003. Although the treaty deals primarily with the effects of enlargement on EU institutions, it also reaffirms the Union's commitment to environmental policy. At the December 2000 Nice conference that led to the treaty's formation, a declaration was adopted affirming Member States' determination "to see the European Union play a leading role in promoting environmental protection in the Union and in international efforts promoting the same objective at global level."[4]

Efforts to establish an EU constitution were blocked by "no" votes in referendums held in France and the Netherlands.[5] Failure to obtain agreement on a constitution resulted in efforts to forge a new treaty, the Treaty of Lisbon, that amends the Maastricht Treaty and the Treaty Establishing the European Community. The final holdout signature was that of Czech president Vaclav Klaus, a Euro skeptic and opponent of the treaty. He finally acquiesced to international pressure to sign the treaty after the Czech constitutional court ruled that the treaty did not conflict with the Czech constitution. The Lisbon

Treaty entered into force on December 1, 2009. It increases the issues subject to qualified majority voting in the European Council, strengthens the role of the Parliament in decision making, and creates new positions for a president and foreign minister. The treaty specifically states that combating climate change is a goal of the EU.

EU Institutions and Policymaking Processes

Institutions

The EU's primary institutions are the European Council and the Council of Ministers, the European Commission, the European Parliament, and the European Court of Justice (ECJ). There are also numerous secondary agencies, including the European Environment Agency (EEA).[6]

The European Council and the Council of Ministers are often simply called "the Council." Technically, when the heads of government meet, which they must do at least twice a year, it is known as the European Council or "European summit." Broad policy directions are set at these summits. More specific policy decisions are made in meetings of the relevant Council of Ministers. Thus, for example, environmental decisions are reached by the Council of Environment Ministers, which as the name suggests is made up of Member States' environment ministers. In the past, the presidency of the Council rotated among the Member States every six months. The Treaty of Lisbon created a permanent president of the Council with a two-and-a-half-year term. The first permanent president is Herman van Rumpuy. In addition, the Treaty of Lisbon empowers the Council to appoint a High Representative of the Union for Foreign Affairs and Security Policy with a five-year term. Catherine Ashton is the first to hold this post.

The Council is the most important EU body because it must approve all legislation. Council directives must be adopted by the individual Member States and incorporated into national law within a specified period of time, usually two years. The Treaty of Lisbon has eliminated the ability of member states to veto.

In general, the Council's actions reflect the national interests of the Member States. The 1986 Single European Act introduced qualified majority voting on some environmental matters (rather than requiring unanimity of all members), and subsequent treaties have expanded greatly the range of environmental matters where qualified majority voting applies. Qualified majority voting (a form of weighted voting) is a special procedure that gives greater weight to states with large populations but protects smaller states by requiring a majority of votes. Since the latest round of enlargement in 2007, a qualified majority requires at least 255 out of a total of 345 votes, or close to 74 percent for a measure to pass, plus a coverage of at least 62 percent of the EU's population. Due to changes introduced by the Treaty of Lisbon, from 2014, qualified majority voting will be based on a double majority of Member States and people. It will require 55 percent of the Member States representing at least

65 percent of the EU's population. Qualified majority voting is an important development in EU procedures as it limits the ability of a single or very small number of Member States to block action at the Union level that the majority desires while it provides minority interests with considerable power to check the actions of the majority.[7]

The European Commission, which functions partly as an executive branch and partly as an administrative bureaucracy, is led by twenty-seven appointed commissioners and includes more than forty directorates-general and services that are somewhat analogous to ministries and agencies of national governments. Starting in 2014, the number of commissioners will be equal to two-thirds the number of Member States. The Commission's task is to initiate EU legislation and to oversee its implementation by Member States. The Commission is also empowered to negotiate international agreements on behalf of the Union. The Treaties of Amsterdam and Nice strengthened substantially the powers of the Commission president. Romano Prodi held this position from 1999 to 2004. Since then the position has been held by José Manuel Barroso. A multinational bureaucracy of somewhat less than 25,000 civil servants serves the Commission and its directorates in Brussels.[8] For the period 2002–2012, the Directorate-General for the Environment, with approximately 750 staff, has four priority areas: climate change; nature and biodiversity; environment, health, and quality of life; and natural resources and waste.

The European Parliament is elected directly by voters in each country and tends to reflect the diverse interests of political parties and groupings across Europe. Because of the accessions of new Member States in 2004 and 2007, the number of parliamentarians has been in flux. Since the 2009 election, there have been 736 members of the European Parliament and 18 observers. The Parliament holds plenary sessions in Strasbourg, France, but much of its staff is in Luxembourg, and most of its committee meetings are held in Brussels. Draft legislation from the Commission is submitted to the Parliament, which can either accept the draft as is or propose amendments. The Parliament also must approve the Commission budget and EU treaties, and it votes on the appointment of the president and commissioners.[9]

The European Parliament lacks the power of legislative initiative, but citizens and national parliaments over time have gained greater influence over the EU's legislative agenda. The Treaty of Maastricht added a provision allowing a majority of Member States to request that the Commission develop a proposal if a piece of legislation concerns implementation of the treaty. The treaty also extends "co-decision" procedures to many policy areas: if the Parliament does not agree with the Council position after a second reading, a conciliation committee is formed to resolve differences. If agreement still cannot be reached, the Parliament can reject the proposal by majority vote, giving the Parliament a de facto veto. Co-decision has increased the Parliament's role in policymaking, resulting in more transparent decision making and reducing the so-called democratic deficit. The Treaty of Lisbon states that with one million signatures EU citizens can petition the Commission to submit a proposal in

any area of EU competence. National parliaments have eight weeks to examine legislative acts, and if one-third (or one-quarter, in issues pertaining to
Justice and Home Affairs) oppose a draft, the Commission is obliged to
review it. In addition, if more than one-half of national parliaments oppose an
act subject to co-decision, the European legislature (meaning, a majority of
the European Parliament of 55 percent of the votes in the Council) must
decide to move forward with the legislative process or to end it.

The European Court of Justice, located in Luxembourg, considers cases
brought before it by the Commission, the Council, or Member States concerning the application of EU treaties. At times, the ECJ is requested to
provide interpretations of law. In July 2008, for example, in response to the
request by the Federal Administrative Court of Germany for interpretation of
a Council directive on air quality assessment and management, the ECJ in case
C-237/07, *Dieter Janecek v. Freistaat Bayern,* ruled that individuals have the
right to require national authorities to draw up action plans when there is a
risk that emission limit values or alert thresholds may be exceeded.[10] In other
cases, the ECJ brings infringement cases against Member States for failure to
comply with Union law. The ECJ also has protected the right of Member
States to keep national laws that exceed Union-wide standards.

The European Environment Agency, approved in 1990, was established
in 1994 in Copenhagen after a long battle over its location. The EEA does
not have regulatory and enforcement powers; rather, it is tasked with helping
the Union and Member States with making informed decisions about the
environment. Its membership includes, in addition to the EU Member States,
Iceland, Liechtenstein, Norway, Switzerland, and Turkey. The six Balkan
countries—Albania, Bosnia and Herzegovina, Croatia, the former Yugoslav
Republic of Macedonia, Montenegro, and Serbia—are cooperating partners.
The EEA also collects and distributes environmental data through the European Environment Information and Observation Network (EIONET),
which consists of about three hundred environmental bodies, agencies, and
research centers.[11] It issues a substantial number of reports about the European environment each year, including emissions inventories and many types
of environmental assessments and scenarios.

The Policy Process

Policymaking within the EU is more "political" than a description of the
institutions might suggest.[12] Because the EU is a fluid and developing set of
institutions, policymaking is complicated by uncertainty over roles, powers,
and decision rules. The Treaty of Lisbon sets an upper limit of 751 parliamentarians. No Member State can have fewer than six or more than ninety-six
seats. Although scholars still debate whether the EU is primarily an "intergovernmental" organization dominated by the interests of individual Member
States or a "functional" regime that represents common transnational interests
and actors, it is increasingly regarded as a competent environmental actor
functioning as a "multilevel governance structure."[13]

The Commission and the Parliament can be viewed as supranational bodies, whereas the Council remains essentially intergovernmental. The Commissioners and their staffs are international civil servants who are not supposed to serve any national interest; therefore, the Commission's proposed legislation tends to favor greater harmonization of European policies. Parliament also tends to favor stronger EU policies, especially in fields such as environmental and consumer protection that are popular with the electorate. The Council, in contrast, is usually more cautious because of its sensitivity to national political interests and the costs of implementing EU policies (which largely devolve on national governments). The Council is more likely to invoke the principle of *subsidiarity*, under which actions are to be taken at the EU level only if they cannot be carried out more efficiently at the national or local level.[14]

Agenda setting in the EU is complex. Numerous actors at different levels may try to get EU policymakers to pay attention to an issue and frame how issues are viewed and discussed.[15] Being a first mover on an issue can be an important aspect of the agenda setting process. To stimulate discussion on an issue, the Commission sometimes issues a green paper, such as the green paper on a common fisheries policy issued in 2001 that boldly criticized EU fishery policy as being unsustainable and argued for a dramatic shift in policy.[16] This green paper was meant to put reform of the common fisheries policy on the agenda while also stimulating stakeholder debate prior to the issuing of policy proposals. It has led to a series of action plans, communications, and regulations. White papers may be issued to lay out policy recommendations, such as the Commission's 2009 white paper, "Adapting to Climate Change: The European Union Must Prepare for the Impacts to Come."[17]

At other times, the Parliament's Environment Committee may push for proposals stronger than those emanating from the Commission.[18] This has been the case with a wide range of issues, including adding the airline industry into the emissions trading scheme, illegal timber imports, packaging waste, and climate. The Parliament, for example, issued a resolution calling upon the Council to speak with one voice on climate change and maintain a leadership role on climate during the Copenhagen climate negotiations in December 2009.[19]

Conflicts of interest among the states are most evident in the Council.[20] Industrial and other lobbies within a country or countries might fight to prevent or weaken EU legislation pushed by the Commission or other Member States that they see as detrimental to their own interests. This was the case, for example, after the Commission argued for EU carbon dioxide standards for new cars, given that the automobile industry had failed to meet the voluntary targets it had itself earlier established. Germany's and France's powerful automobile industries were opposed to the Commission's proposed timetables and standards, however, arguing that the costs would be too high in terms of jobs, especially at a time of financial crisis.[21] The French president, Nicolas Sarkozy, and the German chancellor, Angela Merkel, bowed to this pressure and proposed an alternative but weaker proposal. In the end, a coalition of Member States led by the Netherlands and backed by Belgium, Denmark, Finland, Sweden, and the United Kingdom opposed the French and German move and backed the Commission's proposal. France and Germany were forced to back down.[22] In April 2009 the countries agreed on a regulation establishing carbon dioxide emission standards for new light-duty vehicles effective as of January 2012, with standards becoming even more stringent for 2020.[23]

Yet, it is also the case that industries may have an interest in getting the EU to adopt standards that have been adopted already at the national level—a process that has been called "regulatory competition."[24] For example, Germany was influential in pushing for the EU to adopt air pollution controls on large combustion plants (Council Directive 88/609/EEC), packaging waste requirements (Council and Parliament Directive 94/62/EC), and renewable energy standards (Council and Parliament Directive 2009/28/EC). After domestic legislation was put into place, Germany had an interest in assuring that other Member States were subject to similar environmental controls. It has been argued that this is one reason that there is not an inevitable downward spiral to lowest-common-denominator legislation.[25] Success is not, however, always guaranteed. It remains to be seen whether the Netherlands will be successful in getting the EU to adopt a tax on the carbon content of packaging similar to national legislation that went into effect in January 2008.

Enlargement and the Acquis Communautaire. One of the principal challenges facing the EU has been finding ways of accommodating different levels of environmental commitment and regulatory capacity without weakening ultimate goals. This has become an even bigger challenge because of the accession of the central and eastern European states that tend to be less wealthy than their western neighbors and have different priorities and concerns. Various strategies have been adopted to ease the transition of the new Member States into the EU and to bring their environmental programs into line with the demands of the *acquis communautaire*.[26] Particularly important were the assistance programs that were set up to assist accession states prepare for enlargement. These included instruments such as the Poland-Hungary: Assistance for Restructuring their Economies (PHARE), which was later broadened to include other accession countries, and the Instrument for Structural Policies for Pre-Accession (ISPA), which focused on environmental and transportation infrastructure priorities. For EU Member States three main sources of funding exist to help with adjusting to EU regulatory expectations: structural funds (for agriculture, social, and regional development), cohesion funds (for support of environmental and infrastructure projects in the poorest Member States), and the financial instrument for the environment, known as LIFE.

Burden Sharing. Another strategy that has been used to deal with Member States' differing capacities is the development of burden-sharing agreements. In the case of the Kyoto Protocol, the EU agreed to reduce its combined emissions of greenhouse gases by 8 percent of 1990 levels by 2008–2012. Under an internal burden-sharing arrangement that covered the fifteen Member States of the EU at the time the Kyoto Protocol was signed, different national targets were formulated based on a mix of factors that included national capabilities, the existing energy mix, and per capita economic wealth. Some countries were expected to make large cuts relative to their 1990 emissions level (Austria -13 percent, Belgium -7.5 percent, Denmark -21 percent, Germany -21 percent, Italy -6.5 percent, Luxembourg -28 percent, Netherlands -6 percent, United Kingdom -12.5 percent), others were given relatively mild targets (France and Finland 0 percent) while other poorer Member States were permitted to increase their emissions (Greece +25 percent, Ireland +13 percent, Portugal +27 percent, Spain +15 percent). Sweden adopted a +4 percent target but later adopted national legislation that imposed a -4 percent target by 2010.

A similar kind of burden-sharing agreement has been formulated to meet the EU's 20 percent renewable energy target as a share of the total energy mix by 2020 that affects all twenty-seven Member States. Member States' targets were determined on the basis of a formula that included a flat rate increase in renewables of 5.5 percent and an additional increase based on per capita gross domestic product.[27] Ten states have renewable energy targets ranging from 10 to 15 percent, eleven states targets from 16 to 25 percent, and six states targets of 30 to 49 percent.

Lobbying. Lobbying by private interests is omnipresent in the EU,[28] so much so that the Commission has established a voluntary register of lobby groups.[29] Industry is very concerned about the impact of new environmental legislation on competitiveness and maintains armies of lawyers and lobbyists in Brussels. Both the Commission directorates and parliamentary committees regularly consult such interests, which tend to represent the largest companies and trade associations. Environmental, consumer, and other public interest groups also have representation and actively try to shape policy outcomes.[30] An umbrella organization in Brussels, the European Environmental Bureau, represents more than 140 environmental organizations from the EU and some neighboring countries.[31] It closely monitors the Directorate-General for the Environment and tries to influence proposed legislation. Other international environmental nongovernmental organizations (NGOs), such as the World Wide Fund for Nature and Greenpeace, also lobby intensely and are regarded as among the most effective pressure groups.[32] A broad range of stakeholders and policy networks influences the EU policy process at all levels.

Environmental policy is closely related to other issues such as economic competition, taxation, research and development, energy, agriculture, and transportation.[33] Effective policymaking therefore requires interaction and cooperation among many EU directorates and parliamentary committees. The development of efficiency standards for electrical appliances, for example, involved a working group of members from the environment and energy directorates. The divergent perspectives of these directorates often lead to different policy preferences. The requirement introduced first by Article 3d of the Amsterdam Treaty that environmental protection must be integrated into all fields of EU policy has given new weight to environmental considerations.

The Directorate-General for the Environment has become stronger and more successful with time. It is, however, still often in a weak position in negotiating with its counterparts, especially the leading economic directorates for industry and trade. Final policy resolution by the Commission and Council usually involves extensive political compromise. This includes sometimes lengthy periods of "derogation" to allow a Member State more time to comply with EU directives and, in some cases, opt-outs. In early 2009, for example, nine Member States requested air quality derogations to be allowed more time to come into compliance with EU air quality limits on particulates.

Harmonization of Environmental Standards

One general rationale for creating common environmental policies and "harmonizing" standards across Member States has been to level the economic playing field. One danger with such logic is that the lowest common denominator will prevail and, in the case of environmental standards, result in Union norms that are considerably weaker than those of the leading states. To mitigate this problem, the Single European Act added to the Treaty of Rome three new articles: 130r, 130s, and 130t—now articles 174, 175, and 176, respectively, of the Consolidated Treaty. Article 174 guarantees that the EU will take action for "preserving, protecting, and improving the quality of the environment, protecting human health, prudent and rational utilization of natural resources, and promoting measures at (the) international level to deal with regional or worldwide environmental problems." Article 175 allows the Council to decide which measures can be decided by qualified majority voting. Article 176 specifies that protective measures taken at the Union level "shall not prevent any Member State from maintaining or introducing more stringent protective measures" so long as these measures are compatible with treaty law.[34]

Lead states are able to retain higher environmental standards than other countries so long as the Commission or the ECJ does not find them in violation of other treaty rules. Numerous EU states now have carbon taxes, including Denmark, Finland, Germany, Italy, the Netherlands, Poland, Sweden, and the United Kingdom, albeit of various levels and breadth. Naturally, those that have introduced carbon taxes would prefer that others introduced carbon taxes as well, so as not to be at a competitive economic disadvantage.[35] Sweden and France are pushing for the introduction of an EU-wide carbon tax for areas not covered under the EU carbon emissions system.

The Maastricht Treaty allowed most environmental legislation to be enacted by a qualified majority in the Council, whereas previously unanimity was normally required. In an offsetting provision, the treaty placed greater emphasis on the principle of subsidiarity. According to Article 5 of the Consolidated Treaty, the EU can take action only "if and in so far as the objectives of the proposed action cannot be sufficiently achieved by the Member States and can therefore, by reason of the scale or effects of the proposed action, be better achieved by the Community."[36] Since 1992 some states have used this principle as a rationale to challenge some Union-wide environmental legislation. The Lisbon Treaty maintains this limit on Union competences.

The Sixth Environmental Action Programme

Since 1972 the Commission has developed environmental action programs to guide its activities for multiyear periods. Although these programs are not legally binding, they have had substantial influence on policy development at the EU level and among Member States. The Fifth Environmental Action Programme (1992–2002), "Towards Sustainability," focused on the need to integrate environment into other economic and sectoral policies. In line with this, the commission's "Communication on Environment and Employment," issued in November 1997, spelled out for the first time how environmental protection and job creation can be mutually reinforcing.[37] The sixth program, "Environment 2010, Our Future, Our Choice," continues this theme. It calls for the EC to integrate environmental concerns into all its policies and to promote sustainable development within the enlarged Union. The program is based on "the polluter-pays principle, the precautionary principle and preventive action, and the principle of rectification of pollution at source." Its four priority areas are climate change, nature and biodiversity, environment and health, and natural resources and waste. Progress in achieving goals is to be measured in relation to targets and timetables covering a ten-year period.

The program also places great importance on the achievement of sustainable development in the accession countries through implementation of the environmental *acquis,* promotion of the transfer of clean technologies, exchange of information, and promotion of civil society. In responding to criticism that the Union needs to do more to fulfill its own environmental goals, the program encourages greater emphasis on effective implementation.[38]

Legislative Action

With an extensive body of EU environmental legislation—more than two hundred pieces of legislation on the environment—the EU has created the most comprehensive regional environmental protection regime in the world.[39] The EU has enacted legislation on many aspects of environmental protection, including noise; environmental impact assessment; control of chemicals and other dangerous substances; hazardous waste transfer and management; development of renewable energy; protection of forests, wildlife, and biodiversity; and action to limit climate change.[40] EU environmental legislation is anything but static. There is a continual process of amendment and revision.

For new and would-be Member States, understanding EU legislation can be a daunting task. The *Handbook on the Implementation of EC Environmental Legislation* was developed to assist officials in candidate countries and potential candidate countries to obtain an overview of existing legislation. The handbook includes ten chapters covering horizontal legislation, air quality, waste management, water protection, nature protection, industrial pollution control, chemicals and genetically modified organisms, noise, and civil protection legislation and is more than one thousand pages long![41]

The chapter on horizontal legislation addresses cross-cutting, integrative, and participatory aspects of environmental protection. It includes, for example, information on the Environmental Impact Assessment Directive, the Strategic Environmental Assessment Directive, the Directive on Access to Environmental Information, the Public Participation Directive, the Environmental Liability Directive, Regulation on European Pollutant Release and Transfer Register, among numerous others. The waste management chapter includes information about the many different directives for different kinds of waste: titanium dioxide, oil, hazardous waste, sewage sludge, batteries, package and packaging, end-of-life vehicles, electrical equipment, extractive mining, and ships. In addition, numerous directives lay down rules regarding the disposal of chemicals and the shipment, landfilling, and incineration of waste.

Regulations, Directives, Action Plans

EU legislation takes the form of either regulations or directives. Regulations are directly binding on Member States and require no further legislation at the national level; they are used when technical standardization is necessary. In contrast, directives are EU legislative acts that must be transposed into national law. Member States are allowed a degree of freedom in choosing the rules to be adopted. Under Article 249 of the Treaty of Lisbon, directives "shall be binding, as to the result to be achieved, upon each Member State . . . but shall leave to the national authorities the choice of form and methods."[42] Directives address such matters as environmental impact assessment, nature protection, chemicals in the environment, and genetically modified organisms.

Framework directives, which provide a framework for subsequent legislation in an area or that consolidate and rationalize earlier directives, have been established for a wide array of environmental problems, including air quality, integrated pollution prevention and control, waste, and water quality. Framework directives establish comprehensive long-term environmental quality goals and standards that can be used to measure progress across a wide range of specific policy instruments and actions. They provide a mechanism for consolidating, integrating, and simplifying related pieces of legislation (for example, separate directives on drinking water, bathing water, and protection of shellfish) to encourage more comprehensive and efficient management of resources. While allowing countries greater flexibility in pursuing these goals (because states have discretion to determine strategies for achieving the goals), framework directives can also serve as catalysts to force states to adopt a more integrated approach to environmental protection. Another explicit purpose of the framework directives is to increase transparency in environmental regulation by ensuring public access to information in a timely fashion.

The EU also issues action plans such as the Climate and Renewable Energy Action Plan and the Animal Welfare Action Plan, 2006–2010, both initially put forth by the Commission and later agreed upon by the Council and the Parliament.

The evolving nature of EU environmental law and the different rationales behind EU legislative developments can be tracked in various issue areas:

Integrated Pollution Prevention and Control. The Integrated Pollution Prevention and Control Directive of 1996 was updated in 2008 (Directive 2008/1/EC). The directive imposes common requirements for issuing permits to large industrial and agricultural sources of pollution throughout the EU. Member States must require all new and existing facilities to obtain operating permits that ensure that all appropriate measures are taken to prevent or minimize pollution of the air, water, and land. The directive calls for use of both environmental quality and emission standards (the "combined approach"), which accommodates different national systems; for example, the British rely on ambient quality standards, but the Germans insist on strict emission limits. Emission standards are to be based on the "best available techniques," but state authorities are given discretion to determine specific technologies appropriate to local conditions. The directive, however, reserves the Parliament's and the Council's right to set Union-wide emission limit values for certain categories of installations and pollutants if necessary.

The larger significance of the directive is that states are encouraged to take a comprehensive, integrated approach to pollution reduction at the source, including waste minimization, efficient use of energy, and protection of soil and groundwater as well as surface waters and air. This approach is in line with the shift evident in Europe from end-of-the-pipe controls to pollution prevention; more integrated, long-term environmental management; and greater flexibility in the use of policy instruments.

Air Quality. EU legislation to protect air quality goes back to 1970, when the first directive to regulate emissions from automobiles was passed (70/220/EEC). Since then, dozens of directives on air pollution covering, among other things, diesel engine emissions; the lead and sulfur content of fuels; and emissions from large industrial facilities, power plants, and waste incinerators have been established. Ambient air quality standards also have been set for sulfur dioxide, nitrogen dioxide, particulates, and lead; and regulations to limit chlorofluorocarbons and other ozone-depleting gases have been implemented under the Montreal Protocol.

In 2008, Directive 2008/50/EC on ambient air quality and cleaner air was formulated. It consolidates four earlier directives plus a Council decision, with the rationale of incorporating "the latest health and scientific developments and the experience of the Member States" as well as "in the interests of clarity, simplification, and administrative efficiency." The earlier directives set limit values for nitrogen dioxide, oxides of nitrogen, sulfur dioxide, lead, particulate matter, carbon monoxide, benzene, and ozone in ambient air. The earlier Council decision addressed reciprocal exchange of information and data from networks and measuring stations. The Sixth Environment Action

Programme determined that pollution levels should be reduced to levels that minimize harmful effects on human health, especially for sensitive populations, and the environment. It also called for improved monitoring and assessment of air quality and provision of information to the public. The new directive states not only that "it is particularly important to combat emissions of pollutants at source and to identify and implement the most effective emission reduction measures at local, national and Community level" but also that "emissions of harmful air pollutants should be avoided, prevented or reduced. . . ." A major addition of the new directive is its setting of tough standards for fine particulate matter (2.5 micrometers in diameter), which are particularly dangerous for human health.[43]

Water Resources Management. EU water quality has been protected since 1975 by directives covering drinking and bathing water, fish and shellfish, groundwater, urban wastewater, and protection against nitrates from fertilizers and various dangerous chemicals. Other policies covered pollution of European seas and rivers under various international maritime conventions and agreements. A new drinking water directive was adopted in 1998.

In February 1996 the Commission called for a water framework directive that, like the air framework, would establish broad guidelines for the protection and management of all freshwater resources. In October 2000 the EU Water Framework Directive (Directive 2000/60/EC), which replaced seven existing directives, was finally adopted after years of sometimes tense discussion and debate. The directive is based on a river basin management approach, with the idea that water quality can best be protected if an entire ecological system's pollution problems are dealt with in an integrated fashion that combines emission limits and quality standards. States were to have transposed the directive into national policy by 2003. In the coming years, they are to conduct studies of the characteristics of river basins, establish a monitoring network, finalize their river basin management plans, and introduce pricing policies. The ultimate goal is to obtain "good status" for water quality throughout the EU by 2015.[44]

Packaging and Recycling. Beginning in the 1970s, a number of European countries began to enact laws to reduce the volume of solid waste by requiring the use of returnable beverage containers, encouraging recycling of materials, and limiting waste in packaging. Denmark led the way by banning the use of aluminum cans and requiring that beer and soft drinks be sold in reusable bottles. Denmark's action eventually led to the seminal ruling by the ECJ in 1988 that such restrictions on trade may be justified on environmental grounds, provided that they do not unfairly discriminate in favor of domestic producers. Other countries subsequently passed legislation mandating the reduction or recycling of certain materials, including packaging. In 1991 Germany gained international attention for its novel packaging ordinance (*Verpackungsverordnung*), which required retail stores to take back all used packaging materials from consumers and process them. The ordinance allowed business and industry to set up a private collection system (the green dot system) on condition that it could meet ambitious recycling targets for various materials; otherwise a mandatory deposit would be levied on the sale of relevant products. The Netherlands also established an ambitious recycling program that required industry to reduce its volume of packaging by 2000.[45]

The EC had adopted a directive on beverage containers in 1985, but in the wake of the German and Dutch laws and the Danish bottle decision it was moved to draft a packaging directive that would accommodate recycling of other materials while preventing the development of potential trade restrictions. After much haggling over German and Dutch approaches mandating higher recycling targets and a coalition led by the United Kingdom that objected to such rigid quotas, a compromise was reached that lowered the mandatory targets to 50 percent recovery, 25 percent overall recycling, and 15 percent minimum recycling for each material. While states were allowed to exceed these targets, Germany's experience suggested that too-high recovery rates could lead to excessive accumulation and export of waste materials because of inadequate processing capacity. In the end, the EU packaging and packaging waste directive (94/62/EC), passed in 1994 over the objections of Denmark, Germany, and the Netherlands, set a "maximum recovery" rate of 65 percent, and set a recycling rate of 45 percent.[46]

In view of the enlargement of the EU as well as growing pressures to further reduce waste, the European Parliament and the Council agreed on amendments to the directive in February 2004 and March 2005. The February amendments strengthened the recovery and recycling targets for packaging waste to 60 percent recovery and between 55 and 80 percent recycling by the end of 2008.[47] The March 2005 amendments gave new Member States additional time (ranging from 2012 to 2015) to meet the new recovery and recycling targets.[48]

Environmental Liability. The White Paper on Environmental Liability, issued in February 2000, called for the establishment of a Framework Directive on Environmental Liability that would introduce the possibility of NGOs bringing suits for environmental harms.[49] The subsequently proposed EU Environmental Liability Directive dropped this provision, however, in favor of a system that focuses on environmental restoration and cost recovery.[50] Directive 2004/35/EC of the European Parliament and of the Council became the first EC legislation whose main objectives include the application of the polluter-pays principle to prevent and remedy environmental damage. On account of the numerous contaminated sites in the Union that pose health risks and contribute to loss of biodiversity and on the basis of the polluter-pays principle, the directive states that "an operator causing environmental damage or creating an imminent threat of such damage should, in principle, bear the cost of the necessary preventive or remedial measures. . . . It is also appropriate that the operators should ultimately bear the cost of assessing environmental damage and, as the case may be, assessing an imminent threat of such damage occurring."[51]

In 2008 the Council and the Parliament further agreed to Directive 2008/99/EC on the protection of the environment through the body of criminal law. The new directive requires Member States to treat as criminal offenses activities that breach EU environmental legislation, such as the illegal shipment of waste, trade in endangered species or ozone-depleting substances, and the significant deterioration of wildlife habitats that are part of the Natura 2000 network of protected sites. Other criminal offenses include significant damage to the environment caused by unlawful emissions to the air, water, or soil; the unlawful treatment of waste; and the unlawful manufacture or handling of nuclear materials.[52]

Nuclear Safety. In November 2000, the Commission adopted a Green Paper on Security of the Energy Supply, which raised issues regarding the position of nuclear energy vis-à-vis other energy sources in lieu of concerns about meeting goals for reduction of greenhouse gas emissions on the one hand, and concerns about aging nuclear power plants on the other. Starting in December 2001 the Council requested regular reports on nuclear safety, and in December 2002 the ECJ confirmed in a judgment that the Community has the authority to legislate in relation to nuclear safety. In January 2003 the Commission adopted two proposals for directives for a Community approach to issues of nuclear plant safety and radioactive waste disposal.[53] It was not until June 2009, however, that the EU environment ministers agreed on the Nuclear Safety Directive.[54] The directive sets expectations regarding nuclear safety and protection of workers and the general public and establishes the license holder as responsible for assuring safety.

Eco-Labeling. Another approach to limiting waste and environmental damage generally is to encourage consumers to purchase more ecologically benign products by providing better information. Germany had introduced an eco-labeling system, and several other countries were planning to do so when in 1990 the Council asked the Commission to prepare a regulation establishing criteria for an EC labeling scheme. The initial criteria used for granting a "green" label took into account the environmental impact of the product throughout its entire life cycle, including the materials used, manufacturing technologies, health and safety of workers, and ultimate disposal costs. Under the Council regulation (92/880/EEC) of March 23, 1992, Member States were authorized to appoint a competent body to award the EC eco-label to manufacturers or importers whose products met the criteria. Participation by industry was voluntary, but it was hoped that consumer demand for green products would drive producers to compete for the label (symbolized by a flower) by designing better products.

In July 2000 a revised eco-labeling regulation (1980/2000/EC) was passed. It authorizes a new EU Eco-Labeling Board, consisting of eco-labeling bodies in each Member State, consumer groups, environmental NGOs, trade unions, industry, and small and medium-sized enterprises, to jointly develop eco-label criteria for different product groups. As of 2009, there were twenty-three product groups, ranging from furniture and household appliances to cleaning products, electrical equipment, and bedding that are covered by eco-labeling requirements. Consumers can learn about products bearing the eco-label on the eco-label catalogue Web site.[55] National eco-labeling bodies remain in charge of implementing the system.

Climate Change

Concern over global climate change owing to the accumulation of carbon dioxide and other greenhouse gases in the atmosphere has been particularly strong in Europe and has led to a search for effective means of reducing dependence on fossil fuels. Climate change has arguably become the single most important global environmental issue on the EU's agenda. The EU has become a major force in pushing for global action on greenhouse gas emission reductions, with its 20 percent energy efficiency, 20 percent renewable energy, and 20 percent greenhouse gas emission reduction goals by 2020 (the latter relative to a 1990 base year and to be increased to 30 percent if other countries agree to comparably stringent measures). Over time, efforts to address climate change have resulted in increasingly ambitious new policies and programs. These policies and programs have put Europe at the forefront of global efforts to tackle climate change. Yet, these efforts have also elicited a degree of resistance from various Member States, and not all Member States have been equally enthusiastic about implementing programs and regulations to reduce greenhouse gas emissions.

Environmental and Energy Taxes. Environmental tax rates vary considerably among Member States, in both level and content. In 2005 the share of environmental taxes stood at 11.6 percent of the total tax revenue and social contribution in Denmark but 5.2 percent in Belgium.[56] Relatively early on, several countries in northern Europe enacted extensive green taxes to promote waste reduction and energy saving.[57]

For many years, the Commission sought to win acceptance of the idea of a carbon tax and made numerous proposals to this effect, but to no avail. In 1997 the Commission for a third time proposed the establishment of a directive on energy taxation. The plan would have extended the existing harmonized excise tax duties on mineral oils to coal, natural gas, and electricity, while allowing national governments to offer rebates for environmentally friendly forms of energy production. In the spring of 2003, EU finance ministers finally agreed on a watered-down version of the Commission's proposal. They called for a directive on minimum rates of energy taxation to curb the use of fossil fuels and encourage sustainable transportation.

Energy Efficiency and Renewable Energy. The European Union has no explicit competence in the energy field. The necessary legal basis for Union action on energy issues stems from other policy areas. EU policy on electricity and gas markets is premised on the Union's competence for forming a common market. Its competence related to renewable energy is tied to articles on the environment.

Improving energy efficiency has become a key component of EU climate policy. This goal has been embodied in a series of action plans, programs, and communications from the Commission. In October 2006, for example, the Commission released a communication entitled "Action Plan for Energy Efficiency: Realising the Potential, COM(2006)545." The plan called for a reduction in primary energy consumption by 20 percent by 2020, corresponding to a 1.5 percent saving per year. A subsequent Commission communication, COM(2008)772, calls for reforms in EU legislation related to energy efficiency in the building sector, proposes reforms to the Energy Labelling Directive, the establishment of a directive for the setting of eco-design requirements for energy-related products, and reinforcement of a directive on cogeneration.

In March 2007, the European Council endorsed a Commission communication that called for a 20 percent target for renewable sources in the overall share of energy and a 10 percent target for energy from renewable sources in the transport sector. Directive 2009/28/EC embodies these goals, setting a common 10 percent target for fuel from renewables in the transport sector for each Member State and differentiated national targets for renewables in the overall share of energy owing to the different starting points, renewable energy potential, and energy mix of the different Member States. The new directive points to the importance of reducing greenhouse gas emissions, promoting the security of energy supply, promoting technological development and innovation, and providing regional opportunities for employment and development.

Emissions Trading. The idea of a carbon emissions trading scheme was originally proposed by the United States during the negotiations leading to the Kyoto Protocol but was initially strongly resisted by the EU. After the George W. Bush administration announced it would withdraw from the Kyoto Protocol in the spring of 2001, however, the EU unanimously resolved to move forward in trying to put the agreement into force even without the United States and began to look more positively at emissions trading schemes.

In October 2001 the Commission proposed a greenhouse gas emissions trading scheme to the Parliament and the Council.[58] Modeled on the successful sulfur dioxide emissions trading system employed in the United States, the EU scheme became the first international carbon emissions trading system in the world. It came into effect in 2005 and covers the Member States of the EU as well as members of the EEA. It covers more than twelve thousand major emissions sources (for example, utilities, manufacturing industries, cement industry, pulp, paper) and covers approximately 40 percent of all EU carbon dioxide emissions. The first phase of the emissions trading scheme, which ran from 2005 to 2007, ran into serious problems stemming from an overallocation of permits by individual Member States to their industries. The number of permits national governments issued during the second phase, which runs from 2008 until 2012, was controlled more closely by the Commission.

Nature Conservation, Marine Environmental Protection, and Biodiversity Protection

Europe's dense population and long history of settlement mean that there is relatively little land still in its natural state. Among the most important pieces of legislation aimed at protecting Europe's remaining nature are the Birds Directive, 79/409/EEC, and the Habitats Directive, 92/43/EEC. A new development of significance is Directive 2008/56/EC establishing a framework for Union action in the field of marine environmental policy.

Natura 2000. The Birds Directive, signed in 1979, is the EU's oldest legislation for nature protection. It recognizes habitat loss and degradation as the largest threats to bird protection and sets up special protection areas. The Habitats Directive set up a European ecological network of special conservation areas that was given the title Natura 2000. Each Member State is expected to designate and protect areas that are habitats to special plant and animal species as defined by the directive. Since 1994 all of the special conservation areas set up by the Birds Directive have been incorporated into the Natura 2000 ecological network. The aim of Natura 2000 is to assure the long-term survival of species and habitats that are of special importance to Europe.

Biodiversity Action Plan. As a party to the United Nations Convention on Biological Diversity, in 2001 the EU established a Biodiversity Action Plan that called for a halt in the decline of biodiversity within the EU by 2010 and a restoration of habitats and natural systems. A midterm assessment report issued in 2008 concluded, however, that the EU was "highly unlikely to meet its 2010 target of halting biodiversity decline." The report found that 50 percent of species and as much as 80 percent of habitat types protected under the Habitats Directive have an "unfavourable conservation status." The conclusion is that Europe must do much more to halt the loss of biodiversity and natural habitats caused by conversion of land for agricultural and development purposes and by pollution.

Genetically Modified Organisms (GMOs). Based on the precautionary principle, and in an effort to minimize risks associated with the release of GMOs into the environment, the EU has adopted a directive (2001/18/EC) controlling the deliberate release of GMOs into the environment and into the market. A number of countries are eager to pursue GMOs, however, and the Commission itself has supported some specific GMOs for market release. Looking to the future, a group of eleven EU countries has, in an interesting development, called for the right to opt out of EU legislation allowing the growth of genetically modified crops. These processes may be contributing to the creation of a "multispeed" Europe despite efforts to integrate and harmonize policies.

EU Environmental Compliance

The environment is one of the most developed areas of EU law. The EU has done much to protect and improve the quality of the environment in Europe and to put the breaks on environmental deterioration. Still, there are many compliance problems that continue to hinder the overall effectiveness of EU environmental legislation even within the most environmentally conscious of the Member States. New challenges for the enforcement of EU environmental regulations have arisen, moreover, on account of enlargement.

The central and eastern European countries had far higher levels of pollution than western European countries because of the failure of their former communist governments to enforce environmental standards. In addition to outdated coal-burning power plants and factories, and in many cases a lack of adequate sewerage and waste disposal systems, several of these countries relied heavily on Soviet-designed nuclear plants that posed substantial safety risks. The cost of coming into compliance with EU environmental standards has therefore been very high. This combined with the new Member States' strong interest in economic development and their typically more limited environmental capacity have contributed to compliance problems.[59]

The success of the EU commitment to environmental protection depends on the extent to which Member States transpose EU law into national law and apply and enforce the law in practice.[60] EU treaty compliance and enforcement have been a matter of concern for decades.[61] The Commission monitors policy implementation and seeks to detect violations of EU law. More than 20 percent of all Commission dossiers are related to the environment. In 2007, 461 new cases dealing with noncompliance were opened, of which approximately one-quarter were cases opened by citizens and NGOs.[62]

The EU has legal enforcement mechanisms at its disposal. Citizens, local authorities, businesses, or interest groups have the right to make inquiries and lodge complaints on the inadequate application or transposition of EU law directly before the Commission. Once a complaint has been brought, efforts are made to mediate the dispute or to informally persuade the national government to take appropriate action. If a party is found to be in violation of EU law, the Commission can issue a formal notice to the state. If all else fails, an infringement case can be brought before the ECJ to force compliance. ECJ decisions are binding on Member States. Steps have been taken to strengthen the ECJ's reach. The Maastricht Treaty gave the ECJ the authority to fine Member States for noncompliance. In a landmark 2005 ECJ ruling France was fined €20 million for repeated failure to comply with EU fishery conservation policies described above. It was also subject to a €57.8 million fine for every six additional months that it failed to comply. France chose to pay the €20 million fine on time.

Some of the variation in compliance among states is related to different levels of awareness of citizens and interest groups.[63] Some states may have proportionately more complaints lodged because their citizens are more alert, informed, and able to bring matters to the attention of the EU. But differential enforcement is also the result of variations in the budgets and other resources of governments to carry out EU mandates. Because states choose their own means of compliance, differences are inevitable in the instruments used and in the severity of penalties levied against violators.[64]

The Commission is seeking to manage its high case load more effectively by targeting serious categories of breaches. These include bad transposition of directives; breaches of core, strategic obligations under EC legislation, including concerning the designation of Natura 2000 sites or the adoption of national allocation plans for emissions of greenhouse gases; and breaches concerning big infrastructure projects. In addition, it is focusing on more horizontal approaches, where breaches involve, for example, failure to comply with nature conservation or impact assessment regulations across a large number of individual cases.[65]

The Commission also works with an informal network of national environmental officials, known as the Implementation and Enforcement of EU Environmental Law (IMPEL) network.[66] In October 1996 the Commission also issued a communication on implementation that proposed guidelines for states to follow in carrying out inspections, handling public complaints about legal enforcement, and guaranteeing access by NGOs to national courts.[67]

Conclusion

The EU is at a critical stage in its evolution because of the further "deepening" of integration and the largest "widening" in its history.[68] Without question, the EU has made great strides toward environmental protection during the past four decades, but it has also entered a transition phase in this policy area. After several decades of imposing increasingly detailed environmental directives and regulations from Brussels, the EU has begun to revise its approach since adoption of the Maastricht Treaty in 1992 and its emphasis on the principle of subsidiarity. Member States have pressed for greater freedom in implementing EU legislation while supporting the general principles of sustainable development. The European Commission has responded by turning toward the use of broader framework directives that set long-term environmental goals while allowing more flexibility in the choice of means to achieve them; it also has encouraged the introduction of new policy instruments such as emissions trading, burden-sharing agreements, and labeling to improve environmental performance and cost-effectiveness. At the same time it backed the Kyoto Protocol over U.S. opposition, developed the world's first international carbon emissions trading scheme, and challenged the global community with far-reaching proposals, it was unable to continue its international leadership role and achieve anticipated results at the Copenhagen conference in December 2009.

Despite these accomplishments, the EU faces major challenges if it plans to remain an environmental leader. Economic stagnation and high levels of unemployment have dampened public and government enthusiasm for increased environmental protection. Implementation of EU environmental laws at the national level still leaves much to be desired. The addition of the twelve primarily central and eastern European states, which are economically behind the western European states, threatens to shift attention away from major global environmental concerns. Nevertheless, from a global perspective enlargement of the EU has resulted in markedly improved environmental conditions and capacity in the new Member States.

Within the EU generally, sustainable development will require much greater integration of environmental perspectives into other policy areas such as energy, transportation, agriculture, and tourism.[69] Article 6 of the

Consolidated Treaty legally obligates all EU bodies and Member States to pursue such integrated sustainable development strategies. Major tests of the EU governance system therefore still lie ahead.

Notes

1. On the general history and development of the EC/EU, see Clifford Hackett, *Cautious Revolution: The European Community Arrives*, rev. ed. (New York: Praeger, 1996); Desmond Dinan, *Ever Closer Union? An Introduction to the European Community* (Boulder, Colo.: Lynne Rienner, 1994); David M. Wood and Birol A. Yesilada, *The Emerging European Union* (White Plains, N.Y.: Longman, 1996); Neill Nugent, *The Government and Politics of the European Union*, 5th ed. (Durham, N.C.: Duke University Press, 2003); Michelle Cini, ed., *European Union Politics* (Oxford: Oxford University Press, 2003).

2. For a summary of the programs, see Stanley P. Johnson and Guy Corcelle, *The Environmental Policy of the European Communities*, 2nd ed. (London: Kluwer Law International, 1995); and David Judge, ed., *A Green Dimension for the European Community* (London: Frank Cass, 1993). See also John McCormick, *Environmental Policy in the European Union* (Basingstoke, UK: Palgrave, 2001).

3. Consolidated Versions of the Treaty on European Union and the Treaty Establishing the European Communities, *Official Journal of the European Communities*, C321, December 29, 2006: E46.

4. See "Treaty of Nice Amending the Treaty on European Union, The Treaties Establishing the European Communities and Certain Related Acts," 2001/C 80/01, *Official Journal of the European Communities*, C80/78, March 10, 2001.

5. The European Convention, The Secretariat, "Draft Treaty Establishing a Constitution for Europe, CONV 850/03" (Brussels, July 18, 2003). The changes to the draft treaty, agreed upon in June 2004, can be found in "Conference of the Representatives of the Governments of the Member States," CIG 85104, PRESID 27 (Brussels, June 18, 2004). All Member States would have had to ratify the constitution for it to have gone into force.

6. Useful introductions to the institutions of the EU include Nugent, *The Government and Politics of the European Union*, 5th ed.; and *The Government and Politics of the European Union*, 6th ed. (Durham: Duke University Press, 2006); Simon Hix, *The Political System of the European Union*, 2nd ed. (Basingstoke, UK: Palgrave, 2005); Michael Wallace, *Policy-Making in the European Union*, 5th ed. (Oxford: Oxford University Press, 2005); and Michelle Cini, ed., *European Union Politics*, 2nd ed. (Oxford: Oxford University Press, 2007).

7. Daniel Naurin and Helen Wallace, *Unveiling the Council of the European Union: Games Governments Play in Brussels* (Basingstoke, UK: Palgrave Macmillan, 2008).

8. Gerhard Sabathil, Clemens Joos, and Bernd Kebler, *The European Commission: An Essential Guide to the Institution, the Procedures and the Policies* (London: Kogan Page, 2008).

9. Simon Hix, Abdul G. Noury, and Gérard Roland, *Democratic Politics in the European Parliament* (Cambridge: Cambridge University Press, 2007). On the role of political parties, see Simon Hix and Christopher Lord, *Political Parties in the European Union* (New York: St. Martin's, 1997).

10. Judgment of the Court (Second Chamber) of July 25, 2008 (reference for a preliminary ruling from the Bundesverwaltungsgericht, Germany), *Dieter Janecek v. Freistaat Bayern*, Case C-237/07, *Official Journal of the European Union*, September 13, 2008: 3.

11. See the EEA at http://org.eea.eu.int.

12. See, for example, Jeremy J. Richardson, ed., *European Union: Power and Policy-Making* (London: Routledge, 1996); Helen Wallace and William Wallace, *Policy-Making in*

the European Union (Oxford: Oxford University Press, 1996); Stephen George, *Politics and Policy in the European Community* (Oxford: Oxford University Press, 1991); and Carolyn Rhodes and Sonia Mazey, eds., *The State of the European Union: Building a European Polity?* vol. 3 (Boulder, Colo.: Lynne Rienner, 1995).

13. Adrienne Héritier, *Explaining Institutional Change in Europe* (Oxford: Oxford University Press, 2007).

14. See Regina S. Axelrod, "Subsidiarity and Environmental Policy in the European Community," *International Environmental Affairs* 6 (Spring 1994): 115–132.

15. Miranda A. Schreurs and Yves Tiberghien, "Multi-level Reinforcement: Explaining European Union Leadership in Climate Mitigation," *Global Environmental Politics* 7 no. 4 (2007): 19–46; and Sebastiaan Prince, *Agenda Setting in the European Union* (Basingstoke, UK: Palgrave Macmillan, 2009).

16. European Commission, "Green Paper on the Future of the Common Fisheries Policy," vol. 1, COM (2001) 135 Final, Brussels, March 20, 2001.

17. European Commission, "Adapting to Climate Change: The European Union Must Prepare for the Impacts to Come," IP/09/519, Brussels, April 1, 2009.

18. David Judge, "'Predestined to Save the Earth': The Environment Committee of the European Parliament," *A Green Dimension for the European Community*, a special issue of *Environmental Politics* (Abingdon: Frank Cass Publishing, 1993): 186–212.

19. European Parliament Resolution of 11 March 2009 on an EU Strategy for a Comprehensive Climate Change Agreement in Copenhagen and the Adequate Provision of Financing for Climate Change, P6_TA-PROV(2009)0121.

20. Mikael Skou Andersen and Duncan Liefferink, eds., *European Environmental Policy: The Pioneers* (Manchester, England: Manchester University Press, 1997); and D. Liefferink and M. S. Andersen, "Strategies of the 'Green' Member States in EU Environmental Policy-Making," *Journal of European Public Policy-Making* 5 (June 1998): 254–270.

21. "Commission Snubs German Auto Industry over CO_2 Emissions," *Euractiv*, January 30, 2007.

22. "French Phase in Plans for Car CO_2 Opposed," *Euractiv*, October 22, 2008.

23. "Cars & CO_2," *Euractiv*, September 19, 2007; Regulation EC No 443/2009 of the European Parliament and of the Council, of April 23, 2009, setting emission performance standards for new passenger cars as part of the Community's integrated approach to reducing CO_2 emissions from light-duty vehicles, *Official Journal of the European Union*, L140/16, June 5, 2009: 0001–0014.

24. Adrienne Héritier et al., *Ringing the Changes in Europe: Regulatory Competition and Transformation of the State: Britain, France, Germany* (New York: Walter de Gruyter, 1996); Katharina Holzinger, Christoph Knill, and Bas Arts, *Environmental Policy Convergence in Europe: The Impact of International Institutions and Trade* (Cambridge: Cambridge University Press, 2008).

25. David Vogel, *Trading Up: Consumer and Environmental Regulation in a Global Economy* (Cambridge: Harvard University Press, 1995).

26. JoAnn Carmin and Stacy D. VanDeveer, *EU Enlargement and the Environment: Institutional Change and Environmental Policy in Central and Eastern Europe* (New York: Routledge, 2005).

27. Directive 2009/28/EC of the European Parliament and of the Council of April 23, 2009, on the promotion of the use of energy from renewable sources and amending and subsequently repealing Directives 2001/77/EC and 2003/30/EC, *Official Journal of the European Union*, L140/16, June 5, 2009: 16–62.

28. Sonia Mazey and Jeremy Richardson, eds., *Lobbying in the European Community* (Oxford: Oxford University Press, 1993); Sonia Mazey and Jeremy Richardson, "The Logic of Organisation: Interest Groups," in Richardson, *European Union*.

29. Dave Keating, "EU Lobby Register Fails to Impress," *ENDS Daily Europe*, July 10, 2009.

30. Elizabeth Bomberg, "Policy Learning in an Enlarged European Union: Environmental NGOs and New Policy Instruments," *Journal of European Public Policy* 14 (March 2007): 248–268.

31. See the European Environmental Bureau, http://www.eeb.org/.
32. "Pressure Groups Become a Political Force," *European Voice*, June 11–17, 1998.
33. See Andrea Lenschow, ed., *Environmental Policy Integration: Greening Sectoral Policies in Europe* (London: Earthscan, 2002).
34. Consolidated Versions of the Treaty on European Union and the Treaty Establishing the European Communities, *Official Journal of the European Communities*, E1-331.
35. European Environment Agency, "Environmental Signals 2002," Environmental Assessment Report no. 9 (Copenhagen: European Environment Agency, May 14, 2002), 127.
36. Consolidated Versions of the Treaty on European Union and the Treaty Establishing the European Communities, *Official Journal of the European Communities*, E1-331.
37. Commission of the European Communities, *Communication on Environment and Employment*, COM (97) 592 Final (Brussels, November 18, 1997).
38. "Decision No. 1600/2002/EC of the European Parliament and of the Council of July 22, 2002, laying down the Sixth Community Environmental Action Programme," *Official Journal of the European Communities*, L242/1, vol. 45, September 10, 2002.
39. See, for example, McCormick, *Environmental Policy in the European Union;* Andrew Jordan, ed., *Environmental Policy in the European Union: Actors, Institutions and Processes*, 2nd ed. (London: Earthscan Publications, 2005); Albert Weale et al., *Environmental Governance in Europe: An Ever Closer Union?* (Oxford: Oxford University Press, 2002); Andrew Jordan, ed., *Environmental Policy in the European Union* (London: Earthscan, 2002); and Anthony R. Zito, *Creating Environmental Policy in the European Union* (Basingstoke: Palgrave Macmillan, 2000).
40. See Norman J. Vig and Michael Faure, eds., *Green Giants? Environmental Policies of the United States and the European Union* (Cambridge: MIT Press, 2004); and Miranda Schreurs, Henrik Selin, and Stacy D. VanDeveer, eds., *Transatlantic Environment and Energy Politics: Comparative and International Perspectives* (Burlington, Vt.: Ashgate, 2009).
41. Regional Environmental Centre and Umweltbundesamt, eds., *Handbook on the Implementation of EC Environmental Legislation* (European Communities, December 2008).
42. Consolidated Versions of the Treaty on European Union and the Treaty Establishing the European Communities, *Official Journal of the European Communities*, E151.
43. For a more detailed discussion of auto oil legislation in the 1990s, see Regina S. Axelrod, Norman J. Vig, and Miranda A. Schreurs, "The European Union as an Environmental Governance System" in *The Global Environment*, ed. Regina S. Axelrod, David L. Downie, and Norman J. Vig, 2nd ed. (Washington, D.C.: CQ Press, 2005).
44. "Directive 2000/60/EC of the European Parliament and of the Council of 23 October 2000," *Official Journal of the European Communities*, L 327, December 22, 2000: 0001–0073.
45. Markus Haverland, "Convergence of National Governance under European Integration? The Case of Packaging Waste" (paper presented at the Fifth Biennial Conference of the European Community Studies Association, Seattle, May 29–June 1, 1997).
46. Thomas Gehring, "Governing in Nested Institutions: Environmental Policy in the European Union and the Case of Packaging Waste," *Journal of European Public Policy* 4 (September 1997): 337–354.
47. Directive 2004/12/EC of the European Parliament and of the Council of 11 February 2004 amending Directive 94/62/EC on Packing and Packaging Waste, *Official Journal of the European Union*, L47, February 18, 2004: 0026–0031.
48. Directive 2005/20/EC of the European Parliament and of the Council of 9 March 2005 amending Directive 94/62/EC on Packing and Packaging Waste, *Official Journal of the European Union*, L70, March 16, 2005: 0017–0018.
49. Commission of the European Communities, "White Paper on Environmental Liability," COM (2000) 66 (Brussels, February 9, 2000).
50. Timothy Swanson and Andreas Kontoleon, "What Future for Environmental Liability? The Use of Liability Systems for Environmental Regulation in the Courtrooms of the US and the EU," in Vig and Faure, *Green Giants?*

51. Directive 2004/35/CE of the European Parliament and of the Council of 21 April 2004 on Environmental Liability with Regard to the Prevention and Remedying of Environmental Damage, *Official Journal of the European Union*, L143, April 30, 2004: 0056–0075.
52. Directive 2008/99/EC of the European Parliament and of the Council of 19 November 2008 on the Protection of the Environment through Criminal Law," *Official Journal of the European Union*, 328, December 6, 2008: 0028–0037.
53. Derek M. Taylor, "The Directives of the Nuclear Package," European Commission, ftp://ftp.cordis.europa.eu/pub/fp6-euratom/docs/euradwaste04pro_1-taylor_en.pdf.
54. Council Directive 2009/71/Euratom of 25 June 2009 Establishing a Community Framework for the Nuclear Safety of Nuclear Installations, *Official Journal of the European Union*, L172/18, July 2, 2009: 18–22.
55. See Eco-Label Catalogue, www.eco-label.com.
56. European Environment Agency, *Energy and Environment Report 2008*, No. 6/ 2008, 62.
57. Mikael Skou Andersen, *Governance by Green Taxes: Making Pollution Prevention Pay* (Manchester: Manchester University Press, 1994); Timothy O'Riordan, ed., *Ecotaxation* (London: Earthscan, 1997). For a fuller discussion of energy taxes, see Regina S. Axelrod and Norman J. Vig, *Global Environment: Law, Institutions, and Policy* (Washington: Congressional Quarterly Press) 1999, 89–90.
58. Commission of the European Communities, "Proposal for a Directive of the European Parliament and of the Council Establishing a Scheme for Greenhouse Gas Emission Allowances Trading within the Community and Amending Council Directive 96/61/EC," COM (2001) 581 Final; 2001/0245 (COD) (Brussels, October 23, 2001).
59. See EcoTec Research and Consulting Limited, "The Benefits of Compliance with the Environmental Acquis," DGENV Contract: Environmental Policy in the Applicant Countries and Their Preparation for Accession. Service Contract B7–8110/2000/159960/MAR/H1, Final Report, Executive Summary, July 2001, C/1849/PtB.
60. See Peter M. Haas, "Compliance with EU Directives: Insights from International Relations and Comparative Politics," *Journal of European Public Policy* 5 (March 1998): 17–37.
61. Alberta Sbragia, "Environmental Policy in the European Community: The Problem of Implementation in Comparative Perspective," in *Towards a Transatlantic Environmental Policy* (Washington, D.C.: European Institute, 1991); Jeremy Richardson, "Eroding EU Policies: Implementation Gaps, Cheating and Re-Steering," in Richardson, *European Union;* Wyn Grant, Duncan Matthews, and Peter Newell, *The Effectiveness of European Union Environmental Policy* (London: Macmillan, 2000).
62. Commission Staff Working Document, *Situation in the Different Sectors*, accompanying the Commission of the European Communities, *25th Annual Report on Monitoring the Application of Community Law (2007)*, COM (2008) 777 Final, SEC(2008)2855 (Brussels, November 18, 2008).
63. See also Tanja A. Börzel, *Leaders and Laggards in European Environmental Policy* (Cambridge: Cambridge University Press, 2003).
64. See also Jonathan Golub, ed., *New Instruments for Environmental Policy in the EU* (London: Routledge, 1998); and Matthieu Glachant, ed., *Implementing European Environmental Policy* (Cheltenham, England: Edward Elgar, 2001).
65. Commission Staff Working Document, *Situation in the Different Sectors*.
66. The European Union Network for the Implementation and Enforcement of Environmental Law (IMPEL), http://ec.europa.eu/environment/impel.
67. Commission of the European Communities, *Implementing Community Environmental Law*, COM (96) 500 (Brussels, October 22, 1996).
68. See Pierre-Henri Laurent and Marc Maresceau, eds., *The State of the European Union, Deepening and Widening*, vol. 4 (Boulder, Colo.: Lynne Rienner, 1998).
69. See Lenschow, *Environmental Policy Integration*.

12

The View from the South: Developing Countries in Global Environmental Politics

Adil Najam

This chapter examines the collective behavior of developing countries in global environmental politics. In the now burgeoning literature on global environmental politics there is no single aspect whose importance is acknowledged as consistently, but treated as casually, even shabbily, as the role of developing countries. Although very good work has been produced on the behavior of specific developing countries with regard to particular environmental issues, there is little analysis of how this group of countries—often referred to as the "South" or the third world—tends to behave collectively in global environmental politics, or even if it makes sense to talk about this group of countries as a collective.

Of course, it would be wrong to suggest that developing countries are a monolithic or entirely united bloc. Indeed, individual developing countries often differ, and sometimes bicker, on particular environmental issues. However, despite such specific differences and despite the growing significance of emerging economies within the South (for example, China, India, and Brazil), there is a generally acknowledged and easily identifiable sense of shared identity and common purpose among the developing countries of the South. Developing countries do not forfeit their national interests in choosing to act collectively, but in doing so they do form a distinct and identifiable collective within global environmental politics.

This chapter explores the nature of this shared identity and common purpose and how it manifests itself in global environmental politics. Its four sections will (a) outline a historical and conceptual understanding of "Southness," (b) highlight the motivations and aspirations that developing countries have invested in global environmental politics, (c) review the experience of the developing countries in key aspects of these politics since the UN Conference on Environment and Development (UNCED)—also known as the Earth Summit—held in Rio de Janeiro in 1992, and (d) explain why developing countries harbor a certain sense of frustration with global environmental politics. A core argument of the chapter is that the South's current desire for what could be described as a new international *environmental* order stems from the same hopes and fears that had prompted its call in the 1970s for a new international *economic* order.

Understanding the Collective South

Since the mid-1990s, the term "South" has once again become a descriptor of choice for the set of nations variously referred to as developing countries, less-developed countries, underdeveloped countries, or the third world. Especially in the context of global negotiations—and even more so in global environmental negotiations—these countries often choose, and sometimes demand, to be referred to as the South. This is more than a matter of semantics. The term reflects a certain aspect of their collective identity and their desire to negotiate as a collective.[1]

The term, and its use in the concept of the North-South divide, was a staple of scholarly and populist political discourse during the 1970s, particularly as a rallying cry in the demand by developing countries for a new international economic order (NIEO).[2] After having spent most of the 1980s in hibernation, the phrase again gained currency during the 1990s. In particular, the term's wide use by governments, nongovernmental organizations, the media, and officials during the Rio conference in 1992 revitalized it in popular environmental contexts.

Writing in the 1980s, the then secretary general of the Organization for Economic Cooperation and Development (OECD) pointed out that the North-South concept, "like all powerful ideas . . . has the virtue of grand simplicity" and described it as a divide between the developed countries of the North, which have "advanced or relatively advanced income levels and social conditions and a more or less completed process of national integration," and the developing countries of the South, "where the development process is still very much in train, where dual economies and dual societies are characteristic, and where, in many cases, hunger and poverty remain the dominant way of life for millions of people."[3] This still popular view of the North-South divide as a binary distinction between haves and have-nots is a powerful, and not untrue, way of understanding the concept—so long as one remembers that the South seeks not simply economic development but also a say in the political decisions affecting its destiny.[4] The 1990 South Commission Report defined the term in a decidedly more political context by talking not merely about economic poverty but also the "poverty of influence."[5] For the commission, the defining feature of the South is not just its economic weakness but also its political dependence. The self-definition of the South, therefore, is a definition of exclusion: these countries believe that they have been bypassed and view themselves as existing on the periphery. To redress what they consider to be an imbalance of influence, the developing countries have sought the vehicle of global negotiations, often referred to as the North-South dialogue.[6]

From the moment the term was coined, there have been those who consider it largely irrelevant or inaccurate. Such views have been as resilient as the term itself. For example, a 1994 headline in the *New York Times* proclaimed, "The 'Third World' Is Dead."[7] Such unwarranted obituaries have been, and remain, an enduring feature of the collective's decidedly rocky history. For those who define the third world, or the South, solely in terms of Cold War polarizations, the conclusion is obvious: the emergence of Southern unity, they insist, was a result of Cold War politics; now that the Cold War is dead, the alliance should also be buried.[8] Others who see the term simply as an economic differentiator similarly find the term irrelevant as some Southern countries show signs of building economic muscle.

Yet at the simplest and most pragmatic level, what Roger Hansen had to say about the validity of North-South thinking thirty years ago seems equally valid today: "If over [130] developing countries time and again, in forum after forum, act as a diplomatic unit, they would seem to merit analysis as a potential actor of major importance in the international system."[9] At a deeper level of analysis, it is important to remember that for many of these countries— including countries like China, India, and Brazil—the desire for unity in the face of an international order that they believe continues to place them at a systemic disadvantage still outweighs the internal diversity or differences. Most important, even if some Northern observers consider the South's agenda of the 1970s "discredited,"[10] it remains unfinished business for much of the South and a goal believed to be well worth pursuing.[11]

A sense of new vulnerabilities, the persistent pangs of an unfinished agenda, and the opportunity to renew a North-South dialogue under environmental auspices have served to rally the countries of the South and have translated into a renewed assertiveness, especially around the broad issue of sustainable development.[12] The reinvigoration that the South seems to have enjoyed during and since the 1992 Earth Summit and the prominence regained as a relatively cohesive negotiating collective took many by surprise. Indeed, at many turns during the 1992 Earth Summit, and in global negotiations since then, differences within the developing countries of the Group of 77 (G-77) have led to apparent fractures and frictions in the collective. This has been evident, for example, in climate change negotiations where the interests of major oil-producing countries, of growing energy users, and of small island states that belong to the Alliance of Small Island States (AOSIS)— often poorer as well as especially vulnerable to climatic changes—have been at odds.[13] Negotiations on the Biosafety Protocol to the Biodiversity Convention saw developing countries take significantly different positions on the basis of their trade priorities.[14] In the negotiations on desertification, a dispute between African and non-African members nearly brought G-77 coordination to a halt.[15] The dramatic economic rise of China, and to a lesser extent of India, has also again induced much speculation about whether the South has—or is about to—disintegrate. Indeed, on the climate change issue there seems to be a deliberate effort from the North to break the Southern coalition by seeking dialogue with components of the South rather than the collective as represented by the G-77.[16]

However, the empirical evidence is that, at least until now, even when developing countries have different national priorities on specific issues in global negotiations—something that should not be surprising—they almost always have chosen to pursue these interests within the framework of the Southern collective, that is, the G-77. Historically, the collective has remained remarkably resilient in the face of conditions that could have led to its disintegration. This might well change in the future, but it has not changed just yet. Analysts trace this to a common view of the nature of environmental issues and their placement within a North-South framework, which suggests that the collective South will continue to play an important role in future global environmental politics. As Porter, Brown, and Chasek note, "Despite growing disparities among the developing countries between rapidly industri-alizing countries such as China, India, Malaysia, and Brazil, and debt-ridden countries that have experienced little or no growth since the 1980s, such as most of sub-Saharan Africa, Vietnam, Myanmar, and Nicaragua, developing countries share a common view of the relationship between global environ-mental issues and North-South economic relations."[17] China and India may well eventually orbit out of the Southern collective, but at least at this point the benefit of being wooed individually by the North while also speaking for and through the larger collective remains in their interest, as well as in the interest of other developing countries.[18]

Institutionally, the South consists of two distinct organizations—the Non-Aligned Movement (NAM) and the Group of 77—which have played different but complementary roles in furthering the Southern agenda. As Sauvant has noted, "While the Non-Aligned Countries [have] played a key role in making the development issue a priority item of the international agenda, the Group of 77 has become the principal organ of the Third World through which the concrete actions . . . are negotiated within the framework of the United Nations system."[19] An instrument of political summitry, the hundred-plus members of NAM meet every three years at the summit level to renew (or redefine) their vows. Meetings of foreign ministers are held every eighteen months. Operating through ministerial committees, NAM has no permanent institutional infrastructure to manage its activities between these meetings. On environmental issues, NAM has made some—but relatively few—declaratory statements of aspiration, and it is the G-77 that remains the collective voice of the developing countries in global environmental politics.

The Group of 77 has been described by Julius Nyerere, former presi-dent of Tanzania, as the "trade union of the poor."[20] It functions as the negotiating arm of the developing country collective during global negotia-tions. The G-77 describes its goal as "provid[ing] the means for the develop-ing world to articulate and promote its collective economic interests and enhance its joint negotiating capacity on all major North-South interna-tional economic issues in the United Nations system, and promote economic and technical cooperation among developing countries."[21] Although the G-77 emerged around the same time as NAM, it has distinctive origins and, unlike NAM, was born within—and was primarily a result of—the changing composition of the United Nations in the 1960s. Starting as a temporary caucus of seventy-seven developing countries, it has now grown into an ad hoc but quasi-permanent negotiating caucus of 132 members, plus China, which has the status of associate member but plays an influential role in the collective (see Figure 12–1).

Map 12-1 The Group of 77 plus China

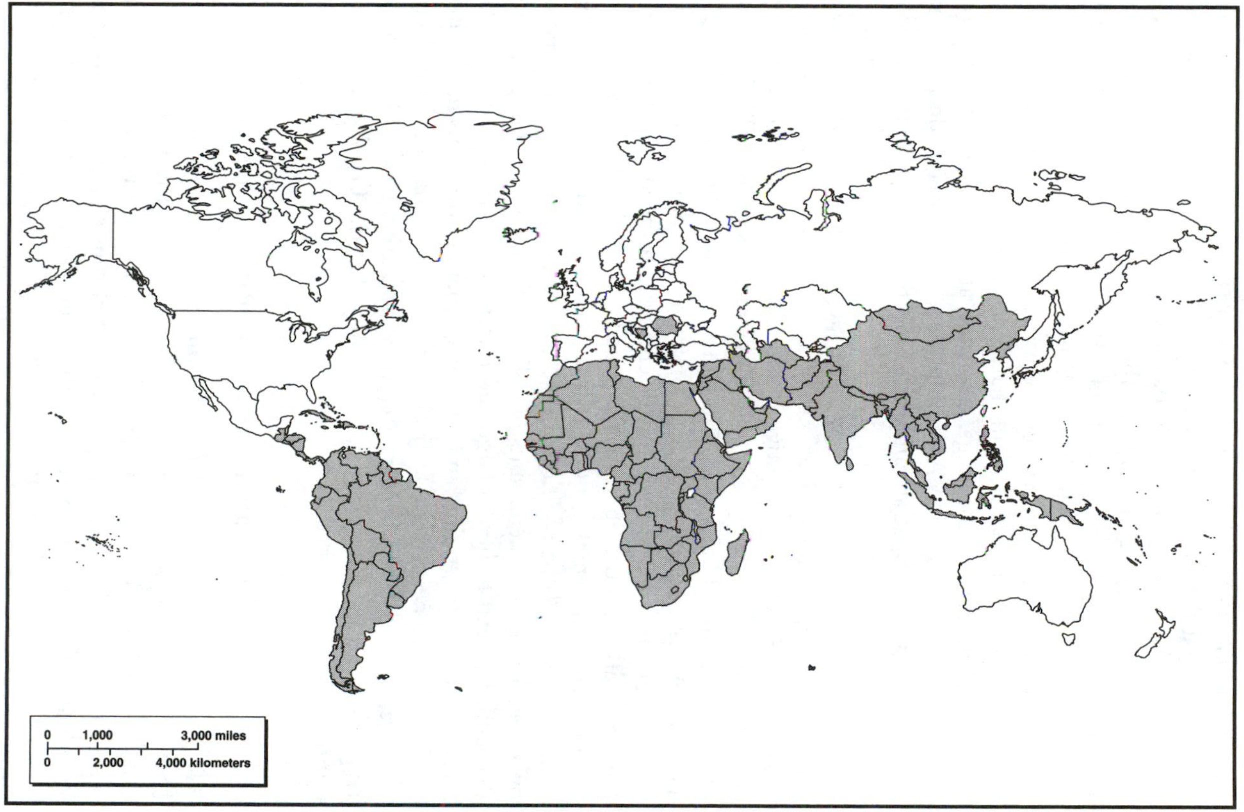

One of the main historical achievements of the G-77 was its role as chief negotiator for Southern demands for a new international economic order. Although the NIEO never achieved its goals, the G-77 has remained a negotiation collective and has exerted influence in agenda setting within various United Nations forums. It enjoyed particular successes in shaping final compromises during the 1992 Earth Summit and in a series of subsequent global environmental negotiations.[22] Indeed, the G-77 has remained, and remains today, the main negotiating voice of the Southern collective in every major environmental negotiation since then. As a negotiating vehicle, the G-77 does not override the individual national interests of its member states; instead it becomes a potent vehicle for aspects of those national interests on which the member states maintain shared positions.

Annual ministerial meetings, convened at the beginning of the regular sessions of the UN General Assembly, serve as the major decision-making body for the G-77. Special ministerial meetings are periodically called to focus on particular issues or to prepare for important global negotiations. G-77 hubs have sprung up in New York, Geneva, Rome, Vienna, Paris, Nairobi, and Washington, where various international organizations are based. In addition, G-77 caucuses are active in most international negotiations, where they adopt joint bargaining positions and strategies. The G-77 chairmanship rotates on an annual basis among its three regional subgroups—Asia, Africa, and Latin America—and the delegation from the chairperson's country serves as the designated spokesperson for the entire caucus in all negotiations during that year. Although the South has emerged as a stable and resilient collective in global environmental politics, it has often been forced to adopt lowest-common-denominator positions because of the impulse for risk reduction, low expectations, assumed habits of collaboration wrought out of a long history, and the need to herd a large and differentiated collective in the face of chronic resource constraints and no management effort. This has limited the G-77's ability to negotiate effectively for the shared goals of the collective or the differentiated interests of its members. The unity of the G-77, while not insignificant, is forever tentative; it is a unity that the G-77 stumbled into— a unity that it has learned to stumble into.

Southern Motivations in Global Environmental Politics

The timing of the 1992 Earth Summit was opportune for the South. The UNCED preparatory process coincided with the withering away of Cold War politics. The end of the Cold War not only instilled a sense of new vulnerabilities in the developing world but also provided the motivation for revitalizing the collective South. At the same time, Rio offered an opportunity to engage the North in a new dialogue. UNCED gave the South a forum, an issue, and an audience that it had been denied since the 1970s. The South—represented by an energetic G-77—succeeded not only in reopening the North-South dialogue but also effectively made that dialogue the focus of the Rio conference. Ultimately, the achievements at Rio and its legacy did not match the South's exaggerated hopes.[23] However, it is also true that Rio and subsequent global negotiations provided the South with opportunities to influence the global environmental agenda, particularly within the context of sustainable development.

A close examination of the goals and actions of developing countries during global environmental negotiations suggests that the South currently seeks what can be described as a new international *environmental* order (NIEnvO) and that this goal stems from the same concerns and ambitions that had prompted its call for a new international *economic* order in the 1970s.[24] Roger Hansen defined the original NIEO debate as a conflict over "conceptions about the management of society."[25] Rallying its newfound unity and negotiating as a tight bloc, the G-77 gained a major victory when a 1974 special session of the United Nations General Assembly legitimized the South's demand for the creation of a NIEO by passing a resolution to that effect and drawing up a plan of action. However, the optimism reflected in the UN resolution proved misplaced, and the differences persisted—North accusing South of being confrontational, and South blaming North for perpetuating an unjust order. By the 1980s it was obvious that the momentum had been lost and, as Mahbub-ul-Haq put it, "North-South negotiations [had] deteriorated to a ritual and a skillful exercise in *non*-dialogue."[26] In subsequent years, as the North's perception of the economic importance of natural resources in the South (particularly mineral and agricultural products) diminished, so did the perceived leverage enjoyed by the G-77. The NIEO agenda rapidly receded from world attention, as did discussions about North-South dialogue. It wasn't until the Earth Summit in 1992 that the relevance of and need for North-South negotiations once again became the subject of broad academic, policy, and even public discussion.

One should note, however, that the environmental issue as an exemplar of the North-South divide actually predates Rio by at least twenty years. It is, in fact, striking that the vast literature on the history of the North-South conflict, as well as the now bulky scholarship on international environmental politics, treats the role of developing countries in the United Nations Conference on the Human Environment (UNCHE), held in Stockholm in 1972, as a mere footnote. In fact, UNCHE was one of the first global forums at which the South consciously negotiated as a unified collective and adopted many of the very same substantive arguments and negotiation strategies that were soon to become the hallmark of the NIEO debates.[27]

From the very beginning, many developing countries perceived environmental concerns as a distinctively North-South issue and, in some cases, as an effort to sabotage the South's developmental aspirations. The intellectual leadership of the South very poignantly set out to redefine the environmental issue area in a decidedly North-South context. The most telling example was the so-called 1971 Founex Report, produced by a distinguished group of Southern intellectuals as part of the UNCHE preparatory process.[28] The tone and substance of the report foreshadowed, nearly exactly, what was soon to become the rhetoric of the South not only during the NIEO debates in the early 1970s but also during UNCED in 1992 and in other major environmental forums before and since then.

The constancy in the South's position at Stockholm and at and since Rio is striking and demonstrates that the original NIEO ideals of the South not only have survived but have resurfaced in these new rounds of global environmental negotiations. For example, Chris Mensah, himself a G–77 negotiator at UNCED, points out that the Southern leadership explicitly formulated its negotiation strategy around two key goals: first, to "ensure that the South has adequate environmental space for its future development," and, second, to "modify global economic relations in such a way that the South obtains the required resources, technology, and access to markets which would enable it to pursue a development process that is both environmentally sound and rapid enough to meet [its] needs and aspirations."[29] In short, developing countries have consistently contextualized environmental issues as being part of the larger complex of North-South concerns, particularly concerns about an iniquitous international order and their desire to bring about structural change in that order. This has become more poignant in recent years and environmental negotiations on issues such as climate change have become increasingly focused on trade and economic aspects. Developing countries have sought from these negotiations the same type of systemic considerations that they had during NIEO debates.

The experience in global environmental politics in the last decade seems to suggest that polarizations across North-South lines are unlikely to disappear by either ignoring them or wishing them away.[30] Even as some individual countries will become individually more active on specific environmental issues, they and the G–77 collective will find collective bargaining an effective strategy for those interests that are, and will remain, broadly shared by the South. The resilience that the South has shown in pursuing what it considers its legitimate agenda of economic justice and international systemic change suggests that international environmental negotiations will continue to be influenced by a Southern agenda that looks very much like a call for a new international *environmental* order. As Gareth Porter and Janet Brown note, "Many developing countries, particularly the more radical members of the Group of 77, have viewed global environmental negotiations as the best, if not the only, opportunity to advance a broader agenda of change in the structure of North-South economic relationships."[31] Marc Williams elaborates, "The possibility of linking negotiations on global environmental change with demands for change in other areas of North-South relations is one crucial reason for the continued participation of developing countries in negotiations of environmental problems."[32] He adds, "It is not . . . a question of environment being co-opted into the North-South debate. It already exists in this debate and is conceived in North-South terms."[33]

If the new vulnerabilities brought forth by the end of the Cold War were what motivated the developing countries to reinvigorate the collective South, it is the all-encompassing rubric of sustainable development that has enabled them to pursue the new North-South dialogue without having (yet) lost the

North's attention. For some, the global politics of sustainable development, loosely defined as it is—and, in fact, because it is so loosely defined—provides a broad framework within which to build a global compact to address both the North's concern for environmental sustainability and the South's desire for economic and social development. For others, including many G-77 negotiators, this new politics encompasses "a struggle between the developing and developed countries to define sustainable development in a way that fits their own agendas. The developed countries, most of which are relatively rich, put environment first. By contrast, the developing countries, most of which are poor and still struggling to meet basic human needs, put development first."[34]

Around the time of the Rio Earth Summit, many in the North and South argued that sustainable development might be the trump card that the South had been seeking all along. The North's new concern for global environmental problems, it was argued, provided the South with considerable leverage and bargaining power because without the participation of the developing countries many such problems cannot be addressed effectively.[35] For example, a Caribbean official suggested that "for the first time in more than a decade, the developing countries have an issue [the environment] where they have some real leverage," while India's environment minister went even further to proclaim that "the begging bowl is [now] really in the hands of the Western world."[36]

In retrospect, such Southern enthusiasm proved decidedly exaggerated, and with time it has certainly mellowed.[37] Although the South enjoyed influence in the Rio process, it soon found that its leverage lay less in influencing what went into the treaties than in what was kept out of them. Evidence since Rio confirms that while the South may have some leverage in the global politics of sustainable development, its extent is limited, its application is largely to avoid defeat, and its use is conditioned by the existence of a high level of concern, even alarm, in the North for the environmental issue under discussion. For example, Marian Miller's research on global regimes relating to the ozone layer, hazardous waste, and biodiversity found that "when there is a shared perception of environmental vulnerability, the Third World is able to gain a modest bargaining advantage."[38]

From the South's perspective, such assessments are sobering but not melancholy. Although the desire for systemic change endures in many quarters, it has been tempered by more realistic assessments. Moreover, part of the defining essence of the collective South is a desire to minimize risk rather than to maximize gain. From this standpoint, the Southern collective has been able to do exactly what it set out to do: minimize the risk of being bulldozed by a Northern environmental agenda, maintain a North-South focus on the global environmental dialogue, and eke out little victories (in terms of global transfers) whenever possible. Importantly, Southern hopes persist for a new North-South bargain constructed around the global politics of sustainable development; the importance that countries like China and India now have in environmental negotiations, for example on climate change, only underscores this potential further. This potential emanates from two important differences between the first generation of North-South dialogue and its current incarnation.

First, unlike its predecessor, this new generation of North-South inter-action is characterized by both sides wanting to establish a global dialogue, albeit with differing interests and agendas. For the South, such a dialogue is itself a long-standing goal. For the North, it is necessitated by the realization that global action on the environment, especially in the age of climate change, cannot be successful without the active participation of the developing coun-tries. This is a major sea change from the 1970s, when the South was calling for a dialogue and the North actively resisted. Furthermore, there is a certain sense of urgency on both sides as the effects of both environmental devasta-tion and abject poverty compound visibly over time.

Second, by their very nature, it is often difficult to conceive of global environmental problems in terms of victory and defeat, especially in the long run. Although the jury is still out on whether and how the global environ-ment might become a win-win issue, all indications suggest that it can very easily be transformed into a lose-lose proposition. This, too, marks a differ-ence from aspects of earlier North-South dialogues, such as the oil or debt crises of the 1970s, which failed partly because the issues were perceived as zero-sum games.

At the heart of North-South politics of sustainable development are debates about the costs to be borne, the ability to bear these costs, the respon-sibility for causing the problem, and the ability to influence future decisions. These can be reduced to contentions about past responsibility, present ability, and future priorities. Serious differences persist between North and South on all three. Bridging the deep differences is not an easy task and would require, at a minimum, innovative strategies from both North and South. One pro-posed strategy for the South would build upon the lessons of negotiation theory and the experiences of the South. The eight-point strategy can be paraphrased as: "Stop feeling angry at the North and sorry for yourself."[39] It recommends that the South focus on interests, not positions; cultivate its own power; be hard on issues, not on people; redefine the international environ-mental agenda; organize itself; develop its constituency; clean up its own act; and remember that good agreements are more important than "winning." Such a strategy would also lead to a more productive international negotiation process.

Given the deeply felt interests that the South has resiliently pursued for so long, it is unlikely that it will voluntarily forsake its demands or be argued out of them. Given a realistic assessment of the South's bargaining leverage, it is equally unlikely that the South will be able to browbeat the North into simply accepting its positions. If meaningful headway is to be made, it will have to come through some mechanism that allows the interests of both sides to be met. In this regard, sustainable development can be a potentially fortu-itous term in that it can (given the right conditions) allow efficient packaging of issues of concern to North and South—issues that they might otherwise be hesitant to deal with individually. Issue linkage, however, can be fraught with both dangers and opportunities. Some, such as Christopher Stone, fear that "adding cards to the deck raises the risk that the environment will get lost in the shuffle."[40] However, Lawrence Susskind reminds us that issue linkage can be "crucial to the success of negotiation[s]" that involve complex, multi-party, multi-issue bargaining.[41] While there is certainly the danger of issue linkage turning into blackmail—either by the North arm-twisting the South to follow its environmental dictates or by the South threatening environmental inaction in the absence of a restructured international system—there is a strong case for both sides to seek issue linkages in their pursuit of meaningful dialogue. After all, the very term *sustainable development* is the embodiment of creative issue linkage.

Southern Views on Global Environmental Politics since Rio

The 1992 UNCED conference is widely viewed as one of the high points of the last thirty years of global environmental politics. Rio's legacy probably owes as much to the many disappointments since that conference as it does to its actual achievements. For example, in a survey of 252 scholars and practitioners from seventy-one countries conducted ten years after Rio, nearly 70 percent of the respondents viewed the Rio Earth Summit as having been "very significant" or "monumental," even though only 6 percent believed that significant progress had been made toward implementing Rio goals. The survey suggests that Rio's greatest impact came from its indirect outputs: its success in giving a higher global profile to issues of environment and development; spurring the growth of national and international institutions, policies, projects, and multilateral agreements for environment and development; and giving more prominence to the views of developing countries on global environmental policy.[42]

For developing countries, a key manifestation of these indirect outputs was the so-called Rio bargain. Although difficult to define—and embraced with varying degrees of conviction by various parties—the Rio bargain is generally understood to be an attempt to bridge lingering North-South differences through two key mechanisms: the concept of sustainable development and a set of design principles for global environmental agreements that addressed key concerns of the South.[43]

More than fifteen years after Rio, it is easy to forget that the notion of sustainable development—which has since become somewhat of a Southern mantra—was not the South's idea but rather a conceptual device used to appease developing countries apprehensive, since before the 1972 Stockholm conference, that environment protection would be used as a reason to stall their economic development. Indeed, the official name of the Rio Earth Summit—the United Nations Conference on Environment and Development—was crafted, after some debate, to signify that environment and development were complementary rather than contradictory categories.

Still, many in the South came to UNCED and viewed the notion of sustainable development with doubt and in some cases outright trepidation.[44]

Eventually, however, developing country negotiators came to see this concept and the broader Rio process as good opportunities to reopen the North-South dialogue, which had languished through the 1980s, and to move toward a grand North-South bargain for which the South had been striving since the 1970s.[45]

Thus, for the G-77 (but perhaps not for many in the North), the most important legacy of the Rio process was a global commitment to sustainable development, which the South sees as providing an emphasis on development equal to environmental protection, and to three critical, subsidiary principles: additionality, common but differentiated responsibilities, and polluter pays.[46] Embodied in the frameworks of various Rio documents, these principles arose out of Southern fears that even though they had not been historically responsible for creating the major global environmental problems, the cost of global environmental action would somehow be transferred to them either in terms of forgone developmental opportunities or actual remediation and adaptation costs. This section reviews the state of global environmental politics from the perspective of the South.[47]

Sustainable Development

Sustainable development was never a clear concept.[48] Indeed, it was never meant to be clear. It was a political compromise, and a rather good one at that. Its greatest strength was constructive ambiguity; actors that might otherwise not talk to one another could accept the concept for very different reasons and agree to talk.

The World Commission on Environment and Development had gravitated toward the concept of sustainable development in a conscious attempt to resolve developing country apprehension about the environmental agenda. The Earth Summit found the concept useful in getting the North and the South to sit at the same table. As a result, use of the concept began to evolve. By the time Rio ended, many saw sustainable development not as a nebulous ideal or vague goal but as a policy prescription, a desired if not mandatory pathway for future national and international policy.[49]

In practical terms, the good news is that many in the South have now totally internalized the concept of sustainable development and have become staunch advocates. This denotes a significant evolution. Many government as well as citizen organizations in developing countries have adopted sustainable development as a guiding principle for implementation and action. As a result, at the local level the concept of sustainable development is far more real today than it was a decade ago.[50]

The bad news is that at the level of intergovernmental debates, the concept has become more, rather than less, murky since Rio. The term stands in danger of being reduced from an innovative framework for negotiation to an empty declaratory aspiration. Thus, while sustainable development was once seen in some quarters as a potentially powerful and even threatening concept—because it suggested the possibility of change in the status quo—it is today on the verge of becoming ineffectual and divorced from its initial action orientation. For those in the South who had come to accept and even embrace the term because of its embedded promise of systemic change, this dilution of the concept has been particularly disturbing.[51] The current climate change debate is a good indicator of this unease. Much of the public discourse as well as the policy debate highlights the environmental parameters much more than the developmental impacts. However, the impacts of climate change, and the need for many developing countries to adapt to these impacts, will be a practical test for the concept of sustainable development and of Northern commitment to the concept. Because adaptation policy is mainly about development, it will either force environmentalists to take development concerns more seriously or could bring new North-South fissures on sustainable development to the fore.

Additionality

The principle of additionality arose out of the Southern concern that environmental issues would divert international aid from traditional developmental matters. Developing countries feared that instead of raising new funds for dealing with global environmental issues, the North and international institutions would simply transfer to the environment resources that had been previously targeted for development. The principle of additionality sought to ensure that new monies would be made available to deal with global environmental issues.

Despite assurances given to the South, however, this principle was abandoned soon after UNCED, during negotiation of the UN Convention to Combat Desertification (CCD). Early in these negotiations it became clear that few if any new funds would be made available for implementation of the treaty. This dismayed developing countries, particularly those in Africa, and became a major source of contention in the negotiations. Ultimately, a global mechanism was established under the CCD in order to, essentially, use existing resources more efficiently in order to meet the action needs of the CCD.[52] Even though the Global Environment Facility eventually decided to include desertification activities in its funding, the CCD negotiations severely damaged the principle of additionality. Since then, negotiations on several other multilateral environmental agreements—including, for example, those addressing climate change and toxic chemicals—have also been subjected to arguments from Northern nations that utilizing market forces and managing existing resources in a better way are adequate substitutes for at least some portion of the original promise of additionality. Additionality is a particular concern in the context of climate adaptation. Many poorer countries fear that not only will climate adaptation drain their own developmental resources away from other immediate needs, but international assistance for other development issues will also be diverted to climate-related investments. The fascination with climate change has already drained much attention away from issues that are more immediately important for developing countries, and many in the South fear that it will also drain away resources.[53]

Common but Differentiated Responsibility

This principle acknowledges that some nations have a greater and more direct responsibility for creating and, therefore, addressing global environmental problems. Although these problems are the concern of all nations, and all nations should work toward their solution, responsibility for action should be differentiated in proportion to the responsibility for creating the problem and the available financial and technical resources to take effective action.

Although this principle places the primary responsibility for action on industrialized countries, it was actually a concession of sorts made by the developing countries. Placing responsibility for action on the North had been a major argument of the South since before the 1972 Stockholm conference.[54] In accepting this principle, the South agreed that it, too, would address global environment issues—provided that the primary burden of action, investment, and implementation was not shifted to the very countries that are least responsible for creating the problem and least able to resolve it.

The principle of common but differentiated responsibilities enjoys generally broad support and has been explicitly acknowledged in nearly all international environmental agreements since Rio. At the same time, one could argue that it faces an important assault in the context of the UN Framework Convention on Climate Change. The United States has taken the position that it cannot accept mandatory targets for greenhouse gas emissions unless some type of restrictions are also placed on major developing countries such as China and India. Industrialized countries account for the vast majority of historical greenhouse gas emissions. In addition, although aggregate national greenhouse gas emissions are growing significantly in many developing countries, the per capita emissions of citizens in these countries will remain significantly smaller than those in the North for decades to come. Although understanding the need for the growing economies within the South to take on some additional responsibilities, many in the South worry that we have already seen a shift from past responsibility as a yardstick for future action— a change that would, from their perspective, make global environmental regimes even less equitable.[55]

Polluter-Pays Principle

This principle has deep roots in domestic environmental policy in the North, particularly in the United States. It seeks to ensure that the costs of environmental action, economic and other, will be borne by those who created the need for that action. As with the principle of common but differentiated responsibility, the polluter-pays principle is rooted in concerns about fairness and constitutes a key component of the Rio bargain.

Along with other aspects of the Rio bargain, many in the South believe that the polluter-pays principle has been steadily diluted in the last fifteen years and is being further diluted as we attempt to create a new post-Kyoto climate regime. They point to an increasing pattern of pushing implementation of multilateral environmental agreements steadily Southward, including in the climate, desertification, and biodiversity regimes, by seeking relatively fewer changes in behavior patterns in the North and relatively more in the South—even though it was Northern behavior that gave rise to many problems in the first place.[56]

Consider, for example, the Clean Development Mechanism (CDM), a provision of the Kyoto climate agreement that allows industrialized countries to meet some of their responsibilities for greenhouse gas reduction by investing in projects in the South. In the name of efficiency, the CDM moves a great deal of climate action to developing countries where emission reductions are likely to be cheaper rather than imposing greater costs in the countries responsible for past greenhouse gas emissions. Although the logic of economic efficiency is potentially compelling, the CDM arguably threatens the core moral element of the polluter-pays principle in that it allows industrialized countries to avoid taking more significant and expensive action domestically—essentially allowing the polluters to buy their way out of their responsibility. In addition, while capturing efficiencies in the South may be enticing in the short term, it leaves subsequent generations in the developing countries with potentially ever more arduous tasks in the future, as they would have already sold away their rights to cheaper solutions. On the other hand, it is clear that as the developing country contributions to carbon emissions increase, the polluter-pays principle should equally apply to them. However, if the integrity of the principle is compromised by the North in trying to find cheap and quick fixes for their pollution, we may find the South much less willing to accept the principle when their turn comes.

Southern Frustrations in Global Environmental Politics

Global environmental politics has yielded mixed results for the Southern collective. On the positive side, one could argue that the South, which had largely rejected the global environmental agenda at Stockholm in 1972, has today internalized and accepted much, if not most, of that agenda. Indeed, developing countries are today integrated into the global environmental system far more than many would have expected them to be at Stockholm in 1972, or even at Rio in 1992. The concept of sustainable development has allowed developing countries to incorporate long-standing concerns about economic development and social justice into the emerging environmental agenda, and by doing so they have influenced the nature of global environmental discourse. More broadly, global environmental politics has afforded the South a new arena in which to advance its persistent demand for radical, structural reform of the international system.

Yet the dominant feeling within the South remains one of frustration with global environmental politics. There are few tangible benefits to show for its continuing and increasing involvement and investment in this issue. The South has been no more successful in crafting a new international *environmental* order than it had been in building a new international *economic* order. Most of the concessions the South thought it had negotiated from the North have proved largely illusionary, and the so-called Rio bargain has not exactly delivered. Much of the attention in terms of North-South environmental relations since UNCED is focused on what the South sees as the failure of the North to deliver what had been promised or implied at Rio, such as additional resources, technology transfers, and capacity building. The inability of the North to fulfill these commitments—and the lack of attention to this failure in the policy discourse—is a major contributor to the South's prevailing sense of frustration. The achievements of individual countries notwithstanding, the Southern collective has little to celebrate except its survival. As the concept of sustainable development loses clarity and purpose at the global level, and as the key principles of additionality, common but differentiated responsibility, and polluter pays are steadily eroded (at least from the South's standpoint), developing countries have a diminishing interest in staying engaged in these processes. These issues defined the raison d'être for the South's engagement in global environmental negotiations. While Southern disenchantment is unlikely to turn into total disengagement, it is certainly not conducive to meaningful North-South partnerships for what still remain very pressing global environmental challenges.

Parallel to this unraveling of the Rio bargain is the negotiation overload that has characterized the world of global environmental policy since the Rio Earth Summit.[57] It is not without irony that the less we are able to implement existing multilateral environmental agreements, the more frantic we seem to become in trying to create new ones. Proliferation of such agreements has led to a severe case of negotiation fatigue among all countries, particularly developing countries.[58] The limited and already stretched human resources available to these countries are further thinned by increasing demands of even more, and more complex and demanding, negotiations for multilateral environmental agreements. While major Northern countries have responded to the negotiation proliferation by deploying more human and knowledge resources, most developing countries are unable to do so, compounding the systemic disadvantage they already face in the negotiations.[59]

As we end the first decade of the twenty-first century, developing country negotiators are much more involved in global environmental politics than they ever expected to be, but they often consider themselves disenchanted, disadvantaged, and disempowered.[60] For the Southern collective, the sense of frustration stems not only from global environmental negotiations having yielded many agreements but very little implementation; it also stems directly from having seen the North-South bargain, a cherished legacy of the Rio Earth Summit, unravel slowly. Yet the key assumption that led to the forging of the original bargain—meaningful progress on the great environmental challenges of our times, including climate change but not limited to it—is more valid today than ever before; however, such progress is unlikely, if not impossible, without the full and active participation of the developing countries. Meaningful participation by the developing countries is much less likely to come from trying to break up the Southern collective (which has always been resilient to such attempts) than it is by addressing the acknowledged and much articulated needs of the developing countries. The view from the South is not without hope, but it contains many challenges that cannot be wished away.

Notes

1. For a more elaborate treatment of the argument made in this section, see Adil Najam, "The Collective South in Multinational Environmental Politics," in *Policymaking and Prosperity: A Multinational Anthology*, ed. Stuart Nagel (Lanham, Md.: Lexington Books, 2003), 197–240.

2. For discussion, see Craig Murphy, *The Emergence of the NIEO Ideology* (Boulder, Colo.: Westview Press, 1984).

3. Emile Van Lennep, "North-South Relations in the 80s: A Constructive Approach to New Realities," in *Global Development: Issues and Choices*, ed. K. Haq (Washington, D.C.: North-South Roundtable, 1983), 15.

4. See Stephen D. Krasner, *Structural Conflict: The Third World against Global Liberalism* (Berkeley: University of California Press, 1985); and Caroline Thomas, *In Search of Security: The Third World in International Relations* (Boulder, Colo.: Lynne Rienner, 1987).

5. South Commission, *The Challenge to the South: The Report of the South Commission* (Oxford: Oxford University Press, 1990), 1.

6. See B. P. Menon, *Global Dialogue: The New International Order* (London: Pergamon Press, 1977); and Murphy, *The Emergence of the NIEO Ideology*.

7. Barbara Crossette, "The 'Third World' Is Dead, but Spirits Linger," *New York Times*, November 13, 1994, sec. A.

8. Examples include A. Oxley, "North/South Dimensions of a New World Order," in *Whose New World Order?* ed. Mara Bustelo and Philip Alston (Annandale, Va.: Federation Press, 1991).

9. Roger Hansen, *Beyond the North-South Stalemate* (New York: McGraw-Hill, 1979), 2. See also Marc Williams, "Re-articulating the Third World Coalition: The Role of the Environmental Agenda," *Third World Quarterly* 14, no. 1 (1993): 7–29; Cedric Grant, "Equity in International Relations: A Third World Perspective," *International Affairs* 71, no. 3 (1995): 567–587.

10. James K. Sebenius, "Negotiating a Regime to Control Global Warming," in *Greenhouse Warming: Negotiating a Global Regime*, ed. Jessica Tuchman Mathews (Washington, D.C.: World Resources Institute, 1991), 87.

11. South Commission, *The Challenge to the South;* Mohammed Ayoob, "The New-Old Disorder in the Third World," *Global Governance* 1, no. 1 (1995): 59–77; Adil Najam, "An Environmental Negotiation Strategy for the South," *International Environmental Affairs* 7, no. 3 (1995): 249–287.

12. Dennis Pirages, *Global Ecopolitics: The New Context for International Relations* (North Scituate, Mass.: Duxbury Press, 1978); Hayward R. Alker Jr. and Peter M. Haas, "The Rise of Global Ecopolitics," in *Global Accord: Environmental Challenges and International Responses*, ed. Nazli Choucri (Cambridge: MIT Press, 1993), 133–171; Najam, "An Environmental Negotiation Strategy for the South."

13. William R. Moomaw, "International Environmental Policy and the Softening of Sovereignty," *Fletcher Forum of World Affairs* 21 (Summer/Fall 1997): 7–15.

14. Aaron Cosbey and S. Burgiel, *The Cartagena Protocol on Biosafety: An Analysis of Results*, IISD Briefing Note (Winnipeg, Canada: International Institute for Sustainable Development, 2000).

15. Anil Agarwal, Sunita Narain, and Anju Sharma, *Green Politics* (New Delhi: Centre for Science and Environment, 1999); Elisabeth Corell, *The Negotiable Desert: Expert Knowledge in the Negotiations of the Convention to Combat Desertification*, Linkoping Studies in Arts and Sciences, no. 191 (1999), Linkoping University, Linkoping, Sweden.

16. John Humphrey and Dirk Messner, "China and India as Emerging Global Governance Actors: Challenges for Developing and Developed Countries," in *IDS Bulletin* 37, no. 1 (2006): 107–114.

17. Gareth Porter, Janet W. Brown, and Pamela S. Chasek, *Global Environmental Politics,* 3rd ed. (Boulder, Colo.: Westview, 2000), 179.

18. For related discussion, see Humphrey and Messner, "China and India as Emerging Global Governance Actors."

19. K. P. Sauvant, *The Group of 77: Evolution, Structure, Organization* (New York: Oceana Publications, 1981), 5.

20. Julius K. Nyerere, "Unity for a New Order," in *Dialogue for a New Order,* ed. K. Haq (New York: Pergamon Press, 1980), 3–10.

21. *Principles and Objectives of the Group of 77 for the Year 2000 and Beyond* (New York: Office of the Chairman of the Group of 77, 1994), 1.

22. See Najam, "An Environmental Negotiation Strategy for the South"; Adil Najam, "A Developing Countries' Perspective on Population, Environment and Development," *Population Research and Policy Review* 15, no. 1 (1996): 1–19; Tariq Banuri, "Noah's Ark or Jesus's Cross?" Working Paper no. WP/UNCED/1992/1, Sustainable Development Policy Institute, Islamabad, Pakistan, 1992; Makhund G. Rajan, "Bargaining with the Environment: A New Weapon for the South?" *South Asia Research* 12, no. 2 (1992): 135–147; and Agarwal, Narain, and Sharma, *Green Politics.*

23. See Banuri, "Noah's Ark or Jesus's Cross?"; Najam, "An Environmental Negotiation Strategy for the South"; Adil Najam, "The Case for a South Secretariat in International Environmental Negotiation," Program on Negotiation Working Paper no. 94–8, Program on Negotiation at Harvard Law School, Cambridge, 1994; and Richard Sandbrook, "UNGASS Has Run Out of Steam," *International Affairs* 73, no. 4 (1997): 641–654.

24. Najam, "An Environmental Negotiation Strategy for the South."

25. Hansen, *Beyond the North-South Stalemate,* vii.

26. Mahbub-ul-Haq, "North-South Dialogue: Is There a Future?" in *Dialogue for a New Order,* 270–287.

27. See Wade Rowland, *The Plot to Save the World* (Toronto: Clarke, Irwin & Co., 1973).

28. *Development and Environment,* Report and Working Papers of Experts Convened by the Secretary General of the United Nations Conference on the Human Environment, Founex, Switzerland, June 4–12, 1971 (Paris: Mouton, 1971).

29. Chris Mensah, "The Role of Developing Countries," in *The Environment after Rio: International Law and Economics,* ed. L. Campigio, L. Pineschi, D. Siniscalco, and T. Treves (London: Graham and Trotman, 1994), 33–53.

30. Banuri, "Noah's Ark or Jesus's Cross?"; Caroline Thomas, *The Environment in International Relations* (London: Royal Institute of International Affairs, 1992); Williams, "Re-articulating the Third World Coalition"; Tariq Osman Hyder, "Looking Back to See Forward," in *Negotiating Climate Change: The Inside Story of the Rio Convention,* ed. I. M. Mintzer and J. A. Leonard (Cambridge: Cambridge University Press, 1994), 201–226; Agarwal, Narain, and Sharma, *Green Politics;* and Adil Najam, "Trade and Environment after Seattle: A Negotiation Agenda for the South," in *Journal of Environment and Development* 9, no. 4 (2000): 405–425.

31. Gareth Porter and Janet Brown, *Global Environmental Politics* (Boulder, Colo.: Westview Press, 1991), 129.

32. Williams, "Re-articulating the Third World Coalition," 19.

33. Ibid., 25.

34. Hyder, "Looking Back to See Forward," 205.

35. For example, G. J. MacDonald predicted that "the views of the developing nations will determine the direction, and probably the ultimate significance, of UNCED"; see "Brazil 1992: Who Needs This Meeting?" *Issues in Science and Technology* 7, no. 4 (1992): 41–44. The *New York Times* (March 17, 1992) noted that "for the first time . . . the

developing countries have an issue where they have some real leverage." Oran Young argued that the South has "substantial bargaining leverage" and that "Northerners will ignore the demands of the South regarding climate change at their peril." See Oran Young, "Negotiating an International Climate Regime: The Institutional Bargaining for Environmental Governance," in *Global Accord: Environmental Challenges and International Responses*, ed. N. Choucri (Cambridge: MIT Press, 1993), 447.

36. Both statements quoted in Rajan, "Bargaining with the Environment," 135–136.
37. Ibid., 147.
38. Marian A. L. Miller, *The Third World in Global Environmental Politics* (Boulder, Colo.: Lynne Rienner, 1995), 141. Others have reached similar conclusions, including Susan Sell, who examined North-South environmental bargaining on ozone depletion, climate change, and biodiversity, and V. de Campos Mello, who analyzed the forestry negotiations at UNCED. See Susan Sell, "North-South Environmental Bargaining: Ozone, Climate Change, and Biodiversity," *Global Governance* 2, no. 1 (1996): 97–118; and V. de Campos Mello, "North-South Conflicts and Power Distribution in UNCED Negotiations: The Case of Forestry," Working Paper no. WP-93–26, International Institute for Applied Systems Analysis, Laxenburg, Austria, 1993.
39. Najam, "An Environmental Negotiation Strategy for the South," 249–287.
40. Christopher D. Stone, *The Gnat Is Older than Man: Global Environment and Human Agenda* (Princeton: Princeton University Press, 1993), 115.
41. Lawrence E. Susskind, *Environmental Diplomacy: Negotiating More Effective Global Agreements* (New York: Oxford University Press, 1994).
42. Adil Najam, Janice M. Poling, Naoyuki Yamagishi, Daniel G. Straub, Jillian Sarno, Sara M. DeRitter, and Eonjeong M. Kim, "From Rio to Johannesburg: Progress and Prospects," *Environment* 4, no. 7 (September 2002): 26–38.
43. See, for example, Martin Khor K. Peng, *The Future of North-South Relations: Conflict or Cooperation?* (Penang: Third World Network, 1992).
44. Edward Kufour, "G-77: We Won't Negotiate Away Our Sovereignty," *Third World Resurgence* 14–15 (1991): 17; *Environment and Development: Towards a Common Strategy of the South in UNCED Negotiations and Beyond* (Geneva: South Centre, 1991); Banuri, "Noah's Ark or Jesus's Cross?"; Najam, "An Environmental Negotiation Strategy for the South."
45. A. O. Adede, "International Environmental Law from Stockholm to Rio," *Environmental Policy and Law* 22, no. 2 (1992): 88–105; Williams, "Re-articulating the Third World Coalition"; Najam, "An Environmental Negotiation Strategy for the South."
46. For more on each, see David Hunter, James Salzman, and Durwood Zaelke, *International Environmental Law and Policy* (New York: Foundation Press, 1998).
47. This section builds upon the discussion in Adil Najam, "The Unraveling of the Rio Bargain," *Politics and the Life Sciences* 21, no. 2 (2002): 46–50.
48. Sharachchandra M. Lélé, "Sustainable Development: A Critical Review," *World Development* 19, no. 6 (1991): 607–621.
49. See Adil Najam and Cutler Cleveland, "Energy and Sustainable Development at Global Environmental Summits: An Evolving Agenda," *Environment, Development and Sustainability* 5, no. 2 (2003): 117–138.
50. Tariq Banuri and Adil Najam, *Civic Entrepreneurship: A Civil Society Perspective on Sustainable Development*, vol. 1: *Global Synthesis* (Islamabad: Gandhara Academy Press, 2002).
51. Banuri and Najam, *Civic Entrepreneurship*; Wolfgang Sachs, H. Acselrad, F. Akhter, A. Amon, T. B. G. Egziabher, Hilary French, P. Haavisto, Paul Hawken, H. Henderson, Ashok Khosla, S. Larrain, R. Loske, Anita Roddick, V. Taylor, Christine von Weizsäcker, and S. Zabelin, *The Jo'burg Memo: Fairness in a Fragile World* (Berlin: Heinrich Böll Foundation, 2002).
52. Pamela S. Chasek, "The Convention to Combat Desertification: Lessons Learned for Sustainable Development," *Journal of Environment and Development* 6, no. 2 (1997): 147–169; Corell, *The Negotiable Desert*.

53. Adil Najam, David Runnalls, and Mark Halle, *Environment and Globalization: Five Propositions*, (Winnipeg: International Institute for Sustainable Development, 2007).

54. *Development and Environment.*

55. See Adil Najam and Ambuj Sagar, "Avoiding a COP-out: Moving Towards Systematic Decision-Making Under the Climate Convention," *Climatic Change* 39, no. 4 (1998): iii–ix; Adil Najam and Thomas Page, "The Climate Convention: Deciphering the Kyoto Convention," *Environmental Conservation* 25, no. 3 (1998): 187–194; and Adil Najam, Saleemul Huq, and Youba Sokona, "Moving beyond Kyoto: Developing Countries, Climate Change, and Sustainable Development," *Climate Policy* 3 (2003): 221–231.

56. See, for example, Anil Agarwal and Sunita Narain, *Global Warming in an Unequal World: A Case of Environmental Colonialism* (New Delhi: Centre for Science and Environment, 1991); and Agarwal, Narain, and Sharma, *Green Politics.*

57. Adil Najam, Mihaela Papa, and Nadaa Taiyab, *Global Environmental Governance: A Reform Agenda* (Winnipeg: International Institute for Sustainable Development, 2007).

58. Miguel Munoz, Rachel Thrasher, and Adil Najam, "Measuring the Negotiation Burden of Multilateral Environmental Agreements," *Global Environmental Politics* 9, no. 4 (November 2009): 1–13.

59. Adil Najam, "Knowledge Needs for Better Multilateral Environmental Agreements," WSSD Opinion Paper, International Institute for Environment and Development, London, 2002.

60. Najam et al., "From Rio to Johannesburg."

13

Energy and Environment in China: Achievements and Enduring Challenges

Joanna I. Lewis and Kelly Sims Gallagher

China faces development and environment challenges, particularly those stemming from its coal-reliant energy system. China relies on coal for more than two-thirds of its energy needs, including approximately 80 percent of its electricity needs. Although coal has helped to fuel China's rapid economic growth, it has done so at the expense of the local—and the global—environment. Coal combustion causes most of China's air pollution, including sulfur dioxide and particulates, and also affects human health, agriculture, ecology, and infrastructure. In addition, China's coal-fueled power sector is the largest source of carbon dioxide emissions in the world and, therefore, is a major contributor to global climate change. China's transport sector, while still accounting for a relatively small share of China's energy consumption, is responsible for most of its urban air pollution.

China faces serious challenges in addressing the environmental impacts of its energy use. Energy demand is growing so quickly that the government can barely monitor technology decisions, resulting more often than not in the construction of additional conventional coal plants. Despite relatively stringent environmental regulations, enforcement of central government policies is often overlooked at the local level. A lack of capacity and transparency in emissions monitoring and energy consumption data means policymakers do not have in hand all the information needed to make strategic decisions about China's energy future.

Despite these real challenges, China has made significant progress in many key areas, including promoting energy efficiency and renewable energy. Armed with aggressive national-level energy intensity reduction targets, a national renewable energy law mandating and supporting the use of low-emission or emission-free technologies, and a suite of other policies targeting the industrial and transportation sectors, the Chinese government has numerous tools in place to address the environmental impacts of its current energy system. Perhaps most promising is the attention China is placing on the development of advanced, low-emission technologies, including renewable-power technologies and higher-efficiency motor vehicles. Chinese firms have used creative strategies to obtain access to advanced technologies, often from the United States and Europe, and in some instances have been able to leapfrog older technologies, shifting directly to more advanced, more energy-efficient, or cleaner ones.

Examining the successes and failures in China's strategies to address the environmental impacts of its energy consumption can provide insights into where China may be headed in the years to come. Understanding how current domestic challenges shape China's positions in international environmental negotiations is also crucial for productive engagement with China to improve its environmental situation. This chapter explores China's current energy and environmental challenges, its successes to date, and prospects for China's future energy development pathways.

Energy, Environment, and Development

China's economic development during the past thirty years has been remarkable by nearly all metrics. Since 1978, China has consistently been the most rapidly growing country in the world.[1] On the basis of purchasing power parity, China is now the second-largest economy in the world, and it is the fifth-largest according to market exchange rates.[2] As a result of this steady and rapid economic growth, an estimated 200 million people have been pulled out of absolute poverty since 1979.[3]

Despite these impressive achievements, the Chinese government continues to face difficult economic development challenges. China's overall economic development statistics reveal that, despite the emergence of modern cities and a growing middle class, China is still largely a developing country. Although rapid economic growth has made China the fourth-largest economy in the world, its gross domestic product (GDP) per capita is still below the world average.

Economic growth is not just a crucial part of China's development strategy, but it is also crucial to the political stability of the country. A fundamental target of the current development plan articulated by China's leadership is an annual economic growth rate of 7.5 percent.[4] Many have argued that continued rapid economic growth in China is critical to the Communist Party's legitimacy. The Communist Party leadership in China "considers rapid economic growth a political imperative because it is the only way to prevent massive unemployment and labor unrest."[5]

Energy is directly tied to economic development. The relationship between energy use and economic growth matters greatly in China. Although China quadrupled its GDP between 1980 and 2000, it did so while merely doubling the amount of energy it consumed during that period. This allowed China's energy intensity (ratio of energy consumption to GDP) and consequently the emissions intensity (ratio of carbon dioxide–equivalent emissions to GDP) of its economy to decline dramatically, marking a dramatic achievement in energy intensity gains not paralleled in any other country at a similar stage of industrialization (Figure 13-1). This has important implications not just for China's economic growth trajectory but also for the total quantity of China's energy-related emissions. Reducing the total quantity of energy consumed also contributes to the country's energy security. Without this reduction in the energy intensity of the economy, China would have used more than three times the energy than it did during this period (Figure 13-2).

Figure 13-1 Energy Intensity Trends in China, United States, European
Union, India, Japan

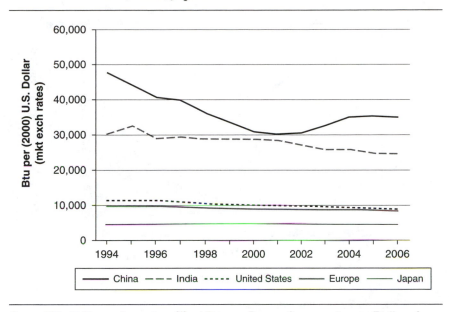

Source: "World Energy Intensity—Total Primary Energy Consumption per Dollar of
Gross Domestic Product Using Market Exchange Rates, 1980–2006," *International
Energy Annual* 2006, U.S. Energy Information Administration, Table E.1g, www.eia.doe
.gov/emeu/international/energyconsumption.html.

The current decade has brought new challenges to the relationship
among energy consumption, emissions, and economic growth in China.
Starting in 2002, China's declining energy intensity trend reversed, and
energy growth surpassed economic growth for the first time in decades. This
trend continued until 2005. This reversal has had dramatic implications for
energy security and greenhouse gas emissions growth in China during the
past few years. In 2007 China's CO_2 emissions were up 8 percent from
the previous year, making China the largest national emitter in the world for
the first time (surpassing U.S. emissions that year by 14 percent).[6] China's
long-term energy security is dependent not only on having sufficient supplies
of energy to sustain its incredible rate of economic growth but also on being
able to manage the growth in energy demand without causing intolerable
environmental damage.

Currently, China emits 35 percent more carbon dioxide per dollar of
output than the United States and 100 percent more than the European
Union. China's increase in energy-related pollution in the past few years has
been driven primarily by industrial energy use, fueled by an increased percentage of coal in the overall energy mix. Industry consumes about 70 percent of
China's energy, and China's industrial base supplies much of the world. As a
result, China's current environmental challenges are fueled in part by the
global demand for its products. China today produces about 35 percent of the

Figure 13-2 China's Energy Consumption: Actual and at Frozen 1977
Intensity

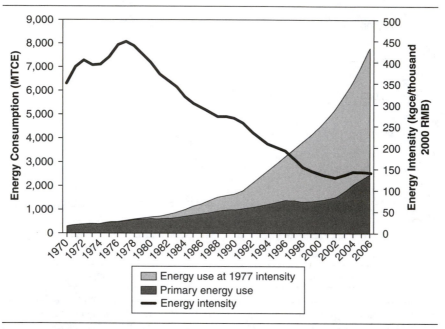

Source: China Energy Databook, vol. 7 (Berkeley: Lawrence Berkeley National Laboratory, 2008), Table 4B.2, Actual Primary Energy Consumption and Projected Energy
Consumption at Frozen 1977 Intensity.

world's steel and 28 percent of its aluminum, for example, up from 12 percent
and 8 percent, respectively, a decade ago.[7] The centerpiece of the current five-
year plan is to promote the service industries—the so-called tertiary sector—
because of their higher value-added to the economy and the energy and
environmental benefits associated with a weaker reliance on heavy manufacturing. The current goal is to move the economy away from heavy industry
and toward the service-based industries. In so doing, energy use should
decline, and environmental quality should improve. The recent resurgence in
heavy industry in China, responsible for the rapid emissions growth in the
past few years, illustrates the challenge of facilitating this transition.

Energy and Local Air Pollution

China's rapidly growing economy, population, and energy consumption
are all threatening its future environmental sustainability. China faces many
environmental challenges, including water scarcity, exacerbated by water pollution, and releases of toxic substances in the environment. Although most
sources of pollution in China can be traced back to energy use, we focus in this
section on the relationship between energy consumption and air pollution,
particularly from coal combustion and oil consumption by motor vehicles.

Table 13-1 Characteristics of China's Coal Power Plants

Technology	Availability	Cost (dollar per kilowatt)	Efficiency (%)	Use in China
Subcritical	Now	500–600	30–36	Most of current generation fleet
Supercritical	Now	600–900	41	About half of current orders
Ultra-supercritical	Now, but needs further research and development to increase efficiency	600–900	43	Two 1,000-megawatt plants in operation
Integrated gasification combined cycle (IGCC)	Now, but faces high costs and needs more research and development	1,100–1,400	45–55	Twelve units awaiting National Development and Reform Commission approval

Sources: "CO$_2$ Emissions from Fossil Fuels," International Energy Agency, 2007; "China Coal Report," International Energy Agency, 2009.

Note: Efficiency is lower heating value (LHV), gross output.

Coal

Coal is at the heart of China's environmental woes, with major implications for human health. Most of China's air pollution emissions come from the industrial and electricity sectors. In 2006 China installed 101 gigawatts of new power plants, 90 gigawatts of which was coal-fired power. In 2007 China installed an additional 91 gigawatts for a total in 2008 of 713 gigawatts. To put these astounding numbers in perspective, Germany's entire electricity system in 2005 was 124 gigawatts.

Although China is building a few state-of-the-art coal plants, most of its existing power plants are relatively inefficient (Table 13-1). In 2006, 20 percent of new Chinese plants built that year were supercritical, and the rest were subcritical. The average efficiency of today's coal fleet in China is 32 percent, but this ratio is expected to increase to 40 percent by 2030. Today, the average efficiency of U.S. coal-fired plants is slightly higher than the average efficiency of Chinese power plants. Some of China's newest plants are more efficient than American plants, however, and China is rapidly closing the gap by using some of the world's most advanced designs.[8]

Particulate matter from coal is a major air pollutant. Concentrations of PM-10 (particles the size of 10 microns or less that are capable of penetrating deep into the lungs) in China's cities are extremely high, ranging from the extreme of Panzhihua's average concentration of 255 to 150 in Beijing, 140 in Chongqing, and 100 in Shanghai. These numbers can be compared with 45 in Los Angeles and 25 in New York. PM-10 can increase the number and severity of asthma attacks, cause or aggravate bronchitis and other lung diseases, and reduce the body's ability to fight infections. Certain people are especially vulnerable to PM-10's adverse health effects; they include children, the elderly, exercising adults, and those suffering from asthma or bronchitis.[9] In addition, each year more than four thousand miners die in China's coal mines, mostly in accidents.[10]

Sulfur dioxide emissions from coal combustion, a major source of acid deposition, rose 27 percent between 2001 and 2005. Acid rain affects southeastern China especially, and Hebei Province is most severely affected, with acid rain accounting for more than 20 percent of crop losses. Hunan and Shandong provinces also experience heavy losses from acid rain. Eighty percent of China's total losses countrywide are estimated to be from damage to vegetables.[11]

The economic costs of China's air pollution are very high. According to a recent report from China's government and the World Bank, conservative estimates of morbidity and premature mortality associated with ambient air pollution in China were equivalent to 3.8 percent of GDP in 2003 if premature death was valued at 1 million yuan per person. Acid rain, caused mainly from sulfur dioxide emissions from coal combustion, is estimated to cost $30 billion yuan in crop damage (mostly to vegetables) and $7 billion yuan in material damage annually. This damage is equivalent to 1.8 percent of the value of the crop output. Although water pollution is less directly tied to coal consumption, it is still fundamental to human well-being, and it too has become a major drag on overall economic growth. Health damages from water pollution are estimated to equal 0.3–1.9 percent of rural GDP, not including the morbidity associated with cancer.[12]

Why does China use so much coal? Coal is China's main energy resource endowment, accounting for 93 percent of China's remaining fossil fuel resources. In China, 74 percent of the electricity is derived from coal, at 526 gigawatts in 2007. Hydropower provides 20 percent of electricity capacity; nuclear power, 1 percent; and wind power, 0.5 percent. Although nuclear and wind power have been growing rapidly in recent years, coal is so dominant that it is unlikely that the current mix of electricity supply can be significantly altered any time soon. Natural gas is not commonly used for power generation owing to its high price and lack of availability because of limited domestic resources. In addition, China has always been reluctant to import natural gas from its most obvious supplier, its neighbor Russia. China is aggressively pursuing renewable energy, and it ranks number one in the world in some respects, such as in its installation of solar hot water and small hydropower. It ranks fourth in the world in terms of installed wind capacity, and fourth in terms of ethanol production.[13] Still, China's non-hydro renewable capacity is a tiny fraction of primary energy supply, which is completely dominated by coal.

Motor Vehicles

In China's biggest cities, including Shanghai and Beijing, most of today's urban air pollution comes from motor vehicles. The car population in China has grown dramatically, from fewer than a total of 100,000 autos in 1990 to approximately 37 million in 2008.[14] Although the growth in new passenger cars has been astounding, the total number is still quite small compared with the number of vehicles in the United States, which has a car and sport-utility vehicle population of 230 million. With 20 percent of the world's population, the Chinese own only 1.5 percent of the cars in the world.[15]

The increased demand from all the new cars on the road is causing oil imports to rise. By 2000 total Chinese automobile oil consumption equaled total oil imports at 1.2 million barrels per day, and today China is now the second-largest consumer of oil in the world and the third-largest oil importer.[16] In only the last decade China has emerged as a major global consumer of oil, and there is strong potential for China to become a major natural gas consumer as well, especially if it tries to reduce its greenhouse gas emissions (because natural gas is much less carbon intensive than coal). About half of China's oil imports come from the Middle East, but Angola became the largest supplier in 2006, and China has invested heavily in energy resources in Africa. Although there have been several new oil discoveries in China recently, Chinese reserves are on the decline.

Many projections about future level of car ownership in China exist—the International Energy Agency projects there will be 203 million light-duty vehicles and 66 million trucks by 2030—but these estimates are speculative.[17] China's population, degree of affluence, fuel price levels, and extent of available alternatives are all key factors in the possible levels of future car ownership in China. As China imports greater amounts of energy, prices of these commodities will rise until supply catches up, and price spikes will be especially likely during supply disruptions. China has imposed aggressive fuel economy standards for cars and other types of motor vehicles, which will significantly reduce demand for oil below what it could have been absent these policies (Figure 13-3). China's fuel economy standards are more aggressive than those in the United States, and the government plans to implement new standards that are as much as 18 percent more stringent.[18] These fuel economy standards will greatly benefit the cause of combating global warming as increased efficiency means reduced fuel consumption and fewer greenhouse gas emissions (unless people drive their cars more on account of the lower cost of driving).

Although relatively late to do so, China has taken many steps to reduce pollution from motor vehicles since 2000. In July 2000, leaded gasoline was banned, and China's first emission standards were implemented at the Euro I level. In 2005 China moved to Euro II, and then to Euro III in 2007. These Chinese standards still lag U.S. and EU standards, and a key hurdle has been China's relatively poor fuel quality, which must be improved to reduce emissions further. Also, public transportation was scaled up in China's major cities, most notably in Beijing in advance of the 2008 Olympic Games and again through China's economic recovery stimulation package. Despite these actions, emissions of nitrogen oxides, carbon monoxide, and ozone from vehicles continue to increase. As the number of vehicles in China continues

Figure 13-3 International Comparison of Actual and Projected Fuel
Economy Standards for New Passenger Vehicles, 2002–2016

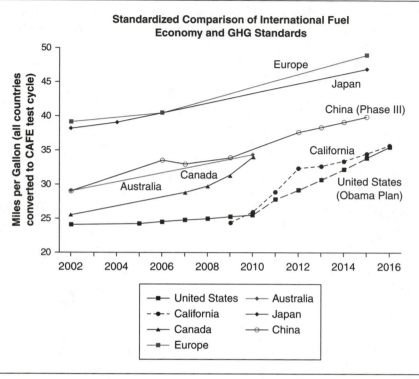

Source: Feng An, Innovation Center for Energy and Transportation.

to increase, additional regulations will be necessary just to maintain current
pollution levels.[19] The rapidly growing vehicle fleet in China is driven by
population growth, urbanization, and rising standards of living.

Environmental Regulation in China

In 1972 China signed the United Nations Stockholm Declaration on the
Human Environment, which became the impetus for legislative reforms under
Deng Xiaoping as the government sought to demonstrate that it could keep
its promise to the international community. More immediately, the declaration
had the effect of raising environmental concerns among China's leaders,
particularly Zhou Enlai.[20] For these reasons, in 1973 the central government
held its first national conference on environmental protection. The result of
this conference was the publication of the "Rules on the Protection and
Improvement of the Environment," which became the blueprint for subsequent environmental lawmaking in China.[21] In 1978 the state's responsibility
for the protection of the environment was added to the constitution, but it

was not until 1979 that the first comprehensive environmental law in China, the Environmental Protection Law, was written.[22]

China has an extensive range of environmental laws, including six over-arching environmental laws, nine natural resources laws, twenty-eight environmental administrative regulations, twenty-seven environmental standards, and more than nine hundred local environmental rules.[23] The key challenge with environmental laws and regulations in China is in their implementation. Many environmental regulations are top-down in nature, meaning they come from the central government, but their implementation must take place at the local level, where the environmental problems occur. The relatively weak central government authority that oversees environmental regulation in China has not been very successful at encouraging implementation at the local level. The enforcement of environmental regulations is generally less of a priority for local officials than ensuring that economic growth targets are met. In March 2009, the State Environmental Protection Agency (SEPA) was upgraded to the Ministry of Environmental Protection (MEP), although it remains to be seen whether this increases the leverage of the environmental mandate or helps with the challenge of implementation of current laws and regulations.

China has some very stringent environmental regulations in place, but many of the standards and targets are not being met. Table 13-2 shows the targets from the tenth five-year plan for air pollution (2005 target levels) and the actual emissions for that year.[24]

Although many of China's laws and regulations are somewhat weaker than those of their counterparts in the United States and Europe, some of the Chinese government's policies are actually stricter or more far-reaching than most equivalent industrialized countries' policies. Enforcement of China's environmental policies is, however, highly uneven. Some cities—like Beijing

Table 13-2 China's Tenth Five-Year Plan Targets for Air Pollution (Planned and Actual Emissions)

Air pollution	Planned 2005	Actual 2005	Percentage greater or lesser than planned
Sulfur dioxide	17.9	25.5	42
Industry	14.5	21.7	50
Domestic	3.5	3.8	9
Soot	10.6	11.8	11
Industry	8.5	9.5	12
Domestic	2.1	2.3	10
Industrial dust	9.98	9.1	1

Sources: World Bank, Washington, D.C.; State Environmental Protection Agency, Beijing, 2007.

in its run-up to the 2008 Olympics—have gone to tremendous lengths and expense to clean up their local factories and reduce air and water pollution. But typical local environmental enforcement is lax and undermines the relatively good policies that have been issued by the central government. For its part, the central government has thus far failed to provide adequate resources to strengthen the MEP so it can improve its own capacity to enforce regulations. There is no adequate system of environmental data collection, distribution, and analysis, which further complicates the enforcement effort because without irrefutable data about pollutant emissions and effluent releases, the government lacks a fundamental tool that would enable it to judge and act on noncompliance with the law. All of these deficiencies demonstrate the need for improved environmental governance and, especially, more effective government institutions to promulgate and enforce regulations.

Few environmental nongovernmental organizations (NGOs) exist in China because of the government's close control over NGO activities. More and more environmental NGOs are being formed all the time, however, and their role is more often viewed by the Chinese government as complementary to achieving government goals rather than contradictory. In fact, Chinese environmental NGOs can play an important watchdog role in overseeing the implementation of environmental regulations at the local level and reporting violations to the central government. Even with improving NGO relations, however, in recent years there have been an increasing number of protests driven by environmental problems. High-profile incidents driven by environmental catastrophes include the algal bloom in Taihu Lake, caused by factory pollution, that cut off drinking water to thousands of people and a large benzene explosion at a chemical plant that was initially denied by the government, causing public protests.

In Europe and the United States, the environmental movement was and continues to be critically important to the passage and enforcement of landmark environmental laws. In China, environmental groups are allowed to form, but usually only for the purposes of public education. The government has apparently given the media permission to report on environmental abuses, and it has established hotlines for citizens to call to report environmental infractions. Still, it is clear that criticism of government policies and, especially, the Communist Party itself is not acceptable. Average citizens and NGOs are not yet potent political forces with respect to the formation of environmental policies today in China.

There is, however, a growing reliance on academia to inform environmental policy making, and university and research institute experts are encouraged to make suggestions, recommendations, and even relatively modest constructive criticisms to the government. At the beginning of 2009, for example, the government established a new Center for Climate and Environmental Policy under the MEP to conduct policy-related research on climate change, sustainable energy, and environmental protection. It is difficult to imagine that China will be able to forge a sustainable path without the help of NGOs and research institutions, given the large size of its economy and population.

Energy and Greenhouse Gas Emissions

Now the world's largest emitter of greenhouse gases, China must play a crucial role in any solution to the global climate change problem.

Energy and Climate Policy

China has ratified the primary international accords on climate change—the United Nations Framework Convention on Climate Change (FCCC) and the Kyoto Protocol—but as a developing country, China has no binding emissions limits under either accord. China is, however, an active participant in the Clean Development Mechanism (CDM) established under the protocol, which grants emissions credits for verified reductions in developing countries, which can be used by developed countries toward meeting their Kyoto targets. The Kyoto Protocol requires developing countries to implement measures to mitigate climate change as is feasible for them "in accordance with their common but differentiated responsibilities and respective capabilities."[25]

In the early 1980s, the Chinese government treated climate change as a primarily scientific issue and gave the China Meteorological Administration the responsibility of advising the government on policy options. However, the start of the international climate negotiations meant the engagement of the Ministry of Foreign Affairs and the gradual politicizing of the climate change issue. As both political awareness and sensitivity surrounding the climate change issue increased, the primary role of representing the Chinese government was shifted to the more powerful National Development and Reform Commission (NDRC), the main government agency responsible for studying and formulating policies for economic and social development. The move indicated a shift in the relative importance given to the issue as well as a shift in perspective; initially viewed as primarily a scientific issue, climate change had now become recognized as predominantly a development issue.[26]

China's domestic climate strategy remains centered on its energy development strategy as driven by its overall economic development goals. Although attention to climate change has recently increased among China's leadership, climate change has not surpassed economic development as a policy priority. Now the largest emitter of greenhouse gas emissions measured on an annual basis, China can no longer ignore its contribution to this challenge, even with its relatively low per capita emissions rates (Figure 13-4).

China released its national climate change report on June 4, 2007.[27] Referred to as China's climate change plan, the report has provided a comprehensive synthesis of the policies that China currently has in place that are serving to moderate its growth in greenhouse gas emissions and to help the country adapt to the impacts of climate change. Most of the policies and programs mentioned in the plan are not climate change policies per se, but policies implemented throughout the economy, and particularly in the energy

Figure 13-4 China's Emissions of Greenhouse Gases Compared with Emissions in the Rest of the World and Selected Countries and Regions, 2007

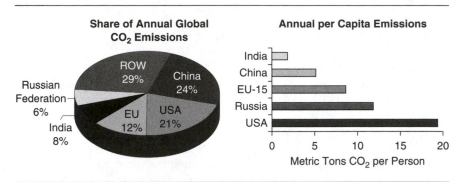

Sources: "China Contributing Two-thirds to Increase in CO_2 Emissions," Netherlands Environmental Assessment Agency, June 13, 2008, www.mnp.nl/en/service/pressreleases/2008/20080613ChinacontributingtwothirdstoincreaseinCO2emissions.html; BP, 2008.

Notes: Data are for 2007; figure includes CO_2 emissions from fossil fuels only.

sector, that have the effect of reducing greenhouse gas emissions. Many of these policies have been enacted to help the country meet its broader economic development strategies, and, if implemented effectively, will also serve as policies to mitigate China's greenhouse gas emissions. Three of these key policy areas are energy efficiency, renewable energy, and industrial policy.

With the hope of achieving energy intensity improvements between 2000 and 2020 similar to what it had done the previous two decades, China has a broad national goal of quadrupling economic growth while doubling energy consumption. Beijing's eleventh five-year plan includes a near-term goal of reducing national energy intensity 20 percent below 2005 levels by 2010. Implementation of such centrally administered government targets has proven challenging, particularly at the local level. In an attempt to improve local accountability, the NDRC is allocating the target among provinces and industrial sectors, and energy efficiency improvement is now among the criteria used to evaluate the job performance of local officials. As of the end of 2009, it appears that these elevated implementation efforts, along with the shutdown of inefficient plants and the economic slowdown from the global financial crisis, have made China well positioned to meet its energy intensity target by 2010.[28]

Under the National Renewable Energy Law adopted in 2005, China has set a target of producing 15 percent of its primary energy from renewable and other low-emission sources by 2020, up from about 7 percent at present. There are also aggressive targets for different renewable energy technologies, including a target for 100 gigawatts of wind power by 2030.[29]Although increases in wind power in particular have been impressive in recent years, leading to 12 gigawatts installed by the end of 2008, this energy source is still dwarfed by large-scale hydropower at 171.5 gigawatts; and hydropower capacity is projected to more than double by 2020.

The Renewable Energy Law offers financial incentives, such as a national fund to foster renewable energy development, discounted lending, and tax preferences for renewable energy projects. Policies to promote renewable energy also include mandates and incentives to support the development of domestic technologies and industries by, for instance, requiring the use of domestically manufactured components. Spurred by a requirement that newly installed wind turbines contain 70 percent local content, by the end of 2008 Chinese manufacturers were producing about 70 percent of the wind turbines being sold in China. Tax and other incentives have targeted the solar photovoltaic industry, and in 2008 China produced about 40 percent of the photovoltaic panels used worldwide.

Climate Change Impacts

The impacts of climate change on China are likely to be serious. A synthesis report compiled by China's leading climate change scientists stated, "It is very likely that future climate change would cause significant adverse impacts on the ecosystems, agriculture, water resources, and coastal zones in China."[30] Impacts that are already being observed in China include extended drought in the north, extreme weather events and flooding in the south, glacial melting in the Himalayas endangering vital river flows, declining crop yields, and rising seas along heavily populated coastlines.[31] As a result, China's agricultural system, trade system, economic development engines, and human livelihood all will face new risks under a warming world.

Post-2012 International Climate Negotiations

Although China has made significant advances in some areas, the major part of energy development in the next few decades is likely to be based on fossil fuels and, consequently, will have profound implications for global greenhouse gas emissions. China is showing increasing recognition of a responsibility to engage with the rest of the world on issues related to climate change, but this transition is likely to be a gradual one.

The Chinese government has stated that it is unwilling to accept firm limits on its national greenhouse gas emissions in an international treaty. This has led many to criticize China's position and claim that China is unwilling to take on its fair share of the climate change solution. It is important to understand, however, that while the government may argue against such caps based on an equity principle—after all, a person in China is responsible for far fewer emissions than a person in the United States (Figure 13-4)—China may in fact implement binding domestic policies to limit greenhouse gas emissions in the near term. In such a case, China would be more likely to

translate these domestic policies into voluntary commitments under the UN
Framework Convention on Climate Change. There are also technical reasons
why China is unlikely to agree to cap its greenhouse gas emissions by committing to an absolute emissions reduction target in a binding international
treaty. Committing to a quantifiable emissions limit is challenging for a country that has little prescience into its future emissions pathway, as recent emissions trends well outside the bounds of expert modeling projections have
illustrated. The 2004 *International Energy Outlook* projected that China's carbon dioxide emissions would not surpass those of the United States until after
2030. In 2006 this date was revised to approximately 2013, and in reality it
happened in about 2007 (Figure 13-5).[32] This inaccuracy is due to the fact
that China's emissions grew much more rapidly during this period than any-
one had predicted. There is perhaps understandable concern in China about
agreeing to bind itself internationally to targets for the future if they cannot
quantify their emissions today.

Figure 13-5 Upward Revisions in Carbon Dioxide Emissions Scenarios
for China

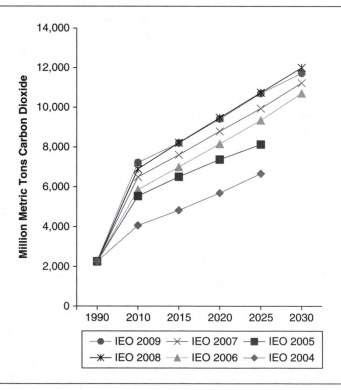

Source: Energy Information Administration, 2004–2009.

Note: Forecasts shown are for EIA's reference case.

China needs international assistance to reduce its greenhouse gas emissions, and not just in the form of the financial assistance and technology transfer it publicly demands at the international climate negotiations. It is therefore critically important for the international community to ratchet up bilateral and multilateral collaboration with China on a wide range of issues ranging from technology development and cooperation to more basic technical assistance with collecting and processing data, establishing accurate domestic systems to quantify and monitor emissions, and modeling and projecting future emissions growth. Such baseline information is crucial for informing any domestic climate change policies as well as for setting any international climate change commitments. In November 2009, President Hu Jintao and President Barack Obama in an important first step announced an initial package of climate and energy cooperation agreements to foster cooperation between the two countries.[33]

It is uncertain how China will respond politically to the climate change threat and to its role in the challenge. While dramatic, path-changing action is unlikely in the near future, it is most probable that gradual changes will be instituted to begin to address domestic greenhouse gas emissions. These changes are most likely, however, if they address other pressing issues simultaneously. The Chinese government is already under pressure to reduce severe local air and water pollution, for example; and addressing these pollutants by using less coal could also be a climate change mitigation strategy. Likewise, current policies to promote energy efficiency and renewable energy are in line with domestic priorities and are also crucial for reducing greenhouse gas emissions. Several proposals are being discussed in the context of the post-2012 UN climate negotiations that would require China's commitment to the international community to be in the form of policy actions or sector-specific actions rather than national mandatory emissions limits.[34] Other studies have attempted to quantify the potential for greenhouse gas mitigation from China through such ongoing policy activities.[35] Because of the challenges in quantifying and projecting emissions trajectories in China, it may be more technically and politically feasible for China to commit to policies that will lead to absolute emission reductions, and to carbon intensity targets that are indexed to economic growth. The Chinese leadership announced in November 2009 its intention to implement a domestic carbon intensity target of a 40–45 percent reduction below 2005 levels by 2020. Depending on the stringency of the domestic carbon intensity target, growth in absolute emissions could continue. Whether such a target would reduce emissions below "business as usual" is an open question, and it depends, among many other factors, on future economic growth rates, rates of deployment of low-carbon technologies, the evolving structure of the Chinese economy, and the types of energy supply. For the fifteen-year period from 1991 to 2006, for example, China reduced its carbon intensity by 44 percent, but Chinese carbon dioxide emissions more than doubled.

These win-win actions, or mitigation actions with other co-benefits, may not be sufficient in the eyes of the international community as we approach 2030. Although the EU is the only region in the world to date that has implemented mandatory national measures to reduce greenhouse gas emissions, several countries are expected to soon follow, including Australia, New Zealand, Japan, and the United States. International pressure on China is likely to stem primarily from the United States and the EU under a scenario in which both regions have adopted mandatory climate action. The White House announced in November 2009 that "in the context of an overall deal in Copenhagen that includes robust mitigation contributions from China and the other emerging economies, the President is prepared to put on the table a U.S. emissions reduction target in the range of 17 percent below 2005 levels in 2020 and ultimately in line with final U.S. energy and climate legislation."[36] Several U.S. states already have adopted mandatory greenhouse gas reductions at the state level.[37]

Developing countries have for the most part remained unified over time in their approach to the international climate change negotiations, representing their positions in the context of the Group of 77 (G-77).[38] Additional pressure could mount if other non–Annex I countries (the group of developing countries currently exempt from binding mitigation commitments under the FCCC) opt to take on mitigation commitments in the current round of negotiations for the post-2012 period. For example, Brazil and Mexico have already signaled their willingness to pledge national actions in an international framework.[39]

Achieving Sustainable Development in China: Two Cases

It is not, in fact, difficult to imagine environmental conditions being vastly improved in China, nor is it hard to imagine China formulating a new mode of industrialization that is far cleaner and more efficient than the U.S. model. Indeed, one could even envision a future in which the Chinese government decided to embark on a completely new growth strategy that championed sustainable development precisely because the environmental woes currently afflicting China are so severe and costly to its society.

To achieve dramatic environmental improvements in China, a comprehensive and far-reaching incentive system would have to be created. The gap between the best available technologies worldwide and what exists in China is still large, although advanced energy technology is increasingly available and in many cases is being developed indigenously. Even though advanced energy-efficient and cleaner technologies have been developed (and are often manufactured and used both within China and internationally), they are not widely adopted in China.

The proposition that late-industrializing countries like China would leapfrog to the most sustainable technologies available has often not been borne out, and, in fact, many limits to leapfrogging have been identified. Most important, it is clear that the processes of leapfrogging, technology transfer and cooperation, and accelerated deployment of environmental technologies are not automatic.[40] Many barriers to technological leapfrogging exist in different contexts, including the higher costs of some cleaner technologies, lack of knowledge about or access to those technologies, and insufficient incentives to adopt such technologies. Indeed, without clear and consistent incentives for firms to produce and consumers to purchase cleaner products and services, they often fail to do so. Especially because environmental quality is a public good, government has a special role to play in the design and enforcement of environmental laws and regulations, which in turn create the appropriate incentives for producers and consumers alike.

The following two cases illustrate the challenge of technological leapfrogging in China. One highlights a failure in the area of clean vehicles, but the other highlights a success in the development of wind power.

Case 1: Environmental Challenges of Developing a Domestic Auto Industry

The auto industry has been enormously helpful to the Chinese economy. As of 2003, 16 million people were employed directly in China's burgeoning car industry, not including spillover industries such as the manufacture of steel and rubber. According to the China Automotive Technology and Research Center (CATARC), the auto industry makes up 3 percent of the country's total manufacturing employment and 6 percent of manufacturing output—this is a tripling of the percentage since 1990.

Before World War II, China manufactured very few automobiles. Some trucks were manufactured for government officials but most automobiles were imported. Immediately after World War II, there was a great deal of technology transfer from the Soviet Union, yet after the Sino-Soviet split, around 1960, passenger car production virtually ceased. After the Cultural Revolution, the Chinese leadership debated whether China should copy the South Korean and Japanese auto-industry model or simply focus on importing cars. The government initiated an experiment of auto manufacturing, beginning with vehicles licensed from Japan, a policy that later sparked the formation of joint ventures (JVs) (Figure 13-6).

Auto Industry JVs—Partnerships out of Balance

Beijing-Jeep was China's first JV company. The lack of experience with such a partnership led to a steep and painful learning curve for both the Chinese and U.S. firms. Some of the difficulties stemmed from the lack of a clear auto industry policy in China until 1994. Even the 1994 guidance policy was very broad and simply stated that China would form a national pillar auto industry and attempt to gain its own technological capabilities. In the mid-1990s, there was also much talk within the Chinese government of consolidating the auto industry, which today is still quite fragmented, with 160 manufacturers. The government issued another major auto policy in 2004, which stated that China wanted technology transfer to turn auto manufacturing into a world-class industry, although

Figure 13-6 Growth of Passenger Car Production in China, 1991–2008

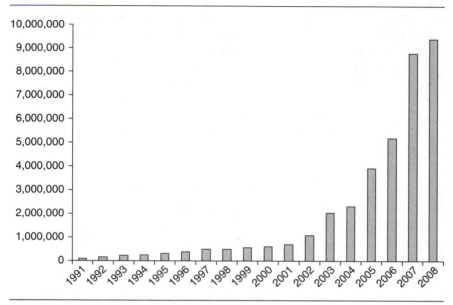

Sources: "2005 Auto Industry in China," China Automotive Technology and Research Center; *China Auto* (Tianjin: China Automotive Technology and Research Center), January 2006, January 2007, February 2009; and MSNBC, January 2008.

the government had lost most of the tools to do so when China entered the World Trade Organization (WTO).

Except for Chery and Geely, all the major Chinese auto companies have been created via JVs, with some partnering with two or three international automakers. This extensive web of partnerships (illustrated in Figure 13-7) led some foreign companies to worry about their intellectual property "slipping" to other international automakers, although technologies transferred by outside firms were rarely, if ever, updated once a model was in production until the late 1990s. For example, Shanghai-Volkswagen produced a 1980s version of the Santana when it first began manufacturing in China. Years later the company put a different shell on this same model and called it the Santana 2000.

Another obstacle to greater transfer of clean vehicle technologies stems from the conditions China agreed to under the WTO. During WTO accession talks, the United States and Europe were greatly concerned about the auto industry, which led Chinese negotiators to concede all of China's policies requiring technology transfer and local content requirements. Yet China was creative about re-establishing what were in effect local content requirements through tariff policies. Although the United States and Europe successfully disputed these tariffs in the WTO, the Chinese bought themselves some time to further develop their parts manufacturers.[41]

Lack of technology transfer was a major irritant to JV relations in some cases. A Chinese engineer at Beijing Jeep Corporation (BJC) once

Figure 13-7 Investment in China's Auto Industry: Partnerships and Linkages between Chinese and Foreign Companies

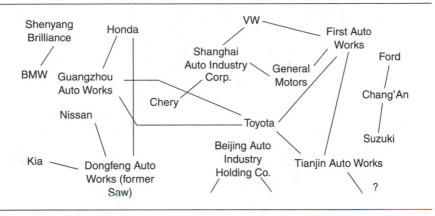

Source: Kelly Sims Gallagher, "Foreign Direct Investment as a Vehicle for Deploying Cleaner Technologies: Technology Transfer and the Big Three Automakers in China," PhD dissertation, Fletcher School of Law and Diplomacy, June 2003.

commented, "Top executives in big [foreign] companies only see China as a market to sell vehicles. They don't see China as a place to develop vehicles." At Shanghai-GM, the Chinese developed a tracking system to ensure that they were getting all the information and technology they had been promised. Although GM is viewed as one of the most generous in terms of technology transfer, the Chinese were still dissatisfied—although both sides have profited from the venture. One Chinese manager stated bluntly, "the foreign companies are not good teachers, and the Chinese companies are not so clever." Ford Motor waited until WTO negotiations were over to close its JV agreement with Chang'An so Ford would not have to deal with technology transfer requirements. The Chang'An–Ford relationship was initially very troubled because of dissatisfaction with the kind of autos Ford was bringing to China, beginning with the first car—the Fiesta. Realizing the challenges associated with foreign technology transfer, China's eleventh five-year plan for the auto industry emphasizes the need for more autonomous development, better Chinese branding, and less dependence on JVs.[42]

Lack of Clean Vehicle Technology Transfer

In terms of U.S.-China vehicle technology transfer, U.S. automakers did not substantially contribute to improving the technological capacity of Chinese firms because within the JVs very little knowledge was transferred about the technology. The Chinese government also failed to design and implement an aggressive and consistent strategy for the acquisition of technological capabilities from foreigners in the auto industry. Even though technology transfer has been slow, foreign direct investment undoubtedly contributed to the growth of the Chinese auto industry. For example, the Chinese firms have acquired good manufacturing skills and some product adaptation capabilities. While Chinese parts and components manufacturers have benefited from local content requirements, Chinese automakers have lagged on engine design and innovation because foreign automakers hesitate to share this technology. The most glaring example of a failure to leapfrog was that no foreign auto company transferred any kind of pollution-control technology such as a catalytic converter to China until 2000, the year the Chinese government imposed its first pollution-control standards for vehicles.[43]

On the positive side, China issued its first vehicle fuel efficiency standards in 2005, and they were strengthened in 2008 (see Figure 13-3). These fuel efficiency standards are more aggressive than current U.S. standards and will result in the Chinese passenger car fleet being much more energy efficient than the U.S. fleet in only a few years.

Case 2: Developing a Domestic Wind Power Industry for a Low Carbon Economy

Still primarily dependent on coal for electricity generation, China is perhaps one of the least likely places you'd expect to find a burgeoning wind power industry. Spurred by aggressive wind power targets and policy incentives, China has in fact emerged in 2008 as the second-largest wind market in the world after the United States. The more than 6 gigawatts of new capacity installed in China in 2008 alone represented 22 percent of global installations for that year and doubled the amount of 2007 existing capacity. By the end of 2008, China had installed 12.20 gigawatts of wind power capacity, as shown in Figure 13-8. Although China is still behind the United States, Germany, and Spain in terms of total installed wind capacity, it is projected to surpass both Germany and Spain by 2010.

Wind Turbine Technology Development

China has only recently entered the wind power technology industry and capacity increases have been large, but the share that wind power contributes to China's total electricity generation is still less than 1 percent. While civilizations have been harnessing wind energy for centuries, modern, utility-scale wind turbine technology originated from research and development that began in the late 1970s, most notably in Denmark, the Netherlands, Germany, and the United States. The Danish manufacturer Vestas—one of the first wind turbine manufactures in the world—still has the largest global market share of any one company, but each year it is losing market share to competitors, including those in the emerging economies of China and India. China's first leading wind turbine manufacturer, Goldwind, entered the list of top ten manufacturers for the first time in 2006. It has recently been joined by several other Chinese manufacturers, including Sinovel and Dongfang Electric, to make up the top three in the Chinese market.

Figure 13-8 Growth of Wind Power Installations in China, 1999–2008

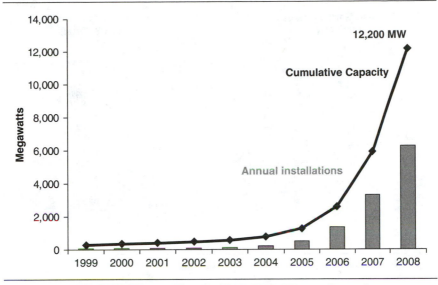

Source: Global Wind 2008 Report (Brussels: Global Wind Energy Council).

Models of Technology Transfer in the Wind Sector

As recently as 2004, the Chinese wind power industry was comprised of predominantly foreign-owned companies that relied on various models of technology development for the Chinese market. Many early Chinese wind turbine companies formed joint ventures with foreign companies, but almost all such ventures failed. Leading foreign wind companies continued to export their technology to China, and some began to relocate their own manufacturing bases there, but none transferred technology to Chinese companies.[44] Chinese firms were left to look to smaller foreign firms that were more willing to share their technology, most frequently via licensing agreements.

In only four years the market structure of the Chinese wind industry has changed dramatically. In 2004 just one Chinese-owned company manufactured wind turbines, but in 2008 ten manufacturers held at least 1 percent of the Chinese market share (Figure 13-9), and several more had technology at various stages of research and development. In addition, several new foreign-owned manufacturers have entered the Chinese market, no doubt attracted by the scale of wind development taking place in China. In 2009 all foreign-owned firms selling to the Chinese market were locally manufacturing their turbines in China rather than exporting to China turbines made elsewhere. This change was primarily driven by China's policy requiring the use of local content in wind turbines installed in China as well as by China's relatively low-cost labor base and the overall opportunity the sheer size of the Chinese market presented.

Figure 13-9 Sales of Wind Turbines in China, 2006 and 2008

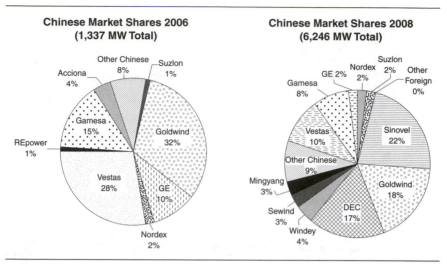

Source: Shi Pengfei, China Wind Energy Assocation.

Several new technology transfer agreements are behind the emergence of many new Chinese manufacturers, primarily in the form of licensing agreements worked out with smaller foreign wind power technology development or design firms. Goldwind, the early leader, has continued to acquire advanced technology through additional licensing arrangements as well as by acquiring ownership of its international technology partners outright. The new entrants, including Sinovel and Dongfang, have also pursued licensing agreements with foreign firms that allowed them access to advanced technologies and the associated intellectual property.

Few foreign companies that are operating within the Chinese market have transferred wind power technology to Chinese companies, likely in order to maintain their competitive edge in the marketplace and protect their intellectual property rights. Other foreign firms not directly involved in the Chinese market—in particular, smaller firms that focus on overseas markets and would otherwise not have access to the Chinese market—continue to license their technology to Chinese-owned firms. In addition, Chinese firms are increasingly acquiring intellectual property via direct acquisition of firms, giving them full ownership of the technology as well as access to skilled labor in many cases. In Goldwind's case, such acquisitions have also given it control over the technology that has been licensed to their competitors.[45]

An examination of wind turbine development in China illustrates how substantial technical advances are indeed possible in relatively short amounts of time. It took China less than a decade to go from having companies with no wind turbine manufacturing experience to companies capable of manufacturing complete wind turbine systems, with almost all components produced locally. This was done within the constraints of national and international intellectual property law, and primarily through the acquisition of technology licenses or via the purchasing of smaller wind technology companies. Many Chinese companies are now beginning to export their turbines abroad, including to the United States. This case illustrates the successful development of a crucial low-carbon technology in China and provides one example of how China might be able to leapfrog to advanced energy technologies, improve its local environmental conditions, and reduce its greenhouse gas emissions.

Outlook and Conclusions

Providing modern energy services for 1.3 billion people in an environmentally sustainable manner is a profoundly daunting challenge. Fortunately, the Chinese central government is demonstrating increasing awareness of the problems posed by local pollution, climate change, and an interest in altering China's current energy development trajectory. Clearly there is new urgency and opportunity to address climate protection, energy security, and economic development issues, especially among the world's largest energy consumers. It is doubtful, however, that the Chinese government will be able to significantly alter this trajectory without meaningful international engagement during the critical time period of the next one to two decades.

China possesses the ingenuity and the institutional capital to meet certain elements of the climate challenge better than others. It has the technical, engineering, and increasingly the innovation capacity that many other developing countries lack. China is expected to gain from developing many of the technologies that will be crucial for dealing with climate change. This includes both renewable energy technologies as well as carbon capture and storage technologies, the latter of which would allow China to continue to rely on fossil fuels while avoiding severe impacts of climate change.

For China to transition to a more environmentally sustainable development pathway, several overarching issues will need to be addressed. First, because of its reliance on coal, China faces a large incremental cost in moving toward higher-efficiency coal technology and in capturing and storing the emissions from these plants. Large financial resources will be needed because, even though China is already a successful industrializing country, there are competing demands for available financial resources. Second, key capacity limitations in China's ability to collect accurate and transparent energy and emissions data are at the root of China's challenge in enforcing environmental regulations and of its hesitancy to commit to quantifiable greenhouse gas emissions targets. Third, limitations on the use of foreign investment and foreign technology to achieve its domestic development goals cause ongoing bilateral trade disputes and tensions in discussions over international technology transfer.

Recognizing the unique challenges that China faces in addressing the transition to a more sustainable development pathway can inform what China will be willing and able to undertake in its own domestic energy and environmental policy and within a multilateral climate agreement.[46] China's local environmental challenges are increasingly global in their impact, and as a result the entire world is watching to see how China responds to its challenges. While the interest in China is global, its government still primarily looks inward in shaping its domestic policy decisions; thus, national energy security and local environmental concerns still rank above global greenhouse gas emissions in relative importance. In the end, the decision of how to deal with climate change will hinge on the government's ability to find a way to reduce local and global emissions while continuing to grow its economy and bring a better quality of life to the citizens of the People's Republic of China. Improved human well-being is key to maintaining domestic stability, and that will be the guiding principle for China's leadership in local and global environmental politics.

Notes

1. Barry Naughton, *The Chinese Economy: Transitions and Growth* (Cambridge: MIT Press, 2007).
2. Kevin Watkins, *Human Development Report 2007/2008: Fighting Climate Change: Human Solidarity in a Divided World* (New York: United Nations Development Programme, 2007).
3. "World Bank Says China Is Poverty Reduction Model," Xinhua, February 25, 2003, www.china.org.cn/english/2003/Feb/56694.htm.
4. "Facts and Figures: China's Main Targets for 2006–2010," *People's Daily Online*, March 6, 2006, http://english.people.com.cn/200603/06/eng20060306_248218 .html.
5. Susan Shirk, *China: Fragile Superpower* (New York: Oxford University Press, 2007).
6. Netherlands Environmental Assessment Agency (MNP), "China Contributing Two Thirds to Increase in CO_2 Emissions," Press release, June 13, 2008, www.pbl.nl/en/ news/pressreleases/2008/20080613ChinacontributingtwothirdstoincreaseinCO2emi ssions.html.
7. Trevor Houser, "China's Energy Consumption and Opportunities for U.S.-China Cooperation to Address the Effects of China's Energy Use" (testimony before the U.S.-China Economic and Security Review Commission, June 14, 2007), www.uscc .gov/hearings/2007hearings/written_testimonies/07_06_14_15wrts/07_06_14_ houser_statement.php.
8. Keith Bradsher, "China Outpaces U.S. in Cleaner Coal-Fired Plants," *New York Times*, May 10, 2009, www.nytimes.com/2009/05/11/world/asia/11coal.html.
9. "Air Pollution—Particulate Matter" (Sacramento: California Air Resources Board, May 2003).
10. David Biallo, "Can Coal and Clean Air Co-Exist in China?" *Scientific American*, August 4, 2008, www.sciam.com/article.cfm?id=can-coal-and-clean-air-coexist-china.
11. *Cost of Pollution in China: Economic Estimates of Physical Damages* (Washington, D.C.: World Bank and China State Environmental Protection Administration, 2007).
12. Ibid.
13. Eric Martinot, *Renewables 2007 Global Status Report* (Paris: REN21 Renewable Energy Policy Network, 2007).
14. Data compiled with information from *China Auto* (Tianjian: China Automotive Technology and Research Center) and MSNBC.com, various years.
15. S. C. Davis and S. W. Diegel, *Transportation Energy Data Book*, Report no. ORNL-6978 (Oak Ridge, Tenn.: U.S. Department of Energy, Oak Ridge National Laboratory, 2007).

16. "Statistical Review of World Energy," BP, June 2008, www.bp.com/statisticalreview.
17. International Energy Agency, *World Energy Outlook 2007* (Paris: IEA/OECD, 2007), 20.
18. Keith Bradsher, "China Is Said to Plan Strict Gas Mileage Rules," *New York Times*, May 27, 2009, www.nytimes.com/2009/05/28/business/energy-environment/28fuel .html.
19. Michael P. Walsh, "Motor Vehicle Pollution and Fuel Consumption in China," in *Urbanization, Energy, and Air Pollution in China: Proceedings of a Symposium* (Washington, D.C.: National Research Council, National Academy of Engineering, National Academies Press, 2004).
20. Stefanie Beyer, "Environmental Law and Policy in the People's Republic of China," *Chinese Journal of International Law* 5, no. 1 (2006): 185–211; Lynn Kirshbaum, "Environmental Law in China: Challenges to Implementation (paper prepared for Robert Sutter, Georgetown University, December 12, 2008).
21. Kirshbaum, "Environmental Law in China."
22. Beyer, "Environmental Law and Policy in the People's Republic of China" and Kirshbaum, "Environmental Law in China."
23. Xielin Liu, "Building an Environmentally Friendly Society through Innovation: Challenges and Choices" (background paper, China Council for International Cooperation on Environment and Development, Beijing, 2007).
24. World Bank and State Environmental Protection Agency. *The Cost of Pollution in China: Economic Estimates of Physical Damages* (Washington, D.C.: World Bank, 2007) http://siteresources.worldbank.org/Inteapregtopenvironment/Resources/China_Cost_of_Pollution.pdf.
25. The Kyoto Protocol to the United Nations Framework Convention on Climate Change, http://unfccc.int/resource/docs/convkp/kpeng.html.
26. Joanna I. Lewis, Jeffrey Logan, and Michael B. Cummings, "Understanding the Climate Challenge in China," in *Climate Change Science and Policy*, ed. Stephen H. Schneider et al. (Washington, D.C.: Island Press, 2010).
27. *China's National Climate Change Programme* (Beijing: People's Republic of China, National Development and Reform Commission, June 2007), http://en.ndrc.gov.cn/newsrelease/P020070604561191006823.pdf.
28. Wu Chong and Si Tingting, "Bar for Climate Change Goals Set High for China," China Daily, November 26, 2009, www.chinadaily.com.cn/china/2009-11/26/content_9052416.htm.
29. Julieta Mendoza, "China Aims for 100 GW of Wind-Power by 2020, Wants Growth Lead in 2009," *International Business Times*, December 3, 2009, www.ibtimes.com/articles/20090504/china-set-conquer-worlds-wind-power-growth-market-triples-2020-target.htm.
30. Lin Erda et al., "Synopsis of China National Climate Change Assessment Report (II): Climate Change Impacts and Adaptation," *Advances in Climate Change Research* 3 (2007): supp. 6J11. This paper is a synopsis of Sec. II of China's *National Assessment Report on Climate Change*, published in February 2007.
31. "Fourth Assessment Report on Climate Change: Working Group 2, Impacts, Adaptation and Vulnerability," Intergovernmental Panel on Climate Change (IPCC), 2007.
32. *International Energy Outlook, 2004–2007* (Washington, D.C.: U.S. Department of Energy, Energy Information Administration, 2007), www.eia.doe.gov/oiaf/ieo/ieo-archive.html. Note that revisions to U.S. emissions projections were also made, but by a much smaller total amount during this time period.
33. U.S. Department of Energy, "US-China Clean Energy Announcements," November 17, 2009, www.whitehouse.gov/the-press-office/us-china-clean-energy-announcements.
34. See Joanna Lewis and Elliot Diringer, "Policy Based Commitments in a Post-2012 International Climate Framework," Pew Center on Global Climate Change, 2007, www.pewclimate.org/working-papers/policy-based-commitments; and Jake Schmidt

et al., "Sector-Based Approach to the Post-2012 Climate Change Policy Architecture," *Climate Policy* 8 (2008): 494–515.

35. Jiang Lin et al., "Taking Out 1 Billion Tons of CO_2: The Magic of China's 11th Five-Year Plan?" *Energy Policy* 36 (2008): 954–970; "Greenhouse Gas Mitigation in China, Brazil and Mexico: Recent Efforts and Implications" (Washington, D.C.: Center for Clean Air Policy, 2007).

36. White House Office of the Press Secretary, "President to Attend Copenhagen Climate Talks," November 25, 2009, www.whitehouse.gov/the-press-office/president-attend-copenhagen-climate-talks.

37. Regional Greenhouse Gas Initiative (RGGI), http://rggi.org/home; "Global Warming Solutions Act," California Assembly Bill 32, www.arb.ca.gov/cc/ab32/ab32.htm.

38. The Group of 77 (G-77) was established on June 15, 1964, by seventy-seven developing countries that were signatories to the "Joint Declaration of the Seventy-Seven Countries" issued at the end of the first session of the United Nations Conference on Trade and Development (UNCTAD) in Geneva. Although the number of members of the G-77 has increased to 130 countries, the original name was retained because of its historic significance. See www.g77.0rg/doc.

39. National Plan on Climate Change: Brazil (Brasilia: Government of Brazil, December 2008), www.mma.gov.br/estruturas/imprensa/_arquivos/96_11122008040728.pdf; "National Strategy on Climate Change: Mexico: Executive Summary" (Mexico City: Intersecretarial Commission on Climate Change, 2007), www.semarnat.gob.mx/que essemarnat/politica_ambiental/cambioclimatico/Documents/enac/sintesis/sintesiseje cutiva/Executive%20Summary.pdf.

40. Stephanie B. Ohshita and Leonard Ortolano, "The Promise and Pitfalls of Japanese Cleaner Coal Technology Transfer to China," *International Journal of Technology Transfer and Commercialisation* 1, nos. 1 and 2 (2002): 56–81; Kelly Sims Gallagher, "Limits to Leapfrogging? Evidence from China's Automobile Industry," *Energy Policy* 34, no. 4 (2006): 383–394; Joanna I. Lewis and Ryan H. Wiser, "Fostering a Renewable Energy Technology Industry: An International Comparison of Wind Industry Policy Support Mechanisms," *Energy Policy* 35 (2007): 1844–1857.

41. Keith Bradsher, "After Carmakers Adapt, China Trade Dispute Ends," *New York Times*, August 31, 2009.

42. "Limits to Leapfrogging," 383–394.

43. Ibid.

44. Joanna I. Lewis, "From Technology Transfer to Local Manufacturing: China's Emergence in the Global Wind Power Industry" (Ph.D. dissertation, University of California–Berkeley, August 2005).

45. Joanna I. Lewis, "Technology Acquisition and Innovation in the Developing World: Wind Turbine Development in China and India," *Studies in Comparative International Development* 42, no. 3 (December 2007).

46. Joanna I. Lewis, "China's Strategic Priorities in International Climate Negotiations," *Washington Quarterly* 31, no. 1 (Winter 2007–2008): 155–174.

14

Democracy and Nuclear Power: The Czech Case and the Global Nuclear Renaissance

Regina S. Axelrod

How could it have happened that we let ourselves be led too far by the old totalitarian megalomania? Why with Temelin did we proceed on a steep slope at whose foot everything is different, not only the relationship with the environment, but also the relationship between the citizen and the state? How could we miss the juncture from which a road led to savings, sustainable development and to an uninhabitable country?

Petr Pithart, former prime minister, Czech Republic, and former chair of the Czech Senate, translated from *Listy*, 5 1994, by Mirka Jehlickova

The environmentalists' attitude towards nature is analogous to the Marxist approach to economics. . . . Like other utopias, this one can never materialize, and efforts to make it materialize can only be carried out through . . . the dictate of a small, elitist minority.

Vaclav Klaus, president, Czech Republic
Blue Planet in Green Shackles: What Is Endangered? Climate or Freedom? (Competitive Enterprise Institute, 2008), 5

This chapter focuses on nuclear energy, which has been used to provide electricity for the last fifty years and is often perceived as a technological breakthrough without negative environmental impacts compared with traditional energy sources. It was promoted in the capitalist world as cheap energy and was built in communist countries as a monument to the socialist industrial state. Today its cost-effectiveness is questioned, and there is opposition to its continued use and development for environmental and security-related reasons.

This chapter explores the completion of the 1,000-megawatt Temelin nuclear power plant in the Czech Republic. It also examines the extent to which sustainable development policy has been addressed in a country still undergoing political transformation and also offers insights into the problems of building democratic institutions. In 1989 the Iron Curtain fell and communism as it was known ended in central and eastern Europe (CEE), but the transition to democracy and a market economy has been more complex than most westerners anticipated. This chapter begins by examining energy policy and then discusses, more specifically, nuclear policy in the CEE region. The European Union (EU) has played an increasingly important role in these policies, as CEE states applied for membership. The chapter then addresses sustainable energy and environmental policy in the Czech Republic, utilizing the Temelin controversy as a model for analysis.

These events are now influenced by changing international conditions with the confluence of energy and environmental imperatives. States, globally, are confronting the consequences of global warming and climate change as well as higher prices for fossil fuels. Nuclear energy, however, is not without potential impact on air and water resources and introduces additional problems of long-term waste disposal and terrorism. The Czech Republic has become a proponent of nuclear energy expansion in the EU (it became a member in 2004) as a means to reduce dependence on fossil fuels. This argument has been adopted by many states in the international community, many of which are already nuclear states and some that are aspiring to be. It is in this changed global context of potential nuclear energy renewal that this analysis takes place.

The Czech experience exemplifies a state involved in the burgeoning nuclear renaissance—now a global phenomenon. States seeking to expand or develop nuclear energy can look to the Czech Republic as an example. The range of states includes India, China, Belarus, Vietnam, Egypt, Jordan, Turkey, Qatar, Saudi Arabia, Venezuela, Chile, and Morocco—countries that span the globe. The argument that nuclear energy would help solve the climate change–global warming problem was taken up by nuclear industries in many states as well as the Czech Republic. But there was an irony: nuclear energy expansion was proposed in the 1980s and promoted throughout the 1990s with no reference to climate change. In fact, President Vaclav Klaus, who was prime minister in the early 1990s, is a proponent of the view that global warming has been exaggerated by left-thinking environmentalists who want to destroy the free market.[1] In the Czech case nuclear power was promoted not because of climate change concerns but because of the revenue from electricity exports that it provides the government as well as opportunities for construction and business for industrial companies and developers. Various interests also want nuclear energy to be the key to Czech energy independence from Russia and see it as an opportunity to be a technology leader in Europe. Czech governmental leaders promised to retire the polluting coal-burning plants, but the results have been quite different. Nuclear energy has been a constant; only its rationale has changed.

The Czech Republic was in the first group of CEE candidates to join both the EU and the North Atlantic Treaty Organization. In December 1997 the Czech Republic, Estonia, Hungary, Poland, and Slovenia were invited to begin negotiations for EU accession. The Czech Republic harmonized its environmental and energy legislation with the EU as a prerequisite for membership. The country's ability to develop the necessary democratic attributes familiar to western Europe was also a prerequisite. The adoption of the *acquis communautaire*—the body of European Community law—presented financial difficulties for the nations of CEE joining the EU because of the huge financial investment necessary to meet EU standards.

Austria, a nonnuclear state, has consistently and aggressively opposed construction of the Temelin nuclear power plant. As Temelin is approximately fifty miles from its border, the Austrians have made this proximity an issue in the Czech accession proceedings. Other states such as Germany, which closed its Russian-made nuclear plants in the eastern part of the country, also have a stake in the future of Temelin.

The Czech experience with nuclear power has been a test case that affected the viability and future marketability of nuclear power in CEE. Upgrading Temelin was part of a Group of Seven (G-7; Canada, France, Germany, Italy, Japan, the United Kingdom, and the United States) commitment to take action in response to the legacy of unsafe Russian-built nuclear power plants. The Chernobyl accident in Ukraine is a constant reminder of the danger to human life and the environment. The international nuclear community also has a stake in the outcome, as there is intense competition among American and European nuclear engineering companies for contracts to upgrade, build, and complete new nuclear plants in the region.

Of the ten candidate states that joined the EU in 2004, eight are nuclear. The EU does not have a policy regarding nuclear power reactor safety because of the divergent policies of nuclear and nonnuclear states. Austria, Greece, Ireland, Denmark, Portugal, and Luxembourg have no nuclear plants. Some Member States, for example, Belgium, Spain, Germany, Sweden, and the Netherlands, have declared a phasing out of nuclear power; however, the nuclear industry is lobbying heavily to expand the nuclear sector.

As a condition for EU accession, CEE states pledged to decommission their Russian-designed nuclear plants or upgrade the more modern ones with aid and loans for CEE states in the EU through Euratom loans and PHARE and TACIS programs—programs that assisted in the transition to market economics and democratic political systems. Without the prospect of joining the EU, these actions would never have been taken. In October 2002, for example, Lithuania's parliament voted to close the first two units as a precondition for beginning EU negotiations. Bulgaria, because of extensive modifications, contested the closing of Kozloduy 3 and 4 but did close units 1 and 2 on December 31, 2002. The upgrading of units 5 and 6 was covered by a loan from the European Bank for Reconstruction and Development (EBRD). In neighboring Ukraine (which borders on the enlarged EU), the population demanded the reopening of Chernobyl to provide jobs and electricity.[2] They wanted the G-7 states to provide promised funds to cover the social impact of Chernobyl. Western states and the EU pledged more than $700 million to replace the sarcophagus, which is leaking, but only a small portion has been spent. Local protesters advocated restarting the closed plant if funds were not forthcoming.

EU energy commissioners have been generally supportive of nuclear power as one of a mix of energy sources to meet Kyoto Protocol goals. The EU position is to leave such decisions up to Member States, but the position of the president of the EU Commission has been positive toward nuclear power.

In addition to safety, another concern was that these Russian-designed plants that produced and exported electricity to the West would be abandoned just when the demand for electricity would be increasing. This has happened, and in Bulgaria and Lithuania, for example, there is pressure to build new nuclear plants to secure adequate electricity and protect their economies.

Energy Policy in Central and Eastern Europe

Building large nuclear power plants to produce electricity was consistent with the former Soviet Union's communist vision of progress. Throughout the CEE region, energy-intensive industries were supported by cheap energy: the higher the energy intensity, the greater the inefficiency in the use of energy, and the higher the energy demand for a given level of output. According to 1996 statistics from the Ministry of Environment, Czech energy intensity was much higher than that in western countries that were members of the Organization for Economic Cooperation and Development (OECD) and one-third higher than that in the United States. The Stalinist model required maximum production levels, and economic incentives encouraged increased energy consumption.[3] The results were distorted economies and overdependence on low energy prices.

Central and eastern European countries paid a high price to the former Soviet Union for their energy. They needed oil and natural gas, for which they paid less than the market price, but in return these nations sold goods to the former Soviet Union at less than market prices. The former Soviet Union controlled the natural gas and oil pipelines and could close them without notice. This power was a type of blackmail, and the CEE regimes took the threat seriously. They could not risk the political instability that could result from a cutoff of oil. Since 1990 these states have actively sought ways to free themselves from energy sources in the former Soviet Union. This situation remains as the Czech Republic fears that its supply of Russian oil and gas may be cut if the country acts against Russia's interest in other areas. At the same time the Czech Republic has moved closer to American interests, for example, in its agreement to host a U.S. defensive radar installation within its borders. The Czechs, adding a new area of dependence, also signed an agreement to purchase nuclear fuel from the Russians. There is still concern about Russian power and its control over Czech energy and supplies. Throughout the EU, Russia is a major supplier of oil and natural gas. As North Sea supplies decline in the future, the EU may further increase its dependence on supplies from Russia.

The soft brown coal with high sulfur content used in many CEE countries is a source of severe air pollution. The crude mining practices, larger plant size, and absence of desulfurization equipment have led to a catastrophic situation in northern Bohemia in the Czech Republic, an area termed the

Black Triangle that extends to the German and Polish borders. Children have been forced to stay home from school because the air is too dangerous to breathe, and cars have been banned from city centers. In the winter, there is permanent smog. Nuclear energy proponents argued that it would be beneficial to the environment to substitute nuclear power for coal, thereby reducing harmful air emissions.

The Eastern Movement of Nuclear Power

Nuclear power advocates saw the opportunity and accepted the challenge. The former Soviet Union, with compliance or agreement from the CEE states, had planned dozens of nuclear power plants for the region. Skoda, a Czech company, was named the prime contractor. The success of the Temelin project would now give the Czech electric utility Ceske energeticke zavody (CEZ) and Skoda a future in the modernization of these partially completed plants throughout the area.

The former Soviet Union's monopoly over nuclear reactors in the CEE region has left enormous problems. The reactors are considered to be poorly engineered, lacking many of the safety features mandatory in the West. To restore public confidence in the safety and reliability of nuclear power, foreign assistance was sought to improve safety through the upgrading or closing of these plants located in Bulgaria, the Czech Republic, Hungary, Lithuania, Slovakia, and Ukraine.

A G-7 summit held in July 1992 focused on the safety of these plants, especially in view of the 1986 Chernobyl disaster. The industrialized states wanted many of them closed, and an emergency plan was developed. "A longer term goal of the assistance program is to shut down the most dangerous nuclear power reactors and replace them with alternative energy sources."[4] Almost $1 billion was pledged by the EU, the International Atomic Energy Agency (IAEA), the OECD, the EBRD, and individual states to develop alternative energy sources and energy efficiency programs. Because these funds promised new life to the nuclear industry in the form of orders for new equipment, instrumentation, control systems, and nuclear waste storage facilities, the focus shifted to temporarily increasing the safety of the plants instead of closing them. Indeed, although a few plants have been taken offline since the collapse of communism, a vast new market benefiting suppliers of nuclear technology has emerged.[5]

One of the major problems encountered by the nuclear industry is grafting western technology onto Russian-designed reactors. Temelin was to be the first such redesign project on a Russian VVER 1,000-megawatt plant. Skeptics were concerned that Russian reactor containment designs cannot be properly retrofitted. A 1993 IAEA study of the VVER 440 and 230 reactor models concluded that the containment structure could not withstand a primary circuit pipe breach.[6] The cooling systems are also inadequate, and the reactors are prone to metal fatigue. Even more recent versions, for example, the 213 model, did not meet western safety standards.

The nuclear industry consulted with Russian nuclear engineers to facilitate western financing of new projects. The irony is that the nuclear industry in the western countries found itself in the awkward position of supporting the use in eastern Europe of a technology it had criticized only a few years earlier. Plant designs considered too dangerous for the West are still in use in CEE countries. Germany, however, closed a former East German VVER 440/213 plant and canceled upgrading a VVER 1000 plant because the government considered them too expensive and problematic to upgrade safely.

Pressure to turn to nuclear energy has resulted in party coalition discussions in Germany, which had pledged in 2000 to phase out its nuclear reactors. In Ireland, along with Norway and Austria, some groups are calling for renewed discussion about the nuclear energy option. At the same time, however, there is concern among environmental advocates about environmental impacts, waste disposal, liability, safety, and nuclear proliferation. There is concern that nuclear energy is being portrayed as a clean and safe alternative.[7]

Sustainable Development and the Environment in the CEE

The most widely used definition of sustainable development is "development that meets the needs of the present without compromising the ability of future generations to meet their own needs."[8] It was popularized by the 1987 UN Brundtland Commission report, *Our Common Future* (see Chapter 1).

From Communism to a Free Market

In the CEE region, the transition from a centralized economy run by an economic and technocratic elite to one based on free market principles and pluralism has been swift as well as often painful and marked by uncertain policy. The demise of central planning left a vacuum in policy direction. Decisions about energy production, supply, and consumption were made in the absence of environmental criteria. "The application of Marxist ideology in practice led to environmental devastation in all Communist countries but its low point was probably reached in the Czech Republic."[9]

Under communism, environmentalists were labeled right wing because they were accused of trying to destroy socialist dreams by imposing costly demands on the government. After 1992 they were branded left-wing extremists trying to ruin the free market economy by advocating a role for the state in protecting the environment.

One major difference between western democracies and communist systems and states undergoing political transformation is that in the West the public has more opportunities to influence policymaking. Greater public participation encourages problems to surface and solutions to be considered early in the decision-making process. However, such supports as an active civil society, transparency, and existing environmental remediation programs were not readily available in the Czech Republic. "Environmental transition, like the more general political and economic transitions, engenders needs for different skills, information and knowledge as well as different organizational structures and social institutions than were common in the Communist era."[10] A sustainable development program that includes the environmental impact of energy usage could call on the expertise of interest groups, nongovernmental organizations (NGOs), and the general public, resulting in not only better decisions but also popular support for them.

Embracing Sustainable Development in the Czech Republic

The first postcommunist government of Czechoslovakia (which split into the Czech Republic and Slovakia in 1993) enthusiastically developed policies consistent with principles of sustainable development. Environmental issues had been part of the pre-1989 opposition, and some of the dissidents held government positions. Bedrich Moldan, the Czech environment minister—the Czech and Slovak republics had their own environment ministers—instituted a Green Parliament, which was a forum for environmental interest groups to discuss and recommend proposals. The period was full of optimism and a sense of mission. Influenced by the Brundtland Commission, the new government issued a report, "Concept of State Ecological Policy" (also known as the Rainbow Program), which called for the integration of the environment into all policy sectors. Air and water pollution, solid waste disposal, and the cleanup of highly contaminated areas were given priority.[11]

During that period an environmental code of ethics for business was proposed and endorsed by many. It called for the rational use of natural resources, the internalization of environmental costs, and the establishment of a Czech environmental protection agency. A proposed eco-tax on fossil fuels would provide funds to clean up contaminated areas such as northern Bohemia.[12] The overall strategy was to use economic and financial instruments to change the behavior of the polluters rather than rely on end-of-the-pipe solutions. The national-level Federal Committee for the Environment wanted to make environmental recovery a central concern in the shift to a market economy. Its chair, Josef Vavrousek, raised his committee's activity to the international arena by hosting a pan-European EU-sponsored conference on the environment at Dobris Castle in 1991. The conference produced a notable EU report on the state of Europe's environment, called the "Dobris Assessment," in 1995. Additional conferences followed.

All of this changed following the elections of 1992, which brought to power a new Czech government headed by Vaclav Klaus. Institutional capacity never developed. The Czech Environment Ministry became demoralized while it lost political clout. The ministry's dedicated environmentalists were replaced by party stalwarts. There were no monitoring systems or inspection programs to follow up and enforce legislation. Other issues such as crime, inflation, and the Czech-Slovak split replaced the environment on the government agenda, although a majority of people still believed environmental problems were urgent.[13]

The Klaus government ignored the work of the earlier government, focusing instead on free market rationalizations for ignoring the environment. During the preparation of the State Environmental Policy document in 1995, Prime Minister Klaus refused to allow the term "sustainable development" to be used. A ministry official explained that the term was dropped for domestic political reasons, because support of the concept could be perceived as a way for socialists to return to greater state-directed activity.[14] But Klaus wanted to limit any government responsibility for environmental matters. The document stated, "The Czech Republic's environmental policy is conceived as a dynamic approach which will facilitate identifying ecologically, economically, socially and politically optimal policies as opposed to establishing an inflexible system which could hamper economic development and lead to State control."[15] The government's perspective was that environmental problems would be solved in the marketplace and that it was the environmentalists who were the problem.[16] The optimal level of pollution was proclaimed to be whatever was socially acceptable, although few mechanisms existed for determining what that was.

The 1995 State Environmental Policy document referred to the Temelin nuclear facility as a remedy for the air pollution caused by coal-burning units. It also projected that the Czech Republic would achieve a level of environmental quality comparable to that in the countries of western Europe by the year 2005—an unrealistic expectation given the state of the environment and the level of administrative infrastructure, resources, and expertise necessary to realize that goal. The *2005 Report on the Environment in the Czech Republic*[17] admitted that it would be very difficult to meet limits for suspended particulates, carbon dioxide, and ground-level ozone. The report does not mention the concept of sustainability and does not articulate any plans for increasing renewable and alternative energy and thus does not reduce air pollution. In the Czech Republic economic development has been more important than developing and meeting sustainable environmental goals. The competition between these goals in the Czech Republic demonstrates the rocky path of post-communist states in the region as they build competitive market economic systems.

After 1992, NGOs no longer had access to the Environment Ministry, and relations became strained. Some environmental groups discovered they were on a list of extremist NGOs (the list also included skinheads and anarchists) compiled by the Security Information Services, presumably to discredit them and deny them the opportunity to address the public. According to the government, it was an unofficial list, but environmentalists insisted that their names be removed. The list was given to the police, who apologized and said that the responsible person would be punished. Many of these environmental activists were pre-1989 dissidents but were now labeled enemies of the state.

Perhaps the diminished interest in environmental issues was due to a "lack of social basis for the pursuit of advanced environmental policies typical of the first two years of the 1990s."[18] Czech scholar Petr Jehlicka maintains that the lack of public involvement and information provided by the media and government, as well as the absence of an educated and economically secure middle class, strongly influenced the public perception that environmental concern meant no more than reducing pollution.[19] What was also lacking was capacity building, including not only well-functioning institutions but human resources encompassing skilled personnel to run programs and monitor performance in the public sector on all levels of government.[20] Moreover, the embracing of a free market system and "neo-liberalism" or liberalization resulted in not only the closure of inefficient plants but also the increase of consumerism with its negative environmental impact.[21]

Energy Policy in Transition

The government stated it would retire coal-burning plants when Temelin came on line. However, these plants are still needed as backup when Temelin is off-line for maintenance and repairs. The closing of coal-burning plants also has the unpopular prospect of increasing unemployment. The Ministry of Industry and Trade policy has been to offer subsidies to encourage switching to home electric heating, which has the unfortunate consequence of increasing consumption of electricity.

The Road to Temelin

The Decision to Upgrade

The Temelin nuclear facility was approved in 1978. Construction started in 1986. It was part of a massive project to build at Temelin four 1,000-megawatt reactors designed in the former Soviet Union, with others to be located throughout Czechoslovakia. Because of the Chernobyl accident, construction was suspended in 1989 pending a review of the reactor design. The government was under pressure to take action because of general concern about the safety of Russian-designed reactors. The plan was scaled back in 1990 for several reasons: the Czech government wanted to use the opportunity to build ties to the West; the Russians could not deliver the designs on schedule; and environmental problems surfaced.

During this period Petr Pithart, the first postcommunist prime minister of the Czech Republic, complained about the lack of information essential to making a decision about the plant's future. He reduced the number of reactors from four to two and tried to initiate a public debate but left the final decision to the next government. In the spring of 1992 new data indicated that energy consumption would not increase substantially from 1989 to 2005. It could have been used to show that Temelin was unnecessary, but the Klaus government, led by the Ministry of Industry and Trade, favored the nuclear facility. Not even the parliament could initiate a public discussion of the issue.

A 1990 analysis by the IAEA found design flaws in the VVER 1000 and recommended changes: for example, replacement of the instrumentation and control systems and fuel assembly. This provided the rationale for upgrading

Temelin. In the fall of 1992 CEZ and Westinghouse signed letters of intent for supplying nuclear fuel and replacing the instrumentation and control systems subject to U.S. Export-Import Bank (Exim Bank) loan guarantees. Halliburton NUS, an American company, completed a probabilistic safety assessment that examined issues such as commercial policy and personnel issues.

In March 1993 CEZ awarded the contract to Westinghouse after two rounds of bidding. Controversy erupted over the bidding process in 1996, when it was revealed that information may have been leaked to Westinghouse about the bids of its competitors, allowing it to enter a second bid that was just under the next lowest bid.[22]

The U.S. Role

U.S. support for Westinghouse's bid to upgrade Temelin was critical. There was intense lobbying by Westinghouse to get the Exim Bank to approve the loan guarantees in support of a seventeen-bank consortium headed by Citibank. For Westinghouse, the goal was to replace Russia as the supplier of nuclear fuel and provide the instrumentation and control systems. CEZ and the Czech Ministry of Industry and Trade told the United States that the Temelin project could lead to additional upgrading contracts. According to U.S. officials, without the support of the Exim Bank, Westinghouse would not have won the contract because other bidders had the support of their governments. The United States promised that if Westinghouse won the contract, it would encourage increased cooperation between the United States and Czech firms in nuclear and other industries.[23] The U.S. embassy in Prague assured Czech officials that Westinghouse would have access to competitive financing through the bank for the instrumentation and control systems and the specially designed nuclear fuel assembly. It is clear that both the Czechs and the Americans were interested in making the deal.

At the request of the Exim Bank, the U.S. National Security Council began an interagency review of the reactor design and the technical ability of the Czech regulatory authorities to ascertain compliance with U.S. environmental policy. The unified procedures established for interagency review of projects were not triggered, however, because the exports for Temelin did not include "the entire nuclear reactor or nuclear steam supply system."[24] An environmental impact assessment (EIA) of the redesigned Temelin project was therefore never performed.

The Exim Bank's nuclear engineer reviewed the project to assess safety, environmental risks, and feasibility. To learn about Soviet reactors, he relied on U.S. Department of Energy (DOE) reports, IAEA analyses, Czech officials in Prague and Temelin, and a DOE study of VVER reactors. However, officials at IAEA and DOE deny that "any such assessment had actually been made."[25]

Although the Nuclear Regulatory Commission (NRC) did not perform its own evaluation of the reactor design, it lent its support. Temelin opponents alleged that the NRC's cautious report was rewritten to obtain the approval of Vice President Al Gore. Moreover, the Exim Bank consultations with Czech officials were frustrating because the information requested was not freely forthcoming. One bank official complained, "It is absolutely unacceptable to have a situation where we don't get a document or are not otherwise informed of something because we didn't ask exactly the 'right' question in the 'right way.'"[26]

Nevertheless, in March 1994 the Exim Bank's board of directors approved the loan.

Under NGO and Austrian pressure, Congress decided to investigate the project. By then, more than one million Austrians had signed a petition protesting the loan. The Austrian government had offered to pay the Czech government to switch from nuclear power to natural gas at Temelin. It had also called for an EIA with public comment, or at least a preliminary safety review—the procedure that would be followed if the reactors were located in Cuba or Mexico. Thirty-two members of the U.S. Congress sent a letter to Kenneth Brody, the Exim Bank chairman, strongly recommending that Temelin be required to meet western health and safety standards as a condition for the loan guarantee.[27]

Congress expressed concern about potential liability in the event of a nuclear accident, as well as the potential costs of more projects to upgrade Russian plants with American tax dollars. Committee chairman John Dingell, D-Mich., was concerned about an information gap "because the Russians refused to relinquish the documentation with design specifications of the Temelin plant."[28] Dingell requested all communications between the Exim Bank, the Czech Republic, the DOE, the NRC, and Westinghouse concerning safety and cost. The Czech government was unwilling to produce any documents.

The newly elected Republican-controlled Congress replaced Dingell as committee chair, and Congress was no longer interested in pursuing the issue of safety at Temelin.

Exim Bank officials recommended that in the future "unified nuclear procedures"—which require extensive analysis and an environmental assessment—should be applied to the export of major parts of nuclear power plants, with the participation of relevant U.S. agencies. On December 3, 1996, the Exim loan guarantee for the consortium was signed at the U.S. embassy in Prague. The project had support in the United States—from former president George H. W. Bush, Vice President Gore, the NRC, the DOE, and the State Department—on the grounds that it benefited American competitiveness.

Problems at Temelin

The many delays in the construction of Temelin contributed to an escalation of costs, and they exceeded the break-even point established by CEZ.

Summary of Administrative, Safety, and Technical Problems at the Temelin Plant

1. Lack of adequate documentation from the Russians necessitating redrawing of designs.
2. Safety goals not well defined. Too many suggestions and insufficient standards to assess degree of change necessary.
3. CEZ underestimated magnitude and complexity of integrating western and Russian technology.
4. Westinghouse had no incentive for timely completion.
5. Inadequate communication and coordination of activities on site and with Westinghouse Pittsburgh headquarters.
6. Russian and American cables were incompatible, requiring total replacement.
7. Russian and American safety codes differed.
8. Russian and American assumptions about equipment capability differed.
9. Westinghouse designs lacked level of detail familiar to Czech workers.
10. Absence of plans for long-term storage of nuclear waste.
11. Westinghouse misplaced two nuclear fuel rods that were found in the airport.
12. State Office of Nuclear Safety inspections revealed some noncompliance with safety standards.
13. Tritium could be released in the Vltava River, which supplies drinking water to Prague.

Westinghouse asked for increased compensation, claiming it had underestimated its charges because of safety and design changes, salary increases, and prolonged labor contracts.[29] CEZ blamed Westinghouse for insisting on about 2,000 design changes—Temelin went through its six major rounds of changes.

CEZ admitted that experts had underestimated the work needed to upgrade the Russian design to meet western standards.[30] A summary of administrative, safety, and technical problems is given in the box on this page.

The first unit finally came on line in October 2000.

Even after the first unit opened, problems continued to plague Temelin, including leaks in the steam supply pipes. The Czech solution used restraints or covers for the pipes that would not meet American or German standards, which required separation by a wall. Other problems surfaced in the nonnuclear system, including improperly fitted safety valves (Russian-designed) and improperly connected welded pipes. Technical problems caused unit 1 to be shut numerous times, and unit 2, launched in May 2002, also experienced many shutdowns for repairs, including replacement of its turboset rotors. There has also been leakage of low-level radioactive water, causing additional problems.[31]

Opposition to Temelin

Little public discussion surrounded the decision to resume construction of Temelin. Two groups, Hnuti Duha (Rainbow Movement) and the South Bohemian Mothers against Temelin, developed a small but substantial presence. Within sight of the plant, the Temelin Nuclear Power Plant Civic Association tried to arouse interest in the local community.

Numerous protests against the Temelin plant occurred in the 1990s, especially on the anniversary of the Chernobyl accident. In 1995 former prime minister Pithart was among the demonstrators. Civilian groups such as Children of the Earth, Citizens against Temelin, and Greenpeace often cooperated. The Austrian Green Party, accompanied by citizens from Germany, Denmark, and Austria, also held demonstrations. Petitions were presented to the government, which made no official response.

Austria has a strong interest in the plant because of Temelin's close proximity to its border. Low-level radiation and the risk of major accidents make the location of nuclear power plants a transboundary issue. The Greens in Austria were vocal in their opposition, gaining political party support. They wanted the Austrian government to make the decommissioning of Czech nuclear plants a condition for EU membership. The provincial governor of Upper Austria tried to arouse public awareness of the dangers of nuclear power and supported antinuclear groups.

Government studies in the late 1990s opened public discussion of the future of energy policy, including Temelin. Public hearings were held and covered by the media. The result was to continue Temelin's construction.

EU Membership as a Force for Change

The prospect of becoming a full partner in the EU has been a catalyst for change in the Czech Republic. As part of the accession process, the Czech Republic had to demonstrate that it adopted European Community legislation. Environmental and energy legislation presented the greatest challenges. Although EU law was transposed into national law, it was not an easy task because Czech legal practices and culture were not compatible with new approaches in some EU directives.[32]

By 2000 the conflict over Temelin switched from a domestic debate to the international arena in the context of EU enlargement. Protests from Germany and Austria, with blockades of the Czech-Austrian border at various sites, increased when Temelin was launched in October 2000. Austrian protesters, fueled by the Freedom Party led by Jörg Haider, demanded that Austria veto the closing of the energy chapter of the *acquis communautaire*, thereby preventing the Czech Republic from joining the EU unless it closed Temelin.[33] The Austrians, as inhabitants of a nuclear-free state, claimed they had the right to protect their citizens against a potential threat. Relations between Austria and the Czech Republic became strained. In December 2000 the EU enlargement commissioner volunteered to serve as a mediator, and a process began that included hearings in both countries, an EIA completed by the Czech government, and an expert trilateral mission to assess safety issues. The Czech Republic agreed to establish a hotline between the two countries to exchange information. On November 21, 2001, the heads of government of Austria and the Czech Republic signed an agreement, concluding what became known as the Melk process, after the city in which the document was signed. The Czechs agreed to improve security at Temelin. The commission report stated that, after examination of the environmental impacts on soil, water, minerals, climate, and health, damage was not probable. This was the only case in the EU in which a finished project was assessed using an EIA.

That EIA process concluded with the Austrians still dissatisfied with the level of safety guarantees. The two reactors at Temelin have been operational but not without continuing problems, for example, defective fuel rods.[34] Austrian and German opposition to Temelin provided the EU with a unique opportunity to broker a solution that resulted in the Melk Protocol.[35] The goal was to provide greater safety assurances to Austria.

The Czech entry into the EU gave it a prominent role in promoting nuclear energy. The lack of harmonized safety standards for nuclear reactors in the EU gave the Czech Republic an opportunity to showcase its nuclear expertise. Most of the electricity the Czech Republic generates is still exported to EU countries, giving the Czech Republic greater access to an expanded electricity market and greater opportunities for nuclear collaboration.

Building Democracy and Environmental Protection through Public Participation

When democratic attributes such as public participation are compared in the countries of CEE, similar deficiencies may be traced to the influence of Soviet political and bureaucratic structures and patterns of interaction. Nevertheless, one must keep in mind that these states have distinctive histories and cultures that temper the Soviet influence. Much of the reluctance to participate directly in politics can be traced to the dearth of real opportunities for public involvement prior to 1989. The "highly centralized structure of the state itself" was constraining.[36] In fact, individuals were punished if they challenged or questioned government decisions. The public was discouraged from making demands on their leaders because the state, in theory, provided for their needs. There were no means to link people to their leaders other than through the Communist Party.

The public therefore lacked experience in civic life, including membership in intermediary organizations such as NGOs and political parties. Information was the property of the technical elites, and criticism was denied to citizens. General apathy and passiveness were pervasive; people appeared content and remained withdrawn from public life.

Some experts on the CEE region, scholars such as Keith Crawford and Piotr Sztompka, point out the difficulty of changing this political culture.[37] Since the political transformation of 1989, the average Czech citizen has been preoccupied with economic issues. Membership in political parties or NGOs is still low; political parties are still considered a dirty business.[38] The problem is how to create political efficacy so that the public has the resources and motivation to play an active role in the policymaking process. Unfortunately, there is still a reluctance to seek information or challenge authorities.

Accountability

The hierarchical government structure originating in the Austro-Hungarian empire and reinforced under communist rule not only discouraged public participation but also influenced bureaucratic behavior. Bureaucrats were not regarded as public servants but as servants of the state. Bureaucratic accountability meant that no one took responsibility.[39] Administrators could be severely disciplined, even at the local level, for a small deviation, so a poor decision that did not have the intended result could be costly for the decision maker. Administrators disliked making decisions for which they might be blamed and held accountable. Therefore, most orders were passed orally, with no written record. The reluctance to take responsibility for actions was typical of the communist legacy and is a continuing problem.

Since 1989, people have been encouraged to take responsibility for themselves, yet the policymaking process does not provide sufficient opportunities to make decisions about their future. People hesitate to become involved in problems they do not believe they can solve or assess properly because of a lack of expertise, for example, the building of a nuclear plant. Polls by the Institute for Public Opinion Research in Prague in 1993 and 1995 indicated that a majority of people trusted the government to make the right decision on nuclear power.[40] (Those younger than twenty-nine and older than sixty were more distrustful than the other age groups.) Ironically, 65 percent also agreed with demonstrators supporting environment protection! Because most information is still controlled by the government, it is difficult to make independent judgments without countervailing facts. Even some academic elites do not feel qualified to have an opinion about nuclear power because it is outside their particular expertise.

The Relationship between Czech Political Culture and Temelin

Political culture involves attitudes, values, and beliefs about political institutions and practices. The Czech political culture described in the previous section influenced policymaking at Temelin as follows:

• The low level of information about nuclear power contributed to the belief that it was safe. Some residents near the Dukovany nuclear power plant do not respond to alarms because they say they cannot see any pollution. The public has been unable to challenge government pronouncements about safety at the Temelin plant. The public is unaware of alternative energy resources that would be compatible with sustainable development while reducing air pollution in northern Bohemia. Information was not used to shape public opinion and encourage public interest and debate.

• The media often discredit NGOs and protest activity, giving minimum coverage to their activities. Television showed foreigners at a Temelin demonstration to raise questions about the power plant's legitimacy. The media have begun to challenge this complacency and increase public debate. In the spring of 1998, for example, the future of Temelin was finally explored on television with discussion from representatives of government ministries, CEZ, and other experts.

• The lack of public debate left decision making to special stakeholders such as bureaucrats. Public activity is considered an impediment to government decisions. Even the parliament never debated the decision to complete Temelin. The lack of communication among members of the parliament, NGOs, scientists, researchers, professional associations, and bureaucrats inhibits sharing of information and, consequently, the development of a civil society.

• Local governments were not involved in the licensing process for Temelin. Communities were denied an opportunity for public discussion even after requests were made to the central government. Local authorities' opinions were not considered. The decision to grant a construction license was approved by the state office, which evaluated only the building plans and not the environmental impact of the plant.

• The lack of individual responsibility within the organization's decision-making hierarchy contributed to delays at Temelin. Difficulties in obtaining clearance or approval on highly technical issues potentially can compromise safety levels if decisions are made under pressure and without proper oversight.

• Administrative practices and rules were loosely enforced. There is a poor history of monitoring and implementing environmental legislation. Nuclear energy technology requires a high level of safety and low levels of risk and uncertainty, with a decision structure that provides for extensive monitoring, oversight, and redundancy.

• Because discussion of the decision to continue construction of Temelin was suppressed, with government officials refusing to engage in open debate, the potential for latent conflict remains. "There existed no legitimate alternative political grouping able to offer a fresh approach to dealing with a particular problem such as the environment, and the leadership was thus trapped and prevented from seeking solutions to the worsening ecological situation."[41] The NGOs are weak, with low membership and few resources. Except for the Rainbow Movement and Greenpeace, most have dropped Temelin from their agendas.

• The attitude that there is an objective nonpolitical solution to Temelin that is best made by experts ignores the political aspects of a conflict. It is as if the truth were waiting to be found by a divine expert. According to this view, the public should not have a role in decision making on a technical issue, and the government should not ask them. Some decision makers lack the understanding that participants in any conflict have particular biases and that any decision will reflect those biases as well as the objective analysis.

• The media, such as newspapers and television, have been timid and reluctant to carry out investigative reporting. There is little critical analysis, and the media are reticent if embarrassing the government might be the outcome. The public is therefore deprived of the ability to make informed choices.

Despite all of this, it is also true that the Czech political culture is undergoing a transformation. With EU membership, Czechs enjoy close ties with western Europe. The adjustment will not be easy; beliefs and attitudes that worked well in the past are slow to change. According to eastern European scholar Klaus von Beyme, the peaceful revolution of 1989 led by "intellectuals and their followers" did not transform political systems.[42] There is still a lack of trust between authorities, accompanied by a low level of political efficacy. As people become more familiar with democratic forms of political activity, they may begin to challenge existing bureaucratic and technocratic elites.

Comparison with the American Nuclear Experience

The United States provided loan guarantees as well as technical assistance to the Czechs during the construction of Temelin, and U.S. Nuclear Regulatory Commission (NRC) manuals, held up as a model, were on the desks of Czech nuclear inspectors. The Czech Republic has 6 nuclear power plants, and the United States has 104. In the United States most nuclear power plants are aging and must be replaced. The energy generated will have to be replaced while existing plants are decommissioned and radioactive materials are sent to disposal sites. The nuclear industry has been dormant for more than thirty years. The NRC provides safety oversight to U.S. nuclear power plants that are primarily privately owned. The safety record of these plants is variable and the NRC needs more resources to be effective.

The three major problems associated with the expansion of nuclear energy in the United States are safety and terrorism, cost, and the long-term disposal of nuclear waste. The second issue, financial cost, is not a major concern in the Czech Republic because the utility, CEZ, is owned primarily by the government and provides substantial revenues through the export of most electricity generated to the rest of Europe. The other two issues apply to both countries; therefore, the issue of cost will be discussed first.

In the United States, the DOE supports the nuclear industry by funding research and development projects. Legislation caps the liability of private utilities, which some critics argue would not even cover a meltdown.[43] Decommissioning may cost even more than building a nuclear power plant and, ironically, provides additional profit for nuclear engineering and construction companies. The nuclear industry itself considers investment in new plants risky and expensive, and without government aid, such as loan guarantees and tax credits, investment is a hard sell. The industry refers to these as incentives, not subsidies. They represented billions of dollars of support. According to the chief executive officer of Exelon, a major owner of seventeen nuclear power plants, "We're not big enough to build nuclear plants into the market without the initial government assistance that's in the loan guarantee program. Exelon has taken a very clear position that unless we get the federal loan guarantees of equivalent financing we will not go forward."[44] Moreover, costs are rising owing to shortages of skilled labor and increases in the price of materials, cement, steel, and copper.[45] Insurance companies consider investments in nuclear power plants risky. But as motivation to solve the global warming crisis grows, costs may be discounted. The bottom line is that consumers of electricity will pay more as state utility regulations allow rate hikes to cover the cost of the construction of nuclear power plants. Some states—Florida, for example—are already passing enabling legislation to allow this practice.

Safety and protection from terrorism have been ongoing issues in both the Czech Republic and the United States.

The problem of disposal of nuclear waste took on a new aspect after September 11, 2001. It was feared that trains transporting nuclear material—spent fuel, which needs to be safely stored for hundreds of thousands of years—could be attacked by terrorists with shoulder-fired weapons that could pierce protective casks and cause explosions that would lead to radioactive emissions. In the United States it has been proposed that trains laden with nuclear waste travel on tracks through cities on their way to waste disposal sites. Terrorism and the waste problems are intimately related.

No country yet has successfully developed or implemented a long-term storage program. In the United States, most waste is stored in cooling ponds or in above-ground casks. In the Czech Republic, spent fuel is stored on site in casks. Until the waste problem is solved, some critics feel that a nuclear renaissance makes no sense. To accumulate thousands of tons of additional radioactive material without safe disposal creates a problem as serious as global warming. Some scientists have confidence that geologically safe sites will be found. The Czech Republic has identified six such sites, but local public opposition has deterred officials from moving forward. The government is supposed to locate a facility by 2065. The Czech Nuclear Waste Repository Authority would like the EU to change its legislation so that states could share a site instead of having to locate sites within each country's boundaries. They would even consider being designated a host EU site.[46] Prime Minister Mirek Topolanek was of the opinion that environmental groups opposing siting of nuclear waste facilities are ideologically motivated and that nuclear waste is a political, not a technical, problem.

In the United States, opposition from the state of Nevada and concerns that Yucca Mountain, the only designated long-term waste disposal site, is unsuitable because of leakage and other environmental uncertainties have left nuclear waste dangerously accumulating on-site and open to sabotage and

Safety Issues in U.S. Nuclear Power Plants

1. Guards found sleeping.

2. Nuclear power plants are vulnerable to airplane attacks; the price tag for extra containment measures is in the millions of dollars.

3. Nuclear power plants are understaffed and are at such low levels that power downs or brown-outs are possible.[a]

4. Fatigue is a problem because of excessive overtime.

5. Drought could force shut-downs because of a lack of needed cooling water; the least-talked-about problem is that 24 of the 104 U.S. nuclear power plants are in potential drought areas.

6. Clear data on safe limits of radioactive exposure are lacking; what is the acceptable level of frequency and each occurrence?[b]

7. There are problems with safety valves.

8. Fuel rods have been lost.[c]

9. Plants routinely fail when mock attacks are carried out, even when plants are given six months advance notice.[d]

10. Lack of a culture of safety.

Safety issues are also a concern in other countries; for example, Bulgaria has experienced emergency shutdowns, Switzerland has a shortage of inspectors, Japanese workers have been exposed to radioactivity, and in France there was a uranium leak of 1,000 times the normal level into the river in Vaucluse.

Notes

[a]*Palm Beach Post*, May 14, 2008.

[b]*International Herald Tribune*, March 31, 2008.

[c]*Reuters*, August 17, 2004.

[d]*Catalyst*, Spring 2008, 6.

terrorism. In June 2008, DOE formally filed for an application for a license with the NRC. Frank Bowman head of the Nuclear Energy Institute, said, "Americans can and should be proud of our international leadership. . . . The filing of this application continues down a path to properly meet our obligation to future generations to safely and reliably manage the by-product of this highly efficient form of electricity production."[47] Private utilities have proposed temporary backup sites in the neighboring state of Utah. If the waste keeps piling up, building new plants in the United States and the Czech Republic could be delayed. Deputy director-general for nuclear safety and security at the IAEA, Tomihiro Taniguchi, said, "If this doubt is not ameliorated soon, it could well lead to all the ambitious plans to expand the use of nuclear power on a global scale being significantly delayed."[48] President

Barack Obama dashed the hopes of the nuclear industry in February 2009 when he announced the withholding of funds from Yucca Mountain and stated that he wanted an alternative plan for the disposal of existing nuclear waste. He appointed an opponent of the Yucca Mountain repository site, Gregory B. Jaczko, to head the NRC.[49]

The alternative to waste disposal is recycling, but that has problems of its own. A major one, and the reason the United States has banned recycling, is because it produces plutonium, which is used in nuclear weapons. The risk is that plutonium and other transuranic material could be used to develop nuclear weapons. The list of countries aspiring to begin nuclear energy programs includes countries with oil resources as well as countries in the Middle East and Africa where political stability is a concern. States want to compete with India, Pakistan, and Iran for the political stature that a nuclear arsenal provides. States need skilled technicians, engineers, and specialized personnel to construct and run nuclear plants. Moreover, the more that nuclear fuel supplies and spent fuel are transported, the greater the opportunity that material could be diverted for weaponization. This is a more serious problem if enrichment facilities are available. Establishing a nuclear nonproliferation regime would be a first step to control possible repercussions of the rush to nuclear energy.

Although in the Czech Republic nuclear energy was developed by the government with support from the major political parties, in the United States the government continues to support the resurgence of the industry by streamlining the licensing process, giving loan guarantees, and funding the application process. Such support may not be forthcoming given new global economic realities. If the solution to the problem of safe nuclear waste disposal had been solved before the construction of the nuclear reactor, the urgency and risks that regulators now face would not exist.

Safety: The NRC

The Energy Policy Act of 2005 (PL109-58) directed the DOE to offer financial incentives to the nuclear sector to develop more nuclear plants. The nuclear industry has invested billions of dollars to prepare NRC licensing applications. The NRC also streamlined the licensing process, merging the construction and operational licenses.

For the NRC, additional staff and resources are needed to review these applications for new reactors and on-site inspections. The Office of New Reactors created in 2006 to review applications needs five hundred employees and millions of dollars a month to hire contractors such as DOE laboratories and commercial companies to perform the reviews; approximately one-third of this work is contracted out. NRC is funded primarily through fees charged to licensees and applicants. That money is used to offset congressional appropriations.

NRC will have to train employees to perform these technically difficult tasks with training courses yet to be developed. There is concern that some critical needs—digital instrumentation and control and project management—will not be met. A formidable challenge will be to update and monitor new applications, evaluate them, and assess progress. In addition, most public comments regarding design, safety, and environmental criteria have come from the industry sector. This could result in bias favoring those stakeholders. According to a report by the Government Accountability Office, the NRC "will face a daunting task in implementing this new process while at the same time facing a surge in applications over the next 18 months."[50]

Global Implications

Global warming has emerged as the strongest argument in environmental terms to support nuclear energy. Nuclear energy is being portrayed in both the United States and the Czech Republic as a sustainable policy. The rise in fuel prices, the independence from Russian oil supplies in the Czech Republic, and independence from Middle Eastern petroleum are other arguments made by nuclear proponents. But oil supplies will eventually be depleted. Middle Eastern states such as Jordan, Morocco, Egypt, Saudi Arabia, Libya, and the United Arab Emirates may recognize that, but, instead of investing in solar and renewable energy, they also want to join the nuclear club. States seeking to offset fossil fuels that produce greenhouse gases do not suggest reducing demand or increasing investments in renewable technologies. Meanwhile the IAEA publicly supports increasing the expansion of nuclear energy. An increase in the number of nuclear states will overstretch the IAEA's ability to monitor and regulate the transport and use of nuclear materials and waste disposal procedures of additional countries. In individual states, national authorities need to be created to regulate reactor safety, personnel training, licensing, siting, and overall oversight. Whether some governments would submit to such international norms is problematic; for example, it is known that Asian governments underreport accidents to the UN International Labour Organization.

In both the Czech Republic and the United States, the nuclear industry and government regulators propose building more nuclear power plants. In the Czech Republic the level of public debate is low. It is similar in the United States even though thirty years ago NGOs and the public were able to thwart the building of new plants. In fact, in the Czech Republic, public support for nuclear energy has increased.[51]

Temelin Controversy Continues

The two Temelin reactors are operational, but problems continue. The coalition government (in power from 2006 until 2009), which included the Green Party as the junior coalition member, agreed with the Green Party that no new nuclear plants would be built; this was part of the price for the Green Party's participation in the government. While the Greens promote renewable energy and conservation, the majority party, the Civic Democratic Party or ODS, has been pro-nuclear and sees its role as a major nuclear energy player. In October 2008, Prague hosted the second European Nuclear Energy Forum sponsored by the EU to discuss the promotion of nuclear energy and harmonization of safety standards within the EU. Prime Minister Mirek Topolanek supported nuclear energy: "New reactors meet all parameters not only for Czech Greens, but also for all normal people, who want to have energy supplies guaranteed."[52] He also perceived any opposition by NGOs as ideological and did not see as problematic the lack of a long-term waste disposal site. He referred to it as a pseudo-problem, not a technical one.

Another study to recommend an energy policy, commissioned by the government in September 2008 and headed by Vaclav Paces, director of the Czech Academy of Sciences, did little to resolve the controversy as it suggested that nuclear energy was acceptable.[53] However, the environmental minister, Martin Bursik, who was also head of the Greens, threatened to pull out, saying the study was similar to the one done ten years earlier by the Ministry of Industry and Trade. At the same time, CEZ announced that it planned to construct two more 1,000-megawatt reactors at Temelin and extend the life of the Dukovany nuclear plant (which was also recommended in the Paces Commission report). CEZ is still majority owned by the government, and its decisions reflect their joint compatibility. The fact that CEZ is profitable is also a factor that contributes to its independence because the government benefits in real terms.[54] The role of the Ministry of Environment is to prepare an EIA: a determination of what should be examined and the response of CEZ to the screening. It is expected that this will take about one year.[55] The major issues are disposal of nuclear waste and transmission of electricity on existing wires. Other issues are improving energy security and closing plants that burn lignite coal. One does not find sustainability yet in the discussions on energy policy; it is a sensitive concept because there is no agreement on its definition.

The Czechs are slowly developing energy efficiency programs and wind energy, but not enough to meet the EU directive of having 20 percent of energy coming from alternative and renewable sources by 2020. Although the Czechs are concerned about security of energy supplies and dependence on their Russian neighbor, they have a contract with Russia for nuclear fuel and transport of nuclear waste, a contract that has put Westinghouse out of the uranium fuel supply market for plants of this type.

Domestic politics may have a significant role in how energy policy and sustainability play out. The population supports nuclear energy and does not want outside interference from other states. NGOs have only a limited role.

CEZ has now become a major exporter of electricity to the rest of Europe and one of the most profitable energy producers in the world.[56] While the current two units at Temelin export 50 percent of electricity produced, 100 percent of electricity generated at the two proposed nuclear plants would be exported. RusAtom, Westinghouse, Mitsubishi, and Areva have expressed interest in bidding for the contract. There is concern that if the Russians win, they will require Russian fuel. There is also discussion of opening new uranium mines.

CEZ and the Czech government are discussing a new energy scenario. The Czech Republic has not met the renewable targets set in 2003, and sustainable energy development is not on the agenda. CEZ considers nuclear energy to be a renewable source. The plan under discussion is vague, without specific renewable targets. As in the United States, a long-term repository is lacking and the state has responsibility for final waste disposal. CEZ pays into a state fund for such an eventual disposal project and maintains that disposal is not a problem. New plants will be built without a solution to the nuclear waste disposal problem.

The proposal by CEZ for nuclear expansion carefully warns of environmental and technical costs of renewable energy but mentions no downside for nuclear energy or coal. For example, it does not include any requirements to restore land to its natural state after coal mining. Coal is considered a primary source, and plans exist for new mines in environmentally protected areas and the removal of any restrictions to lignite mining because of environmental factors. In the past, whole towns have been demolished and inhabitants forced to leave.

Coal-burning plants continue to produce electricity; none are expected to be closed, and some have been retrofitted. The rationale of building nuclear plants to enable coal plants to shut down and thereby reduce greenhouse gas emissions has proven deceptive.

Conclusion

For several reasons, nuclear energy is still controversial in the Czech Republic and the United States. First, nuclear power plants alone cannot be built fast enough to fulfill the energy needs of developing economies, and those countries with existing plants need to retire some of them. The hundreds of projected plants will not be on line in time to meet projected demands. Second, any increase in the number of states with nuclear energy capacity increases the likelihood of nuclear proliferation. Third, there is little discussion among states about reducing electricity demand, which would be good for the environment because less harmful by-products or waste would be produced. The myth that nuclear energy is without environmental impact persists. Fourth, a false choice has been put forward that one has to choose between fossil fuels or nuclear energy, when ultimately renewable alternative energy will be the future energy source because of limits to supplies of fossil fuels. That is where massive investment by both public and private sectors should focus. Global warming has been the issue that nuclear enthusiasts in the United States and the Czech Republic have embraced. The nuclear industry frames the nuclear energy renaissance as environmental stewardship.[57]

Concepts such as sustainability are new to the Czech Republic as they are to many other countries around the globe. But the issue is not just the difference between a communist system or a free market system; serious environmental problems such as air pollution have plagued both economic systems, and environmental criteria have been given minimal attention.

Sustainability requires group or collective action with a concern for the public interest; it is future oriented. Sustainable development can succeed only if public support emerges and Czechs participate more fully in civil society. Public participation transfers legitimacy to sustainability. But the discredited planning legacy of the past may also have to be revitalized to develop environmental policies consistent with the principle of sustainability. Planning and public input can be compatible, but this requires an educated and informed public willing to make the investment. The challenge for the Czech government is to develop an energy policy that is consistent with sustainable environmental goals in a democracy that includes a greater role for the public through a variety of participatory mechanisms.

Former prime minister Pithart summarized the dilemma: "The construction of Temelin does not only change our attitude to energy saving, nature, and our health; it changes the whole social, economic, and political climate. With Temelin producing energy on a large scale, we are closer to a centralized, strong state and further away from regions, municipalities, and from citizens. . . . With Temelin, 'small is beautiful' is not valid, the statement which is valid says 'huge is also powerful.'"[58]

Notes

1. Regina S. Axelrod, "Reflections on the Writings of President Vaclav Klaus," *Listy* 38 (2008): 3, 105–107.
2. Associated Press, December 17, 2002.
3. For a discussion of energy policy in central and eastern Europe, see Peter Rutland, "Energy Rich, Energy Poor," *Transition* 3, no. 9 (1996): 5; and John M. Kramer, "Energy and the Environment in Eastern Europe," in *To Breathe Free*, ed. Joan DeBardeleben (Washington, D.C.: Woodrow Wilson Center, 1991), 57–79.
4. "Nuclear Safety: International Assistance Efforts to Make Soviet Designed Nuclear Reactors Safer," *Report to Congressional Requesters*, report no. GAO/RECD 94–234 (Washington, D.C.: General Accounting Office, September 1994), 1.
5. Colin Woodard, "Western Vendors Move East," *Transition* 17 (November 1995): 24.
6. Ibid.
7. *Irish Times*, March 27, 2007.
8. World Commission on Environment and Development, *Our Common Future* (London and Oxford: Oxford University Press, 1987), 43.
9. Peter Jehlicka and Jan Kara, "Ups and Downs of Czech Environmental Awareness and Policy: Identifying Trends and Influences," in *Protecting the Periphery: Environmental Policy in Peripheral Regions of the European Union*, ed. Susan Baker, Kay Milton, and Steven Yearly (London: Frank Cass, 1994), 154. See also Barbara Jancar-Webster, "Environmental Politics in Eastern Europe in the 1980s," in DeBardeleben, *To Breathe Free*, 25–56; and Andrew Tickle and Ian Welsh, eds., *Environment and Society in Eastern Europe* (New York: Longman, 1998).
10. "CEE From Transition to Accession," in *EU Enlargement and the Environment: Institutional Change and Environmental Policy in Central and Eastern Europe*, ed. JoAnn Carmin and Stacy D. VanDeveer (London: Routledge, 2005), 9.
11. Richard Andrews, "Environmental Policy in the Czech and Slovak Republics," in *Environment and Democratic Transition: Policy and Politics in Central and Eastern Europe*, ed. Anna Vari and Pal Tamas (Dordrecht, Netherlands: Kluwer Academic Publishers, 1995), 28.

12. Ibid., 31.
13. "Status of National Environmental Action Programs in Central and Eastern Europe," *Country Reports* (Szentendre, Hungary: Regional Environmental Center, May 1995), 28.
14. Brian Slocock, "Paradoxes of Environmental Policy in Eastern Europe," *Country Reports* (Szentendre, Hungary: Regional Environmental Center, May 1995), 43.6
15. "State Environmental Policy," document approved by the Government of the Czech Republic, Ministry of the Environment, August 23, 1995.
16. For an excellent discussion of environmental policy in the Czech Republic, see Bedrich Moldan, "Czech Republic," in *The Environmental Challenge for Central European Economies in Transition,* ed. Jurg Klarer and Bedrich Moldan (West Susses, England: Wiley, 1998), 107–130.
17. *2005 Report on the Environment in the Czech Republic* (Prague: Ministry of Environment, 2006).
18. Peter Jehlicka, "The Development of Czech Environmental Policy in the 1990s: A Sociological Account" (paper presented at the Summer Symposium of the University of Bologna, July 1997), 14.
19. Ibid., 12–14.
20. Carmin and VanDeveer, eds., *EU Enlargement and the Environment,* 12.
21. Ibid., 8.
22. Czech News Agency (CTK), May 11, 1996; and *Prague Post,* June 5, 1996.
23. "Nuclear Safety: U.S. Assistance to Upgrade Soviet-Designed Nuclear Reactors in the Czech Republic," Report of the Ranking Minority Member, Committee on Commerce, House of Representatives (Washington, D.C.: Government Accounting Office, June 1995).
24. Ibid., 7.
25. S. Jacob Scherr and David Schwarzbach, "Turning Points," *Amicus Journal* (Winter 1995): 14.
26. "Nuclear Safety," 11.
27. *East European Reporter,* March 25, 1994.
28. *Energy Daily,* March 17, 1994.
29. *Prague Post,* January 14, 1998.
30. *Nucleonics Week,* August 24, 1995.
31. CTK, April 3, 2008.
32. See Eva Kruzikova, "EU Accession and Legal Change: Accomplishments and Challenges in the Czech Case," in *EU Enlargement and the Environment,* 99–113.
33. For a comprehensive analysis of the Austrian opposition to the Temelin nuclear power plant, see Michael Getzner, *Nuclear Policies in Central Europe* (Frankfurt am Main: Peter Lang Gmbh, 2003).
34. BBC Monitoring International Reports, December 20, 2007.
35. For a fuller discussion of the role of the EU and Temelin, see Regina Axelrod, "Nuclear Power and EU Enlargement: The Case of Temelin," in *EU Enlargement and the Environment,* 153–171.
36. Adam Fagin and Petr Jehlicka, "Sustainable Development in the Czech Republic: A Doomed Process?" *Environmental Politics* 7 (Spring 1998): 119.
37. Keith Crawford, *East Central European Politics Today* (New York: St. Martin's, 1996); and Piotr Sztompka, "The Intangibles of the Transition to Democracy," *Studies in Comparative Communism* 24, no. 3 (1991).
38. Z. Vajdova, "Politicka kultura lokalnich politickych elit: srovani ceskeho a vychodonemeckeho mesta [Political culture of local political elites: a comparison of Czech and East German cities]" (working paper, Institute of Sociology, Academy of Sciences of the Czech Republic, 1997, 38).
39. Jehlicka and Kara, "Ups and Downs of Czech Environmental Awareness and Policy," 156.
40. CTK, November 29, 1995.

41. Adam Fagin, "Environment and Transition in the Czech Republic," *Environmental Politics* 3 (Autumn 1994): 481.
42. Klaus von Beyme, *Transition to Democracy in Eastern Europe* (New York: St. Martin's, 1996), 41.
43. *Wall Street Journal*, May 12, 2008.
44. "An Interview with John Rowe," *Bulletin of the Atomic Scientists*, September/October 2008, 10.
45. *Wall Street Journal*, May 12, 2008.
46. *Prague Post*, April 9–15, 2008.
47. PR Newswire, June 3, 2008.
48. *International Herald Tribune*, November 8, 2007.
49. Daniel Whitten, "Obama Rejects Nuclear Waste Site after 20-Year Project," Bloomberg Press, February 26, 2009.
50. "Nuclear Energy: NRC's Workforce and Processes for New Reactor Licensing Are Generally in Place, but Uncertainty Remains as Industry Begins to Submit Applications," report no. GAO-07–1129 (Washington, D.C.: Government Accountability Office, September 2007), 27.
51. *Czech and Slovakia Business Weekly*, May 2, 2008.
52. BBC Monitoring Europe, September 12, 2008.
53. CTK, July 7, 2008.
54. European Daily Electricity Markets, August 15, 2007.
55. *Prague Post*, July 16, 2008.
56. *Prague Post,* November 4, 2009.
57. PR Newswire, June 3, 2008.
58. *Listy* 5 (1994).

15

Consumption, Commodity Chains, and the Global Environment

Stacy D. VanDeveer

Our Material World*

Consumption uses things up. By now it is well known that we humans are consuming vast quantities of natural resources and changing our local, national, and global environments in the process. Furthermore, everything comes from somewhere. Whether the things we consume are grown, captured, mined, or manufactured—or some combination of all of these—they come from somewhere. People and communities are involved in the complex processes that create, harvest, distribute, and sell the things we use in our daily lives. Every transaction along these chains or webs of economic and social relations consumes resources. And, frankly, the social and environmental conditions in which things are grown, harvested, and mined are often quite grim—in ecological and humanitarian terms—and often unregulated.

Concern about global ecological limits and the ramifications of scarcity date back to at least the 1970s, continuing through the end of the twentieth century with a spike in interest around the 1992 Rio Earth Summit.[1] For much of this same period, resource politics was central to understanding global geopolitics and interdependence as energy, environmental, food, and other natural resource issues grew in importance among many political and economic elites in the "North" and "South."[2] By the early twenty-first century, the global environmental movement and the international social justice movement were beginning to see more shared interests and concerns under broader conceptions of sustainable development.[3]

Contemporary concern about consumptive and social justice aspects of globalization has resulted in a host of state and nonstate attempts to address the negative environmental and social conditions in producer communities around the globe. In recent years, scholars' attention to consumption issues has grown as the aggregate demand of our species continues to increase and as the environmental and human health implications of global resource consumption mount.[4] Environmental and social justice advocates have also turned their attention to combating overconsumption and the ecological and humanitarian costs of unregulated, or badly regulated, agricultural production, mining, and manufacturing around the world.[5] Organizations such as

*I am grateful for valuable research assistance on this topic from Eric Nitschke and from the insights and information produced during several years of teaching global resources and energy politics to students at the University of New Hampshire and the Harvard University Summer School.

Worldwatch Institute, Friends of the Earth, Oxfam, WWF, Global Witness, Fair Trade International, and thousands of other nongovernmental organizations (NGOs) are working tirelessly to reduce the environmental damage and human exploitation accompanying the growth of global wealth and trade. Furthermore, some states are working together and with international organizations, NGOs, and private sector organizations to attempt to reduce corruption and improve governance, in the areas of diamond mining and in the oil and gas sector, for example.

Social critics from Socrates to Madonna have reminded us that we live in a material world, and environmental analysts have become increasingly concerned about the scale of human material consumption. According to one recent estimate, humans consume about 50 percent more natural resources than they did thirty years ago, with people in wealthier countries consuming five to ten times as many resources as those in poorer ones.[6] The same study also notes that we have become more economically efficient over time, using 30 percent fewer resources to produce each dollar or euro of gross domestic product. North American consumerism has begotten a lifestyle that is associated with ravenous consumption of resources—energy, minerals, foods, and products of all types. We also know such consumptive patterns and institutions are being replicated around the world by (mostly) wealthy urbanites in many countries as, for example, consumption of fossil fuels, beef, and bottled water continues to grow and the number of automobiles in the world passes one billion on its way to two billion.[7]

Such lifestyle choices globalize some of the most ecologically damaging and inefficient aspects of Northern consumer culture. Can this process continue? By 2005 Americans had used 50 billion bottles of water, this in a country where tap water is safe to drink in almost every location.[8] How many bottles will be used globally if the taste for bottled water globalizes? How many bottles will end up floating in the oceans and littering ecosystems, or incinerated, or piled in landfills? In addition to increasing material throughput, biodiversity is declining, deforestation and habitat loss continue, and greenhouse gas emissions continue their global climb. In North America and Europe some debate is again emerging about the ways that consumerism may harm the consumers as well as the Earth's ecosystems.[9]

On top of growing global consumption of resources, the world is a very unequal place. About 40 percent of the world's 6.7 billion people live in poverty (defined by the World Bank as living on less than $2 per day). Almost one billion people live in even more desperate poverty—on less than $1 per day. In fact, about 80 percent of the global population lives on less than $10 per day—about what it costs to see a movie or buy two beers in the United States. More than fifty countries (over one-quarter of the total number of countries in the world) are actually poorer, per capita, than they were in the 1970s. Hundreds of millions have no access to clean water or medical care, regularly experience hunger and malnutrition, and live with little or no hope of improvement in these conditions.[10] These people's lives are nearly unimaginable for most North Americans and Europeans: try to imagine living every day on less than the cost of a Starbucks coffee. Chronic hunger is normal, and large portions of your time would be taken up by trying to get water to drink and fuel for cooking and heating. These "bottom billion" tend live in countries without good government, economic opportunity, or much help from the international community.[11] These countries are "falling behind and falling apart."[12] And it is not, generally speaking, the consumption of the world's poorest people that drives ever-growing consumption of the Earth's resources.

If global sustainable development is also about improving the lives of the world's poorest and most marginalized, then addressing issues of over-consumption in some societies cannot simply mean consigning others to perpetual, grinding poverty. The challenge of sustainability, then, is to ensure or engender a high quality of life for all of the nearly seven billion people of today and the nine to ten billion expected in midcentury, without exceeding the capacity of our planet's ecosystems.

This chapter begins with two sections outlining some basic concepts used to understand how globalizing patterns of consumption and production operate. Next, three brief sections present basic information about environmental and humanitarian concerns related to agricultural commodities; extractive industries such as mining, oil, and natural gas exploration; and finished goods. The final section reviews a number of possible policy responses to the challenges of consumption presented here.

Consumption, Commoditization, and Social Embeddedness

Consumption proves to be one of the most difficult issues to confront in environmental politics—for individuals and for authorities from local to global levels. Who benefits from curbing consumption? Consumers like cheap and plentiful products; leaders of wealthy consumer societies are unlikely to curb consumption; neither are the globe's most prominent business leaders or corporations. After the attacks of September 11, 2001, President George W. Bush told Americans to get out there and spend money to help fight international terrorism. Americans' consumer debt is credited with slowing the economic recovery from the 2007–2009 recession. Meanwhile, Chinese are criticized at home and abroad for saving too much and spending (read consuming) too little. We are living in a material world.

Because the total human population has grown so dramatically over the last century, it is tempting to blame the number of humans for our species' growing global impacts on the environment. Yet, the evidence suggests otherwise. While the human population has grown more than fourfold in the last century, our per capita use of resources has grown much more than this.[13] Globally, our consumption of most foods, water, fossil fuels, forest products, fish, and most other resources grows faster than our numbers. Furthermore, in the unequal world of the early twenty-first century, it is in the poorest parts of the world where human population is growing most rapidly, while consumption is driven by the wealthy societies and the urbanites around the world (in the North and the South) whose consumption increasingly mirrors that of North America and Europe. Again, it is not the world's poor and lower-income citizens who drive growing consumption around the world.

Let us use carbon emissions as an example. While the average U.S. citizen emits almost twenty metric tons of carbon each year, the average European or Japanese citizen, with similarly high standards of living, emits less than half of that. Yet, Chinese per capita emissions are about five metric tons, and average per capita emissions for India and most of Africa are less than two metric tons per year.[14] So, while the African population grows faster than the populations in North America, Europe, and China, it is not Africans whose consumption is rapidly changing the global climate. Nevertheless, Africans will suffer the consequences of the global climate change they did not cause.

North Americans, Europeans, and Japanese have used up billions of barrels of oil—not to mention coal and natural gas—from all around the globe and flushed the pollution into the global atmosphere. They are also depleting their own oil and gas supplies. Now joined by China, India, and a small number of other rapidly growing economies, they are engaged in a mad rush to secure access to the remaining oil from offshore and on-land oil reserves around the world.[15] Again, the significance of North American consumptive lifestyles should not be lost in this example. Although Chinese consumption has grown rapidly (like the Chinese government's involvement in global petro-politics), China's 1.3 billion people consume about 3.5 million barrels per day while 300 million Americans use more than 20 million barrels per day.

Many factors cause our collective material consumption to grow over time. This chapter highlights two aspects of contemporary consumer societies and economies: *commodification* (or *commoditization*) and the *social embeddedness of consumption*.[16] One of the many impressive characteristics of capitalism is its endless capacity to induce commodification. Capitalism gives us concrete incentives to develop goods and services most suited to buying and selling—such goods and services can be entirely new, or they can replace things that used to be free or were less amenable to buying and selling. Capitalism engenders creativity and innovation for new goods and services, but it also means that we tend to convert things that are not commodities into things that are.[17]

The example of children's play helps to illustrate the implications. Children (like other mammal youth) have been playing as part of their development, as far as we know, for thousands of years. Our grandparents tell stories of playing things like stickball, of having one doll, of making a toy gun, or of pretending to be cops and robbers or cowboys and Indians. They did not grow up in 2,000–4,000-plus-square-foot houses with several rooms strewn with hundreds and hundreds of toys—most of them made with petrochemicals and transported thousands of miles via fossil-fuel-based transportation. This image of contemporary North American childhood reveals a number of things about the typical North American lifestyle: the material throughput of everyday life tends to grow over time, as does the size of the average house although the size of the average North American family has gone down over time. We have larger houses for fewer people, and a lot more stuff.

Commoditization dynamics may also facilitate inequality and injustice in the world, even as they drive impressive levels of innovation and wealth creation. Thus, water privatization may shift water resources from local community control to the control of firms or the state, further marginalizing poorer citizens or communities.[18] Perhaps the best example of commodification's frequently unequal outcomes can be found in medical research and product development. Much more money is invested in the development of treatments for the maladies of the world's wealthy than is spent curing and treating things that kill people in the world's poorest societies. Growing markets for treatments for balding and erectile dysfunction and diet programs and pills offer enormous potential for the development of profitable products. The profit potential for treatments of diarrheal and other treatable diseases that sicken or kill many of the world poorest is much lower. So too is the profit potential for preventive treatment regimes for people in the North and the South.[19]

Such dynamics also play out in agricultural production, research, and investment. It is not uncommon for people to be malnourished in communities where coffee, roses, or other international commodities are grown for export. Attention to commoditization dynamics is not about spinning conspiracy theories, but about understanding that institutionalized incentives have consequences and outcomes in the world.

Patterns of North American material consumption and related commoditization processes also reveal the importance of our second concept, the social embeddedness of consumption. This concept refers to the fact that what individuals consume is heavily determined by a host of social influences and institutions. Unlike the assumptions often made in economic theories and models, social embeddedness suggests that "a consumer's choices are not isolated acts of rational decision making."[20] Rather, what we consume may help us find meaning, social status, or aspects of our identity. Furthermore, our consumer choices are shaped by advertising and myriad media images, and they are very much influenced by a complex, larger web of social and political institutions around us. So, for example, think of a decision to purchase a car, a phone, or an item of clothing. Which of the choices seems cooler? Sexier? More eco-friendly? More professional? More fun? Which choice seems more like you (or me) or more like the person you want to be? The answers to these questions and the perceptions on which they rest connect our buying decisions to the social worlds around us. We live in a material world.

Beyond individual purchasing choices among the options before us, consumption is also embedded in broad social and political institutions. The cars, phones, and clothing choices presented to us are shaped by government policies; corporate structures and cultures; long histories of product development; and a host of other interrelated social, political, and economic factors.

In other words, the choices consumers have are not determined simply by the aggregate preferences of consumers but by myriad other factors. For example, can I choose not to have a car if there are no transportation alternatives? I can reduce the amount of energy I use in my dorm room or apartment, but I usually have no control over whether my electricity is generated with wind power or the dirtiest coal. The social embeddedness of consumption means that, by my individual choices, I can reduce my ecological footprint somewhat through changes in my purchasing and other behaviors. Doing so may positively affect the environment, my life, and the lives of others. Yet, because consumption is socially embedded, I can make a substantial impact on the consumption levels of my lifestyle and my community only by working to change social and political institutions. As Michael Maniates observes, we cannot simply recycle cans, plant a tree, buy a few green products, and save the Earth.[21] Political and social change is required.

Chains, Chains, Chains

Commodity chains have long been of interest to business practitioners and scholars alike.[22] Traditionally, a commodity chain was viewed as a set of connections or processes through which a product went from the provision of raw materials at one end of a chain to the final purchase and use of a product at the other end. Processes along the chain might include harvesting or mining, processing, manufacturing, distribution, marketing, and so on. Then, at some point, a product is likely to be discarded. If we are trying to understand ever-expanding use of material resources, several problems arise with this traditional understanding of commodity chains. First, the traditional notion suggests that consumption happens only at the end of the chain—when we buy something or use it. But, if we are to understand ever-expanding material throughput in our world, we must remember that *consumption happens at every stage or within every transaction along these chains.*[23] At every stage, with every interaction, things are used up.

The second problem with the traditional formulation is that it downplays the social embeddedness discussed above. In other words, every point or transaction along a chain of relations involves, and is shaped by, social interaction and institutions. So, for example, how resources are grown or extracted from the earth—how wasteful, environmentally sensitive, or dangerous to the workers and community members—is contingent in large part on social institutions. The same is true of how things are manufactured and transported. These aspects of social embeddedness mean that commodity chains are better thought of as complex webs of social relations connecting people, institutions, and ecosystems across geographies, societies, and markets.

Thought of as complex webs of social relations that consume resources at every point or transaction, commodity chains help us understand the growing complexity of the globalizing world in which we live. Through these chains, the environmental and social implications of the things people consume are hidden or distanced from their everyday lives. *Distancing* of the implications of consumption severs feedback of information and ideas between social groups involved in commodity chains. It obscures the costs (often called the ecological and human externalities) of our activities.

Tom Princen argues that distancing has multiple facets or dimensions— including geographic, cultural, bargaining power, and agency dimensions—in the contemporary global political economy.[24] In other words, information feedback or knowledge about the costs of our consumption is inhibited by the sheer physical distances (and the geographic complexity) of where the things we use come from. Culturally, most modern consumers know almost nothing about the communities or the practices used in agriculture, mining, or even manufacturing. For example, if we do not associate agriculture with massive amounts of industrial chemicals and the need for stringent regulations on their use we may not think about whether particular foods come from communities where such regulation (and knowledge about chemical risks) may not exist.

The bargaining power and multiple agency dimensions refer to social and economic institutions associated with complex transnational commodity chains. For example, if local farmers or pickers growing a fruit or coffee in a developing country have no choice about to whom to sell their crop, they have no leverage over the price they can ask. There is no competition to buy their goods. Too often, each is forced to take whatever low price is offered. If local workers do not have enforceable rights to organize themselves in attempts to raise their wages, the prices they are paid for the goods, or the standards in which they work, they cannot bargain for their interests. To make things more difficult, transnational commodity chains are now so complex and so dynamic as they experience constant change that neither the buyers of a finished good (at one end of the chain) nor growers or miners or manufacturers at earlier stages of the chain could ever hope to trace the relations or the costs throughout the chain.

The commodity chains of the early twenty-first century are exceedingly complex webs of relations that result in the distancing or obscuring of cost information from consumers at all stages of the chain. And the impediments to improving these feedback breakdowns are significant. If, for example, we assume that each of us reading this chapter wants to be an informed, environmentally and socially conscious consumer, what would we need to know and do? First, we might want to find out where everything we consume comes from (geographic dimensions). For a start, we would need to determine the origins of every ingredient in the food and beverages we consume; every component of the clothing, books, and electronics we purchase; and every electron of electricity and transportation fuel we use (to say nothing of the where the energy used to make and transport the things we buy comes from). Probably none of us could accomplish this task. But, if we managed to find where most of these components originated, we would also need to know about the environmental and social conditions in which every component was made and assembled if we were to consider buying the environmentally and socially superior product.

An example of the challenges presented to the environmentally and socially concerned consumer can be found in a pair of blue jeans. In 2001, the British newspaper *The Guardian* published a story about the writers' attempts to trace a pair of jeans from their point of sale in a shop in the United Kingdom to the origins of the jeans and their components.[25] They found that cotton for the jeans was grown in Pakistan and Benin; the copper and zinc used for the rivets and buttons came from Namibia and Australia, respectively; and the pumice for the stonewashing came from a volcano in Turkey. Furthermore, in terms of where the jeans were made, this answer included the synthetic indigo made in Germany, the thread made in Northern Ireland and dyed in Spain, polyester tapes and wires made in France and Japan, and the denim made in Italy. The jeans were sewn in Tunisia by Ejallah Dousab, who made less than $1.00 an hour; and they were stonewashed there as well (not an environmentally benign process, for the record).

What should a tag in these jeans say about where they were made? How many geographic locations are involved in even a handful of the many hundreds of things each of us owns right now or the hundreds more we will purchase in the coming weeks or months? How many consumers know enough about dyes, pumice, copper mining, stonewashing, Tunisian garment factories, minimum wages, and labor unions to determine what the environmental and social costs of the jeans are? In addition, the jeans story outlined here did not even look into the resources consumed by energy generation and transportation, marketing and retailing, and a host of other consumptive aspects associated with consumer items. Finally, how much more complex than a simple pair of jeans is the chain of relations behind a laptop, a cell phone, or an automobile likely to be?

The *Guardian*'s "Story of the Blues" told of growing cotton, mining zinc and copper, and the production of the finished product. Building on the chain described in the story, the next three sections briefly discuss three overlapping types of commodity chains: agricultural commodities, extractive industries in mining and oil and gas sectors, and finished consumer goods of all kinds.

Bitter Harvests

The foods we eat and the beverages we drink all come from somewhere. So, too, do a host of other agricultural commodities from feedstock for the beef and poultry we consume, to cut flowers for our dates and weddings, and many forest products for the construction industry and finished goods. Some are grown and shipped as is, like many fruits and vegetables. Other agricultural commodities like wheat, sugar, coffee, tea, cacao, or palm oil require much more extensive processing before humans can use or consume them. This processing, like their growth and transportation, involves the consumption of material resources. Frequently, agricultural commodity chains also involve substantial ecological harm and human exploitation.

That agricultural commodities are associated with massive environmental degradation and exceedingly high humanitarian costs is not a new story and is not confined to the twentieth and twenty-first centuries. Coffee, tea, sugar, spices, and bananas, to name only five of the most famous examples, have been associated with empire building, colonial oppression, economic dependence, and large-scale environmental change for centuries.[26] Today, such commodities are associated less with explicitly imperialist rule and more with the environmental and humanitarian costs that their growth and production may involve.

Chief among the environmental concerns related to agricultural commodities are ecological harms caused by the widespread use of herbicides and pesticides and excess nutrients engendered by fertilizer use; the deforestation, land-use changes, and biodiversity losses associated with converting lands into industrial-scale agriculture; concerns about overuse of surface and groundwater resources; soil degradation and desertification; and the growing demand for fossil fuels engendered by the industrialization of agriculture around the world.[27] This diverse list of environmental harms illustrates that no one policy or behavioral change is likely to supply the magic bullet for a transformation to more sustainable agriculture. So, for example, less chemical use or better-regulated use of chemicals is unlikely to slow the deforestation or soil degradation or water exploitation engendered by expanding agricultural demands. Multiple strategies are needed, and many of these will need to be specific to sector, commodity, or place.

The humanitarian and public health concerns most frequently listed by activists and analysts alike include the following: human health risks from widespread and often unsafe use of chemical pesticides and herbicides, exploitation of child labor, the general lack of labor rights and worker safety institutions, and the widespread low pay and poverty in grower-producer communities. For example, the International Labour Organization (ILO) estimates that 69 percent of child laborers work in agriculture.[28] The fair trade movement and fair trade certification were launched to try to address the widespread poverty in developing country agricultural communities as well as the lack of labor rights, bargaining power, and information common in such communities. Table 15-1 lists a number of illustrative examples of agricultural commodities and the environmental and humanitarian implications associated with such commodities.

NGOs such as Oxfam and the Fairtrade Labelling Organization International and its affiliates and international organizations like the ILO have catalogued myriad examples, including Liberian children working with their parents in rubber tapping, more than a million Egyptian children handpicking pests from cotton, the more than three hundred thousand children weeding and picking commercial crops in the United States, and the well-documented and extensive use of child labor and child trafficking in the West African cocoa industry.[29] The latter example led some NGO activists to ask consumers if they knew whether their chocolates were made by child slaves. In 2004 the ILO estimated that child laborers numbered about 218 million, with more than 125 million of these engaged in work that was quite hazardous to their health.[30]

Table 15-1 Agricultural Commodities and Associated Environmental and Humanitarian Concerns

Commodity	Associated environmental issues	Associated social issues	Major producer areas
Bananas	• Deforestation and habitat loss • Unregulated pesticide, fungicide, and fertilizer use • Soil degradation • Solid waste • Water use	• Low wages and impoverished communities • Child labor • Environmental health and worker safety • Corporate-state collusion and government corruption • Militia funding and violence • Gender discrimination	• Coastal areas across Central America, Caribbean, South America, India and South Pacific, Central Africa
Cacao and chocolate	• Deforestation and habitat loss • Unregulated pesticide, fungicide, and fertilizer use • Soil degradation	• Low wages and impoverished communities • Child labor, child slavery, and child trafficking • Lack of labor rights • Environmental health and worker safety	• West Africa (Ivory Coast, Ghana, Nigeria, Cameroon) • Latin America
Coffee	• Deforestation and habitat loss • Unregulated pesticide, fungicide, and fertilizer use • Soil degradation	• Low wages and impoverished communities • Lack of labor rights • Environmental health and worker safety	• Tropical zones of Latin America, Asia, and central Africa
Tea	• Deforestation and habitat loss • Unregulated pesticide, fungicide, and fertilizer use • Soil degradation	• Low wages and impoverished communities • Lack of labor rights • Environmental health and worker safety	• China, India, Sri Lanka, Kenya, Indonesia, Turkey

Sources: Jason Clay, *World Agriculture and the Environment: A Commodity-by-Commodity Guide to Impacts and Practices* (Washington, D.C.: Island Press, 2004), and information compiled by the author.

One extremely thorough review of the environmental issues raised by global agricultural commodities covers the ecological and human health risks of twenty-one major commodities: bananas, beef, cashews, cassava, cocoa, coffee, corn, cotton, oranges, palm oil, rice, rubber, salmon, shrimp, sorghum, soybeans, sugarcane, tea, tobacco, wheat, and wood pulp.[31] Yet, even this impressive list is incomplete. One might also add grapes, apples, and many other fruits as well as cut flowers, various horticultural products, sugar beets, and cultured pearls. With each of these, ecological risks and harms are incurred; and the people involved in their growth, harvest, and processing may suffer from health or human rights degradation. Take, for example, the often little-known risks to agricultural workers in parts of Latin America and Africa who cultivate fresh flowers for homes and businesses in North America and Europe and for bouquets used to express love and beauty. Few if any labor rights, poor working conditions, and repeated exposure to dangerous chemical pesticides are not uncommon for the (mostly) women cultivating and processing the flowers. Like many commodities issues, conditions in parts of the cut-flower industry illustrate the overlapping nature of the ecological risks and the humanitarian concerns.

In addition to the commodities listed in Table 15-1, a number of other commodities are experiencing global overconsumption. Perhaps most famous among these are the world's tropical forests and fisheries, around which the record of international cooperation for environmental protection or sustainable use remains exceedingly poor. For example, the seemingly intractable combination of complex transnational commodity chains associated with forest products, growing global demand for most such products, and poor governance in many exporting countries continues to drive massive environmental degradation, human health risks, and oppression in many countries within tropical forest export sectors.[32]

Few agricultural challenges illustrate the growing material throughput and the social embeddedness of consumer culture better than the global growth in beef consumption. For several decades, consumer tastes have increasingly turned to beef as consumers have become wealthier. The industry engages debates about World Trade Organization rules and the use of genetically modified organisms and antibiotics in industrial production, and often drives land degradation, deforestation, and the use of myriad agricultural chemicals.[33] Large areas of agricultural land must be devoted to growing the feed for cattle, for example, and the chemical inputs, deforestation, and transportation involved in the global beef market drive enormous quantities of greenhouse gas emissions.

The news about seafood is no better. Since 1950 seafood consumption has grown almost eightfold as nearly all major fish stocks around the globe experience dramatic decline.[34] Note, in addition, that although a vegetarian diet is more carbon efficient than beef and reduces pressure on fish stocks, it does not address the many environmental externalities and humanitarian issues associated with globalized and industrialized agriculture.

Imagine then, the aggregate environmental and humanitarian harm that might be associated with a simple date on Valentine's Day: cut flowers, chocolates, dinner (seafood or beef), dessert, and coffee. After the jeans example above, imagine trying to trace the origins, environmental externalities, and working conditions associated with one evening out. Individual consumers, whether carnivores, vegetarians, or green buyers, cannot change the world simply by choosing to buy different things. They can reduce their individual contributions to problems with purchasing decisions. But political action and social change are required if we are to consume less of our environment and do less harm to each other as we eat and drink.

Still Digging

Extracting resources from the earth is essential to contemporary economies and societies around the globe, and the accompanying ecological and human costs are high. Things like stone, iron, and bronze were so important to human history that whole eras are named after them.[35] The environmental externalities associated with mining have long been of concern. One group of minerals comprises the metals iron, bauxite, copper, lead, nickel, zinc, silver, gold, mercury, cadmium, cobalt, titanium, tin, manganese, chromium, tungsten, coltan, lithium, and a host of others—some of them quite rare and highly valuable. But metals are not the only commodities mined from the earth; others include stone, sand, and gravel; clays; salt; phosphates; potash; lime; gypsum; and soda ash. Large-scale mining operations take place on every inhabited continent, often involving some of the largest multinational corporations in the world. While mining and oil and gas externalities have long been known, the growing scale of mining operations and increasing demand for oil and natural gas mean that the cumulative effect of extractive industries is unprecedented.

In the mining industry, environmental and humanitarian concerns are often tightly coupled. Extractive industries require the movement of massive quantities of earth, and they produce stunning amounts of a diverse set of pollutants. One estimate put the movement of earth worldwide at 57 billion tons, an amount that rivals estimates of all erosion around the globe.[36] In other words, humans now move more earth each year, just for mining and quarrying, than the global hydrological cycle does. This, added to global agriculture and urbanization and construction, helps to illustrate the massive land use and habitat changes human activities unleash around the globe. And these changes do not even consider the impacts of climate change.

Extractive industries are also waste intensive and frequently highly polluting of local and regional environments. Mining wastes degrade surface and groundwater in countries across the global North and the global South. North America is littered with areas of local regional ecological damage from mining, and the contemporary scale of mining operations around the world often dwarfs mining operations in North America. Today, a single mine can be extremely large, or small shallow mines may dot a landscape by the hundreds or thousands. Furthermore, most extracted commodities have to be refined substantially in order to be of value. Here, too, resources are used up and enormous quantities of wastes are produced. The ecological damage does not stop there, however. As extraction has moved deeper into mountain and tropical forest regions of the world, thousands of workers and the development of previously undeveloped areas go with it. Mining is therefore also a driver of broader regional and global ecosystem changes.[37]

In terms of social and humanitarian implications, the record of extractive industries is poor. Mining and oil and gas extraction are frequently associated with serious human health risks posed by pollutants released into local and regional environments as well as with damage to indigenous peoples and other groups whose environments, communities, and social and political organization may be substantially altered by the arrival of extractive industries.[38] In fact, the human security and humanitarian-related issues associated with the mining sector and the oil and gas industries are legion. Some high-profile examples include:

• **Diamonds:** Phrases like "blood diamonds" and "conflict diamonds" became famous over the past decade or more, as African diamond mining became increasingly enmeshed with civil war, state oppression, widespread environmental degradation, and severe human rights abuses. Estimates suggest that more than a million unregulated miners were toiling in conditions similar to enslavement while funds from the diamond trade were fueling weapons transfers, war, and terrorism.[39]

• **Coltan:** The technology boom of the 1990s and 2000s drove boom-and-bust cycles in columbite-tantalite (also known as coltan), commonly used in cell phones and other electronics. When the price spiked, a rush to mine for coltan spread rapidly in parts of the Democratic Republic of the Congo, and to extract the mineral individuals and groups dug thousands of giant pits in national parks and reserves, agricultural land, streams and river basins. Money from the coltan trade fueled militias, arms transfers, and activities of local warlords, mixing violence and oppression with ecological damage and dangerous working conditions. After the price collapsed, mining declined but the ecological damage, many weapons, and the legacy of civil violence remained.[40]

• **Gold:** The gold industry, like mining for most commodities, is plagued by reports of substantial ecological damage on a local and regional scale, pollution releases, adverse human and ecological health effects, and violations of basic human and labor rights in a host of countries. Gold is no longer mined by pickax-carrying pioneers but by employees of (or contractors to) multinational corporations in massive open pits that generate staggering quantities of wastes. Working conditions are often unsafe, indigenous peoples and other local communities are often overrun, and funds from mining operations can make their way to militias and oppressive public officials.

• **Oil:** It is difficult to overstate the importance of oil in the economic and political history of the past century. Tremendous wealth has been accrued by nations, corporations, and individuals. Oil's ecological costs include damage via pollution (of land, freshwater, oceans, seas, and air) of local environments and the global atmosphere, ecological changes driven by extraction itself, and damage from pipelines and other transportation. In terms of oil's connection to human rights violations, a recent review included all of the following problems: damage to human health from pollution and climate change, the common connection between oil interests and revenues with public and private sector corruption, lack of transparency and accountability, violation and abuse of indigenous peoples' rights, militarization and violent conflict, organized crime, and damage to community development.[41]

Global competition in the mining sector and the growth in global demand for many minerals have resulted in the dramatic expansion of mining operations and the consolidation and growth of a number of large multinational mining conglomerates, often owned primarily by North American, European, Chinese, Australian, and South African investors. These companies often construct what amount to armed camps around mining and oil and gas extraction operations to protect the investments and the workers from militias and violence engendered by community resentment. Such camps can be seen in many African, Asian, and Latin American facilities.

Perhaps the clearest case of political and economic damage done by oil and gas resources is the extensive research done on the "resource curse." A few recent analyses survey the topic.[42] The resource curse concept refers to the observed relationship between a country's high level of export dependence on a valuable resource and the likelihood that the country will have poorer than average economic performance over time and undemocratic, often corrupt, or ineffective governance. Such oil-exporting states are often called petro-states. For example, of the twenty largest oil exporters in 2000, eighteen were undemocratic. Economically, many highly indebted countries are oil exporters; oil-rich Nigeria ranks among the poorest countries on Earth, and citizens of mineral-exporting countries tend have high levels of poverty and child mortality.[43]

Analysts differ on the exact mix of causes of the resource curse, but important factors include the economic damage done by boom-and-bust dynamics that tend to plague commodity prices and commodity-dependent economies, a lack of economic diversification, and the presence of corruption. Also, political institutions tend to be weak in petro-states and heavily entangled in patronage networks and corruption. State institutions tend to have little independent authority over the oil sector and comparatively low levels of capacity to deliver services to citizens or to build or command their loyalty. Nigeria, Bolivia, Angola, Chad, and several states in the Caspian and Central Asian region are most often mentioned when petro-states are discussed, and many of the dynamics are also seen in the oil-rich states of the Persian Gulf.

Environmental and humanitarian challenges are not simply particular to a small number of extracted commodities in a few places; they are endemic in many parts of the sector and across many countries. So, for example, although the coltan price collapse deprived some Congolese militias of a major source of funding in early 2002, by 2008 the mining of tin ore was funding militia activities. Workers' human and labor rights are exploited, and virtually no environmental regulation exists. In this example, militias make money both by selling the tin (often to the multinational corporation that ostensibly owns the concession for the tin) and by taxing the sales of mineral traders and bars, brothels, and peddlers of everyday goods used by the miners and other people around the mine.[44]

Furthermore, mining is not simply about "old" products and technologies like steel, tin, and aluminum. Concern about the scarcity and concentrated control of some rare minerals used in electronics, wind power, electric and hybrid cars, and missile technologies has led to a rapid global search for additional deposits and increasing investment on several continents.[45]

Lithium, which is used in many types of batteries, is another resource that may also bring new, greener technologies together with the resource curse and geopolitical concerns outlined above, as Bolivia contains perhaps half of the world's lithium deposits even as it already manifests many of the political and economic dynamics common in petro-states.

Although we've all heard, "When you find yourself in a hole the first thing to do is stop digging," we cannot simply stop using oil, gas, coal, and dozens of minerals from the earth. Many new and old technologies rely on minerals. Yet halting the escalating ecological and human costs of these activities and reducing environmental and humanitarian externalities is possible. We know it can be done because some mines already meet much higher environmental and labor standards. High-standard mining operations still have ecological and human health effects, of course, but these can be minimized substantially. Also possible is substantially increasing energy and materials efficiency levels, recycling, and reuse. We can, in other words, use less of some things rather than always using more. The final section of this chapter turns to a discussion of a few of the many policies that might be used to address the environmental and humanitarian damage done by extractive industries.

Products, Chains, and Ecological Shadows

Peter Dauvergne calls global patterns of harm, both ecological and human, the "shadows of consumption."[46] He traces these shadows via five products: automobiles, leaded gasoline, refrigerators, beef, and harp seals. Although these products have brought substantial benefits to humans, they also engender substantial costs. As he notes, people are "dying of consumption." The automobile, for example, extracts a heavy environmental and human price as it transforms societies around the world and increases urban air pollution and the risks to drivers, passengers, and pedestrians—to say nothing of its growing contributions to global climate change. As environmental social movements and government policies demand fewer pollutants and safer vehicles in Northern consumer societies, these risks move—sometimes they are clearly pushed—onto populations and ecosystems in the developing world. This dynamic also is clear in Dauvergne's treatment of leaded gasoline, about which safety concerns were raised when it was introduced in the 1920s. It was the end of the twentieth century before lead was taken out of gasoline in much of the developed world, and only in the early years of the twenty-first century is this happening in much of Africa and parts of Asia.

Dauvergne shows that automobile efficiency and safety have improved globally, over time, and that leaded gas and ozone-depleting substances are being phased out. These developments are very good news for humans and ecosystems. Yet the globalization of other risks and harms continues apace: climate change, beef consumption, e-waste, and the seemingly endless growth in material throughput of consumer societies in the global North and South.

Dauvergne's work on a small number of products, like the blue jeans story above, illustrates that all goods and the chains of consumption that produce and distribute them cast ecological shadows. Although contemporary goods may have very clear benefits for humans in terms of our health, prosperity, entertainment, or knowledge, all also have ecological and humanitarian costs. These costs are usually hidden by the various distancing dynamics discussed above.

Another way to conceptualize the idea that consumption takes place along every point in a product's commodity chain is offered by political scientist Ronnie Lipschutz, who outlines "waste chains" that parallel literally every aspect of a commodity chain, from product design or conceptualization through the mining, growing, processing, and manufacturing associated with the good.[47] This waste chain also includes wastes generated by all of the energy consumed throughout the chain of consumption as well as the eventual disposals of the product itself. A mobile phone, or any other consumer electronics item, illustrates the point. Wastes are generated—in other words, things are consumed or used up—from the mining of minerals and extraction of petroleum used to make both plastics and energy all the way through the toxic e-waste that the phone becomes at the end of its life.

The European Union (EU) has taken a leadership role in the reduction of e-waste and the regulation of its reuse, recycling, and disposal. Yet, without political action in other jurisdictions such as the United States, which lacks similar standards, and without aggressive European and global standards and enforcement, e-wastes will continue to grow in quantity and to be disposed of legally and illegally in ways that damage ecological and human health.[48]

What Can Be Done?

The fact is that many people who grow the bananas, coffee, flowers, and other crops sold in international markets live in impoverished or ecologically damaged communities. The same is true of communities where minerals and fossil fuels are drawn from the earth. A reasonable estimate is that nearly 150 million nonretail production workers and nearly 500 million households depend on production of these commodities, and millions more are indirectly related to these commodities.[49] This number does not include the millions more dependent on the production of the thousands of categories of finished goods. Even if it were possible for higher-income societies and consumers to stop consuming these commodities, throwing hundreds of millions of families out of work and leaving them without any means of support would not beget sustainable development either.

The commodity chains discussed here are complex webs of social relations connecting people and markets across great distances (geographic and otherwise). This suggests that citizens and governments in the South and the North share responsibility for the ecological and humanitarian effects of global markets. We are all consumers—although some of us consume a lot more than others—sharing a measure of responsibility for sustainable development in our own countries and around the world.

The list below contains only a few sets of policy options that could reduce aggregate material throughput in consumer societies or address specific aspects of the ecological and humanitarian damage engendered by the contemporary, globalizing political economy. Note that most of these options can be deployed at multiple levels of government in the public sector; or within the private or civil society sectors; or by some combination of public, private, and NGO actors and institutions.

- **Command-and-Control Regulations:** With policies that reduce the generation of waste, increase recycling, engender cleaner product design, and push energy efficiency and renewable energy development, government mandates remain common and often prove effective. EU law, for example, is mandating a reduction in the use of hazardous substances in a host of products, pushing product redesign to facilitate recycling and reuse, and reducing packaging and other household and consumer wastes. Many U.S. states have mandated increasing minimum amounts of renewable energy in electricity grids, and governments around the world mandate product efficiency. Other ideas include banning individual items (such as disposable bags, leaded gasoline, or inefficient products) or regulating and enforcing standards for international corporations.

- **Adjust Subsidies:** States or companies can reduce subsidies and incentives that encourage waste and inefficient use, or they can subsidize more efficient technologies. For example, states in the North and South use tax codes and other incentives to subsidize oil, mining, and forestry extraction sectors by hundreds of billions of dollars. Similarly, U.S., EU, and Japanese domestic agricultural subsidies damage development prospects in the global South and distort trade in ways that disadvantage the world's poorest economies. Subsidies can also be used to encourage research and development in cleaner technologies or the investment or purchase of efficient technologies or renewable energy.

- **Taxation:** Although citizens dislike taxes, many economists view them as one of the most efficient ways to reduce pollution and other externalities. If, for example, taxes are used to substantially increase the cost of emitting carbon or other pollutants or of extracting resources and degrading ecosystems, then we can expect less pollution, waste, resource use, or biodiversity loss.

Taxes can be applied to packaging, disposable goods of all kinds, and a host of hazardous or unhealthy activities such as smoking.

- **Certification and Labeling Schemes:** Certification schemes have proliferated rapidly over the past decade or more; they have been developed by nonstate actors to address the environmental and humanitarian consequences of international markets. Probably the most widely known of these are the fair trade certification scheme and the Forest Stewardship Council (FSC) certification.[50] Many thousands of people live in communities where fair trade–certified products may help to raise living and working standards, and vast tracts of forests have been certified by the FSC process in dozens countries. Consumers and decision makers in almost any organization can seek to advance the influence of certified products by choosing to buy them or by encouraging organizations such as governments, universities, and companies to set fair trade purchasing policies. In additional to the largely non-state-driven certification programs, such schemes can also be state driven or state backed. Examples of state-coordinated certification systems include the UN- and state-backed Kimberley Process designed to certify that diamonds do not fund armed conflict and violent oppression, and the Energy Star program operated by the U.S. Environmental Protection Agency (and used or copied in many other countries) to rate the energy efficiency of home appliances, office equipment, and heating and air conditioning equipment. Like all policy options, certification schemes have critics and limitations. From the consumer's perspective, the ever-growing list of certification schemes—each including a large and complex set of criteria—makes them difficult to keep straight. Each scheme must build credibility and legitimacy with consumers over time.[51] Yet most analysts have concluded that certification schemes and other aspects of the corporate social responsibility movement, although they have the capacity to build niche markets and alter some environmental and humanitarian conditions, rarely alter the dominant incentives and practices in the global market.[52] In other words, fair trade coffee may well benefit the participating pickers and their families and communities, but it constitutes a small fraction of the global coffee market, and it has little impact on most of the market.

- **Capacity Building and Improved Governance:** In many parts of the world where ecological degradation is accelerating and humanitarian exploitation is extensive, government lacks either the capacity or the will, or both, to curb these problems. Sustainable development, from alleviating poverty and meeting the UN Millennium Development Goals to reversing environmental damage of all types, requires public institutions that work. Multilateral environmental agreements must be implemented if they are to shape outcomes; so too do the other policy options discussed in this chapter and throughout the volume. Lessons can be drawn from successful cases of public and civil society capacity building around the world, and they can be applied more widely to the dual challenge of environmental and social sustainability.[53] Expanded and enhanced capacity development assistance to build states and civil societies that can effectively and sustainably govern people and resources is a shared challenge in the North and South.[54]

This partial list leaves out many other possibilities, including government- and NGO-led consumer awareness campaigns, international standards for financial and governance transparency to reduce corruption and improve effective governance, and a host of options that engage global treaties and other forms of international agreements, possibly involving existing environmental institutions as well as those associated with the World Trade Organization or the ILO, development banks, or myriad other organizations and institutions.

Let us also be clear that not all ideas or initiatives related to environmental governance and sustainable development do (or will) come from the North. The notion that environmental and sustainability policies, movements, ideas, and norms are the purview of the North has been put to rest by activists and policymakers in (and analysts of) countries from central and eastern Europe, Brazil, Costa Rica, India, and China, to name only a few.[55] It is also clear that environmental and resource politics are high politics in the transatlantic relationship, between North and South, and for dozens of commodity-dependent countries.[56] Resource scarcity or conflict can turn violent, or it can engender deepening cooperation and peace building.[57] The stakes can be high.

Consumption issues and trends, like global inequality and the set of global environmental concerns and institutions discussed in this volume, can be shaped by collective action and individual choices and behaviors. As the introduction to this volume notes, whether we are up to dual challenges of globalizing greater and more sustainable prosperity without overwhelming the planet's ecosystems and other species remains to be determined.

Notes

1. See, for example, Donella H. Meadows, Dennis Meadows, and Jorgen Renders, *Beyond the Limits* (White River Junction, Vt.: Chelsea Green Publishing, 1992); and William Ophuls and A. Stephen Boyan Jr., *Ecology and the Politics of Scarcity Revisited* (New York: W. H. Freeman and Company, 1992).
2. Joseph Nye Jr. and Robert Keohane, *Power and Interdependence: World Politics in Transition* (Boston: Little, Brown, 1977); Dennis Pirages, *Global Ecopolitics: The New Context for International Relations* (Pacific Grove, Calif.: Duxbury Press, 1978); and James Harf and B. Thomas Trout, *The Politics of Global Resources* (Durham, N.C.: Duke University Press, 1986).
3. Kate O'Neill and Stacy D. VanDeveer, "Transnational Environmental Activism after Seattle: Between Emancipation and Arrogance," in *Charting Transnational Democracy: Beyond Global Arrogance*, ed. Janie Leatherman and Julie Webber (New York: Palgrave, 2005).
4. Thomas Princen, Michael Maniates, and Ken Conca, eds., *Confronting Consumption* (Cambridge: MIT Press, 2002); Tomas Princen, *The Logic of Sufficiency* (Cambridge: MIT Press, 2005); Peter Dauvergne, *The Shadows of Consumption: Consequences for the Global Environment* (Cambridge: MIT Press, 2008); *State of the World 2004: The Consumer Society* (Washington, D.C.: Worldwatch Institute, 2004); and Dennis

Pirages and Ken Cousins, eds., *From Ecological Scarcity to Ecological Security: Exploring New Limits to Growth* (Cambridge: MIT Press, 2005).

5. SERI (Sustainable Europe Research Institute), *Overconsumption: Our Use of the World's Natural Resources* (Vienna, Austria: SERI, 2009); and WWF, *Living Planet Report 2008* (Washington, D.C.: WWF, 2008).

6. SERI, *Overconsumption*.

7. Worldwatch Institute, *Vital Signs 2007–2008* (Washington, D.C.: Worldwatch Institute, 2007); and Daniel Sperling and Deborah Gordon, *Two Billion Cars: Driving toward Sustainability* (New York: Oxford University Press, 2009).

8. David Abel, "Battle to Expand Bottle Law Heats Up" *Boston Globe*, October 8, 2009.

9. Princen, *Sufficiency*; John De Graaf, David Wann, and Thomas N. Naylor, *Affluenza: The All Consuming Epidemic*, 2nd ed. (San Francisco: Berrett–Koehler Publishers, 2005).

10. Joseph Stiglitz, *Making Globalization Work* (New York: Penguin Books, 2006).

11. Paul Collier, *The Bottom Billion: Why the Poorest Countries Are Failing and What Can Be Done about It* (New York: Oxford University Press, 2007).

12. Ibid.

13. Princen, Maniates, and Conca, eds., *Confronting Consumption*; and SERI, *Overconsumption*.

14. Netherlands Environmental Assessment Agency, "Global CO_2 Emissions: Increase Continued in 2007," www.pbl.nl/en/publications/2008/GlobalCO2emissionsthrough 2007.html.

15. Michael Klare, *Rising Powers, Shrinking Planet* (New York: Metropolitan Books, 2008); and Christopher Flavin and Gary Gardner, "China, India and the New Global Order," in *Worldwatch Institute, State of the World 2006* (Washington, D.C.: Worldwatch Institute, 2006).

16. Princen, Maniates, and Conca, eds., *Confronting Consumption*.

17. Jack Manno, "Commoditization: Consumption Efficiency and the Economy of Care and Connection," in *Confronting Consumption*, ed. Princen, Maniates, and Conca, 67–100.

18. Vandana Shiva, *Water Wars: Privatization, Pollution and Profit* (Cambridge, Mass.: South End Press, 2002).

19. Ibid.

20. Princen, Maniates, and Conca, eds., *Confronting Consumption*, 14.

21. Michael Maniates, "Individualization: Plant a Tree, Buy a Bike, Save the World?" in *Confronting Consumption*, ed. Princen, Maniates, and Conca, 43–66.

22. Alex Hughes and Suzanne Reimer, eds., *Geographies of Commodity Chains* (London: Routledge, 2004).

23. Princen, Maniates, and Conca, eds., *Confronting Consumption*.

24. Thomas Princen, "Distancing: Consumption and the Severing of Feedback," in *Confronting Consumption*, ed. Princen, Maniates, and Conca, 103–131.

25. See Fran Abrams and James Astill, "Story of the Blues," *The Guardian*, May 29, 2001; see also Louise Crewe, "Unraveling Fashion's Commodity Chains," in *Geographies of Commodity Chains*, ed. Hughes and Reimer, 195–214.

26. For recent examples from this large literature on coffee, see Antony Wild, *Coffee: A Dark History* (New York: W. W. Norton, 2005); Mark Pendergrast, *Uncommon Grounds: The History of Coffee and How It Transformed the World* (New York: Basic Books, 1999); and Stewart Lee, *The Devils Cup: A History of the World According to Coffee* (New York: Ballantine Books, 2003). On sugar, see Sidney Mintz, *Sweetness and Power: The Place of Sugar in Modern History* (New York: Penguin, 1986). On bananas, see James Wiley, *The Banana: Empires, Trade Wars and Globalization* (Lincoln: University of Nebraska Press, 2008). On tea, see Roy Moxham, *Tea: Addiction, Exploitation and Empire* (New York: Carroll & Graf, 2003).

27. Jason Clay, *World Agriculture and the Environment* (Washington, D.C.: Island Press, 2004).

28. *The End of Child Labor: Within Reach* (Geneva: International Labour Organization, 2006), 8.

29. Worldwatch Institute, *Vital Signs,* 112–113.

30. Ibid.

31. Clay, *World Agriculture.*

32. Peter Dauvergne, *Loggers and Degradation in the Asia Pacific: Corporations and Environmental Management* (New York: Cambridge University Press, 2001); Peter Dauvergne, *Shadows in the Forest: Japan and the Politics of Timber in Southeast Asia* (Cambridge: MIT Press, 1997); see also extensive information available on the Web site of the NGO Global Witness, www.globalwitness.org.

33. See, for example, Geoff Tansey and Joyce D'Silva, eds., *The Meat Business: Devouring a Hungry Planet* (Boston: St. Martin's Press, 1999); Brian Halweil and Danielle Nierenburg, "Meat and Seafood: The Global Diet's Most Costly Ingredients," in *Worldwatch Institute, State of the World 2008* (Washington, D.C.: Worldwatch Institute, 2008); and Dauvergne, *Shadows of Consumption.*

34. Worldwatch Institute, *Vital Signs,* 26; and B. Worm et al., "Impacts of Biodiversity Loss on Ocean Ecosystem Services," *Science,* November 3, 2006, 787–790.

35. John E. Young, "Mining the Earth," Worldwatch Paper no. 109 (Washington, D.C.: Worldwatch Watch Institute, 1992).

36. Gavin Bridge, "Contested Terrain: Mining and the Environment," *Annual Review of Environment and Resources* 29 (2004): 205–259.

37. Ibid.

38. Ibid.; and Michael J. Watts, "Righteous Oil? Human Rights, the Oil Complex and Corporate Social Responsibility," *Annual Review of Environment and Resources* 30 (2005): 373–407; Dara O'Rourke and Sarah Connelly, "Just Oil? Environmental and Social Impacts of Oil Production and Consumption," *Annual Review of Environment and Resources* 28 (2003): 587–617.

39. For detailed histories and information, see the many Web-based reports by Global Witness (www.globalwitness.org) and the UN-sponsored Kimberley Process (www.kimberleyprocess.com).

40. "Under-mining Peace," Global Witness, June 2005; and Carol Albertyn, "Environment and Conservation, Wildlife and Animals," Carte Blanche Interactive, 2004.

41. Watts, "Righteous Oil?"

42. Paul Steven and Evelyn Dietsche, "Resource Curse: An Analysis of Causes, Experiences and Possible Ways Forward," *Energy Policy* 36 (2008): 56–65; Erika Weinthal and Pauline Jones Luong, "An Alternative Solution to Managing Mineral Wealth," *Perspectives on Politics* 4, no. 1 (2006): 35–53; Stiglitz, *Making Globalization Work,* 133–159; Collier, *Bottom Billion,* 38–52; Terry Lynn Karl, *The Paradox of Plenty: Oil Booms and Petro-States* (Berkeley: University of California Press, 1997).

43. Weinthal and Luong, "An Alternative Solution to Managing Mineral Wealth."

44. Lydia Polgeen, "Congo's Riches, Looted by Renegade Troops," *New York Times,* September 16, 2008.

45. Keith Bradsher, "Chinese Threat Reinvigorates Efforts to Mine Rare Minerals," *New York Times,* September 26, 2009.

46. Dauvergne, *The Shadows of Consumption.*

47. Ronnie D. Lipschutz, *Global Environmental Politics: Power, Perspectives and Practice* (Washington, D.C.: CQ Press, 2004), 122–126.

48. See Selin, this volume; Henrik Selin and Stacy D. VanDeveer, "Raising Global Standards: Hazardous Substances and E-Waste Management in the European Union," *Environment* 28, no. 10 (2006): 6–17; and Elisabeth Rosenthal, "Smuggling Europe's Waste to Poorer Countries," *New York Times,* September 27, 2009.

49. Figures compiled by author.

50. Benjamin Cashore, Graeme Auld, and Deanna Newsom, *Governing through Markets* (New Haven: Yale University Press, 2004); David Vogel, *The Market for Virtue: The Potential and Limits of Corporate Social Responsibility* (Washington, D.C.: Brookings Institution Press, 2005).

51. Cashore, Auld, and Newsom, *Governing through Markets.*

52. Vogel, *The Market for Virtue.*

53. Geoffrey Dabelko and Stacy D. VanDeveer, "It's Capacity Stupid: National Implementation and International Assistance," *Global Environmental Politics* 1, no. 2 (2001): 18–29.

54. Ambuj D. Sagar and Stacy D. VanDeveer, "Capacity Development for the Environment: Broadening the Focus," *Global Environmental Politics* 5, no. 3 (2005): 14–22.

55. JoAnn Carmin and Stacy D. VanDeveer, *EU Enlargement and the Environment* (London: Routledge, 2005); Paul F. Steinberg and Stacy D. VanDeveer, *Comparative Environmental Politics* (Cambridge: MIT Press, forthcoming); Paul F. Steinberg, *Environmental Leadership in Developing Countries* (Cambridge: MIT Press, 2001); Sanjeev Khagram, *Dams and Development: Transnational Struggles for Water and Power* (Ithaca, N.Y.: Cornell University Press, 2004); Kelly Sims Gallagher, *China Shifts Gears* (Cambridge: MIT Press, 2006); Lewis and Sims Gallagher, this volume; Kathy Hochstetler and Margaret E. Keck, *Greening Brazil* (Durham, N.C.: Duke University Press, 2007).

56. On transatlantic relations, see Miranda Schreurs, Henrik Selin, and Stacy D. VanDeveer, eds., *Transatlantic Environment and Energy Politics* (Farnham, UK: Ashgate, 2009).

57. Geoffrey Dabelko, "Uncommon Peace: Environment, Development and Global Security Agenda," *Environment* 50, no. 3 (2008): 32–45; Ken Conca and Geoffrey Dabelko, eds., *Environmental Peacemaking* (Baltimore: Johns Hopkins University Press, 2002).

Index

International environmental governance,
    1–23. *See also* Policy; Regimes; *specific
    aspects and entities*
  developments affecting, 4
  historical perspective, 1–2
  international regimes and, 6, 24
  international relations theory and, 4–6
  sustainable development concept and,
    6–9, 251
  system overview, 2–3
  uncertain future, 19–20
International environmental institutions.
    See also Global institutions;
    Intergovernmental organizations;
    specific entities
  forms of, 9–10
International environmental justice.
    See Environmental justice
International environmental law, 48–69
  air quality, 63–64
  basic rules and emerging legal
    standards, 62–65
  case law, 56–57
  common but differentiated
    responsibility, 18, 60, 252
  compliance and, 15, 188
  criminal law (EU), 228
  customary law, 56, 61
  economic institutions and, 65–66
  flora and fauna protection, 53, 62
  freshwater resources protection, 63
  general principles, 57–62
  global legal systems, 79, 92
  good neighborliness and international
    cooperation, 58–59
  as governance system element, 2
  hazardous substances, 64–65
  historical development, 11, 53–55
  international actors, 50–52
  international legal order, 49–50
  international organizations and, 50, 51,
    53, 56, 57
  international relations theory, 4–5
  judicial domain and, 57–58, 65
  marine environment protection, 62–63
  monitoring implementation of, 102
  nongovernmental organizations and,
    50–52, 53, 109
  polluter-pays principle, 61–62
  precautionary principle, 60–61
  soft law, 11, 32, 57
  sources of, 55–57, 71
  sovereignty and, 49, 52, 57–58, 79

states and, 48, 49, 50–51
sustainable development and, 48,
    59–60, 65
territory, 49, 52, 56, 58
UNEP and, 34
waste management, 64
International equity, 7. *See also*
    Environmental justice; Equity;
    Social justice
International Geophysical Year, 27, 113
International Geosphere-Biosphere
    Program, 29
International institutions. *See also* Global
    institutions; Intergovernmental
    organizations; *specific entities*
  forms of, 9–10
  international relations theory, 4–5
Internationalism, regimes and, 93
International Joint Commission, 9–10, 98
International Labour Organization, 26,
    132, 305, 319, 329
International legal order, 49–50. *See also*
    International environmental law
International management and
    manufacturing standards, 71
International Maritime Organization,
    10, 26, 51, 76
International Monetary Fund (IMF)
  evolution of global institutions, 27
  function of, 38
  international environmental law and, 51
  international regimes and, 96
  voting procedures, 10
International nongovernmental
    organizations (INGOs), 95, 98–100,
    104–105. *See also specific entities*
International Organization for
    Standardization, 71
International organizations (IOs). *See also
    specific entities*
  binding acts, 57
  consumption as concern, 312, 319
  federations of international and
    national organizations, 102, 104
  forms and growth of, 9–10, 95
  Group of 77 caucuses and, 244
  international environmental law and,
    50, 51, 53, 56, 57
  international regimes and, 97
  legal functions and roles, 51
International political system, as obstacle
    to policy, 78–79. *See also* Political
    systems